International Migration, Immobility and Development

International Migration, Immobility and Development

Multidisciplinary Perspectives

Edited by
**Tomas Hammar, Grete Brochmann,
Kristof Tamas and Thomas Faist**

Oxford • New York

First published in 1997 by
Berg
Editorial offices:
150 Cowley Road, Oxford, OX4 1JJ, UK
70 Washington Square South, New York, NY 10012, USA

Berg is an imprint of Oxford International Publishers Ltd.

Library of Congress Cataloging-in-Publication Data

A catalogue record for this book is available from the Library of Congress.

British Library Cataloguing-in-Publication Data

A catalogue record for this book is available from the British Library.

ISBN 1 85973 971 7 (Cloth)
1 85973 976 8 (Paper)

Typeset by JS Typesetting, Wellingborough, Northants.
Printed and bound in Great Britain by
Biddles Ltd, Guildford and King's Lynn

Contents

Acknowledgements

This book is the first part of a research programme 'Migration, Population and Poverty', primarily financed by the Swedish Council for Social Research (SFR), and mainly based at Centre for Research in International Migration and Ethnic Relations (CEIFO). The programme was initiated by three members of the editorial group, Tomas Hammar, Grete Brochmann and Kristof Tamas, as well as Sture Öberg, professor of geography at Uppsala University. The second part of the programme is an ongoing study of the control policies of eight European countries. The preconditions of immigration control, legal traditions and political implications are studied. At the centre of interest is the crucial dilemma: how a liberal democratic state can maintain control over its immigration without denying the human rights of individuals, even though they are foreigners or non-citizens. A team of scholars, headed by Grete Brochmann, at the Institute for Social Research in Oslo, will give answers in a comparative analysis planned for publication in 1998.

A third part of this programme has also been planned, a study of emigration and immobility in one or two selected regions. On the basis of our theoretical assumptions about the causes of immobility, we have suggested an anthropological study of the costs and benefits of not going abroad in comparison with those of emigrating. The study will contrast similar 'twin' regions that differ with respect to high or low emigration. To this end, we have received financial support from the Swedish International Development Authority (SIDA/SAREC) and travel grants from SFR and the Norwegian Research Council. Together with the Union for African Population Studies (UAPS) in Dakar, Senegal, we organised in November 1995 a preparatory conference. A volume of the proceedings, published jointly by UAPS and CEIFO, appeared in 1996 under the title: *International Migration in and from Africa: Dimensions, Challenges and Prospects*, edited by A. Adepoju and T. Hammar.

The present project has primarily been financed by the Swedish Council for Social Research (SFR) from 1994 to 1998. Additional financial and/or institutional support has been received from the Fritz Thyssen Foundation Köln, the Europa-Kolleg Hamburg, the Centre for Economic Policy Research (CEPR) London, University of the Bundeswehr, the Institute for Social Research Oslo, and the Norwegian Research Council.

Notes on Contributors

Ishtiaq Ahmed, Ph.D. and associate professor in political science, Stockholm University, Sweden, specialist in the politics of development, in nation building, state and citizenship, the author of several books on the concept of an Islamic state, regional interest in Pakistan and the Middle East.

Gunilla Bjerén, Ph.D. in sociology and associate professor of social anthropology, Stockholm University, Sweden. Senior researcher and head of the Centre for Gender Research at Stockholm University, specialist on urbanisation and migration, author of a book on migration in Ethiopia.

Grete Brochmann, Ph.D. in sociology, research director at the Institute for Social Research, Oslo, Norway, author of a book on women migration to the Middle East, regional interests in East Africa, Sri Lanka, the Gulf states and Mozambique, recent books on migration policies and the European Community, and on Bosnian refugees in the Nordic countries.

Thomas Faist, Ph.D. and senior researcher, Bremen University, Germany, specialist in comparative policy studies, and in the integration of immigrants in receiving states, author of recent book on social citizenship and immigrant minorities in the USA and Germany.

Peter A. Fischer, Lic.rer.pol., senior researcher at the Institute for Economic Policy Research at the Bundeswehr University in Hamburg, Germany, specialist in policy research and the analysis of international migration, recent book on economic integration in a common market, namely the Nordic labour market (with Thomas Straubhaar).

Tomas Hammar, Ph.D. in political science, professor and director of the Centre for Research in International Migration and Ethnic Relations (CEIFO), Stockholm University 1982–93, specialist in the political analysis of migration, books on European immigration policy, and democracy and the nation-state.

Notes on Contributors

Kenneth Hermele, economist, specialist in economic development, ecological aspects, and policies and policy evaluations, regional interest in Africa (Mozambique, Uganda, southern Africa), recent book on how economists analyse growth and environment.

Gunnar Malmberg, Ph.D. and associate professor in geography, Umeå University, Sweden, specialist in urbanisation and migration, book on metropolitan growth and migration in Peru.

Reiner Martin, MA, researcher at the Institute for Economic Policy Research at the Bundeswehr University in Hamburg, Germany, specialist in the analysis of international migration and regional economics.

Thomas Straubhaar, Ph.D. at Berne University, Switzerland, professor of economics at the Bundeswehr University, Hamburg, Germany. Specialist in international economics, economic integration and migration research, author of books on labour migration and the balance of payments, effects of migration policy in the Mediterranean countries and in Switzerland, and recently on the economics of international labour migration. He is also, together with Peter A. Fischer, author of a book on the Nordic labour market.

Kristof Tamas, MA, political scientist and researcher at the Centre for Research in International Migration and Ethnic Relations (CEIFO), Stockholm University, Sweden, specialist in international migration politics in Europe and policies addressing the causes of migration.

Why Do People Go or Stay?

Tomas Hammar and *Kristof Tamas*

At the end of the twentieth century there are worldwide about 100 million people residing outside their country of citizenship. They have recently or sometime during their lifetime migrated to live in another country than the one in which they were born. In contrast, around 6,000 million have not left their country of birth, or they have returned to their country after a period of emigration. In other words, more than 98 per cent of the world's population remain in the country where they are citizens. Why have many more not emigrated?

Prevailing migration theories would have us assume that migration from poorer to richer countries had taken much larger proportions than the currently estimated volume. Available theories can only partially explain the present situation. They give some clues as to why people emigrate and why they return, but very little about why people stay. They are far from satisfactory and they were conceived at a time when the world was very different.

The causes and consequences of migration are not the same as they were before the First World War, at the time of transoceanic emigration from Europe to the Central and North Americas, or after the Second World War at the time of labour migration to Northern Europe. New emigration flows from countries in Asia, Africa and Latin America have emerged in a process linked to economic development. Meanwhile, the immigration countries of the North have become welfare democracies of a post-industrial era with new technologies and transformed labour markets. The 1990s have everywhere witnessed high unemployment rates and stagnating growth. The new flows go mainly between countries in the South and the flows towards the North face increasingly restrictive immigration control from governments fearful of uncontrollable and unwanted immigration. While South to North migration can be assumed to grow even more in the future, its new global character needs to be analysed with new theoretical tools.

In this book we evaluate old theories in the light of a new global situation. We undertake a systematic review of the theoretical literature on international migration assessing what has been done in relation to the actual and potential migration flows as well as to current migration policies. What we need at this stage is not a new general theory, but a multidisciplinary evaluation of available social science theories in an attempt to apply them to the new world of international migration, or to what we shall call here 'South to North migration'.

The following questions are analysed in this book:

1. Why do some people migrate?
2. Why do most people stay? Why do many emigrants return?
3. How is international migration related to development? Is the volume of emigration dependent on the development process in the country of origin? Is this development process in turn dependent on international migration?

In studies of the causes of international migration, almost all attention has up to now been given to those who actually migrate, although their behaviour under most circumstances is not the normal one, but the deviant case. A parallel might be helpful, although it must not be misunderstood and taken for a value judgement. Just as more attention has recently been paid in medicine to those who are healthy, or in traffic studies to the absence of accidents, we suggest studies not only of those who have emigrated but also of those who have stayed in their country of origin. In other words, we include in our study both those who take part in international migration and those who do not, but stay on, those who are in this sense the *immobile*.

There are indeed many answers to these questions, from several disciplinary perspectives. We have therefore worked on them together as a team of social science researchers with different backgrounds and training. In each of our chapters, we have presented the state of the art in one discipline and its neighbouring territories. We feel that this book is an important contribution towards the theory of international migration, thanks to our team's broad competence and our close and intensive multidisciplinary co-operation.

Chapters 2–4 and 6–8 include the state-of-the-art presentations for geography by Gunnar Malmberg (chapter 2), micro- and macro-economics by Peter A. Fischer, Reiner Martin and Thomas Straubhaar (chapters 3 and 4), political science by Ishtiaq Ahmed (chapter 6), sociology by Thomas Faist (chapter 7) and anthropology by Gunilla Bjerén (specifically exploring gender perspectives on migration, chapter 8). Kenneth Hermele analyses the politico-economic discourse on development and migration (chapter 5). Finally, Thomas Faist ties the many threads together, comparing and evaluating the theories (chapter 9).

This book has gained from the participation of all authors in the planning, writing, discussing and revising. None of us has worked just with her or his own chapter. In a series of meetings of several days, we have given and received comments on drafts and revisions. Each author is, of course, responsible for her or his own chapter and each chapter represents one discipline. Our multidisciplinary method has been of great benefit for the analysis. Each chapter, therefore, gives reference to and shows the influence from the other contributors. The final evaluation, comparison, and conclusion in chapter 9, has likewise been thoroughly discussed by all of us.

South to North Migration

The total volume of South to North migration has grown during the last three decades. The flows to the North have come from a larger number of increasingly diverse countries in the South (OECD 1993b: 15). Since the end of the Cold War, East–West flows have also emerged. Although traditionally restrictive of immigration, Japan has received a growing number of migrants. The total migrant stock or stock of immigrants in the world has increased and is at present approximately 100 million.[1] The rate of growth has been limited in the North, compared to the South. In the period 1965–75 annual growth in the migrant stock of the South was 0.4 per cent, while between 1975 and 1985 the South's migrant stock increased by 2.2 per cent per year. The largest share of this increase has been accounted for by Southern Asia, Western Asia and North Africa. Despite this growth, the share of migrants of the total population in the South, has remained at a level of 1.6 per cent, whereas the proportion in the North is on average 4.1 per cent (UN 1995).

International migration might be expected to grow in the future because of several factors, such as population increase, poverty, structurally caused un- and underemployment, political conflicts or ecological factors. However, there are no obvious causal links between such variables and international migration (Tamas 1996). It has even been hard to find or verify the causal relation between high nativity and South to North migration flows (Muus 1993). Nevertheless, statistics and figures have often led to speculation.

In 1992 alone, 93 million people were added to the world population. According to UNFPA estimates, world population will reach 6.25 billion

---

1. This figure is often quoted, but is a crude estimate. It was presented in an article by Jonas Widgren (1987), and then quoted in e.g. Russel and Teitelbaum (1992) and UNFPA (1993). This is a maximum figure for the population of foreign citizens, but propably a low figure for the population of the foreign-born.

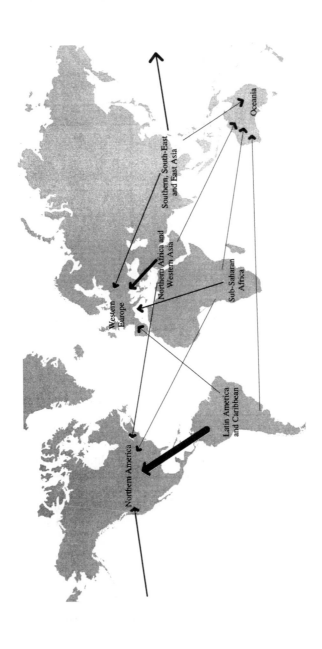

Map 1.1 South to North Migration Flows 1960–4
Data for the maps are taken from the same source as for Figure 1.1, i.e. tables provided by Hania Zlotnik, the UN Population Information Network (POPIN) Gopher of the UN Population Division, Department for Economic and Social Information and Policy Analysis, 1996 (for more details see Figure 1.1 pp. XX).

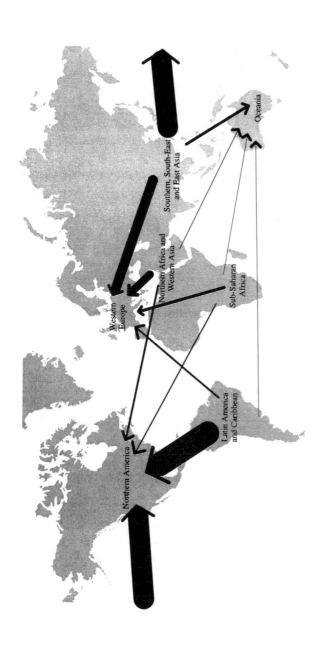

Map 1.2 South to North Migration Flows 1980–5

Data for the maps are taken from the same source as for Figure 1.1, i.e. tables provided by Hania Zlotnik, the UN Population Information Network (POPIN) Gopher of the UN Population Division, Department for Economic and Social Information and Policy Analysis, 1996 (for more details see Figure 1.1 pp. XX).

in the year 2000, and increase to 8.5 billion by 2025. As much as 93 per cent of this population growth takes place in countries in the South. From 1975, the yearly growth in world population has been at around 1.7 per cent. While the average global fertility rate was at 3.8 children per woman between 1975 and 1980, the period 1990 to 1995 showed a decrease to 3.3. However, there were notable regional differences. While most countries in the North have a stagnant or decreasing level of reproduction, average fertility rate in Africa was 6.0 children per woman (UNFPA 1993: 1).

The population increase in the South has not been paired with a growth in employment opportunities. The labour force will grow by an estimated 2.3 per cent in the countries of the South during the 1990s. Such an increase requires a growth in employment opportunities with 260 million jobs. An even larger expansion in employment will probably be necessary as more women may be expected to enter the labour markets in the South (UNDP 1993: 36–7). The present level of unemployment and underemployment will continue and probably grow, and thereby give new incentives to a future increase in South to North migration. However, as shown by the theoretical analysis in this book, the causes of staying may be even more powerful, even with such gloomy prospects. Moreover, intra-South or South to South migration flows, although only partially analysed in this book (see e.g. chapter 3), may be important alternative strategies for those people who will face unemployment. Migration within Africa, for example, has been extensive, particularly as ethnic groups are dispersed over the political borders, and cross-border commuting may be an important alternative to long distance South to North migration.

It is also important to note that more than 90 per cent of South Asian migrants since the mid-1970s have gone to oil-exporting countries in Western Asia as these countries, unlike those in the North, have been actively recruiting migrant labour (Shah 1994: 227). The significance of such immigration in several countries in Western Asia is shown in table 1.2, where the net stock of immigrants and the economic development in all seventy countries have been gathered from various sources. This table is shown here, as it gives an idea of the global spread and size of international migration and of its relation to the level of economic development. This table will be further analysed in chapter 4.

Table 1.1 shows that South to North flows have increased since the early 1960s. Total net migration from the South to the North has increased from 230,000 in the period 1960–4, to almost 940,000 in the period 1985–9. This growth is moderate rather than overwhelming, considering the theoretically assumed reasons for migration. When figures are divided into continents/regions of origin, there is not

Table 1.1 South to North Migration[a]

Total: Developing Countries

Region of destination	1960–4	1965–9	1970–4	1975–9	1980–4	1985–9
North America	128,600	237,000	372,900	605,200	782,200	704,300
Oceania	8,000	14,000	27,200	29,100	36,400	57,700
Western Europe	114,400	274,300	441,400	366,600	336,800	361,700
Total	251,100	525,300	841,500	1,000,900	1,155,400	1,123,700
Net migration [b]						
Oceania	7,300	12,700	25,800	27,700	35,000	56,600
Western Europe	53,200	93,900	176,900	97,600	29,100	156,100
Maximum net South to North migration[c]	230,000	391,800	654,700	763,000	890,100	939,600

Africa and Western Asia

Region of destination	1960–4	1965–9	1970–4	1975–9	1980–4	1985–9
North America	10,400	20,300	29,400	41,900	44,500	52,400
Oceania	4,200	7,500	12,900	10,600	7,100	11,900
Western Europe	99,200	184,300	351,900	242,900	205,500	189,000
Total	113,800	212,100	394,200	295,400	257,100	253,300
Net migration[b]						
Oceania	4,000	7,000	12,300	10,100	6,600	11,600
Western Europe	44,400	52,600	144,900	36,200	-26,900	64,300
Maximum net South to North migration[c]	99,700	128,100	265,800	120,700	68,000	150,900

[a] The tables are modified versions of tables provided by Hania Zlotnik, the UN Population Information Network (POPIN) Gopher of the UN Population Division, Department for Economic and Social Information and Policy Analysis. Figures here have been approximated. The data for Canada and the United States (North America) and Australia and New Zealand (Oceania) are classified by place of birth; the data for Belgium, France and the Netherlands are classified by country of citizenship, and those for Germany, Sweden and the United Kingdom are classified by place of last or next residence. The total for Belgium, Germany, the Netherlands, Sweden and the United Kingdom are presented under the label Western Europe. Figures for France are added under Africa and Western Asia (more precisely for North Africa and Western Asia) and added to the total for developing countries. Data for the United Kingdom are available only from 1965.

The data for the United States include information on the number of migrants legalising their status as a result of the Immigration Reform and Control Act (IRCA) of 1986. Those legalising their status as a result of the General Amnesty Program were redistributed over the 1972–82 period according to linearly increasing trends. Those legalising their status under the special Agricultural Workers Program were redistributed uniformly over the

Table 1.1 South to North Migration[a] (*continued*)

South, South-East and East Asia

Region of destination	1960–4	1965–9	1970–4	1975–9	1980–4	1985–9
North America	17,800	57,700	132,000	198,500	305,300	308,200
Oceania	3,600	5,800	9,700	14,500	27,600	41,600
Western Europe	10,800	68,700	68,700	93,600	107,400	147,200
Total	32,200	132,200	210,400	306,600	440,300	497,000
Net migration						
Oceania	3,100	5,100	9,100	13,900	26,900	41,000
Western Europe	6,400	34,400	26,000	44,500	47,200	80,500
Maximum net South to North migration	27,400	97,200	167,000	256,800	379,400	429,700

Latin America and the Caribbean

Region of origin, region of destination	1960–4	1965–9	1970–4	1975–9	1980–4	1985–9
North America	100,400	159,000	211,400	364,800	432,400	343,700
Oceania	200	700	4,600	3,900	1,700	4,200
Western Europe	4,400	21,200	20,800	30,100	23,900	25,500
Total	105,000	180,900	236,800	398,800	458,000	373,400
Net migration						
Oceania	200	600	4,400	3,700	1,500	4,000
Western Europe	2,300	6,900	6,000	16,900	8,800	11,300
Maximum net South to North migration	102,900	166,500	221,800	385,400	442,600	359,000

1982–6 period. The data has been included in the paper 'Beyond the Numbers: A Reader on Population, Consumption and the Environment', Laurie Anne Mazur, ed. (Washington, D.C.: Island Press), 1994. As the data is collected from a wide variety of sources of differing quality, it must be treated with caution.

[b] Net migration is the volume of immigration minus emigration. Figures for North America are not included as no such data are available.

[c] Figures for France are not included in the sum of net migration.

everywhere a clear, uninterrupted upward curve. There has been a substantial increase in asylum seekers from the South up till the early 1990s, but the countries in the North have become increasingly restrictive towards asylum seekers and the recognition rates have fallen. Many asylum seekers thus do not remain in the North. A large part of migration to the North therefore consists of family reunion or marriage, related to

Table 1.2 Net stock of immigrants and economic development in selected countries

Country	Net stock of immigrants total persons	Real GDP % of pop.	per capita
Europe			
Austria	512000	6.6	16504
Belgium	900000	9.1	16381
Cyprus**	2900	0.3	9953
France	3600000	6.4	17014
Germany	5000000	7.9	18213
Greece	−300000	−3.2	7366
Italy	800000	0	15890
Luxembourg	117300	28.4	19244
Netherlands	692400	4.6	15695
Poland	−250000	−1.7	4237
Portugal	−720000	−6.9	8770
Spain	−985000	−2.6	11723
Sweden	490000	5.7	17014
Switzerland	1200000	17.9	20874
United Kingdom	1894000	3.3	15804
Western Asia			
Bahrain**	132000	51	10706
Iraq	1282000	6.8	3508
Jordan	−400000	−44.4	3869
Kuwait	1499000	71.4	15178
Oman**	442000	70	9972
Saudi Arabia**	2878000	60	10989
Turkey	−2500000	−4.3	4652
United Arab Emirate	805000	89	16753
Yemen	−850000	−7.3	1562
South and Southern Asia			
Bangladesh	−634000	−1.8	872
Hong Kong	300000	5.2	15595
Indonesia	−748000	−1	2181
Japan	1348000	1.1	17616
Korea, Rep.	−231000	−1	6733
Malaysia	890000	5	6140
Pakistan	−1200000	−3.8	1862
Philippines	−1200000	−2	2303
Singapore	300000	10	15880
Sri Lanka	−288000	−4.1	2405
Thailand	−280000	−0.9	3986
Africa			
Algeria	−280000	−4.7	3011
Botswana	−130000	−1	3419
Burkina Faso	−900000	−19.6	618
Cameroon*	250000	5.4	1646
Egypt	−2500000	−16.8	1988

Tomas Hammar and Kristof Tamas

Table 1.2 Net stock of immigrants and economic development in selected countries (*continued*)

Country	Net stock of immigrants total persons	Real GDP % of pop.	per capita
Gabon	300000	25	4147
Gambia, The*	50000	16.7	913
Lesotho	−200000	−10	1743
Morocco	−1600000	−6.4	2348
Senegal	−100000	−4	1248
South Africa*	500000	4.9	4865
Sudan	−500000	−4.9	949
Swaziland	−30000	−16.7	2384
Tunisia	−550000	−6.7	3759
North and Latin America			
Argentina***	1628000	5	4295
Canada***	4000000	15.1	19232
Colombia	−1300000	−3.9	4237
Uruguay	−200000	−6.5	5916
USA***	21000000	8.4	21449
Venezuela	1000000	5.1	6169
Oceania			
Australia***	4000000	23.4	16051
former USSR			
Azerbaijan	255000	4	3977
Belarus	118000	1.5	5727
Estonia	5907000	38	6438
Georgia	1406000	25.7	4572
Kazakhstan	8329000	50.7	4716
Kyrgyzstan	1660000	40	3114
Latvia	1204000	45.2	6457
Lithuania	607000	16.5	4913
Moldova	982000	22.9	3896
Russian Fed.	1910000	2.6	7968
Tajikistan	877000	18.1	2558
Turkmenistan	795000	22.9	4230
Ukraine	7333000	14.4	5433
Uzbekistan	3130000	16.2	3115

* = Population of foreign citizens minus nationals domiciled abroad
** = Economically active foreign citizens minus nationals domiciled abroad
*** = Foreign-born population minus national abroad

Note: The stock of foreign population in a country includes those residents of the country who are not citizens. From this stock we have substracted the stock of the same country's own citizens living abroad. A minus sign in the table means that e.g. Spain has more of its citizens living abroad than foreign residents on its territory. Shown in the table is also the net stock of immigrants, measured as a percentage of the total population of the country. As this table is computed from many sources, data are not fully comparable, and must be treated with caution.
Source: ILO/IOM/UNHCR 1994.

the earlier period of active labour recruitment in these regions. Networks are here of great importance, as shown by Faist in chapter 7. As indicated by the table, new global patterns of international migration have emerged, and with them the need for a theoretical framework that can explain this development.

Perspectives of the North

Many countries of destination (in Europe, North America, Australia and Japan, here referred to as the 'North') fear that the growth in migration is only the beginning of much greater international population movements. To meet future flows, which might threaten the stability and security of states, governments in the North and international organisations have launched new and comprehensive policy programmes. These include not only border controls, visa systems, deportations, and anti-trafficking legislation, but recently also targeted programmes for development assistance, international trade and foreign investments. In the political rhetoric, the 'root causes' of emigration should be addressed, and future refugee flows should be averted also by the promotion of armistices and peace, political stability, democracy and respect for human rights. The complex interrelations between all these factors are not seldom over-simplified and even greatly distorted by wishful political thinking.

The end of the Cold War has given rise to new political divisions in the international system and to reinterpretations of what constitutes conflict and security. Questions about collective identity, nationalism and ethnicity versus internationalisation and globalisation are in focus worldwide (Waever et al. 1993). International migration is often regarded as a carrier of potential conflicts and security risks affecting ethnic and social relations, and in the end, economic and political stability in the countries of immigration (Weiner 1993).

Immigration to the North is no longer invited or tolerated. It has become unwanted and strongly restricted. Although South to North migration has been reduced, it has not come to an end. Immigration of close relatives is often allowed. Asylum seekers may be admitted. Professionals and some specialists are given work permits, and tourists and business people are welcomed. Among all of these, some foreigners on visit will overstay their visas, ask for asylum, or enter the labour market as illegals. Several countries in the North experience a considerable illegal or clandestine immigration. Domestic economic interests often demand cheap immigrant labour to be employed in the black or grey, informal labour market. Migrants there take on jobs which native-born people do not want. At the same time, the fear of 'being flooded' is often more widespread and more politically charged in a society in times of limited economic growth. Dissatisfaction is projected on the foreigner, resulting in xenophobic attitudes and behaviour.

Perspectives of the South

From the point of view of the North, migration from the South is thus often regarded as a threat that should be kept under control. From the perspective of the South, emigration to the North constitutes merely a limited option. From the perspective of both individuals who might consider migration and of policy makers who might see emigration as a means to societal improvement the doors have been closed, but the need or motives for migration are still there.

All the countries that we bring together here under the label 'the South' are internally very heterogeneous and different in most respects, as of course are the countries of the North. The South to North difference is not only the geographic position, indicated by the labels, but primarily the economic gap between the poorer South and the richer North. The 'South' includes countries in Asia, Africa and Latin America that are economically less developed. Both in this introduction and in several chapters, we shall discuss definitions of economic development as well as some of its indicators. Despite the many shortcomings of this term, we shall have to be satisfied in this study with it, vague and broad as it is.

Most countries in the South have not implemented a specific emigration policy, nor have they seen migration as a matter of great relevance for their post-colonial relations to states in the North. There are exceptions, e.g. the Maghreb states in relation to France. A new situation might also emerge elsewhere. Several countries, such as Bangladesh, Pakistan, the Philippines and Sri Lanka, have actively pursued policies of labour emigration. They have wanted to place surplus labour into gainful work abroad in the hope that skills will later on be transferred back again. Most of all they have hoped for and often also obtained substantial amounts of savings from migrants temporarily working in other countries. The economic impact of these remittances has, however, been disputed. It remains unclear how much a country as a whole gains or loses from emigration, remittances and return migration.

The loss of skilled people or "brain-drain" has in some instances been seen as an obstacle to development. In general, less attention has been given to international and more to internal migration as well as to migration between neighbouring states, for instance within Africa. The number of forced migrants and refugees from countries in Africa and Asia has steadily increased. Relatively few have, however, been able to seek protection in the North. Most of them have stayed in refugee camps or have resettled in neighbouring countries in the South (see Adepoju and Hammar 1996).

Theoretical Approaches

International migration is studied within most social science disciplines. We may find large interest in migration within, for instance, anthropology, demography, economy, education, geography, history, political science, psychology and sociology. Contributions are also made within many other fields such as law (international law and legislation about aliens and citizenship) and social medicine. International migration is, in other words, not the domain of any one discipline. It is a field of study where multidisciplinary research is highly needed but lacking. Research is nevertheless frequently undertaken without consideration or consultation of related work in other disciplines.

This book is based on the co-operation of researchers from four Northern European countries. We have divided the work between us mainly according to disciplinary perspectives, but our objective is much more ambitious than a traditional book with parallel chapters. Our main purpose has been to write a multidisciplinary book, where each author broadens her or his own disciplinary range.

Each of our disciplines has developed various schools and traditions in which some prime conceptual aspects or organising ideas have been selected. In geography, for instance, these are principally time and space. Economists often focus on the scarcity of resources, the functioning of markets and the individual maximisation of life-time utility. In political science the prime concept may be said to be power, and here the sovereign state has traditionally been the central unit. Sociologists may in the same vein be said to study social behaviour, while anthropologists have predominantly been occupied with culture. These examples are, of course, simplifications. They nevertheless illustrate that although time and space may be the same when we study a given period in a certain society, we tend to approach the same phenomenon (international migration) with different tools, looking at different aspects. Most importantly, we also tend to make a number of basic assumptions, varying from discipline to discipline, about those relations that we ourselves do not study but take for granted. Economists usually call factors that we assume to be given the '*ceteris paribus*'. In several chapters here they are referred to as the 'black boxes'.

In the economic chapters of this book, these *ceteris paribus*' assumptions are systematically dropped, one by one. Factors that previously were assumed to be constant are in this way brought into the analysis, which is thus made a bit less general and more realistic. Still, even with this method the analysis will not be comprehensive enough, partly because the questions asked are too narrow in scope. An illustration of this is the limitation which we emphasise here, namely immobility. All disciplines have, within their frameworks, focused on the explanandum 'why do people migrate?', neglecting the twin question 'why do they not migrate?'.

We also find a division of labour between various levels of analysis within the disciplines: the macro-, meso- and micro-level. Macro-studies in economics are predominantly concerned with the differences in environmental factors of geo-political units. Micro-studies look at differences as perceived by individual human beings, families, firms, etc. International economy deals with a level of analysis above the national level. Political science and sociology have developed specialised subfields for the study of a whole spectrum of units of analysis ranging from the behaviour of individuals at one end, through families, groups, sub-national organisations, nations, supra-national organisations, and the entire international system at the other end. The meso-level provides links between the macro- and micro-levels (chapter 7). In our view, comprehensive theories about the causes of international migration will have to include all levels of aggregation. We have therefore in this book made a multidisciplinary attempt to cover both micro-, meso- and macro-levels of analysis.

A number of different research strategies are used in the study of international migration, as in social science disciplines in general. There are many examples of both qualitative and quantitative studies of migration flows, both intensive and extensive, idiographic and nomothetic studies of minorities in the host societies, and both inductive and deductive, understanding (hermeneutic) and explicative (analytic) studies of integration and socialization processes. We argue here for the combination of several of these approaches in explanations of the causes of international migration. Social science is about human behaviour, and therefore not likely to develop into an "exact" science, or to become as rigorous as studies in the natural sciences.

This more general discussion is relevant not only for this book, but also for any multidisciplinary project. In research on international migration many disciplines must be involved and work together. As a mono-disciplinary approach operates within certain sets of parameters, it can give only a limited picture of the migration process, be it ever so analytically rigid and consistent. Our aim in this book is therefore to increase the mutual awareness of what has been done elsewhere or in other disciplines, and to confront and compare different approaches, theories and results. With this eclectic method we have attempted to detect not only the unnecessary overlaps and misunderstandings, but also the unexplored and neglected perspectives.

Disciplinary borders have been crossed previously by several authors. The works of major theoreticians in this field are central references in more than one discipline (Ravenstein, Hägerstrand, Hirschman, to mention just three). In each chapter we have brought together similar and disparate interpretations of the theories and models used to explain the causes of migration across national borders as well as the causes of immobility. Summarising the steps we have taken towards a more systematic approach, Faist concludes in the final chapter that transgressing disciplinary borders is a commendable, fruitful method, offering great opportunities for further development of social science theories.

The Conceptual Framework

Throughout this book we discuss various conceptual frameworks. We shall discuss key concepts, and the problem that the same operationalisations are seldom used in the various disciplines. In this introduction, we pay special attention to two sets of concepts, attributed already in the title of the book, one concerning migration and immobility and the other related to development.

International Migration and Immobility

Migration is a spatial phenomenon. People move from one place to another, alone or together with others, for a short visit or for a long period of time, over a long or short distance. As the world is divided into territories of sovereign states, some migration goes across the national borders. It is of course this migration that is called international migration. Migration that takes place within the territory of a state is called internal or intra-national migration. In geography, the term 'regional migration' usually means movements between internal regions of a country (a sub-category of internal migration). The same term may in other literature refer to regions of several states, such as the European Union or Latin America (a special case of international migration) (chapter 2).

The distinction between international and internal migration may be regarded as formal and legalistic, but it has an impact of great significance on the relations between individual migrants and the states on both sides of the border, as well as between these states. International migration is more or less regulated by the destination states and to some extent also by the states of origin. Internal migration is usually free from regulation. Furthermore, when migrants leave the country where they are citizens and enter another country where they are aliens (as well as vice versa when they return), this implies a major change in their legal status, their right to take up residence and work, their social, economic and political rights.

Each state is sovereign to decide about the right of foreign citizens to immigrate, to reside in the country and to take work there. Aliens laws and legislation on naturalisation are highly diverse and constantly changing. We therefore need our own definitions of which movements are international migration and of who is an international migrant.

We shall use the terms *immigrant* and *emigrant*, not as they are determined in the aliens legislations and statistics of the world's countries, but independent of the legal status of migrants. We shall thus include not only those who are acknowledged as legal immigrants, but also those who are asylum seekers, family members, undocumented or illegals. Even citizenship or nationality will be irrelevant in our understanding of these terms.[2]

We shall apply one significant criterion for the definition of movements of people across borders, namely the time of stay spent in the country of arrival. For the purpose of our discussions, we need a distinction between on the one hand those who only pay short visits, and on the other hand those who shift (or at least intend to shift) their residence to the country of destination. It is only the latter category that we want to include. We shall not try to operationalise 'residential intention' here, but we could mention some alternative options (for example, declared intention to take up residence, or a *de facto* stay, lasting a certain period of time, e.g. one year).

An international migrant is thus a person who has moved from one country to another with the intention of taking up residence there for a relevant period of time.

A number of terms are used to designate the countries involved in international migration. An emigration country may be called the 'home country', the 'sending country' or the 'country of origin'. An immigration country likewise may be called 'host country', 'receiving country' or 'destination country'. All these labels are problematic and more or less misleading. Does 'emigration' mean a permanent settlement? Which country is after many years the 'home country', and cannot a migrant have more than one 'home country'? What is the 'origin' and for how many generations? Do countries 'export' people as the notions of sending

---

2. Statistics on international migration are in most countries based on citizenship and not on country of birth. It should therefore be noted that as a consequence, the stock of immigrants in the tables in this chapter are defined by citizenship.

and receiving (not to mention exporting and importing) countries seem to imply? We are aware of these problems, and we have opted to exclude only two, namely 'host' and 'home' countries. One reason for letting the other terms stay in the text is stylistic. We use them only to say that these are countries of *de facto* immigration or emigration. We do not want to imply anything about the self-image or the policy of a country.

In the course of our analysis, we have become convinced that the concept of immobility or non-migration makes a substantial contribution to the theoretical literature, broadening the scope of the analysis of international migration. As shown in chapter 2, there are many time–space strategies available for most people, and international migration is only one among them. Other strategies are staying in the local spatial unit (or full immobility) or some form of internal migration to another spatial unit within the country, as e.g. rural–urban migration, commuting, circulation, or internal refugee migration. For even in the case of forced or reactive migration, various barriers may hinder people from crossing borders. Refugees may have to remain as displaced people within their country of residence, because they are given no opportunity to leave.

Many of these alternative forms of migration can explain why, contrary to many assumptions, there is not much more international migration. As most people of the world remain within the borders of their country or even at their very place of birth, it is most relevant to add the reasons for immobility to any model of the dynamics of international migration. For semantic reasons, we use the terms 'non-migration' and 'immobility' interchangeably.

Finally, two more points concerning types and direction of migration. Economic reasons for international migration are prevalent throughout this book. In several chapters refugee migration and forced migration are discussed. While using the terms 'forced' and 'voluntary' migration or 'political' and 'economic' migration, we do not imply that migrants always can be categorised as either the one or the other. In our understanding we are here faced with a continuum. There may be pure cases. Most frequently, however, there is behind the same migration decision more or less of both voluntary elements and compulsion. Moreover, dichotomies are mostly made by governments and from the viewpoint of the involved states, rather than from the situations or perspectives of the migrants. Several of the chapters in this book attempt to give the perspective of the migrant a more pivotal role in the analysis.

Migration between less developed and more developed countries often goes from certain sending countries to specific destinations, as from the Maghreb countries in North Africa to France, or from Pakistan to the United Kingdom. Some of these 'migration systems' are less bound by geographical distance (such as the British post-colonial system), while others are composed of geographically defined areas (such as the Mediterranean migration system). The direction of the flows is a reflection of post-colonial economic, political, cultural and linguistic links and exchanges. On a more social and personal level, migration systems contain networks and personal contacts between migrants and their families, relatives, friends or traffickers in the country of origin, which may give rise to continued or increased migration, or 'chain migration' (chapters 7 and 8).

Development

While 'change' may be said to be a term that is not value loaded, 'development' often implies an assumption that something is moving from a lower, less differentiated status to a higher, better and more differentiated one. This latter term may also express the belief that societies undergo a 'natural' process of evolution and that some societies may be more and others less advanced in their development.

As the terms 'development' or 'economic development' are much in use in this book, we will here explicitly dissociate ourselves from these interpretations. We do not use 'development' to give such connotations. We use the terms for lack of better alternatives and as a 'black box', into which we cannot go deeply enough in this study. We shall also in more detail in the individual chapters relate to the ideas of change and development in economic, political, anthropological and other literature on international migration. Kenneth Hermele discusses the concept of sustainable development in chapter 5. He also points to the fact that international migration is about the global distribution of people. While total space is limited, and the use of natural resources is most unevenly distributed, the future of the globe depends on how this limited space will be used. The links between migration and development are here of great significance.

Striving for a broad understanding of development, we have abstained from a more distinct definition. In our view development may be regarded as a multidirectional process rather than something which can be defined in terms of subsequent stages and levels. The process of development usually includes a change in the overall welfare, which incorporates social, economic and political conditions in time and space. Development is also about the distribution of welfare. The changes that take place are valued subjectively by each individual or each community. Development takes place when members of a society or a community experience an enhancement of their chances of social, economic and political well-being.

The operationalisation of this controversial term is also a great problem. Economic development is often measured using standardised economic criteria and economic indicators. The traditional measure, the GNP/GDP per capita, has sometimes been adjusted to reflect purchasing power, i.e. to account for the varying purchasing power of money in different countries. The United Nations Development Programme (the UNDP) has presented the Human Development Index (the HDI) as an influential alternative to the GDP per capita. This is not much of an improvement, however, as the HDI is mainly a joint measure of three variables, the GDP per capita, life expectancy at birth and educational achievement. Each of these variables accounts for one-third of the weight of the combined HDI, and this means that we find an important overlap between the GDP and the HDI. In other words, it does not offer a qualitatively different measure.

As we understand development as a process, we are more interested in the dynamic aspects of this process. As development takes place in time and space, the difference over time and the speed of change registered for a country is often more significant than the static level or point of departure from which the change originates. A low but growing GDP or HDI may thus be assumed to affect migration differently than stagnant levels, while on the other hand the level of growth may be important, as a change in GDP or HDI may have different consequences depending on from which level it began (chapters 4 and 5).

As other than economic factors may constitute development, it is important to keep in mind the significance also of factors like democracy, human rights, freedom of expression, welfare and security, environment, optimism about the future, etc. These are clearly less quantifiable dimensions. The multidisciplinary approach in this project is also motivated by the need for a broad and inclusive analysis of the links between development and international migration. When we use the term 'development' in this book, we therefore refer to both the economic measurement of GDP per capita and the broader cluster of non-quantifiable social and political dimensions.

—2—

Time and Space in International Migration

Gunnar Malmberg

The Immobility Paradox

The causes of international migration may seem easy to identify. The income differentials between South and North would be a sufficient explanation for a large portion of the immigration to Europe and North America. From a Eurocentric perspective one might see a long list of motives for 'them' to come to 'us', in the 'El Dorado' of the European welfare-states. But if the perspective is changed and the issues looked upon from African, Asian or Latin American perspectives, probably only a small share of the population on these continents would regard migration to the North as a conceivable, possible and preferable solution to their everyday problems. Most potential emigrants would not be allowed to pass the international borders into the countries of the North. But even if immigration were free, an overwhelming majority would probably stay at home. A large part of the population would not have the means to go. Many would be too firmly rooted in the villages, towns or neighbourhoods where they live. Others would regard a life in the North as inferior to the one they have. Many have probably not even thought about migration as an option and some would prefer other destinations to the countries of the North. Other forms of mobility would appear as a more possible solution. In certain cases, however, migration to the North might be the most feasible alternative, by preference or for compulsory reasons.

Data reveal that migration between countries and continents is only a small segment of the contemporary world migration. Most migrants move within countries and to closely located destinations. Among international migrants people from the poorest countries are underrepresented, and economic development seems to trigger rather than constrain emigration. A substantial part of the migrants from developing countries move to other countries in the Third World. The overwhelming majority of the world's population remain in the country and region where they were born, throughout their lives. Income differentials might be a sufficient explanation of the actual migration, but the large number of non-migrants is rather an anomaly in relation to the economic disparities between the North and the South. This immobility paradox challenges important theories of international migration. Since the late nineteenth century, when Ravenstein (1885) formulated the 'laws of migration', influential theories of migration have regarded regional economic disparities as major determinants of migration. However, in international migration studies three important anomalies can be observed in relation to the dominating theories:

a. Migration from poor to rich countries is not as frequent as might be expected.
b. Economic growth in countries of the South does not seem to reduce emigration.
c. Emigration rates vary considerably between countries and regions on the same economic level and it seems as if, once started, migration tends to continue, partly independent of changing economic conditions.

These are three anomalies that justify the questions raised in this book:

a. Why do people move from South to North?
b. Why do most people in the South remain in their countries of origin?
c. How is migration related to the development process?

The aim of this chapter is to present a few influential geographical theories of migration and to discuss to what extent they may contribute to the understanding of these questions. In the following paragraphs different geographical perspectives are presented. The influential push-pull model and its critique is discussed. This criticism forms a point of departure for presenting alternative geographical perspectives on migration, including theories in the same tradition as the push-pull model (e.g. the gravity model) and theories developed in the alternative structural and humanist traditions. The importance of the different spatial and temporal perspectives of migration and its determinants is stressed, and thereby the questions initially raised are partly reformulated.

Mobility in Time and Space

The dichotomy of moving/staying is a common point of departure in geographical migration research. However, there seems to be no explicit theory as to why people, to such a large extent, reside in their home region and in their country of origin throughout their lives. Staying seems to be the expected outcome, migration the unexpected, i.e. the one to be explained. Migration is often defined as a permanent and long-distance change of the place of residence, as a short-distance move is regarded as local mobility, and moves of short-term residents are regarded as temporary mobility. In studies of international migration, to stay is equivalent to remaining within the national borders. From this point of departure the stayers form a large majority, although most people, even in sedentary agricultural societies, are normally engaged in various forms of spatial mobility (see e.g. Skeldon 1990).

Compared to some other forms of spatial mobility, migration results in a more immediate and fundamental change, a definite relocation of the base of everyday activities. It differs from short-distance mobility in that everyday access to places, environments, resources and people is totally altered. In comparison to temporary mobility, migration also results in a more permanent and thus fundamental change in the life situation. But often the difference between migration and other kinds of spatial mobility is less apparent.

The rapidly changing social and economic conditions in Third World countries create new forms of adjustment and life strategies in the urban and rural areas, including new forms of social organisation, eco-technological organisation, political actions (voice) and spatial mobility (exit). However, the choice is not only between one type of voice, exit or loyalty – to use Hirschmann's (1970) classical concepts – but between a large variety of strategies and actions. To emigrate is only one possible response to changing conditions, and emigration is only one of many kinds of spatial mobility. The alternative to migration – to remain in the area of origin – also includes different forms of mobility in time and space. To many people in Third World countries, the temporary spatial mobility over a day, a week, a month or a year is an important part of the economic and social organisation of that society, and a possible response to what we frequently regard as migration determinants (Chapman and Prothero 1983). Migration is often looked upon as a once-in-a-lifetime event determined by present conditions at origin and destination, but it is often the result of many strategic decisions that form a life course of various types of mobilities through time-space.

In relation to international migration the alternatives include a variety of time-space strategies such as remaining at the place of origin, tem-porary circulation, rural–rural migration and long-distance migration to towns and cities (Chapman and Prothero 1983, Skeldon 1990, Adepoju 1995). Temporary migration is occasionally an alternative, but may also be an important gateway to permanent migration. New ties are

Gunnar Malmberg

established in the place of destination and attitudes to the receiving societies – foreign societies and urban centres – are altered. In many Third World countries migration to new frontier areas, for instance in outer Indonesia (Geertz 1963) or Amazonas (Sjöholt 1988), has offered important alternatives for the rural population. But the main alternative for the rural majority is moving to the cities, rather than going abroad or to some other rural location (Gugler 1988). The opportunities for internal migration might be one of the most important explanations of why international migration does not occur.

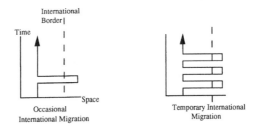

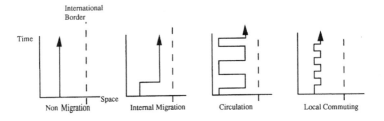

Figure 2.1 Time-Space Mobility Patterns; Examples of Individual Life Paths through Time-Space

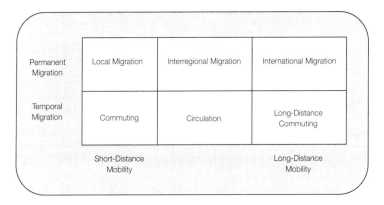

Figure 2.2 Temporal and Spatial Dimensions of Human Mobility

In the so-called *time geography* developed by Hägerstrand (1975), mobility is analysed from a micro point of view; individuals' *life paths* or trajectories through time-space are described and analysed in an everyday or a lifetime perspective. Migration is just one form of *time-space mobility*, while others include for instance staying and commuting (see figures 2.1 and 2.2). Empirical analyses of individuals' time-space mobility in different societies demonstrate the huge variety in human mobility and life paths, but also reveal the frequency of certain forms of spatial mobility and of some dominating *time-space mobility patterns*. To choose a certain path through time-space, for instance to go abroad, occasionally develops into a common established *time-space strategy*. For eighteenth-century European peasants, staying in the home village for a lifetime was one important time-space strategy; for pastoralists circulation is a dominating strategy; and moving to the cities is a common strategy for young Latin American women; while emigration to Europe has been an important strategy for North African men during the last decades.

When we analyse different time-space mobility patterns, determinants of both staying and moving are identified and the distinction between migration and immobility is less apparent. One way to address the topic at hand is to identify the determinants of international migration in relation to other forms of mobility and to analyse how, for instance, internal migration affects (triggers or constrains) international migration. If international migration is regarded not as the opposite of staying but as one form of mobility in time and space, the questions initially raised may be reformulated in the following way:

a. Under what circumstances does emigration become a major alternative to other time-space strategies?

b. Under what circumstances are other kinds of time-space strategy chosen instead of emigration?

c. How are different kinds of time-space strategy related to the development process?

Geographical Perspectives on Migration

Geography is about spatial differentiation, the way it is changed by man and nature, and about the impact of geographical conditions on society and human life. Geographers focus upon the interplay between, for instance, physical, social, economic and political conditions in spatial contexts. The spatial distribution and redistribution of people are decisive for the geographical variations of human activities, and for the role of mankind in changing the face of the earth. Migration as well as other forms of spatial mobility – long-distance, short-distance, everyday mobility and once-in-a-lifetime migration – are thus central themes in population geography. However, geographers have frequently used, integrated and reinterpreted migration theories from economics, sociology and demography, so that it is not surprising that geographical migration studies have followed a path of development similar to that in other social sciences. As in other disciplines, migration theories are often classified into macro- and micro-theories (White 1980, Cadwallader 1992, Massey et al. 1993), where the distinction is related to the actors and the level of aggregation. In macro-theories the actor is the population aggregate responding to conditions at the places of origin and potential destinations, while in micro-theories the explanation is sought in the behaviour and

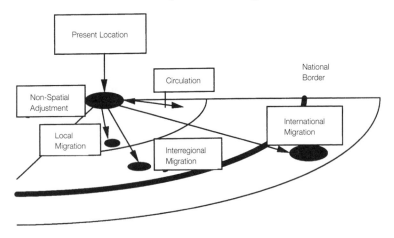

Figure 2.3 Alternative Time-Space Mobility Patterns

decisions made by individuals. In theories influenced by neo-classical ideas the 'economic man' makes his decisions on the basis of a purely economic rationality, whereas in behavioural analyses, for instance, other aspects of migration decision are taken into consideration. Contemporary migration studies also focus on actors at the meso-level (such as households, social networks, institutions) and on the problem of linking the micro- and the macro-level (Massey 1990, Cadwallader 1992)[1].

For geographers the influence on migration of environmental conditions (social, political, economic, physical, etc.) in different time-space settings is a more crucial issue than in other social sciences. One important role of geographers is to emphasise the influence of the spatial dimension and the necessity to adapt different spatial and temporal perspectives on migration studies. Migration analysis is not only carried out on the macro- or the micro-level (analysing population aggregates or individuals), but also on different temporal and spatial levels – on a local, regional, national or global levels using short-term or long-term perspectives (see figure 2.5).

In the first part of this century, geography was dominated by an idiographic tradition, where spatial diversity and the uniqueness of specific places were the focus of attention. In the post-war period many geographers were influenced by nomothetic ideas and positivist ideals, and sought general explanations to spatial phenomena. Measurable

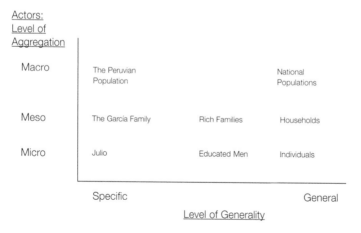

Figure 2.4 Actors in Theories on Different Levels of Generalisation and Aggregation (Macro–Meso–Micro)

1. See chapter 7.

Gunnar Malmberg

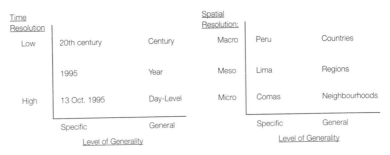

Time Resolution			Spatial Resolution:		
Low	20th century	Century	Macro	Peru	Countries
	1995	Year	Meso	Lima	Regions
High	13 Oct. 1995	Day-Level	Micro	Comas	Neighbourhoods
	Specific	General		Specific	General
	Level of Generality			Level of Generality	

Figure 2.5 Spatial Units and Time Perspectives in Theories of Different Levels of Generalisation and of Different Temporal and Spatial Resolution.

economic and spatial conditions became important explanatory factors in these geographical models (Haggett 1965, Harvey 1969). For a long time, migration research was dominated by a macro-approach, focusing on the population's adjustment to the social, economic and physical conditions on a macro-level (Cadwallader 1992). *Interaction models,* which drew attention to the influence on migration flows of distance and population potentials, became an important tool in forecasts of inter-regional migration (Olsson 1965, Stillwell 1991). The *migration systems* approach, introduced in geography by Mabogunje (1970), focused upon the interrelation between origins and destinations through information flows, personal contacts and social networks, and the way this mutual relationship influenced the destinations of migration flows.

The neo-classical economic approach to migration has also had a strong position in geography and has remained the most influential micro-theory. In reaction to the neo-classical and macro-theories, behavioural approaches were developed in geography – focusing on migration decisions, the influence of selective information, social networks, etc (see e.g. Wolpert 1975, Clark 1981).

Subsequently, structural and marxist theories became another major alternative, emphasising the importance for migration of the *political and socio-economic structure* (Shrestha 1988), and in reaction to the dominance of quantitative geography and structuralism, humanistic approaches have more recently gained a central position in geographical research.

In contemporary migration studies qualitative methods have become more important and the foundations of earlier migration theories have been questioned. Skeldon (1990) has pointed to the disadvantages of a static definition of residence. It has also been claimed that the geographical units signifying migration origins and destinations, such as *places*, *regions* and *nations,* are not only spatially limited areas with objectively defined characteristics, but also socially constructed categories with specific values and meanings for people in various contexts (Jackson and Penrose 1993). In the critique of behavioural approaches to migration, the importance of the meso-level has been stressed, for instance the role of households in migration decisions (Halfacree 1995, Moon 1995). Geographers have also become more aware of the importance of gender relations for migration and of the fact that migration is a gender-specific process (Katz and Monk 1993, Halfacree 1995).[2] The studies of time-space trajectories, biographies and life paths, initially introduced by Hägerstrand, have received increasing attention in geographical migration studies (Katz and Monk 1993). Recent trends in geographical migration studies are to a large extent the same as in neighbouring disciplines, but the emphasis on spatial (and temporal) perspectives is still a unique characteristic of geographers' approaches.

Critique of the Push-Pull Model

A traditional push-pull model based on the assumptions of neo-classical economics has remained an influential perspective within geography (e.g. Lee 1966, Dorigo and Tobler 1983). The basic ideas of this perspective are that migrants respond to primarily economic conditions in the places of origin and destination, that migrants have adequate information about living conditions in the place of destination, that the migration decision is based on a rational economic calculation and that migration is therefore the response to the actual economic conditions in the places of origin and destination. Although this model has been strongly criticised, it has maintained its important position in geographical textbooks, for instance, due to its simplicity and internal logic. To a certain degree, however, assumptions and perspectives in this model draw attention away from factors that might be essential for understanding the mechanisms of international migration. The critique of the model, formulated by researchers from different traditions, has demonstrated its limitations and the possibility of developing new alternative views of migration. A few of these limitations can be mentioned here:

1. The model regards residence in a geographical area as a static condition, although people are always mobile over shorter or longer distances.

2. Some of these perspectives have been important in other disciplines and are more thoroughly discussed in other chapters of this book: the nation-state from a political science point of view by Istiaq Ahmed (chapter 6), gender from an anthropological point of view by Gunilla Bjéren (chapter 8), and the meso-link from a sociological point of view by Thomas Faist (chapter 7).

2. In the push-pull model the concept of migration is not easily transferred from one spatial level to another, since migration, and the alternative to stay, is something quite different when referring, for example, to migration between villages or between nations. In studies on different spatial levels the concepts of origin and destination refer to various types of environments (i.e. nations, regions, cities or villages) that affect migration in different ways.

3. A traditional push-pull model does not sufficiently consider the effects on migration of distance, other migration flows, intervening opportunities, and the size of population potentials.

4. The model does not draw attention to the restructuring of either the demographic, physical, socio-economic or political conditions that create important preconditions for migration.

5. The models fails to deal with the influences on migration of information flows, personal contacts and social networks in migration systems.

6. Assumptions about migration decisions are inadequate, as:

   – Migrants and potential migrants respond not only to changing conditions in the environment and migration decisions are not merely based on economic calculations, but also on other kinds of considerations.
   – Potential migrants have only limited information and migration decisions are based on partially distorted views of conditions at the potential destinations and of a future at the place of origin.
   – A migration decision is neither an exclusively individual affair nor a completely voluntary act, but often a collective and strongly conditioned or constrained decision.

7. The model does not pay attention to the varying opportunities and inclinations of people in different situations (with different sex, age, class or cultural backgrounds) to make 'rational' migration decisions, and to substitute the 'utilities' of one place for those of another. Furthermore, it does not consider the restraining impact on emigration of different constraints and of engagements in various long-term and short-term projects.

These different kinds of limitations draw attention to some alternative perspectives on the issues of South to North migration and non-migration.[3]

---

3. For a further discussion of the critique of the traditional neo-classical migration model, see chapter 4.

Origin and Destination

Living conditions at the places of origin and destination are major determinants in influential geographical theories of migration. The push-pull model (Lee 1966) regards migration as a consequence of attractions in areas of destination and repulsive forces in the area of origin. In studies of international migration, the analysis has often been carried out at the national level. Characterised by the average socio-economic conditions, receiving and sending countries are defined as the origins and destinations. However, resources and constraints in the areas of origin and destination are selectively accessible for people in different life-situations. These individual differences in access might be essential to the mechanisms, character and size of migration. Aggregation to the national level means that information about migration determinants is lost, while alternative levels of analysis, on the local or regional level, might reveal other aspects.

Analyses on a local and individual level focus on the more immediate determinants of migration decisions. If the migration decision is a response to personal economic conditions then it is plausible to assume that migration is strongly affected by local conditions, and if the potential destination is a specific place, then the local economic conditions (rather than the average in the country) will affect the migration decision. Individual migration decisions are formed in everyday life and to a

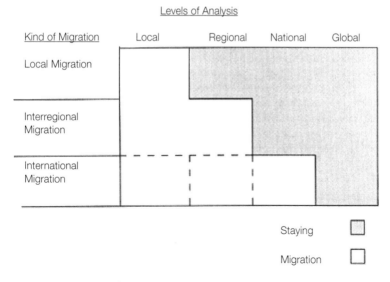

Figure 2.6 Definition of Migration on Different Levels of Analysis

large extent influenced by conditions on the local arena. As certain migrant groups have a tendency to cluster in specific places or to search for employment in limited sectors, migration is influenced only by the specific conditions in these economic sectors or regions. Analyses of international migration on a national level will most certainly miss important explanations to why people move and to why so many remain in the country of origin. However, some emigration determinants might be better analysed on a macro level, for instance the impact of changes in emigration policy or the restructuring of the political economy. The categorization of geographical units – places and nations, origins and destinations – by geographers, journalists, politicians, migrants, etc, is also part of the game that in the end might affect migration. It also affects our image of migration and of what might be regarded as a migration paradox.

In the traditional push-pull model migration is regarded as the response to static conditions, albeit migration decisions are obviously determined by the changing conditions on the micro- and macro-level. The choice of time resolution in migration studies thus similarly affects the identification of determinants. Economic, political or social conditions at the places of origin and destination are to a varying degree changing over time. While immigrant policies might change from one day to another, the average living standard in an industrialised country changes slowly. Individuals' life situations depend on circumstances that change from one day to another and on long-term processes throughout a lifetime. Different temporal perspectives will, on the national as well as on the individual level, reveal alternative migration determinants.

Geographers highlight the importance of location in space, as opposed to other factors that affect people's lives. However, it is important to stress that migration is not only a response to environmental conditions, but is also related to people's individual attributes, qualities and assets, and most certainly to the social relations between people. Age, sex, class and ethnicity also affect migration decisions. Class structure, gender systems, cultural values and racism at places of origin and destinations are factors that strongly affect the opportunities of women and men with different social and cultural backgrounds to make a living, to find employment, to adjust and to migrate. One shortcoming of traditional geographical theory is that place-specific conditions are often overestimated. People's economic or social situation are only partly dependent on where they live.

By analysing international migration on different levels of time-space resolution some possible explanations to the immobility paradox presented earlier can be identified:

- It is obvious that the average income differentials between origin and destination countries do not necessarily reflect the economic differences in the individual life situations and local environments of stayers and movers.
- The opportunities to use alternative strategies, for instance to try to improve the life situation locally or to migrate to other destinations within the national borders, is one important explanation of the 'paradox' of international immobility.

Distance, Barriers and Migration Potentials

The influence of physical *barriers* and *distance* on spatial mobility has been a central theme in geographical migration studies, although contemporary international migration seems to be more strongly influenced by non-physical barriers such as international borders and cultural distance. In the traditional *gravity model*, initially presented by Stouffer (1940), spatial interaction was assumed to be proportional to the population size at the places of origin and destination but decreasing with the square of the distance between the two. There are several explanations regarding the influence of distance on migration: (a) The costs of moving are related to the distance; (b) migration is often triggered by other kinds of international contacts, such as trade, which are strongly affected by distance decay; (c) physical distance is often related to perceived cultural distance, which similarly constrains migration; and (d) the propensity to move to distant locations depends on the number of intervening opportunities.

More sophisticated versions of the gravity model have provided efficient tools for anticipating the spatial distribution of interregional migration (Wilson 1974, Haynes and Fotheringham 1984, Fotheringham 1991). However, these models have been less relevant when applied to international migration, since conditions other than distance seem to have a stronger impact on destinations of international migration (S. Öberg 1994). The development of international networks, communication links and interpersonal contacts has been of greater importance to international migration than physical distance.

In the gravity model it is assumed that migration is proportional to the population size in the places of origin and destination. However, the major population concentrations of the world have hitherto contributed to international migration in only a limited degree. A probable scenario would thus be a rapidly increasing emigration from the world's major population concentration in China, India, Indonesia and the former Soviet Union (King and Öberg 1993). The development of huge immigrant communities might also function as poles of attraction for further migration, so that migration might be proportional to the size of this specific population rather than to the total population in the areas of destination.

Migration is also determined by different types of barriers or intervening obstacles. Physical barriers, such as mountains, oceans and deserts, have had a long-term constraining effect on international migration. Today, the national border is probably the most important barrier influencing international migration. The permeability of the national border, the opening and the closing of the gateways, is one of the most important factors affecting international migration in a short-term perspective.

According to the gravity model, the interaction between locations is also influenced by alternative intermediate locations or *intervening opportunities* (Stouffer 1940). For potential migrants from rural areas in Third World countries, urban centres (and to some extent peripheral frontier lands) provide important intervening opportunities. The attraction of these alternative locations might strongly influence the number of emigrants. Countries with large populations have more intervening opportunities within the national border and in accordance with the theory, emigration rates should be higher from smaller countries.

The interaction theory presents some possible explanations of the immobility paradox:

- The effects of large physical and cultural distances are still, in certain cases, major obstacles to South to North migration.
- The attractions of intervening opportunities (e.g urban areas) within the national borders influence the emigration rates.
- The construction of political (or other) barriers often has a strong restraining effect on South to North migration.

Environmental Change, Population Growth and Migration

The eco-demographic approach to migration has its roots in the environmentalist tradition of geography, focusing on the influence of physical conditions on the subsistence opportunities in different environments (Simkins 1970, Grigg 1980, Wood 1994). This perspective has become increasingly influential as the problems of population growth and environmental change have been linked to the debate about increasing migration pressure (King and Öberg 1993).

The relationship between population change and economic development is a crucial issue in the development debate. *Neo-Malthusian* ideas, which regard population pressure as the major constraint to economic development, maintain a central position in current debate about environmental and demographic change. From the other classical standpoint, it has been argued that population growth is a dynamic factor that triggers development, for instance in agriculture (Boserup 1965, Wilkinson 1977). These positions are based on different views of the opportunities for increasing production and economising with scarce resources in a situation of rapid population growth. Similar pessimistic and optimistic positions are found in the contemporary debate concerning the possibilities for handling environmental problems through new technology and, simultaneously, for maintaining and spreading the Western life-style to countries of the South.[4]

The impact on migration of physical environments and population growth is a central topic within the eco-demographic tradition of geographical research (Simkins 1970, Grigg 1980). In a macro-perspective it is argued that population growth and environmental deterioration trigger migration. However, of more importance for the question of migration is the fact that a large number of the ecological problems affecting people in the Third World are generated at the local level, resulting in over-exploitation and land degradation and thereby heavily influencing the economic situation of the rural population. Wood (1994) argues that forced eco-migration is an increasing problem in the Third World. However, the difference between eco-demographic and economic problems is sometimes vague, and there is always a mixture of compulsory and voluntary components in a migration decision. S. Öberg (1994) talks about soft and hard determinants, for instance, poverty and starvation. Eco-demographic problems usually result in economic problems and the responses – to economise with resources, change the production methods etc – are often the same as in the case of, for example, increasing production costs.

Migration can be the result of short-term ecological changes such as environmental catastrophies, but also of long-term eco-demographic changes such as population growth or long-term resource degradation. But the consequences of such changes are not predetermined. Whether or not population growth triggers migration depends on the availability of alternative strategies to solve the problems. Geertz (1963) emphasised the impact of ecological and social conditions for increasing production through intensified cultivation. Grigg (1980) pointed to the importance of various strategies, e.g. population control, intensified cultivation, increase of non-farm income and migration. Rural societies often use a variety of strategies to handle problems caused by ecological disequilibrium and demographic change. In cases of economic deterioration caused by ecological changes, potential migrants seldom have the means for long-distance migration. As in the case of several other migration

---

4. See further in chapter 5.

determinants, ecological changes will only occasionally result in 'flight migration'.

Another attempt to relate population growth to migration is made by Zelinsky (1971), who links the demographic transition to a mobility transition; a development over time of a different form of migration. From the historical experiences of European migration he presents a generalised stage model of a *mobility transition*, assuming that similar patterns would also be found in the developing world. One assumption was that out-migration is triggered by social, cultural and economic changes in the area of origin. Parallel to this change is an extension of the information fields which links locations to each other and affects migration opportunities. The economic differences between the places of origin and destination thus become the major migration determinant, and people move from poorer to richer regions until the income differences are levelled out.

When the transition theory is applied to the issues of international migration, however, several objections can be made. Firstly, that the hypothesis is mainly concerned with the conditions at the place of origin and not with the influence of preconditions at the destination. Secondly, that emigration is often dependent on a large number of factors, some of which are of coincidental character, for example the ability to cross international borders and to find a place to live and a source of income. These conditions often change over time and vary between places. The preconditions for emigration are not necessarily related to the general economic growth in a country. They are also affected by, for instance, the shifting opportunities to choose other forms of time-space strategies.

In the migration-transition model, international mobility is only included in the early stage of frontier migration. Zelinsky's model thus refers only to the great out-migration from Europe to America and Australia, whereas the last few decades of extensive international migration are not integrated into the model. This clearly demonstrates the problem of the stage models. Apart from the level of economic development or modernisation in a country, mobility is to a large extent determined by the position of that country in the international economic and political systems (Taylor 1989). In the migration-transition model, there are good theoretical explanations for the weak relationship between, on the one hand, emigration and, on the other, economic and demographic development.

Rapid population growth and environmental deterioration could be reasons to regard the relative immobility as a paradox, but:

- Emigration is only one of many possible responses to economic problems caused by population growth or ecological disequilibrium.

- Forced eco-migration is a rare phenomenon and emigration to the North is seldom a possible alternative for those who escape natural disasters.
- Emigration rates are, apart from demographic changes, determined by a variety of conditions in both origin and potential destination areas.

Migration and Structural Change

The push-pull model presents a static view of migration determinants, although it is obvious that the determining factors are changing over time. In alternative approaches the relationship between migration and changes of socio-economic structure on a macro-level has been analysed. The mobility transition model was part of the developmentalist approach and it regarded migration as part of a development process. Demographic transition, modernisation in rural areas and industrialisation were regarded as determinants of the regional differentiation and of the interregional interaction that triggered the increasing long-distance migration.

The alternative structuralist approach also focuses on the impact of the social, economic or political structures that determine the preconditions for migration. Shrestha (1988), however, argues that migration in a Third World context has to be analysed in relation to the development of capitalist labour-market relations, the proletarianisation process, and the regional and international division of labour. The development of colonialism, post-colonialism and an international economy created relationships of dependency, dominance and an exploitation of the South by the North (Taylor 1989). From a geographical point of view, this resulted in new forms of spatial differentiation and spatial interaction that became major prerequisites for interregional and international migration.

In the literature on Third World migration, the expansion of the capitalist economy in rural areas is often regarded as a major precondition for increasing mobility (Gilbert and Gugler 1981). The dependency on the market economy makes rural communities in the Third World more vulnerable to fluctuations in the external economy, resulting in the dissolution of the social structure in traditional local communities, an increased social diversification and a process of proletarianisation and semi-proletarianisation (Chayanov 1966, Roberts 1995). Improvement of interregional and international communications have resulted in a more efficient innovation diffusion and an intensi-fication of public and private information flows, which decreases the cultural distances between rural communities, urban societies and countries in the industrialised world. It is important to stress that the socio-economic transformation of rural areas in the Third World is a diversified process. The way cultural, social and economic changes are interrelated varies in different time-space contexts. Socio-economic change in, for instance, a Mexican community in the 1930s is not equivalent to the contemporary transformation in a Kenyan village. The processes of external penetration and the local conditions are very different but so too, are the opportunities and attitudes to solve the problems through internal migration or emigration.

Migration within and from the Third World is also affected by the social and economic changes in the urban areas which, from a structuralist point of view, are strongly determined by the capitalist penetration of the peripheral economies (Castells 1989). Third World cities function as attractors and alternatives to emigration, but also as an intermediate station in a process of stepwise migration from rural areas to industrialised countries. Urban growth in the Third World is often described as overurbanisation, mainly resulting from a rural push, as a consequence of the huge subsistence problems in rural areas (Sovani 1964, Gugler 1988). It has been assumed that the inflow of people to the cities does not correspond to the attractiveness of the urban areas, as the migrants often face severe social and economic problems in growing squatter and slum areas. However, empirical research on rural–urban migration suggests that the move into Third World cities often results in improved economic conditions, and that the changes in migration intensity are related to shifting economic opportunities in urban rather than rural areas. The poorest people are normally underrepresented among migrants (Gilbert and Gugler 1981, Gugler 1988). Migrants are attracted by opportunities to find well-paid jobs, but also by the possibilities for making a living through self-employment within the informal economy. Informal solutions to problems such as housing and transportation have also become important for the living conditions among migrants in Third World cities (Brown and Sanders 1981).

For a majority of the Third World population today, urban areas represent the major migration alternative, and the future development and attractiveness of Third World cities could be one of the major factors affecting the so-called migration pressure on Europe and other parts of the industrialised world. However, urban areas are also important origins of emigration. Among urban middle-class people in the Third World, migration to Europe or the United States is often regarded as a strategic move in a social and economic career. Emigration from former colonies to, for instance, France, Britain and the Netherlands reinforced the historical linkages between the old metropolises and the urban areas of former colonies. Refugee immigration to Europe in the 1970s also established new migration linkages between, on the one hand, other industrialised countries (e.g. Germany and Sweden) and, on the other, the urban upper and middle classes in some Third World countries (e.g. Chile and Iran). The changing opportunities for crossing the national border are probably a major factor affecting the size of these migration flows.

- Structural theories demonstrate how social, economic and political changes trigger migration from the rural areas of the Third World. However, the consequences of structural changes in developing societies are strongly dependent on contextual factors, and there is no obvious relationship between emigration and, for instance, the expansion of capitalist socio-economic relations. Migration rates also depend on the conditions in, and access to, potential destinations.
- The development in the different Third World cities – in formal and informal sectors – is of crucial importance for the opportunities to make a decent living within the borders of a Third World nation. The restructuring of the urban economy is thus an essential factor in determining the frequencies of emigration from the South to the North, and is a major determinant of international migration and immobility.

Migration Systems

In geography, the migration-systems approach was initially developed by Mabogunje (1970). He argued that migration in the Third World was the response to a combined effect of conditions at origin and destination, and that rural–urban migration was determined by the interrelationship between sub-systems in the rural and urban areas. Migration-systems models were developed in reaction to the shortcomings of push-pull and interaction models in explaining the diversified geographical distribution of migration flows (Castles and Miller 1993). In the original migration systems approach, as well as in some interaction models, specific migration flows are related to other flows. It is assumed, for instance, that migration from one country to another will affect migration to alternative destinations. Migration within a country will influence emigration from that country, immigration to a country might affect out-migration and the migration between two destinations tends to grow over time; migration feeds more migration. According to the migration-systems approach (Gurak and Caces 1992), population mobility is related to other forms of spatial interaction, such as economic, political, historical and cultural linkages. Migration is often affected by events, decisions and activities in the past that created linkages between specific geographical areas. The migration process is often maintained through processes of cumulative causation (Myrdal 1957) in which the networks play an essential role (Massey 1990).[5]

The migration systems approach has focused on social networks from a micro-perspective (Hugo 1981, Gurak and Caces 1992). Ritchey (1976) maintained that friendship and kinship could affect migration in four different ways; with (a) a negative effect, as long as major social relations prevailed within the origin area, (b) a constraining effect, as long as information from emigrated relatives provided a negative image of conditions at destination, (c) a stimulating effect, when this information was positive and encouraged migration, and (d) a positive effect on migration and the migrants' adjustment, when relatives provided assistance in the area of destination. Recent literature has stressed the importance of institutions for the development of a migration process (Cadwallader 1992, Castles and Miller 1993, Goos and Lindquist 1995).

International linkages are not only established between countries but more precisely between specific places or regions. As a consequence of the established individual linkages, emigration from one country is often directed to a specific area within the immigration country. The out-migration rate will be affected rather by conditions in these areas than by those in other potential immigration areas. Furthermore, the development over time of a migration system, through established social networks and a cumulative causation process, will in itself exert a strong influence on the number of migrants.

A geographical interpretation of the migration systems theory provides us with some explanations of the initially formulated questions about the lack of relationship between migration and economic development:

• Migration is determined to a high degree by the conditions and developments in specific places of origin and destination within a given migration system and not by the general development in all potential destinations and origins.
• The dynamics of a migration system strongly influence the development of migration over time, and result in a cumulative causation process, which is one explanation as to why the relationship between migration and economic development is not so obvious.

Migration Decisions

The migration decision approach was developed in reaction to the neo-classical migration theory (Wolpert 1975, Courgeau 1995). It was argued

5. See chapter 7.

that a migration decision is not only based on economic calculations but represents the result of a large number of considerations, that migration was seldom the result of one person's decision and that migrants often had scanty information about conditions at potential destinations. One central conclusion is that the image of alternative destinations is based on personal contacts rather than public information. Migration decisions are also supposed to be influenced by people's *mental maps* or *cognitive maps* (Clark 1981, Gould and White 1986), i.e. the knowledge, image and attitudes present in the minds of individuals or groups of near or remote geographical environments, including the positive or negative attitudes to these places and their characteristics. The construction and reproduction of these images are made through social interaction, in which different forms of biased information about places, regions and countries are interpreted. Important steps in making these images are the delimitation of geographical areas (for instance First World/Third World), the identification of specific locations (Sweden, Paris, Munich) and the evaluation of conditions there ('opportunities', 'problems').

A migration decision is not an exclusive matter for the individual person. Migration acts are often conditioned by more or less imperative decisions of other family members or by the collective family. They can also be strongly affected by other families' decisions. The migration of close relatives or friends may demonstrate both chances and obstacles and sometimes the positive outcome of moving. Rossi (1980) claimed that a large number of migration acts are directly caused by changing demographic and family conditions. More recent research has demonstrated the importance of moving together, marriage, divorces, becoming an adult, having children, growing old, etc (Holm et al. 1989). The role of the family and household structure in migration is one essential issue for migrant researchers.[6] Although these explanations of migration are more easily applied to local mobility than to international migration, it is obvious that, for example, the entry into new stages of the life course is a factor that affects any kind of migration. When families choose between different time-space strategies the combination of the various individual paths has to be considered, and the result of the individual's path is dependent on the plans of other family members. The opportunities for men and for women to migrate depend on the gender system and the structure of the household (Buijs 1993, Katz and Monk 1993).[7]

A major critique of the neo-classical migration theory points to the fact that migration is not influenced solely by economic considerations. In general, a voluntary migration decision is motivated by a wish to

6. See also chapter 8.
7. See also chapter 8.

obtain some kind of change in everyday life, while at the same time most people have a wish to maintain some kind of stability, for instance, to increase purchasing power and still keep the immediate contacts with relatives and friends. The possibility of obtaining the intended change and maintaining a desired stability depends on (a) the differences between the conditions in the places of origin and destination, (b) the possibilities and necessity for the migrant to bring with him/her possessions, relatives, customs, etc, (c) the opportunity to maintain contacts with the home area by return visits, letters, telephone calls, etc, and (d) the inclination to substitute important parts of everyday life in the place of origin with a new situation in the potential place of destination.

Migration often presupposes that there are apparent differences but also important similarities between the area of origin and potential destinations. These differences and similarities might depend on general conditions in the country of origin and destination or on local or individual conditions that affect everyday life. But migration decisions may also bring about unintended consequences resulting from unknown conditions. Besides migration, there are other alternative ways of obtaining the intended changes, maintaining the desired stability and avoiding the risk of unintended consequences of migration. The evaluation of different time-space strategies is thus essential to the decision to move.

International immobility and the lack of relationship between migration and development might be explained by the facts that:

- Migration decisions are to a large extent influenced by factors other than economic considerations.
- Migrants often have limited and distorted information about potential destinations and migration decisions are not made only by independent individuals.

Places

The concept of *place* is central in geography and it has been widely discussed and reinterpreted in contemporary geographical literature (Entrikin 1991, Tuan 1991). In traditional migration literature the *place utility* concept is used to embrace all the conditions in a location that might affect a migration decision (Cadwallader 1992). The place-utility concept thus refers to the sum of qualities, both positive and negative, in a specific location. In contemporary humanistic geography the distinction between *location* and *place* is stressed (Entrikin 1991). The first concept refers to the geographical location where people and things are situated. The latter refers, on the one hand, to the physical features and social life in a limited space and, on the other, to the subjective images, values and meanings that this specific geographical place represents to people. A *place* is a 'whole' and might have values for people that exceed the sum of the various qualities in that location. A place where someone has grown up might represent crucial and positive values which cannot easily be substituted by qualities at another location. In such places people become insiders with a specific understanding of social life, an understanding that they cannot easily transfer to another place. A person's identity might be strongly tied to local places, but also in different ways, to other geographical areas, such as countries or cities (Relph 1976).

Apart from social and economic conditions, people can also be emotionally tied to physical features of a specific place, such as houses, streets or forests. Whereas people may die, move or change, the physical characteristics of a place may often remain relatively unchanged. Place attachment of this kind might constitute an important obstacle to out-migration, and an attraction for return migration. However, places do not necessarily represent something positive, and the attitude to a place might equally well trigger out-migration. When places represent a meaningful 'whole' the choice between moving or staying should not be regarded merely as a comparative calculation of the sum of qualities among these places.

- Strong ties to specific places or geographical units can provide important explanations as to why people prefer to stay in the place of residence and reject emigration despite the economic advantages of moving abroad.

Time Geography

The time-geographical perspective developed by Hägerstrand (1975a, 1975b, 1993) emphasises the importance of location *and* duration of single events, intended actions, activities, projects and constraints. It focuses on the individual's actions and how they are determined in specific time-space situations and contexts. This perspective has drawn geographers' attention to the temporal dimension and has also influenced other social sciences.[8]

One of Hägerstrand's central ideas is that activities are strongly conditioned by physical and social constraints that prevent us from doing certain things but enable us to do others (Hägerstrand 1975b, Pred 1981, Åquist 1992). Hägerstrand draws attention to the importance of certain

---

8. See chapter 8.

time-geographical constraints that affect people's opportunities to carry out various acts and planned projects. He distinguishes between three types of constraints: capacity constraints (when the individual does not have the physical, economic or social means to realise certain acts), coupling constraints (the potential activities are constrained since individuals cannot be engaged in various activities or projects or be at different locations simultaneously) and steering constraints (rules, laws, etc., that are created with the intention of limiting or giving increased access to time-space). In relation to migration, travelling costs and distance provide examples of capacity constraints. The impossibility of moving abroad without immediate access to the home village is an example of a coupling constraint, while immigration laws are examples of steering constraints.

In a lifetime perspective, the individual's path through time and space is strongly conditioned by a number of collectively defined projects in which he/she is engaged (Hägerstrand 1975a, 1975b). Some of these projects are strongly tied to specific places, while others are easily transferred to new locations. Sometimes important goals in life cannot be realised outside a specific place.

In everyday life people take part in a wide range of activities and projects. They are socially linked to other people in more or less institutionalised and long-lasting social groupings. Strategic decisions such as migration are not made independently of these activities, projects and social ties. To move means that a substantial portion of these will have to be cut off and that other people's projects and activities are also affected. When essential projects become footloose or substitutable, it might be easier both to move and to remain in the place of origin.

Projects and events also have a time duration which is often flexible but sometimes given, so-called *embedded time* (Åquist 1992). Growing old, learning a new language, adapting to another culture, becoming a citizen in a new country – these are examples of processes that have an embedded time of importance for migrants. Other examples are the individual or collective migration-decision process, the individual life cycle, the demographic transition and the migration cycle.

While internal migration in general seems to be strongly dependent on fundamental changes in the social and economic structure, international migration may to a large extent be determined by occasional and situational conditions – at least in the initial phase of a migration cycle. The behaviour of a few single pioneer migrants might determine the development of the migration pattern for a whole community. The coincidental timing between a liberal immigration policy in one country and a *coup d'état* in another (as in the case of Sweden and Chile in the 1970s) can result in an unexpected in- and out-migration of significance for both countries for some decades. Structural conditions, such as economic disparities or different political systems, are necessary but not always sufficient to start a migration process. In particular, the strong selectivity in origins and destinations of international migration is related to such 'coincidental' conditions.

Time geography is essentially a micro-perspective, but a time-space perspective is also applicable in the analyses of determinants and processes on the macro-level, since any phenomenon has an extension in time and space. Fielding (1993) demonstrates how different short-term and long-term economic and political changes in Western Europe have affected immigration. Emigration from the South will also be influenced by similar long-term and short-term changes of political and socio-economic conditions in the countries of origin.

Migration is influenced by long-term processes such as the expansion of the capitalist world system or the demographic transition. It is also influenced by the short-term effects of business cycles or immigration policies, as well as by the sudden effects of occasional political decisions. The combined effect of these different processes and their extension in time (long-term, short-term) *and* space (local to global level) determines the individual life paths and the population's mobility patterns to a large degree, and thereby determines the significance of international migration and non-migration.

When looking at the questions raised initially, time geography provides us with some possible explanations:

- If people are strongly engaged in a large number of projects in the place of origin this is a strong constraint on emigration, despite income disparities.
- Processes with an embedded time might restrain migration on certain occasions and make it possible only at specific moments, so that the occasional timing of migration determinants might thus be more important than structural conditions. Emigration is thus a feasible and preferable strategy only when a large number of factors coincide with each other in time and space.

Conclusions

Some geographical perspectives on migration have been presented and discussed in this chapter, with the aim of exploring the initially presented questions: Why do people move? Why do so many stay? How is migration related to the development process? It is maintained that a time-space perspective is essential in the analysis of international migration and immobility. By studying migration at different levels of time-space resolution, alternative explanations of international migration and immobility are identified. Analyses of emigration at a local level will illuminate different aspects of migration from those arising from studies at a national level. Similarly, a long-term perspective on economic and political changes, or on an individual's life course, will also focus on different aspects from those arising from a short-term, day-to-day approach.

From the time-space perspective, South to North migration and immobility are viewed not as a simple dichotomy but as a rough generalisation. There are different forms of emigration and the alternative to emigration is not only to stay but also to move in another way, as a variety of more or less established time-space strategies are often available for people in different situations and settings. This perspective demonstrates some possible explanations of the immobility paradox. Circulation and internal migration (rural–rural, rural–urban, urban–urban, urban–rural) are often well-established strategies and are thus more probable alternatives than moving abroad. If the internal regional variation is great, migration within the country (for instance to urban areas) might result in large income improvements, and might thus provide a sufficiently good alternative to emigration. Internal alternatives may function as intervening opportunities, but could also be a first step towards the development of extensive emigration – from rural areas to cities and then to countries in the North.

In this overview a number of important geographical theories and some further explanations of the so-called immobility paradox have been presented. According to the dominant theories, migration decisions result from the pros and cons of places of origin and potential destinations. If economic conditions alone were considered, the relatively small number of migrants from South to North might seem to be an anomaly. But migration decisions are influenced by a large number of actors (individuals, families or groups), with different objectives and rationalities. A variety of anticipated conditions thus influence the decision, for example personal security, social network, physical and cultural environment. If information about distant countries of the North is scanty or unreliable, migration may be too risky and, despite large income disparities, other time-space strategies are thus chosen and emigration rejected.

To move to a new environment means to substitute resources and relations at a given place for those of another place. This is often difficult, especially if the person is firmly rooted in the place of origin, and closely integrated with people and projects there. If conditions at origin and destination are very different, migration might be too big a step. Migration decisions are often part of a long-term strategy of a family or an individual, and related to other activities and projects. If people are strongly committed to these projects and in other ways tied to the home community or to the physical place where they live, then it is difficult for them to move. However, if people and projects of significance are transferred to a new location this might trigger out-migration. For most people there seem to be obvious advantages in remaining in the place of origin, especially for insiders. By choosing other time-space strategies – short-distance migration, temporary migration or circulation – the pros and cons of both origins and destinations might be combined.

In a long-term perspective the developing countries are facing a period of huge socio-economic, political and demographic change, which will gradually affect, too, the preconditions for migration. Economic, social and cultural linkages are being established between the least developed and most developed parts of the world. Even remote rural areas are being integrated into the world economic system. Traditional production systems are losing their importance as modern technology and the market economy continue to advance. There is a strong tendency towards increasing out-migration and emigration from poorer regions, to cities or to other countries, as the regional and international wage-differentials become more apparent.

However, the consequences of structural changes depend on contextual factors. There is no obvious linear relationship between emigration and, for instance, the demographic transition or the expansion of a capitalist world system into different parts of the Third World; but there are, rather, the combined effects on migration of short-term and long-term processes, on both local and global levels, which have different consequences for migration in alternative contexts. The important international linkages and the diffusion of information have been stressed. For pioneer migrants the information has often been scarce, while in later stages of the migration cycle the picture of potential destinations may be more diversified, as a result of more intensified contacts. Information facilitates the migration decision and it promotes or constrains further migration. Migration often generates more migration. Links between the places or countries of origin and destination are often strengthened over time and are partly independent of changing economic conditions. Consequently many migration cycles seem to follow a specific pattern over time. They develop from a situation with only a few pioneer migrants into an established migration system.

Sometimes, however, migration ceases due to more restrictive immigration policy, unsuccessful adjustment, changing subsistence opportunities, etc. While distance and physical barriers seem to have less impact on contemporary international migration, it is obvious that political obstacles have a substantial, although more discontinuous, effect on migration. The combined effect in time and space of these intervening obstacles and of intervening opportunities would thus provide major explanations for the fact that other time-space strategies are chosen instead of South to North migration.

The theories of migration employed in geography are often a mix of borrowed and genuinely geographical theories. They provide a variety of potential explanations of migration and non-migration. Some are more generally applicable, while others are only valid within a limited domain. One common conclusion drawn by geographers is that well-known mechanisms and processes of migration should be analysed in relation to their contexts, as the outcomes may be fundamentally different in alternative settings. No single explanation of South to North migration or non-migration will be found. Nevertheless, it is possible to identify some important mechanisms and try to anticipate how they will operate in specific time-space contexts in some of the many regions in the many countries of Asia, Africa and Latin America.

—3—

Should I Stay or Should I Go?
Peter A. Fischer, Reiner Martin
and *Thomas Straubhaar*[1]

Introduction: Theories of Migration and the Migration Decision: A Model Framework

This chapter summarises the contributions of economic theory to two increasingly important questions. Why do some people migrate while at the same time most people decide to stay where they are?[2]

Why do people move? Numerous possible explanations have been set forth to answer this question. We are going to demonstrate what they essentially all have in common, namely the belief that differences in environmental macro-factors of geo-political spatial units (countries, regions, locations)[3] influence people's decisions to migrate and thereby cause migration. The exact form of these differences, however, can vary. They are by no means exclusively economic but include also differences in the social, cultural, political and geo-ecological situation. After all, good climate may in some cases be a perfectly valid reason to move to a different place. We call the analysis of migration-inducing environmental differences between geo-political units the 'macro-level' of migration research. Individual human beings, in our terminology the 'micro-level' of analysis, compare the macro-level units on the basis of perceived differences. In a decision-making process, elaborated at greater length below, people weigh the different advantages and disadvantages of their present macro-level unit of residence and potential alternatives and decide whether they want to remain within their present area of residence (decision to 'stay') or whether they want to move to a different geo-political unit (decision to 'go').

---

1. The authors are grateful to Tim Heinzmann for capable research assistance.
2. Definitions of 'migration' as well as some other important concepts related to South to North migration are provided in chapter 1.
3. See chapter 2 for a more explicit treatment and a critical evaluation of the role of space and time for migration.

The above conception of reasons to migrate leads to two major questions which are in effect the essence of a huge part of migration research. On the one hand, one wants to find out which macro-level differences dominate the decision-making process on the micro-level. Is it fair to speak of a dominance of economic motives such as wage differences or employment opportunities, and under which circumstances? Are there other differences between countries which are even more important? On the other hand, it has to be investigated how the decision-making process works, how information is processed and information problems tackled. In this chapter we concentrate on the latter set of questions, which means that we usually assume the causal macro-differences to be exogenously given.[4]

Migration is often categorised as *voluntary* or *involuntary* migration. The latter, depending on the specific situation, could also be defined as flight, expulsion or refugee movement. Causes can, for example, be wars, political terror or ecological disasters. In such situations, the urge of the individual to move to a different country or region is likely to be extremely strong, especially in the case of concrete dangers for life or safety. One can thus argue that involuntary migrants try to minimise their risks rather than maximise their utility. Nevertheless the basic mechanisms of migration decision making as indicated above and explored at greater length below remain in place. We therefore do not see the distinction between voluntary and involuntary migration as particularly helpful. Instead we perceive what one may call 'involuntary' migration as extreme situations where the decision to go is self-evident.[5] The need to decide *where* and *when* to move, however, remains in principle the same as for 'voluntary' migration.

Let us assume a two-unit world, made up of countries A and B. The sum of all 'would like to go'-decisions by the inhabitants of A or B at a given time constitutes the *migration potential* of this unit. Thus all inhabitants of country A who are willing and potentially able to migrate to B make up for A's migration potential at time t. This potential faces B's demand for immigration which is determined by macro-factors and the (politico-economically determined)[6] willingness of B to accept immigrants from A. In a situation where B's demand is high enough and

4. Macro-level issues are dicussed in more details in chapters 4, 5 and – as far as political differences are concerned – chapter 6.
5. For people fearing oppression, the decision whether to go or to stay may actually be on whether to raise their voice in a given society or to exit the system. For an application of Hirschman's (1970) idea of exit and voice to migration theory see chapter 6.
6. The politico-economic approach perceives actual policy action (which is here taken to reflect people's willingness to accept immigration) as the outcome of policy makers' attempts to maximise support from different interest groups. For an introduction to the concept see e.g. Frey (1990).

B is willing to accept all immigrants from A, B's migration potential could entirely transform itself into effective migration. Whether and how fast this would happen depends on the presence and magnitude of *intervening obstacles* like lacking or biased information, legal constraints or procedural requirements. Alternatively, if B's policy actions reflect the intention not to accept immigration from A, a huge part of migration potential ought to transform itself into what we call *migration pressure* (Straubhaar 1993). This term has sometimes been criticised for being an expression of a political threat rather than an analytical tool (Tapinos 1992). As terms like demand, supply and pressure are rather common in economic terminology, and for the simple lack of a better heading, we retain the term migration pressure.

The framework given in figure 3.1 is designed to illustrate the approach we suggest should be adopted in analysing migration.[7] The framework sketches our perception of migration as the result of a process of interaction between macro-level units, with A and B representing the areas of origin and destination. The individual (and the social group one belongs to) is embedded within these units. On the basis of their own needs, desires and aspirations and under the influence of the macro-framework, individuals decide whether they want to migrate from A to B or vice versa. Migration demand and/or intervening obstacles might prevent the full realisation of the migration potential, especially when it comes to South to North migration.

This framework differs from other approaches common in economic migration theory in two ways. Firstly, the model has a richer approach to the micro-level decision making, distinguishing between (a) existential economic needs, (b) needs for security, (c) needs for social integration and acceptance, and (d) needs for self-fulfilment.[8] Secondly, it looks not only at the economic costs and benefits of migration but takes non-economic aspects of life such as peace, freedom, security, love, health and happiness, to mention just a few, explicitly into account.

In what follows, this chapter focuses on the migration decision-making process at the micro-level.[9] The next section is concerned with the decision to go. We start by introducing the classical economic rationales for migration and will then relax them subsequently. Furthermore, the potential migrant will firstly be taken as a completely

7. The approach and outline from the grid model are taken from Fischer (1991), based on Lee's push-pull approach (1966). For more details of the derivation and illustration of the concept, see Fischer (1991).

8. These categories have been originally developed by Maslow (1972) and Allardt (1975).

9. For an investigation of the economic links between the macro-level and migration see chapters 4 and 5.

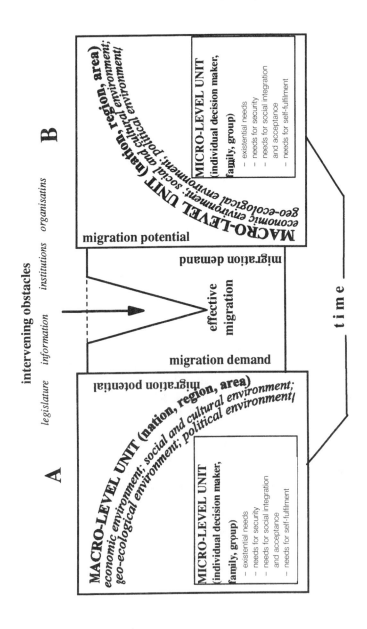

Figure 3.1 Explaining Migration – An Interdisciplinary Framework

independent human being and secondly as part of a larger social group, for example a family. In the next section we move beyond the economic reasoning as to why people are likely to 'go', and look at reasons why they are more likely to 'stay'. In other words, we look at the frequently forgotten (economic) rationales for remaining immobile. The fourth section of this chapter explores dynamic aspects of the individual migration decision, something which we look at in more detail in chapter 4. Major conclusions from the theories discussed are given in numbered implications plotted in italics throughout the text. The final section is a conclusion.

Why Does Migration Start? The Migrant, (More Than) an Economic Person

The Migrant as Individual Utility Maximiser

Economic micro-migration theory is based on a set of assumptions about the behaviour of human beings. Perhaps the most important of these assumptions is the belief that people are rational and that they try to maximise their individual utility or, put in another way, their individual quality of life. As far as migration is concerned, micro-economic behavioural theory assumes that any micro-level decision maker periodically gathers all available information in order to compare the relative advantages and disadvantages of moving to another location or staying at the present place of residence. One should decide to migrate from one place to another if one expects a relative increase in quality of life at a new place of residence. Corresponding advantages from living at another place will be dynamic in nature. Thus time and the time horizon of a decision maker will matter. Therefore, economic migration research usually assumes that individuals exhibit a more or less strong preference for the present: one attributes more weight to costs and benefits occurring soon after a move than to increases in life utility that take place in a distant future. Future costs and benefits are therefore discounted by time.[10] All in all, the (discounted net) increase has to outweigh the benefits of staying immobile plus the actual costs of migration.

Classical micro(-economic) -theories are in one way or another implicitly based on the conception of an individual search process which may be described in the following three stylised steps:

---

10. A more in-depth discussion of the importance of time in migration is provided by Malmberg in chapter 2. With respect to the economic treatment of dynamics in a decision to migrate a more explicit discussion follows below.

Peter Fischer, Reiner Martin and Thomas Straubhaar

a. A person develops a perception of potential locations of destination, including their natural, economic, social and cultural environment.
b. Thereafter this person assesses the advantages and disadvantages of each potential destination. Although many studies approximate 'utility' by wages and other forms of income, a potential migrant's assessment of the advantages and disadvantages of migration will in practice usually also include factors like social integration, appreciation, individual self-fulfilment or natural amenities (Maslow 1972, Allardt 1975).
c. The macro-level determinants are thus the basis for migration decisions. Potential migrants weigh the relative advantages and disadvantages of going or staying and of moving to a certain destination at a given time according to their individual preferences. They are supposed to decide rationally, i.e. to make a decision in favour of the alternative that maximises individual utility or quality of life. With increasing wealth, decision makers are less bound by basic economic considerations and put more weight on more advanced economic gains or even non-economic factors.[11]

The described procedural concept leads to questions that are answered differently by different theories. These are, without being final:

i.   How and when do people derive their perceptions about certain locations?
ii. How do people assess locational advantages and disadvantages?
iii. Which are the locational macro-features people are most interested in?
iv. How do people weigh different kinds of quality-of-life aspects?

The most classical economic theory of migration answers the above questions on the basis of a set of relatively rigid assumptions.

Looking at (i) people are assumed to behave perfectly rational and to consider all feasible alternatives at basically any point of time. Thus, the question when and under which circumstances individuals think about migration is irrelevant; the assumed simple answer is 'in principle always'. This is further eased by the assumption of costless access to perfect information. People are also assumed to have perfect foresight. They know how their environment will change in the future and can therefore act on the basis of security. Last but not least, (neo-)classical theories also assume full employment.

The above assumptions allow decision makers to assess all locational features correctly and without significant investment of time and energy

11. Further steps of the decision-making process are given below.

(question ii). Decision makers are thus supposed to be able to compare locations comprehensively. Moreover, in the classical economic approach there is no room for individual differences. Migrants are assumed to be a homogeneous group of individuals who have the same perfect information and behave in the same way, namely by rationally choosing the best possible alternative. All these are obviously not realistic assumptions. Nevertheless, the resulting basic model will prove helpful in many respects. As we are going to demonstrate, it provides 'clear sight' for some essential features of the migration decision and proves very suitable as a classical 'reference scenario' for more modern and realistic theoretical developments.

Differences between the various strands of economic migration theories influence most prominently the answers to (iii) and (iv).

Standard economic theory assumes that the best (and only feasible) measurement of quality of life is material wealth. People who maximise their personal utility of life are therefore expected to strive for the maximisation of income and wealth. Consequently, the earliest economic explanations of migration have identified differences in disposable income as the crucial macro-feature people are interested in. Most simply, classical economic migration theory supposes that differences in wages cause migration. Ravenstein (1885, 1889) argued nearly a century ago in two seminal contributions that the most important reason for most migration decisions is wage-level differences between macro-level units. Because most economists have nowadays forgotten Ravenstein, his insights are usually credited to Hicks (1932), sometimes even to Harris and Todaro (1970).

Many economists have taken up the wage-difference idea and added different additional features or relaxed some of the above assumptions (Lewis 1954a, Ranis and Fai 1961, Sjaastad 1962, Lee 1966, Harris and Todaro 1970, Todaro 1976). Nevertheless, they all share the idea that different wage-levels come about because of geographic differences in the supply and demand of labour and the endowment with other relatively immobile production factors, usually physical capital. In terms of a two-locations model, it is then assumed that the real wage is higher in the macro-level unit with the lower relative labour/capital ratio and vice versa. This triggers migration from the low-wage country to the high-wage country. As a result of this movement, the supply of labour decreases and wages rise in the capital-poor country, while the supply of labour increases and wages fall in the capital-rich country. At the end of the migration process the wage levels are balanced out and migration comes to a halt.[12]

---

12. For a more detailed treatment of this mechanism see chapter 4.

Peter Fischer, Reiner Martin and Thomas Straubhaar

The economic approach towards explaining migration in its most simple version has the advantage of deriving very general, clear conclusions. Some of them, however, are counterintuitive.

1. *People migrate due to international income (wage) differences.*
2. *Migration equalises wages internationally and therefore brings itself to a halt.*
3. *Given the described restrictive assumptions about the economic man, everybody should be similarly willing to migrate wherever wage differences appear.*

The third conclusion implies that only two different orders of the world can exist: either an environment where wage differences persist due to international economic differences, combined with an *effective control* to assure the absence of international migration, or an integrated world of free international migration where everybody constantly explores wage differences which are thereby levelled out. Newly emerging migration flows can only be explained by changes in control or in wage-levels.

These implications are obviously incompatible with at least two facts. Firstly, migration intensities are conditional on the socio-economic characteristics of migrants, and secondly, many persons are not willing to move despite large wage differences between macro-level units, while others move even in the absence of income differences. Concerning South to North migration, it is puzzling for the simple classical economic view that, given the large income differences between South and North and imperfect immigration control, not many more people migrate from South to North.

In the following sections we will progressively relax the assumptions of our model-theoretic framework, recompiled in box 3.1 below and look at what these relaxations mean for the direction and magnitude of the expected migratory flows. We will also use prior surveys as helpful starting points, although we select and supplement the material provided by these earlier contributions (Borjas 1994, Greenwood, 1975, 1985, 1993, DeJong and Gardner 1981, Cohen 1986, Molho 1986b, Massey et al. 1993, Straubhaar 1995, Ghatak et al. 1996).

In several attempts to explain why so few people move, migration costs have been introduced. Early works of economic migration theory already introduced the costs of transport from the place of origin to the macro-level unit of destination. So-called *gravity models* of migration have incorporated the importance of geographic distance into economic migration research, adding 'some form of distance deterrence function reflecting the degree of spatial separation between origin and destination'

(1) Migration is cost free
(2) Migration is risk free
(3) Potential migrants are a homogeneous group of people
(4) Potential migrants have perfect and costless information
(5) Potential migrants behave in an unconditionally rational manner
(6) The potential migrant is an autonomous human being with no social context

Box 3.1. Assumptions of the classic (micro-)economic model of migration

Assumption 1, that migration is cost-free, is now being dropped.

(Molho 1986b: 406).[13] It is also reasonable to extend the notion of 'distance' beyond its geographic meaning and to include factors like cultural, linguistic or political proximity. Big differences with respect to these variables are bound to increase integration and adjustment costs. Although these are essentially psychic costs and can only partly be expressed in monetary terms, they can significantly reduce the utility of the move.

Distance between two macro-level units, whether narrowly or broadly defined, is likely to reduce the migratory flows between these units. This effect is frequently observable. As far as geography is concerned, one can use Mexico and the United States as classic example of units where the geographic deterrence effect is rather low. It is unlikely, however, that anyone will hear of mass migration from Mexico to Europe. The effect of cultural and linguistic proximity is reflected for example by the relatively high level of 'Southern' migrants in European countries who originate from former colonies. When trying to explain these phenomena additional factors like more generous entry regulations and family ties should not be neglected and will be discussed below.

Another obvious extension is the introduction of non-pecuniary costs and benefits. In our introduction we have already stressed the importance of socio-cultural, political and geo-ecological benefits and costs of migration. Within a general utility-maximisation approach these arguments can explain much of the observable differences in migration and migration dynamics (Straubhaar 1994, Fischer and Straubhaar 1996). There is, however, a certain hesitation among economists to follow that argumentation, not only due to axiomatic objections, but even more so

13. For a more detailed evaluation of these models see chapter 2.

due to the problems of the empirical measurement of non-pecuniary costs and utilities.

While it is rather obvious that 'go' decisions cause various costs for the migrants, it is much less obvious whether they are aware of the existence of these costs and of their true magnitude. Classical economic approaches avoided this problem by assuming free availability of perfect information, an assumption which we will drop below.

When we ask why there is not more South to North migration and why the existing flows suddenly emerge and disappear again, the cost approach adds some explanatory power. Pecuniary and psychic costs may act as powerful deterrents, but subject to change, for example advances in transport, that can be expected to alter the magnitude of migration.

Assumption 2, migration is risk-free, is now being dropped.

Economic theories of migration have heroically assumed full employment. Especially in developing economies this assumption was obviously unjustifiable. Harris and Todaro (1970) deserve the merits of first having dealt with this problem in a formal way. In their contribution, which has become a true cornerstone of neo-classical economic migration theory, they develop a model where migrants care not only about the level of achievable income, but also about the probability of realising it. They approximated the likelihood of realising the expected income by the likelihood of being employed minus the unemployment rate.

Although the basic idea of this so-called Harris–Todaro (HT)-model is rather simple, extensions and refinements of the early models have provided more insights than one might expect. In their 1970 article Harris and Todaro looked specifically at the situation in a developing country with an undeveloped rural and a developed urban sector. Unemployment existed in the latter but was exogenously determined. The higher the wage differential and the lower the urban unemployment rate, the more migration into the urban areas will occur.[14] In empirical investigations vacancy rates in the area of destination as pull factor often explain migration better than unemployment rates.[15]

---

14. Harris–Todaro models were also frequently used in order to examine the welfare implications of migration. See for example Bhagwati and Srinivasan (1974, 1975), Corden (1974), Fields (1975) and Ethier (1985).

15. For example, migration from Finland to Sweden in the 1960s and 1970s has been largely dependent on job vacancies in Sweden and to a much lesser extent on unemployment rates in the two countries (Fischer and Straubhaar 1996).

To the extent that well-educated people have the best chances of avoiding unemployment abroad they should be the most likely migrants (Schaeffer 1985, Stark and Bloom 1985, Galor 1986).

Corden and Findley (1975) introduced capital mobility into the HT-framework but only looked at the comparative static effects of this extension. Dynamic effects were examined by Neary (1981), who questioned the usual prediction of an equilibrium outcome of the migration process. A survey of extensions of the HT-model is provided by Ghatak et al. (1996). Empirical tests of the Harris–Todaro approach reveal that wage differences between macro-level units and differences in unemployment rates are of considerable importance for intra-national migration decisions.

The effect of uncertain employment on migration flows is indeterminate. The obvious effect one would expect is a reduction of the number of migrants. If we take the existence of a certain level of unemployment for granted, though, the fact that people do not normally know whether they will be amongst those unemployed might reduce the deterring effect of unemployment. As long as I can hope to find a job, I can incorporate this hope into my utility calculation which makes a decision to 'go' more likely.[16] If we keep in mind the general utility/disutility framework presented above, it can be stated that uncertainty about finding a job abroad becomes relatively less important the more disutility comes about due to staying in the present location.[17] Put in a simple way, people on the dole at home are less worried about being on the dole abroad.

Other parts of the HT-model, for instance the prediction that wages in the urban sector are persistently higher than in the rural sector, fail to pass empirical tests.[18] As far as international migration is concerned, the empirical evidence on the importance of income differentials is also rather limited (see Lucas 1983). One should keep in mind, however, that the model was not designed in order to explain international migration.

The implications of the neo-classical Harris–Todaro approach for explaining migration go far beyond stating that

4. *not only wage differences, but also the likeliness of getting unemployed or finding a new job in one location relative to another matter for decisions to migrate. The higher the unemployment rate in*

---

16. More considerations on the effects of incomplete and imperfect information will be given below.

17. For an excellent survey of migration and unemployment problems see Herzog/et al. (1993). See also Katz and Stark (1986b), Delbrück and Raffelhüschen (1993) and Stark (1994) for the effects of migration under the assumption of asymmetric information on the labour market.

18. A comprehensive survey of empirical research based on the Harris–Todaro model can be found in Ghatak et al. (1994: 23–8).

the destination area and thus the lower the probability of finding a job and of realising the gains from wage-level differences, the smaller is the expected utility increase of moving there.

More generally, it points to the fact that

5. *a migrant has to weigh all kinds of utility differences between locational macro-units by the probability of realising different, insecure outcomes.*

Because one prefers a known, secure environment at a present location one may abstain from migrating to another location, where expected incomes and other kinds of utilities may or may not be higher. This idea gives another explanation of why South to South or North to North migration is more common than South to North migration. Not only do control and cost differences matter, but the extent to which macro-levels differ from each other also influences the perceived risks for migrants of not succeeding at a new place of residence. The more different locations are, the higher potential migrants usually assess the risk of not managing to realise a higher level of utility by means of migration.

Assumption 3, potential migrants are a homogeneous group of people, is now being dropped.

Another very important contribution in micro-economic migration theory is the human-capital approach (Sjaastad 1962, Becker 1964, incorporated in, among many others, Todaro 1969, 1976 and 1989, and Todaro and Maruszko 1987). This approach implies two theoretical innovations. Firstly, migrants are no longer treated as a homogeneous group of identical individuals. Instead, interpersonal differences in time horizons (e.g. due to age or culture) and preferences for the present (e.g. due to age, wealth or the arrangements of a social security system) are now taken into account. Secondly, migration is regarded as a form of investment in human capital. Both novelties require an explicit treatment of time perspectives and of expectations about the future.[19] Although the human-capital approach essentially remains comparatively static with respect to the decision making itself, it departs from simple comparison

---

19. For alternative concepts of including the time dimension into migration see chapter 2.

of macro-level differences at a given moment in time. Potential migrants compare potential expected future returns in potential destinations with the expected returns in their present macro-level unit of residence, and weigh them with respect to the time period until realisation. Utility advantages in the near future matter more than those one expects to materialise in the far future.

This fundamental change in conception of the migration decision adds two more steps to our stylised migration decision-making process.

d. The effects of migration on the individual's utility or disutility do not materialise immediately but accumulate over time. Micro-level actors thus have to discount future benefits or costs in order to be able to come to a decision. The longer the improvements take to realise, the more the immediate costs of leaving the present location will matter. Discounting future utilities and costs allows us to capture important differences between potential migrants and explains partly why very poor individuals are frequently the least likely to leave; a fact which is of great relevance for South to North migration.
e. The value of an individually weighed and discounted expected quality of life at a macro-level unit 'abroad' compared to the corresponding value 'at home' would thus determine the migration decision from the point of view of the micro-economic behavioural model.[20]

The human-capital approach also changes the implied assumption about people's perception and assessment of different locations and the macro-features they are particularly interested in (compare the fundamental questions on page 54). The answers to all these questions

---

20. A more formal, partially dynamic version of the described migration-decision problem may be summarised and described as follows:

$$_{max}NPV\,(m^{ha})_{t0} = \sum_{t=0}^{x} \left[\left(\sum_{i=1}^{m} (\rho_i^a u_i^a - \rho_i^h u_i^h)_t - \sum_{k=1}^{n} (\rho_k^a c_k^a - \rho_k^h c_k^h)_t \right) \cdot (1+\sigma)^{-t} \right]_t .$$

where the decision-maker's goal is to maximise his $NPV(m^{ha})_{t0}$, the *N*et *P*resent *V*alue at time $t=0$ of migrating from *h*ome to a certain destination *a*broad. It is made up by the difference over time $t= \in \{0 \dots x\}$ between expected utilities abroad (u^a) and at home (u^h) minus the expected difference in costs abroad (c^a) and at home (c^h). With regard to utilities and costs, different categories $i=\in(1 \dots m)$ and $k=\in(1 \dots n)$ may be distinguished. The most simple distinction may be the one between being employed or unemployed. As described above, however, it will hardly be sufficient to distinguish between different kinds of economic benefits and cost only. Because utilities and costs are expected but not certain, the decision maker (implicitly) also has to attribute to each utility and cost a corresponding probability of occurrence (where $0<\rho<1$). The fact of a finite time horizon and preference for the present relative to the future is accounted for by discounting future utilities and costs with a discount factor σ (where again $0<\sigma<1$).

depend to a large extent on the personal characteristics of the potential migrant. Put in another way, this approach is a first step towards a more individualised perception of the potential migrant. The assumptions of autonomous, individual, rational behaviour and perfect information, however, remain up to now unchallenged.

Chiswick (1978 and 1986), Borjas (1985 and 1987) and Hunt and Kau (1985) compare earning levels of natives and immigrants and investigate earning differences among sub-groups of immigrants. They find the predictions of the theory widely supported. The negative influence of age on the decision to 'go' is demonstrated by Goss and Paul (1986) as well as by Plane (1992). Molho (1986a) gives detailed empirical support for the importance of family and education characteristics in shaping migration decisions of young men in Great Britain, thereby demonstrating that the theory is not only applicable to migration emanating from the South. Winter-Ebmer (1994) provides a useful extension of the traditional human-capital approach by looking at the motivational structure of immigrants in Austria. He relates the motivational structure of immigrants to their level of earnings and finds that success-oriented immigrants have on average a better performance on the labour market than 'fear of failure' immigrants.

The human-capital approach provides a theoretical justification for interpersonally different migration propensities. More specifically, it implies that:

6. *The longer one's 'investment horizon', the more likely one is to migrate. Therefore young people should be more willing to migrate than old ones.*
7. *The bigger one's preference for the present, the less likely one is to migrate. People who are primarily concerned with the present, either because they have to struggle in order to satisfy their immediate existential needs or because they have a preference for immediate utility, are less likely to migrate because they will (have to) attribute more value to the immediate (sunk) costs of migration than to long-run utility improvements.*
8. *Migration may be a reasonable strategy even if migrating to a new location in the short run causes a relative loss in life quality. It is sufficient that one can expect to overcompensate this loss by future benefits.*

The development of human-capital theory was a key event in economic-migration theory. Nevertheless, several shortcomings remain. Although introducing dynamic aspects into the analyses of migration decisions, the human-capital approach remains comparatively static with respect to the decision making itself. Migration decisions are not dependent on past decisions or macro-developments, but simply determined by the (perfect, costless) information at a certain point in time.

One of the most striking features of classic economic migration theory as presented above, be it simple HT or human-capital approaches, is the prediction that an equilibrium will be the final outcome of the process. Migration is essentially regarded as a remedy for imbalances in factor markets, in this case the labour market. These imbalances lead to wage differences which in turn trigger migration. As soon as a new equilibrium is reached, which implies that the wage-level differences are cancelled out, these migratory flows are expected to end. Moreover, the adjustment process is usually expected to take place rapidly.[21]

Even casual observation makes it clear that it is extremely difficult to use this theory for the explanation of long-lasting or permanent, as well as of two-way, migratory flows. As we will see below in the section on dynamic aspects of migration, more elaborate theoretical analyses depart from this assumption of an equilibrium outcome. As a matter of fact, even within the basic models of migration the prediction of equilibrium is not very robust. It is sufficient to alter the original Harris–Todaro model in a way that allows urban and rural wage rates to be endogenously determined (Amano 1983) to put the equilibrium outcome into question. The same happens when dynamic effects of capital mobility are investigated (Neary 1981).[22]

Assumption 4, potential migrants have perfect and costless information, is now being dropped.

Generally speaking, the absence of complete and costless information implies that any decision to 'stay' or to 'go' involves not only assessing and weighing different (known) migration alternatives. Potential migrants also have to worry about obtaining and selecting relevant information.

Giving up the assumption of costless and perfect information alters the micro-economic model fundamentally. To gather scarce information requires the use of resources and time. The more information is needed and the more severe the constraints a decision maker faces, the more

---

21. Hunt (1993) argues that adjustment is likely to be time-consuming. He therefore advocates 'disequilibrium' models of migration. The difference between 'disequilibrium' models and conventional equilibrium models is not so much the eventual outcome but the time required until the adjustment process is completed.
22. More details on dynamic effects will be given below.

reasonable it becomes to avoid incurred search costs by not thinking about migration at all. Information costs are therefore an important approach by which to explain immobility. We will come back to that point in the section below that discusses why people stay immobile.

If information is costly and resources are constrained, the individual has to develop an optimal search strategy to gather and select information. This incorporates the need to limit the number of considered alternatives according to cost-benefit criteria. Generally speaking, costly and thus limited information about economic and non-economic factors may lead to second-best solutions. In other words, I may decide to 'stay', although it would be possible to realise a higher level of utility in a different macro-level unit, or I may decide to 'go' but select a location where the obtainable level of utility is lower than somewhere else.

There is obviously a turning point, at which the additional costs of information search are above the additional utility that this information would be likely to produce. The location of this turning point depends on the personal characteristics of the potential migrants. For some professions, for example, less information about labour markets may be required than for others. It also depends on the price of the information. It is reasonable to assume that this price rises with the distance between locations (Maier 1985) and the level of specification of the information required. A weather report, for example, is cheaper than a labour-market analysis for scientists. The introduction of technologically advanced communication, radio and TV, lowers the costs of information. The existence of personal contacts and networks can be even more important than this general information.[23] We will come back to this point below.

The less information people have access to, the more important will *subjective elements* be. If I do not know whether I will get a job at my destination, I will have to make up my mind about the risk that I am prepared to take. Such subjective elements depend partly on (objective) personal characteristics of the potential migrant like age and education – something we emphasised when discussing the human-capital approach – and partly on subjective characteristics like optimism or pessimism. Since incomplete information increases the degree of insecurity, the individual *degree of risk aversion* becomes an important element of the decision to migrate. This is at odds with more simple models of migration where the potential migrant is assumed to be risk-neutral.

The more risk-averse micro-level actors are, the more willing they are to invest in order to obtain more information. Such a purchase of information can be perfectly rational behaviour in a situation where

23. Compare also chapter 9.

information is sparse and the chances of taking suboptimal decisions due to incomplete information are high (Maier 1985). It is likely to be helpful for my economic success if I know as much as possible about the situation in the labour market I plan to go to.[24] Are my personal qualifications in demand or am I likely to encounter unemployment or low-wage employment? Generally speaking, unemployment is one of the biggest insecurities for potential migrants, although it does not apply to all. Molho (1986b: 402) differentiates between contracted migration, i.e. a job is secured before moving, and speculative migration where the job-search process takes place after arriving in the destination area.[25]

Stark and Levhari (1982) try to incorporate the degree of attempted risk avoidance into the decision-making process. Although their analysis is geared towards risks of migration within less developed countries (LDCs), it also applies to migration to and within other macro-level units. Dustmann (1992), looking at the behaviour of people after they have decided to 'go', points to the attempts of temporary migrants to minimise their risks by means of savings.

Related to the problem of limited information and the way people process the information they have at hand is the prevalence of reference groups in general and the relative deprivation of potential migrants in particular (Katz and Stark 1986a, Stark and Yitzhaki 1988, Stark and Taylor 1991). People's concern about their well-being is dependent on their reference group, i.e. the group they compare themselves with, rather than on the average situation of mankind.[26] On the one hand, this may be due to limited information. From their perspective, they do not know as much about the situation of the whole world as about the city they live in. On the other hand, they put more emphasis on information that concerns their close environment. The fact is that the capacity of human beings to process information is limited, something we will discuss shortly. The effect of the two aspects is the same. Put simply, a poor man in a poor society finds it easier to bear this situation than a poor man in a rich one.

---

24. See Xu (1992) for an empirical investigation of the impact of risk aversion on migration in China.

25. On this point see also McCall and McCall (1987) and Franz (1993). Early job-search models were developed by Fields (1975, 1976, 1979). Salvatore (1981) extends and alters the Harris–Todaro model significantly by giving more importance to the problem of unemployment and the uncertainty under which the decision-making process has to take place. A sequential job-search migration strategy is outlined by Berninghaus and Seifert-Vogt (1987, 1992) and commented on by Straubhaar (1987)

26. Note that reference groups may also be decisive in shaping migration decision makers' 'mental maps', a concept common in geographic migration research as described in chapter 2.

There is a huge amount of empirical research on migration with incomplete information. Of particular value are so-called value-expectancy and constraints models, illustrating the importance of such individual assessments of migration alternatives which are only partly based on (constrained) information. DeJong et al. (1983, 1986) demonstrate the importance of expectations for migration decisions of a rural population in the Philippines.

To sum up, the relaxation of the assumption of perfect and costless information alters some counterintuitive results of our analysis of the migration decision. It implies that:

9. *In order to decide to 'go', the costs of staying have to surpass at least the basic information costs. The more the information needed and the more severe the constraints a decision maker faces, the more rational it becomes not to think about migration.*
10. *Gathering and selecting a limited amount of costly information on a selected set of alternative migration decisions frequently requires a shift from first- to second-best solution.*
11. *If, due to the need for a search strategy, migration decisions are only second best, people are likely to face incentives to return and (re)migrate several times.*
12. *People are more likely to migrate the more positive information they have about the economic and social prospects in a potential new location and the less risk-averse they are. If people are not at all risk-averse (rather the exception than the rule), limited information can lead to higher migration than expected.*
13. *Since the availability of information as well as the ability to use it are limited, people put special emphasis on their position within their reference group, for example on their relative level of deprivation.*
14. *Information costs influence the direction of migration flows. In general, people are likely to migrate to locations about which they are already informed or to locations about which it is relatively cheap to obtain information.*
15. *The price of information is likely to rise with the distance between two locations.*

The last two points especially can be regarded as important reasons for the relatively low level of South to North migration actually taking place. Not only will geographical distance tend to limit the amount of available information, with the notable exception of direct South to North frontiers like the Mexico–US and the Moroccan–Spanish borders, but the poverty of most people in the South will also prevent them from rectifying this problem.[27] We would therefore expect only relatively well-off parts of the population to migrate to the North, which is in line with actual events, although technological advances in information transfer might change this in the long run. From the point of view of the theoretical considerations outlined above, scarce information could be migration-enhancing relative to a situation where information is fully available only if decision makers are very risk-loving or if they obtain such a low level of utility at their present macro-level unit of residence that – although having only very limited information at hand – they are easily ready to conclude that they will be better off in another place. At least as far as this latter group is concerned, however, obstacles such as the costs of travel are likely to prevent them from realising their decision to 'go'.

Many people in the South will also abstain from migration because within their reference group their utility is high enough to prevent such a decision. This in turn implies that the income distribution in potential sending countries may be one important determinant of migration decisions. People in a country with a very uneven distribution and a large section of the population which is unsatisfied with their country-specific relative utility level are more likely to 'go' than people in a country where income is more evenly distributed. The same reasoning applies to changes in income levels. A stable low income may be more acceptable than an increasing income level accompanied by a rise in income inequality. Social policy might therefore have a substantial influence on the migration potential of macro-level units.

In addition to the above-mentioned reasoning, the importance of relative income distribution for migration has attracted special attention in economic-migration theory within the particular context of the so-called 'selection-debate' discussing socio-economic characteristics of immigrants and their performance in the United States (Chiswick 1978, Borjas 1987). The key argument states that differences in the relative wage distribution in the country of origin and the country of destination will determine the skill characteristics of migrants. Provided that the wage differentiation between low- and high-skilled jobs is smaller in the country of origin than in the country of destination, high-wage earners are most likely to find it profitable to 'go', provided the two countries do not differ too much in other respects. Migrants will then be 'positively selected'. If, on the other hand, income differentiation is larger in the emigration country, a decision to go is more likely for low-skilled emigrants than for high-skilled ones: migrants will be 'negatively selected'.

---

27. See also chapter 6, by Ahmed, who emphasises that most people in the South cannot use the exit option because they lack the means to do so.

In the last part of this section on economic approaches explaining the decision to 'go' we want to question another standard assumption of economic migration theories, namely the belief that micro-level actors behave in an unconditionally rational manner.

> *Assumption 5, potential migrants behave in an unconditionally rational manner, is now being dropped.*

It is useful to define once more what we mean by the term 'unconditionally rational'. For our purposes rational behaviour means that in a situation where a decision between different options has to be made, a decision maker possessing complete and unconstrained information opts for the alternative that allows him to realise the highest level of utility. As we have discussed in the previous section, the assumption of free and costless information is hardly ever appropriate. Most migration decisions are therefore likely to be suboptimal from an unconditionally rational point of view. Nevertheless, they are likely to be rational with respect to the decision maker's constrained situation. One can call these kind of constraint decisions conditionally (or boundedly) rational, because they are conditional on the incomplete information on which they are based. They cannot be called truly non-rational, although an outsider, possibly in command of more information, might perceive them to be so. The same is true if some people are constrained to base their decisions on short-term costs and benefits only and therefore discount all potential future gains almost entirely. Given this constraint they will never arrive at a decision which might encompass only a small utility reduction in the short term but a very large pay off in the medium term. One has to be careful not to confuse such behaviour with 'true' non-rationality: 'I know that I should opt for A because it is better for me, but I prefer B!' Economics does not have much to say about statements of the truly non-rational kind, but they seem to be the exception rather than the rule.[28] The introduction of conditionally rational behaviour into micro(-economic) -models of migration decision making, however, brings us a good way towards a comprehensive understanding of why migration starts.

What happens if potential migrants have 'too much' rather than too little information? 'Too much' information can still be less than complete information. What we mean by the term 'too much' is that people are

---

28. Touch wood for all economists!!

unable to cope with the amount of information they have to process in order to arrive at an optimal conclusion. In other words, they cannot take all relevant available information into account. The problems associated with tackling complex sets of alternatives, a description which is certainly appropriate for many 'stay' or 'go' decisions, led to the concept of bounded rationality. Simon (1957, 1983) describes the actions of human beings as bounded by the situation they face, the experiences they have acquired before, their emotional patterns and their limited computational abilities. Although this is a more realistic perception of human nature than the 'Olympian' model of human beings who are able to take everything into account, the effects of bounded rationality are similar to those associated with a lack of available information. In both cases human action can appear irrational from the outside although the decision maker does not violate the assumption of rationality as such.[29]

To return to the utility framework developed above, the concepts of imperfect information and bounded rationality imply that not all available macro-level characteristics relevant for the utility or disutility comparison are taken into account by the micro-level actor. This is even more likely with respect to potential destinations abroad, insofar as the main results as well as the implications regarding South to North migration developed in the section above also apply to considerations of conditional, bounded rationality. There is, however, a further implication:

16. *The more different the information relevant for a particular decision is from the information the decision makers are used to processing, the more difficult it becomes for them to employ this information to the full.*

The more 'unfamiliar' or 'strange' an item of information is for decision makers, the less emphasis they are likely to put on this particular aspect of the problem. The cultural difference between the South and the North is, for example, likely to amplify the problem of information availability. In other words, the implications of lack of information for the level of South to North migration are strengthened by the insights of bounded rationality.

---

29. A recent general model of decision making under bounded rationality is provided by Wall (1993). Compare also the survey of earlier attempts by Lipman (1993). These articles do not specifically provide approaches to model migration decisions. They could provide a starting-point for such attempts, though.

Peter Fischer, Reiner Martin and Thomas Straubhaar

Migration as a Group Decision

> *Assumption 6, the potential migrant is an autonomous human being with no social context, is now being dropped.*

To look at migration decision makers not as completely independent individuals but as part of a social group, usually a household or family, is an extension of the classical micro-economic model. But abandoning the independent-individual assumption is bound to have a significant effect on the expected migratory flows (Stark and Bloom 1985). Whether the propensity to migrate will be reduced or increased, however, depends completely on the situation of the group concerned. Nevertheless, there are some rules of thumb concerning the likelihood of people migrating.

Generally speaking, married persons and other individuals strongly attached to someone else are less likely to decide to 'go'. Family ties are also likely to reduce migration-propensity. While these considerations are generally relevant for migration, an alternative scenario exists with respect to migration originating from developing countries. Many families in the South send one or several of their members into a foreign country or region in order to help support the family by means of remittances, a strategy which is obviously likely to increase the level of migration.

Many sociological and political meso-models of migration do introduce migration as a group decision.[30] Economic migration research traditionally focuses on the more pecuniary aspects of group decisions. Its contribution may, however, serve as a further micro-foundation to many meso-models.

Migration based on family decisions is not only a rational way in which to increase the family's income, it can also be regarded as a form of risk-sharing. By locating different members of the social group in different areas and in different labour markets and occupations, the group is able to reduce the overall risks of unemployment, wage-level reductions and so on.[31] After all, economic or non-economic problems are likely to be asymmetrically distributed. In developed countries most risks can be privately insured, while such insurance often is non-existent or non-obtainable for households in developing areas. This makes it more important for households in developing areas to diversify risks by

---

30. See chapters 6 and 7.
31. Indeed, this is one of the key ideas of what has become known as the so-called 'New Economics of Migration' (cf. Stark 1991).

spreading the human resources of the family geographically (see Massey et al. 1993: 435–9). Looked at exclusively from the utility level of the family member sent abroad, the resulting migration decision might appear irrational, because the personal utility of the migrant might have been reduced. From the point of view of the family or group, however, the concept of rational behaviour remains perfectly valid. As Stark and Bloom (1985) call it, this form of migration is 'a calculated strategy and not an act of desperation or boundless optimism' (Stark and Bloom 1985: 175). It is quite conceivable that migrants sent by their families would have remained in the area of origin if their decision had been based exclusively on personal welfare considerations. In this case family ties had a migration-increasing effect.

When looking at family motives for migration, one should also mention approaches which look at the capital rather than the labour market in order to detect causes for migration (Katz and Stark 1986a, 1986b; Morrison 1994). In many countries of the South it is not only impossible to insure risks, it is also impossible to get access to capital markets. This in turn prevents investments aimed at increasing the income opportunities and wage levels of people. For large parts of the population the only chance to obtain capital even for modest investments may be remittances from migrating family members. This has a strongly migration-increasing effect. Eased access to capital markets is therefore a frequently proposed measure to reduce intra-South and South to North migration. Access to capital markets may reduce the urge to use migration to spread risks and earn income from different locational sources. But it may, on the other hand, also provide the means to cover short-term costs of migration, thus helping to realise desires to migrate and thereby leading to more migration. This ought to be especially true if the envisaged destination is further away from the country of origin.

Family motives for migration have been subject to a significant number of empirical investigations. Several studies verified that married persons are less likely to move than singles. This reluctance to migrate is even stronger if the spouse is attached to the labour market (Mincer 1978). Graves and Linnemann (1979) arrive at the same conclusion that marital status and the incorporation of personal social ties into the micro-level migration decision-making process reduces the level of migration. Other examples of the numerous empirical studies in the field are Lauby and Stark (1988), looking at the migration of women in the Philippines, Briody (1987), investigating immigration into South Texas, and Molho (1986b), analysing migration decisions of young men in Great Britain.[32]

---

32. For a more detailed treatment of the particular and changing role of women in shaping group-decision processes see chapter 8.

Generally speaking, the importance of strategic family and group considerations have been verified regardless of whether migratory flows originated from developed or developing areas. For countries at an early stage of development the impact has usually been migration-enhancing, for countries at higher stages of development the impact has tended to be migration-reducing. It depends on the features of the family or household, the level of education of the different members, the income situation, the age and sex structure, and so on, whether the inclusion of family considerations increases or reduces the expected level of migration (Harbison 1981, Schmink 1984, Taylor 1995).

Regardless of the apparent importance of group considerations, one should bear in mind that the personal desires and preferences of a potential migrant still play an important role. They have not been replaced but merely supplemented or augmented by considerations concerning the family as a whole. A migrant whose preference function is strongly dominated by personal rather than family considerations might simply go or stay regardless of the wishes of his or her family. Put another way, there is a danger of 'replacement of an undersocialized view of migration in which all action reflects individual wishes and preferences with an oversocialized view in which people are passive agents in the migratory process projected through time and space by social forces.' (Boyd 1989: 641).

By means of education and general socialisation the family or household has mostly a strong impact on how individuals perceive the information they obtain. In general terms, the family[33] also has in economics-based migration an important mediating function between the macro-level characteristics which provide the framework for potential migrants and the micro-level decision-making of the individuals.

The flow of information from family members abroad to those who initially stay behind is of considerable importance. Such information reduces uncertainty and is likely to ease the decision to 'go' for additional family members. It is also easier to migrate if members of the same social group already live in the destination country, a fact that has given grounds for sociological theories of cumulative causation and migration networks as described by Faist in chapter 7.

Sometimes family ties are the main rationale for migrating. One only has to think about the issue of family reunification in the destination country of the 'pioneering' migrant. Frequently the head of a family is the first to migrate, with the rest of the family following at a later point in time. Such dynamic aspects will be discussed at greater length below.

---

33. Note that the concept and importance of the family or household may be cultural-specific and so may therefore be the influence of collectives on individual migration decisions. For an evaluation and methodological assessment see chapter 8.

Before doing so, we want to summarise briefly the main implications of our discussion about migration as a family decision.

17. *Decisions to 'go' are not necessarily based on the utility consider-ations of an independent individual human being. They are often influenced by considerations about the utility of a family household or another social group.*
18. *With respect to migration originating in the North, family and group considerations are often likely to be an obstacle to migration and therefore to reduce migration propensities. In the South, motives of risk spreading, lack of capital-market access and of information, etc. are more likely to be decisive for migration decisions. Therefore (depending on the social group concerned and contrary to the North) family and group considerations are likely to increase migration potential in the South.*
19. *Public policies geared towards easing access to insurance and to capital are likely to reduce the propensity to migrate from the South.*

Why do Most People Stay Immobile?

On the Value of Immobility

Mobility is a key element and central ingredient of economic analysis in various fields. Economic theory typically analyses the existence and reasons for locational differences in endowments and prices and shows that market mechanisms make it reasonable and beneficial for everybody to even out those differences by appropriate adjustment mechanisms. These can be flows of traded goods, physical capital, financial investment or of migrating people. The axiomatic notion behind that kind of analysis is that the world consists of more or less temporary disequilibria situations caused by exogenous shocks to macro-systems as well as rigidities and imperfections in goods and factor markets. These imperfections disturb the system and should be removed by arbitrage-exchange processes as quickly as possible.

Economic theory usually regards trade, capital and labour flows as important elements of wealth-enhancing adjustment. Temporary disequilibria situations create opportunities for individuals to benefit by reaping disequilibrium profits incorporated in locationally different production costs, interest rates, investment returns or labour compen-sations. From this point of view, mobility is naturally positive and beneficial *per se* because it reduces disequalities and increases aggregate welfare. Immobility, however, reflects the existence of imperfections and rigidities to be removed. What has hardly been asked until now is whether immobility itself could also have a 'positive value' to the individual as well as to the society as a whole. From an economic point of view it is relatively new to look at immobility in this way. There are sound theoretical arguments supporting the idea. As they have not been set forth in this context yet, the first part of this section is intended as a presentation of hypotheses on the 'value of immobility' rather than a review of the 'theoretical state of the art'. The second part will summarise explanations of immobility that are more directly connected to the traditional rigidities and imperfections approaches.

The simple classic economic theories of migration like the Harris–Todaro and human-capital approaches are typical illustrations of the standard economic way of looking at commuting flows. They are – as explained in this chapter – based on the assumption that migration is caused by exogenously determined disequilibria in the labour markets of different macro-level units. Due to these disequilibria individual utility levels, frequently approximated by income, are different from one macro-level unit to another, which induces individual decision makers to migrate into the high-utility areas. Migration rectifies the disequilibria by equalising the labour/capital endowments and levelling out the original wage differences.

As discussed above, classic migration theory in its simple form leaves us with the puzzling implication, that given our contemporary world, we should expect migratory flows of inconceivable magnitude. The existing differences in capital/labour ratios and wage levels between different macro-level units should be a sufficient incentive for the majority of all individuals to change their place of residence. Whereas the number of migrants would be extremely high, the duration of this wave of migration would be very limited. As soon as the migration-induced changes in the supply and demand of labour have levelled out the wage-level differences between the different countries or regions the incentive to migrate would disappear and migration stop.

In the last section we showed how a number of modifications can narrow the gap between 'pure' economic migration theory and the real world, looking on the one hand at obstacles to migration such as the various costs and on the other hand at additional reasons for migration such as the maximisation of a family's utility. These allow economic migration theory to explain different forms of migration. Nevertheless the central paradox of predominant human immobility under conditions of important world-wide, national and regional disparities remained. Although nearly all scholars writing on migration ask why migration does occur, it seems to us a natural question to ask why in our world perhaps 98 per cent of the global population does not move despite massive differences in development and average income.

Most of the presented analyses of migration decision making incorporate an essentially static view of the assets and abilities of the potential migrant. A relaxation of this assumption attributes a more desirable value to immobility. Under the conventional static view the micro-level decision maker compares her/his present and future level or utility in different macro-level units on the basis of her/his present stock of assets and abilities. In most cases this is not a realistic judgement because a certain part of the abilities and assets of every human being are *location-specific*, in other words they can only be used (or are only existent) in a specific macro-level unit and are not transferable to other places of work and residence.[34] An important part of these abilities has to be obtained within a location-specific learning process which requires time, information and temporary immobility. Mobility turns such investments into lost sunk costs, i.e. costs which are tied to a specific project or – in this case – a specific location and lost in the case of emigration. Intertemporally, insider advantages may be reactivable if one returns, but they nevertheless increase the (opportunity) costs of staying away.

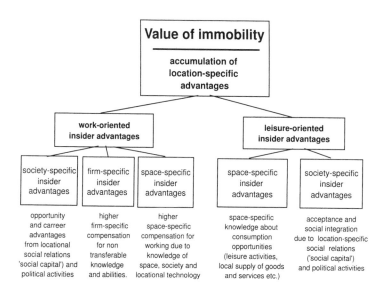

Figure 3.2 The Insider-Advantage Approach Towards Immobility

34. Becker (1962) has already emphasised that part of the knowledge an individual acquires is often firm-specific and cannot be transferred to another employment. Migration may therefore result in a decrease of potentially achievable relative wages because firm-specific abilities are 'sunk' in case of a change of workplace. For a somewhat different treatment of location-specific advantages emanating from the labour-supply side see Chiswick (1986b).

Henceforth immobility makes sense to a majority of people because the loss of location-specific assets and abilities induced by migration would be too severe and because it is immobility which permits the accumulation of insider advantages. These location-specific assets and abilities are not only economic, but also, and perhaps first of all, cultural, linguistic, social and political. For the sake of the label, we would like to call our hypothesis the 'insider-advantage approach' towards immobility. Figure 3.2 gives a graphic presentation of the structure of the idea.

There is some similarity between our 'insider-advantage' approach and the human-capital approach outlined in the preceding section. The human-capital approach emphasises the point that people are very different in their characteristics and their abilities and that migration may be a form of investment on which the return will occur within a given future time span. The insider-advantage approach stresses that during periods of immobility at a particular location individuals invest in the accumulation of location-specific skills, abilities and assets. By this they can increase the realisable individual utility at this location significantly.

Utility gains from immobility can come about in various ways. They can originate on the production as well as the consumption side. Work-oriented gains from staying immobile may be reflected in an improved position of the individual on the regional labour market due to insider advantages. One can differentiate further between firm-specific, space-specific and society-specific insider advantages. Firm-specific advantages make an employee more attractive for the specific firm he works in at present. As far as this firm has production sites at different locations, insider advantages allow for firm-internal locational mobility without causing losses in individual productivity and thus compensation for work. Space-specific advantages on the contrary make the individual particularly attractive for all or at least some firms in his macro-level unit of residence. Examples of such intra-location insider production advantages are expertise in the location-specific preferences, desires and habits of clients or insider knowledge of the peculiarities of the political situation in a country or region. Society-specific advantages broadly emanate from the social relations and political activities an immobile individual builds up within the society she or he is residing in. All of these three work-oriented insider advantages are likely to lead to higher revenues for the individual, in the form of wages or other income.

Leisure-oriented location-specific insider advantages may allow a resident to reach a higher utility level with a given set of monetary or other resources and time. Leisure-oriented space- and society-specific insider-advantages also require a period of immobility and are by and large lost if one moves away. Examples of space-specific advantages can range from information about the 'good-value-for-money' Italian restaurant round the corner to knowledge about cultural events and the local housing market.[35]

Society-specific advantages capture the utility increase one gets from having friends, being socially integrated and accepted at a certain place of residence. They result from what Faist in chapter 7 of this book calls 'social capital'. We attribute them to locational investment in 'social capital' which encompasses a wide range of human contacts, from family relations and friendships to membership of clubs and political parties. Participation in political decision making and democratic activities, including election to a representative body, also need society-specific investments and skills to be acquired during a period of immobility. Once obtained, they open up for the political insider advantages available to relatively permanent residents only. Mobility generally induces the loss of most of these abilities and assets and requires new investments in obtaining a 'ticket to entry' at a new place of residence.

To regain space and society-specific leisure-oriented insider-advantages in a different macro-level unit is costly and time-consuming: to stay immobile has its own value.

There are obviously links between the social and political categories of insider advantages of immobility and the economic pecuniary categories outlined above, especially as far as the work-oriented advantages are concerned. Contrary to categories focusing on monetary advantages, though, the advantages in terms of social relations are for the most part difficult to quantify. Leisure-oriented society-specific insider advantages increase utility from consumption of goods, services, interaction and leisure time, but they are by no means economic or pecuniary only.[36]

In the light of our insider-advantage hypothesis, the extent to which a micro-level decision maker is able to transfer her or his abilities and assets to a different macro-level unit (and eventually back) becomes an important determinant of the individual's propensity to migrate. 'Those who are more adaptable because their skills, broadly defined, are more readily transferable have an easier adjustment. The degree of skill transferability is related to the similarity of the origin and the destination,

35. Especially combined with market imperfections as they are typical for the housing market, leaving and thus being forced to sell one's property at a certain time and buy or rent a new dwelling in another location often reduces gains from investment significantly.

36. Limited mobility may also imply a restriction of social contacts, though. Whether this restriction is perceived as such is essentially a matter of the individual's personal preferences.

as well as the motive for migrating' (Chiswick 1992: 22; see also Chiswick 1986, Greenwood and McDowell 1991).

A rather extreme example of non-transferable abilities is the skills of an Australian aborigine who is an expert at surviving in the desert. He will find it difficult, however, to employ these skills in westernised and urbanised parts of the world where they are to the largest extent devalued.[37]

There are also less spectacular examples, even with respect to groups of individuals who are usually assumed to have a high propensity to migrate. High-school graduates for example, when trying to find a job in their home town, are likely to have location-specific assets simply by knowing many of their fellow citizens and by being accustomed to the peculiarities of their home town. Like the aborigine, they are unable to transfer these assets, which in turn is likely to reduce their willingness to take up residence in a different macro-level unit. This applies to an even higher degree to people in a later stage of their life. Not only are they likely to have a stronger personal attachment to a particular place, over time they have usually also collected a much larger amount of information and abilities than the graduates mentioned above. This increases the disutility arising from the devaluation of these assets when moving to a different place of residence.[38]

One should bear in mind that it is important not only how many location-specific assets people stand to loose from migrating but also how quickly they are able to make good these losses. In other words, how quickly can they acquire new location-specific skills? Not surprisingly those who on average lose little from a migratory move are those who are also able to make good their losses most rapidly; namely the *young* and *well-educated*.

All in all, location-specific insider advantages contribute to an understanding of why most people stay immobile even under conditions of important national and regional disparities. It implies that:

20. *People do not move because the loss of location-specific assets and abilities induced by migration would be too severe and because it is immobility which allows for the accumulation of insider advantages.*

21. *The more location-specific insider advantages one has already acquired, the less likely one is to migrate. Longer periods of immobility allow for higher individual utilities from the use of a given set of resources and time. The longer the stay at a certain*

37. For a related case study see Hoagan, P. (1985), *Crocodile Dundee*, Alice Springs/Hollywood.
38. The mobility-reducing effects of family ties in highly developed societies have already been mentioned above.

location, the less likely one is to (re)migrate. Young people are therefore more likely to be mobile than old people.

22. *The effect of education on the value of immobility is indeterminate, depending on the location specificity of abilities and skills acquired through education.*

23. *The more possible it is to transfer economic, social and political abilities and skills from one location to another, the less valuable is immobility. Differences between location henceforth increase immobility.*

Explaining the widespread absence of labour mobility between the less developed South and the highly industrialised North in terms of our location-specific insider advantages approach implies that most people consider the loss of economic, social and political location-specific abilities and benefits more severe than the potential gains from migrating. This could be explained among others by the great difference between Southern and Northern institutional, organisational and educational systems. Again, we would expect a young western-style educated elite in the South to be most migration-prone especially when their skills do not allow utility gains at home. From this point of view attempts to reduce South to North migration should increase the individual value of staying immobile in the South.

The above considerations provide some important ideas as to why so many people are unlikely to 'go' and in fact will never do so. More empirical research focusing on the transferability of people's assets and abilities as pioneered by Chiswick (1986) would be a most welcome contribution to the analysis of why most people stay immobile.

Additional Reasons for Immobility

Apart from our 'value of immobility' idea, there are other, more traditional explanations for the prevailing dominance of 'stay' decisions. These centre on risk and imperfect-market arguments as well as on intervening obstacles, and they are closer to models introduced in our explanation of why people (start to) move. We would like to look more specifically at four arguments: risk aversion, control, institutional social security systems and discrimination.

Traditional economic models of migration all assume risk neutrality. If, for example, somebody faces the opportunity to gain 1,000,000 dollars abroad with a probability of 0.5 or to lose 200,000 with the same probability of 0.5, risk neutrality implies that he will prefer that opportunity to another possibility at home that promises a sure income of less than 400,000 dollars ($0.5 \cdot 1,000,000 + 0.5 \cdot -200,000$) at a probability of 1.0.[39] An alternative view – in our perception more convincing but difficult to measure and compute – is to assume that most people react with strong aversion to the idea of taking risks. Their hopes of increasing their level of utility at another macro-level unit may be justified but they cannot be sure whether these advantages will really materialise. If they are risk-averse they are bound to 'discount' the chances to increase their level of utility abroad heavily. In terms of our example above, they may only consider moving to gain 1,000,000 or lose 200,000 dollars if they earn for sure less than 70,000 dollars at home. Moreover, informational asymmetries make it generally more difficult to assess risks correctly abroad than at home, and for abroad it will also be more cumbersome to obtain the information needed to reduce risks. In other words, people ought to attribute a relatively higher value to the level of utility which they expect in their present macro-level unit of residence than to the (more uncertain) value they expect abroad.

However, it is difficult to argue that in general people decide to stay because they prefer a secure outcome at home to a probable but insecure outcome abroad. From an objective point of view, their future situation at home may often (and especially in Third World countries) be as insecure as abroad. It seems a conceivable hypothesis to us that most people are not only risk-averse, but, in addition to that, have some (locational) preference for what is given and well known. They incorrectly tend to assess risks abroad to be larger than at home. To a certain extent our insider-advantage arguments could justify such assessments. Insider knowledge may enable individuals to minimise risks at home more successfully than abroad.

Risk aversion is a real factor in economic life, but has never become popular in economic theory because it leads to difficult calculation and assessment problems and produces unstable equilibria in theoretical models. Burda (1995) and Siebert (1993) have developed a different approach in order to explain why potential migrants may consider it beneficial to stay at home and wait even if they are not risk-averse but risk-neutral. Burda and Siebert argue that for risk-neutral decision makers it can be reasonable to *delay* the 'go' decision in order to reduce the uncertainties involved in migrating by collecting more relevant information. To stay and wait has its own value, the 'option value of waiting' (Burda 1995). Such behaviour is only beneficial, though, as long as the opportunity to go is 'non-rival' (i.e. it cannot become obsolete because of the earlier move of somebody else) and as long as

---

39. Note that this is basically an example of the pure stock exchange and portfolio argument in finance which assumes risk neutrality.

the income differences between origin and destination are not increasing. In effect this means that the reduction of certain risks is bought at the price of an additional risk. It can nevertheless be better to wait if, for example, information about income is more readily available than information about employment prospects.

A second 'traditional' explanation of immobility is the control aspect of international migration. As long as policy makers, for politico-economic reasons, are unwilling to accept would-be migrants, they can and will try to curb migration by means of controls. To have the liberty to do so is an important element of nationhood (Hammar 1990). Nevertheless it would be prohibitively expensive in terms of economic – and frequently also political – costs to eliminate undesired in-migration completely (Freeman 1993, Straubhaar 1993). At least for a country with large land frontiers, intense border control is, for instance, bound to create significant problems for trade and non-migration travel. The outcome is therefore more likely a two-tier society with legal immigrants as 'first division' and illegal as 'second'.

From an economic perspective, control by increasing the costs and risks of migration makes immobility more attractive. Illegal transport is much more expensive than regular transport. After arrival illegal immigrants, denied all legal rights and protections, are bound to fall prey to employment practices coming close to slave labour. This is all bound to work strongly against a decision to 'go'.

The final outcome depends not only on the strength of this deterrence effect of illegality, but first of all on the magnitude of the macro-level differences. For intra-European migration, for example, where the differences are not very pronounced, the removal of labour-mobility barriers within the European Union have had only an insignificant impact (Molle and van Mourik 1988). Income differences between the Maghreb countries and Spain or between Eastern Europe and Germany are stronger incentives to migrate. Many individuals are willing to accept the costs and risks of illegal migration, and still migration is smaller than expected. When it comes to preventing South to North migration in the presence of high incentives to migrate, it can therefore be assumed that immigration controls alone are insufficiently effective instruments, although this topic is hotly debated.

The control and illegality aspects of migration are linked to the existence of a system of social security, increasing the attractiveness of destination, for insiders as well as for outsiders.[40] Insiders are less likely

40. For the time being we want to abstract from the disincentives that the costs of a social security system can bring about, especially the higher level of taxation that usually comes along with social services.

to leave and outsiders are more likely to come. In other words, a system of social security should theoretically tend to reduce the propensity of the population of a certain country or region to leave their place of residence but increase the propensity of migrants to take up residence there.

For insiders, a social security system tends to decrease the net gains of leaving and to increase the costs in terms of forgone social rights and benefits. The importance of a social security system for potential immigrants obviously depends on whether they have access to its services, which in turn to a large extent depends on their status. For illegal immigrants even basic public services like school and health assistance may not be accessible. Permanently resident non-citizens (denizens) may be granted most social rights but still not all of them, for example not the same retirement, housing or employment rights. We would expect that constraints in access to the social security system would lead to a reduction in migration and an increase in the relative attractivity of immobility.

The same is true for the fourth area which we would like to mention in this context. Discrimination against immigrants (outsiders) also helps to explain immobility. Discrimination by the native population reduces the attractiveness of a destination.

Discrimination often results in lower wage levels compared to the native population, regardless of the kind of employment and level of qualifications (Hayfron 1993). Rather, immigrants may have to pay discriminatory prices, for example for housing and other services, as well as suffer from psychic costs. Important, although difficult to quantify, is the feeling of being a second-class resident and an unwelcome person.

Therefore, we would expect a negative effect of discrimination on decisions to 'go'. Especially when an individual's decision-making process is on 'knife's edge', where a marginal change of either costs or benefits can be decisive, information about discrimination against immigrants may lead to a negative decision. It is not clear, however, whether negative information is passed on to would-be migrants. Emigrants tend to exaggerate the good parts of their life abroad and say less about the bad parts. Whenever the expected gains substantially outweigh the costs, though, discrimination is unlikely to have a decisive effect. This may be the case with respect to South to North migration, even taking into account that some of these migrants are likely to suffer the greatest degree of discrimination, mainly due to the pronounced cultural differences.[41]

41. The causes of discrimination shall not be addressed at this point although they are a very important area of research in migration. A frequently mentioned economic reason for discrimination against immigrants is the alleged but not normally existing negative effect of migration on the employment opportunities for natives. For a critical analysis of the alleged negative effects see Borjas (1991) and Zimmermann (1993). The

To summarise, in this second part of our discussion of the reasons why most people usually prefer immobility we have put forward the hypotheses that:

24. *Most people are heavily risk averse and thus reluctant to move to another location even if they expect an improvement of their personal quality of life with a high probability but are aware of some risk involved.*

25. *Most people have a (locational) preference for what they know well and thus tend to exaggerate risks abroad as greater than those at home.*

26. *To protect insider advantages (rents), macro-level units usually try to control migration. (Restrictive) Migration control is possibly the strongest intervening obstacle. It increases the costs and risks of a decision to go, but usually not prohibitively.*

27. *The outcome of a system of strict migration control is most likely to be a two-tier society with legal immigrants as 'first division' and illegal as 'second'. Illegal status strongly reduces benefits obtainable from migration, significantly increases the risks and is likely to cause higher costs, e.g. in terms of social security. How far the threat of illegality prevents people from going, however, depends on the magnitude of the other remaining benefits of migration.*

28. *Social security systems reduce the costs of staying immobile and increase the losses in terms of forgone social benefits in case of out-migration of insiders. The level of social protection supplied can therefore be a key element in reducing the propensity to leave. At the same time it may increase the propensity of migrants (non-citizens) to take up residence in this area. The latter effect will depend on the extent to which immigrants are free to benefit from the system, which in turn depends on their legal status. Social security and public welfare systems increase the costs of illegality.*

29. *Discrimination against immigrants by insiders is another reason for immobility. It increases the individual costs and risks of immigration to outsiders and reduces the benefits.*

With regard to South to North migration, control, discrimination and risk aversity combined with a severe lack of information may all help us explain the absence of major migration flows. Actual or perceived

---

analysis of DeNew and Zimmermann (1994) and Franz (1993), however, lends some support to the theory that immigration has negative effects on the labour market. According to Zimmermann (1995) and Razin and Sadka (1995) the effects depend crucially on the overall functioning of the labour market.

changes in these may contribute to an explanation of emerging and vanishing migration flows.

Migration Dynamics in the Early Phases of Migration

From a Comparative-static Towards a Dynamic View of the Migration Decision

In the section above we tried to shed some light on the decision-making process of the individual human beings and evaluated the different reasons influencing their decisions to 'stay' or to 'go'. This analysis was rather simple insofar as it was reduced to a static comparison of alternatives at a given moment in time. It did not take the dynamic effects of migration into account, at least not explicitly, although questions like 'when, why and how does migration start' are dynamic by their very nature. As a matter of fact, dynamic micro(-economic) theories of migration are still rare. The dynamisation of a problem introduces so much additional complexity into the theoretical analysis that it becomes very difficult to derive general ideas and hypotheses. To start with, we would like to sketch some economic hypotheses about migration dynamics. While we are not presenting a more comprehensive theory, we provide some suggestions for future research in the concluding section.

There are two different ways of defining micro-level individual migration dynamics. Firstly, dynamic effects can mean the repercussions which the migratory decisions of individuals have on the determinants influencing the decision-making process of others. Secondly, it can refer to the dynamics of an individual's migration decision itself, by looking at the patterns of decision-making processes as continuous successions of single but interdependent decisions.

With respect to the repercussions of previous migration decisions on present migration decisions we have assumed so far that the determinants of different origin and destination locations are exogenous, a simplifying assumption which we will now drop. Instead we want to outline so-called 'cumulative causation' processes (Massey et al. 1993).[42] Since we focus in this chapter on the micro-determinants of the decision-making process of the individual, we will not extensively discuss issues like the link between migration and development from more broader macro-perspectives, an issue to which we have devoted chapter 4 in this book. For the time being, we restrict ourselves to the question whether these links are migration-accelerating or migration-decelerating.

---

42. See also chapter 7 for an in-depth sociological meso-level treatment.

Some important dynamic aspects of migration have already been implicitly mentioned in the sections above. One such dynamic mechanism is the so-called 'chain migration'. By this we mean the migration-accelerating effect of the flow of information emanating from 'pioneer' migrants. Depending on the content of the information, such an increase may reduce or increase migration. However, the increased amount of information available certainly has the beneficial effect of reducing the level of uncertainty or risk which the decision-making individual faces (Taylor 1986, Massey 1990, Gurak and Caces 1992). The information can be passed on within a family or via any other information channel (Boyd 1989). 'Pioneers' can not only provide information, they are also able to give active support to later migrants, which reduces those later migrants' migration costs (and the relative value of staying immobile). The possibility of obtaining help in a foreign macro-level unit also decreases the costs of migration and tends to increase the number of 'go' decisions: migration accelerates further migration.

The existence of a pioneer group of migrants may not only alter tangible parts of the framework within which 'stay' or 'go' decision are made. It can also in two ways change the perception of those who originally decided to 'stay'. Firstly, given the fact that the 'pioneers' are successful, those who are left behind face a decline in relative income. This is based on the reasonable assumption that the migrants are still part of the reference group of those who opted to 'stay'. Such a relative decline changes the cost/benefit structure and shifts the weight in favour of a decision to 'go'. Secondly, the 'pioneers' are likely to contribute to a general change of the way in which migration is perceived in a society (Massey 1986, Rocha-Trindade 1993). Successful examples of migration will reduce the social 'stigma' which is often initially attached to a change of the macro-level unit. Such a change in attitude accelerates further decisions to 'go'.

The dynamics would have the opposite significance, however, if the experience of the 'pioneers' were negative. If those who opted to 'go' were penalised by a relative decline in the quality of life, be it in the form of economic failure or non-economic hardships, the effect would be a reduction of the migratory flows (provided this failure is made transparent).

A large set of macro-theories discusses the links between migration, migration dynamics and development. In economic terms, there are two different channels through which the migration decision may be influenced. First of all, the expected relative patterns of development at different locations, i.e. convergence or divergence, matter and, secondly, the absolute level of development may influence the character of the migration decision.

Peter Fischer, Reiner Martin and Thomas Straubhaar

In terms of the human-capital model, the relative economic and social development a migration decision maker expects at different locations influences the expected advantages and disadvantages of the move. Expected convergence decreases future relative advantages, while the expectation of continued and stable great differences or even more divergence enforce decisions to go. Chapter 4 provides an in-depth discussion of the links between migration and development and shows how actual migration may change expected convergence patterns.

We have discussed the dynamic effects of migration in the sense of repercussions on further migration improved information or changes in (macro-)economic development. Closer to our micro-treatment of the migration decision itself, however, is the question of the dynamic effects of one decision, taken by an individual at a certain point in time, on the same individual's future decisions. The micro-economic model applied throughout this chapter assumes that individuals rationally ask themselves whether to migrate. It is assumed that the final and unique possible answer to this question has to be either 'yes' or 'no'. But as Hammar (1995) points out, to determine when and why this is asked and how the answers that follow are related to each other may explain an important part of migration dynamics.

The micro-economic method of dynamising the virtually comparative static analysis of the migration decision would have to imagine a continuous flow of single migration decisions and investigate dependencies between actual and past decision making. Suppose an individual or a family every day asks whether to stay or to go: is the 31st answer more likely to be 'yes' than the first?

As far as we know, answers to this kind of dynamics question are still lacking within economic migration research. They may more likely be found within the other social sciences and they will probably represent a promising topic for interdisciplinary research.

Another related field open for further investigation concerns the formation of individual expectations about the advantages and disadvantages of the decision to 'go' or to 'stay'. In terms of our behavioural model, migration propensities depend heavily on whether people form their expectations on the basis of gathered and selected up-to-date information or rather on past experiences. Even if migration decisions are determined by relative macro-level differences, changes in the expectations about future developments may cause migration dynamics to alter, even without any observable actual changes of the determinants. If, for example due to the election of a new political leader, people suddenly change their minds, stop believing in convergence and start to think that the future development within their area is bound to deteriorate, they become more likely to decide to 'go', without any change in the macro-fundamentals.

Quantitative empirical research into the above questions is bound to encounter major obstacles. Nevertheless the formation of expectations of migrants and non-migrants seems to us a very fruitful area of research. We would suggest that findings from such studies should be linked with empirical work on the link between migration and development along the lines sketched above.[43] Let us just point again to the problems encountered by micro(-economic) behavioural theory on the migration decision in attempts to incorporate questions about the dynamics of migration. Although a better understanding of the interdependencies between the development of macro-determinants and the micro-level decision making would be decisive in order to understand more of the dynamics of migration, an important part of these dynamic aspects are determined by macro-economic developments that are outside the scope of this chapter.[44]

With respect to our previous discussion, we may summarise our hypotheses, stating that:

30. *Past migration makes more information available to decision makers about the advantages and disadvantages of certain locations, although the information passed is not neccessarily a complete or neutral picture of the situation abroad. Provided the information conveys the impression that pioneer migrants are relatively successful, past migration accelerates further decisions to 'go' (chain migration). Apparent failure of pioneer migrants, however, has the opposite effect.*

31. *Decisions to migrate are dependent on expectations of relative development convergence or divergence between origin and destination.*

32. *Behavioural dynamics of the migration decision itself are a virtually unexplored field within economic migration research. It is clear, however, that the interdependence of an individual's past and future migration decisions depends on one's information gathering and selection strategy as well as on long-term expectations.*

33. *Changes in expectations can explain altering migration patterns despite the absence of any observable changes of macro-determinants of the migration decision.*

43. Such studies are as yet rare, but some do exist. Such a remarkable example is Mulder (1993), who investigates migration dynamics in the Netherlands.

44. One may refer to general macro-economic and international economic theories as discussed in chapters 4 and 5 of this book as well as to Wallerstein's (1974) world system or Piore's (1979) dual labour market theories, as to many others.

Conclusions

This chapter has reviewed (micro)economic theories in order to explain why people decide to 'go'. Admittedly, *the* classic economic man or woman, continuously computing economic benefits at all conceivable alternative locations, constantly on the move trying to exploit differences between macro-level units and thereby levelling them out, is not realistic. Not surprisingly, the most classical economic model is hardly able to explain the details and dynamics of migration flows, basing its explanations of migration on wage differences and assuming *the* homogeneous economic person to make decisions under conditions of perfect certainty, no costs, perfect information and the absence of risk. Also, the most classical economic migration model fails to explain why world-wide roughly 98 per cent of mankind remain immobile despite large locational differences. The point we make in this chapter is that once we allow for the decision makers to be more complex individuals and the migration decision to be influenced by families or other groups, the micro-economic behavioural model does become a powerful and crucial tool with which to analyse migration, immobility and their dynamics from a multidisciplinary perspective. It meets our ambition of theoretical abstraction and allows us to derive partial as well as general conclusions about who is most likely to migrate, at what time, where to and for what reasons. Applying the behavioural micro-model of migration rectifies a usual shortcoming of most 'general' macro- and meso-models of migration: their lack of a micro-foundation.

Intuition as well as sound empirical evidence support the assumption that decision makers do attempt to maximise their quality or utility of life. Given these premises, we surveyed research contributions by economists and outlined economic arguments which we believe could contribute further to the development of an appropriate behavioural micro-model which can help explain present and future trends in migration and immobility. Apart from the usual intertemporary analysis of pecuniary and non-pecuniary costs and benefits we identified time horizons, preferences for the present, risk assessment, information gathering, information selection and the formation of expectations as dimensions of particular importance for migration decisions.

Immobility is a necessary prerequisite for any 'investment' in the accumulation of *location-specific assets* and *abilities,* which in turn allow for the exploitation of *insider advantages*. Insider advantages not only enable individuals to gain higher incomes, they also allow them to make better use of a given set of resources in order to maximise their quality of life. Gaining knowledge about location-specific economic, social and cultural opportunities, building up a social network, or getting involved in democratic or political activities all require a certain immobility and represent an 'investment' that is lost in case of a decision to 'go'. Such insider advantages are non-transferable. A decision to 'go' leads to their partial or complete loss at least as long as one does not return. Moreover, the basis for further investments in location-specific assets and abilities, for example the social network, is gone and the individual has to start more or less from scratch in another location. To the extent that location-specific assets and abilities are important for decision makers' realisation of life quality, the introduction of location-specific assets and abilities transforms the decision to 'stay' from a paradox into a perfectly rational and understandable behaviour for a major part of the population. So far this idea has been little explored in economic migration research, probably due to its focus on actual migration flows rather than immobility. We believe it deserves further investigation.

Approaches that identify rigidities and market imperfections as causes of immobility are more in line with traditional economic migration theories. Out of those, we have chosen for further discussion *prohibitive initial costs, risk aversity, (locational) preferences for what is given and well known, control policies (causing illegality)* and *discrimination.* All of them make the decision to go less attractive for a decision maker, thereby counteracting the migration incentives provided by macro-level differences such as changes in wage levels between different locations. Only empirical investigations could reveal to what extent and under which circumstances changes of these factors are decisive for migration to emerge or to vanish.

Theoretical analysis of the dynamic effects of migration is still relatively rare in (micro-)economic migration theory. The repercussions which the migratory decisions of 'pioneer' individuals have on the decision making process of future migrants may vary. Chain-migration theories emphasise that past migration increases the level of information for later migrants, which reduces the risks of a decision to 'go'. Macro-economic theories investigate the relationship between migration and development and may explain how actual migration can change expectations about future convergence or divergence processes in sending and receiving areas.

We have also suggested another way to introduce dynamic effects into the analysis of migration, namely the investigation of the *dynamics* of the decision-making process itself. When and why does it make sense for individuals, families or groups to think about whether to 'stay' or to 'go'? How are decision-making processes temporarily interdependent? Does repeated decision making make people more likely to go? Such questions could extend and enrich the simple 'yes' or 'no' framework of the behavioural micro-model described above. Although different theories, looking for example at regulation, information processing and the formation of expectations, may provide further starting-points, a more encompassing analysis has not yet found its way into the body of migration theory. Its development would need multidisciplinary co-operation.

—4—

Interdependencies between Development and Migration

Peter A. Fischer, Reiner Martin
and *Thomas Straubhaar*[1]

Introduction

This chapter discusses macro-economic theories on migration and development in order to contribute towards a multidisciplinary under-standing of migration. As a complement, chapter 3 contains our investigation of determinants, consequences and dynamics of individual migration decisions. There we argue that a number of 'environmental conditions' like economic wealth and risks, political systems, social regulations and networks or environmental amenities all have an impact on whether people are more likely to 'go' or to 'stay'. While in chapter 3 we investigate the importance of these environmental macro-conditions from a micro-level point of view, the present chapter focuses on the macro-level of analysis, presenting theoretical links between the macro-concepts 'migration' and 'development'. When doing this, it is important to bear in mind that macro-concepts, in order to be applied to actual situations, need a micro-foundation of the kind described before. (For a sociological analysis of the meso-link see chapter 7. Another, more contextual mediating micro-macro position is provided by Bjéren in chapter 8.)

A discussion of definitions of 'development' is provided in chapter 1. In the present chapter, however, we will concentrate on economic aspects of development, looking at the efficient use of resources in producing a valuable output and at the relative distribution of this output. Although the term economic aspects of development refers to more than just the available income per head of population, it is an accepted simplification in economic theory to use income as an indicator of

1. The authors are grateful to Martin Wolburg and to participants of seminars at the HWWA Institute for Economic Research in Hamburg, at the Europa-Kolleg in Hamburg and at an ESF workshop on migration and development in Strasburg for helpful comments. Tim Heinzmann provided capable research assistance.

development. As a matter of fact, it is frequently the only available indicator when it comes to comparisons between different macro-level units, be they countries or regions. (For a critical qualification of the wealth-based economic definition of development see contribution by Hermele.)

This chapter has two guiding questions: does migration trigger development and/or does development trigger migration? While most of the academic and policy discussion has traditionally focused on the first question we want to discuss the impact of development on migration first. From a macro-economic point of view, there are clear differences in the environmental conditions prevailing in different macro-level units. The massive international differences in income clearly illustrate this point. This leads to the question whether there is a link between patterns of migration and differences in the economic macro-environment. Is migration dependent on economic development? Do migrants usually move from poor to rich areas? Does an increase in per capita income therefore reduce out-migration, a theory suggested by the statement 'the best migration policy is development policy' (Körner 1987)?

The brief review of major current migration flows presented in chapter 1 shows that the income–migration link is not clear-cut in the way that an increase in income in a macro-level unit would automatically reduce out-migration. In fact, the opposite may be true. From theoretical considerations we suggest that the relation between migration and development ought to be a somewhat more complex story which we would like to call the 'modified inverted U-curve' concept of migration. Development often first enhances and thereafter reduces the scope and incentives for migration, but the sequencing of enhancement and reduction is usually different for different types of migration. In the second part of this chapter we shall sketch the main elements of this 'modified inverted U-curve' hypothesis.

A few individual human beings cannot normally have an impact on the macro-level conditions, but a large number of migrants are likely to do so in the sending as well as the receiving countries. This in turn may influence potential and actual migratory flows during later periods of time. In the third part of this chapter, we are going to introduce some major economic macro theories about how migration can widen or narrow the gap between 'poor' and 'rich' macro-level units. We will put the emphasis on discussing the assumptions underlying these theories and the implications of these assumptions.

Classic economic theory of the so-called 'convergence school' expects sending areas to obtain major benefits from out-migration for their development process. Another school of economic thinking, the 'divergence theory', argues that out-migration may in effect be an obstacle for the socio-economic development of the sending regions. The 'brain-drain' discussion is one important example of the divergence school. As well-educated people are most likely to leave, they drain poorer regions of valuable human capital, needed for development. Thus, under certain circumstances, migration may support development in the advantaged centres at the expense of the disadvantaged, poor periphery.

Whether convergence or divergence effects dominate depends on the economic context, which in turn is largely determined by the (economic) development phase a region is involved in. The empirical studies reviewed in the third section of this chapter indicate that on the whole migration seems to have positive short-term effects for the sending and the receiving countries. The long-term effects, especially for the sending countries, are much more difficult to estimate but the bulk of the empirical studies suggest that migration does not normally have a strong impact on the development process, either in a positive or in a negative way. There seem to be, however, 'turning points' in the development of macro-level units where migration can become decisive.

Although theories are important for our understanding of the mechanisms and predictions, for a deeper understanding of actual migration and development patterns we need careful case-by-case analyses based on country- or region-specific macro-conditions. One cannot expect the effects of migration to be uniform for all countries of the South. After all, the South itself is not and never has been uniform.

Major conclusions from the theories discussed are given in numbered implications plotted in italics throughout the text. Having discussed both sides of the circle we shall summarise the main findings of this chapter and its implications for further research in the concluding section.

Development and Migration

The following discussion is, as mentioned, motivated by two questions. Firstly, we want to ask whether there is a general relationship between development and migration, and secondly, we are interested in whether certain types of migration flows are specific to certain levels of income and forms of macro-economic organisation. When analysing these questions we regard the development of macro-level units and the reasons for the enormous differences in prosperity as exogenously determined. In other words, in this section we do not try to investigate and explain them. Nor do we assume the existence of an automatic mechanism of development. Societies may change over time, they may become more prosperous or less prosperous, they may catch up or fall behind economically, but they may also remain in a steady development state.

Some Stylised Patterns

According to the most simple economic explanation of migration, people move in order to improve their life situation. Internationally, we would therefore expect large numbers of migrants to move from poor to rich locations. This cannot be the complete story, however. Firstly, the total number of migrants is comparatively small; it is estimated that only about 1.5 per cent of the world population are migrants (ILO/IOM/UNHCR 1994: 3). Secondly, most migration is internal rather than international, although international income differences are even more pronounced than national disparities. As far as international migration is concerned, the number of people migrating from countries of the South to countries of the North is small compared to South to South migration. Migration flows are generally rather selective in their direction and show the influence of cultural and historic ties as well as of geographic distance. (For a more in-depth analysis of the dimension of space see chapter 2.) One also finds that the most important sending countries are normally not the poorest and that over time the position of countries within the international migration system changes. With changes of their income levels countries' importance as emigration areas rises or falls. As argued below sending countries can also become receiving countries.

Regardless of these differentiations it has to be emphasised that international migration is *partly* dependent on differences in income and development between macro-level areas. International comparisons of migration populations are extremely difficult due to measurement problems and a lack of comparable data as well as the influence of non-economic and cyclical migration streams. Despite all these problems, comparing migrant populations and development levels still provides relatively clear empirical content to the (theoretical) argument of a (positive) relationship between migration and development. Using the data for major sending and receiving countries provided in chapter 1 we have calculated correlation coefficients between the net number of people born abroad in per cent of total population and relative average real per capita GDP (measured in Purchasing Power Parities – PPP). Net means in this context the stock of people born abroad residing in a country ('immigrants'), minus the number of citizens of this country residing abroad ('emigrants'). Figure 4.1 plots the data in a scatter diagram; correlation coefficients grouped by world regions are shown in table 4.1.

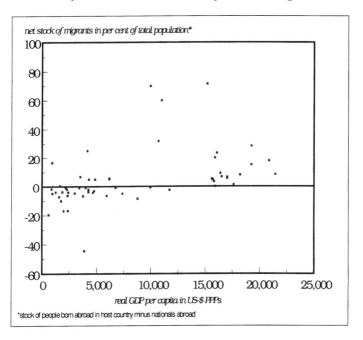

Figure 4.1 Major Immigration and Emigration Countries and Economic Development

Table 4.1 Correlation Coefficients

Region	Note	Correlation Value
World	Ex-Soviet Union excluded	0.46
Europe	Maghreb and Turkey included	0.81
Africa	Maghreb excluded	0.43
America		0.73
Middle East	Turkey excluded	0.89
Far East and Australia		0.73
Ex-Soviet Union		-0.19

Source: ILO/IOM/UNHCR (1994), see also table 1.2. in chapter 1.

Despite plenty of reservations to be made as far as the data used are concerned,[2] the calculations derive a relation between the net stock of foreign-born people and GDP per capita which is overall positive, with a correlation value of +0.46. This correlation is rather weak, but the

2. The data given are always the best available according to ILO/IOM/UNHCR (1994). In some cases, the figure for the foreign-born population had to be substituted by a figure for the non-national economically active part of the population. A few stock figures are gross instead of net. For details see the appendix to the introduction and the original data source. All figures are expressed in per cent of the total population.

migration–development relation becomes much stronger when we look at geographically determined sub-samples. In the case of Europe, for example, combined with Turkey and the Maghreb countries, the correlation is quite strong (+0.81). The same applies to the Middle East (+0.89) and the Americas (+0.73).

For African countries the correlation is slightly below the value for the whole sample. The former Soviet Union is the only subregion where the correlation between development and the net stock of foreigners is negative(!). These two seemingly counter intuitive cases are in fact quite instructive. The value for Africa indicates that political reasons for migration are even more important for migration decisions on this continent than in other parts of the world. There are numerous examples of political turmoil resulting in very large stocks of foreign-born population in countries which are not very attractive from an economic point of view. In the former Soviet Union significant parts of the population were forced to engage in politically determined internal migration. They suddenly became 'foreigners born abroad' when the former Soviet Empire broke up. The very high level of foreigners in the Baltic states, for example, is clear testimony of the political aim to russify these parts of the Soviet Union.

To sum up this first glance at empirical evidence:

1. *Development seems to have an impact on migration. The major sending countries are on average poorer than the major receiving countries.*
2. *Middle-income countries are more likely sources of out-migration than the poorest countries of the world.*
3. *Historical and cultural ties, frequently established in the colonial period, as well as geographic proximity influence the pattern of international migration heavily.*

The Modified Inverted U-Curve Hypothesis

In order to obtain more systematic insights into the link between development and migration, we make two simplifications. Firstly, we define a limited number of types of migration and, secondly, we sketch some elements of (economic) development which affect the micro- as well as the macro-level of migration decision making.

In order to keep things simple we restrict our migration typology to no more than three categories of migration, although these do not cover all possible forms of migration:

a. Internal (short-distance) migration

b. International (long-distance) migration of low-skilled workers
c. International (long-distance) migration of high-skilled workers

The difference between (a) and (b) is fairly straightforward, with the crossing of an international border being the distinguishing event. In some parts of the world, especially in previously colonised areas, international borders cut across economic regions, thereby separating, for example, urban centres from their hinterland. Although this reduces the analytical value of our categorisation, it helps to say that short-distance international migration resulting from such a situation can be regarded as internal. More problematic is the difference between (b) and (c). What is a 'low-skilled' migrant and what is a 'high-skilled' migrant? Educational standards between countries differ significantly and sometimes dramatically despite international attempts to develop internationally comparable qualification levels.[3] Since this chapter does not analyse high-skilled migration empirically, it is sufficient to say that migrants qualified for employment above, say, the level of simple manufacturing jobs shall be regarded as high-skilled migrants.

The question which locational features affect micro-level migration decisions has been addressed in more detail in chapter 3. (Compare also chapter 7 and 9.) For the purposes of the present analysis we assume that the crucial differentiating macro-factor is the average level of per capita income. This in turn influences not only people's desire to 'stay' or to 'go' but also their means to 'go' and their level of information about areas they can potentially go to.

It is far beyond the scope of this chapter to analyse why the income differences between countries or regions are so large. Economic theory usually argues, however, that the spatial allocation of production factors and the production techniques used are of crucial importance. The next section of this chapter will look at this point in more detail, but for the time being, we will restrict ourselves to a purely theoretical derivation of the 'modified inverted U-curve' hypothesis.

Throughout history up to the present time the lowest per capita incomes have been found in those parts of the world where people exploit primarily scarce natural resources or work in agriculture.[4] There is little division of labour and little trade with other economic areas. By definition, in these areas the level of income is low and spatial distribution of the population is primarily determined by ecological

3. One such attempt is e.g. the International Standard Classification for Educational Attainments (ISCED).
4. It goes without saying that neither this nor any of the following is intended as a normative statement, establishing a hierarchical structure among different macro-level units.

factors such as the fertility of the country and the availability of water. There is little wealth differentiation within the area and therefore no economic incentive to engage in internal migration.[5] Due to the lack of financial possibilities and information there is also very little international (out-)migration.

A comparison between the before-mentioned 'areas of lowest income' and parts of the world where per capita income is higher reveals that some features of economic organisations are related to the production of more output and higher income per capita. They in turn influence migration. The increasing use of modern industrial technology is one such process. In most cases trade and other international links with other countries are a source of wealth growing with per capita income. The economic structure of better-off societies is also usually more complex. Finally it is very important from the point of view of migration theory that internal regional income imbalances are usually highest in middle-income areas and decline again in high-income entities.[6]

What do these developments mean for migration between countries and regions at different levels of per capita income? In chapter 3 we have analysed in detail the importance of potential migrants' means to finance decisions to 'go' as well as the influence of the available amount of information on decision makers. As argued above, there is usually very little emigration from the societies with the lowest per capita income where people exploit primarily natural resources or work in agriculture. But countries that have developed somewhat further economically but still belong to the lower range of per capita income are frequently characterised by substantial spatial (rural–urban) imbalances as far as employment and per capita income are concerned. These differences create incentives to move towards better-off parts, in other words they create incentives for internal migration. International migration, however, may be a less feasible option for inhabitants of rural areas. The available financial means to finance a decision to 'go' and the available information are not sufficient. The limited international migration that does take place, though, can contain a disproportionately high share of high-skilled migrants looking for more suitable employment opportunities in other countries. A more detailed discussion of this so-

5. This does not apply to people following nomadic ways of life or to people being forced to move due to the exhaustion of natural resources (hunters, farmers having cut all wood), ecological or climatic change or armed conflicts. In fact, these are the few forms of predominantly internal migration that characterise mobility in our first 'stylised' form of macro-economic organisation.

6. The existence of links between these features and different levels of per capita income does not imply the existence of an automatic process that propels countries or regions towards higher levels of income. Their income level may as well remain immobile or fall.

called 'brain-drain' will be provided in the third section of this chapter.

When moving on to areas with higher per capita income we often find that the internal differences gradually subside, especially in relation to the rising overall levels of wealth. This reduces the incentives for internal migration although this process is likely to be slow. The available means to engage in international migration increase and an increasing number of people can now in principle afford to migrate over long distances. For reasons elaborated in chapter 3, however (increased economic and non-economic opportunity costs of migration), most people will not leave their place of residence. It can be expected, however, that proportionately more high-skilled people will decide to 'go' because the benefits of migration tend to be higher due to higher demand and smaller costs of mobility. In short, low- as well as high-skilled international migration will increase while internal migration will slowly decrease.

In the higher income echelons the incentives to migrate internally or internationally decrease although more people than ever can afford to go. There are, however, two factors that work in favour of more migration. Firstly, high-income parts of the world are usually subject to ever closer international economic integration. Secondly, the increasing division of labour as well as the increasingly international provision of services work specifically in favour of high-skilled migration. Consequently the importance of high-skilled international migrants *vis-à-vis* other forms of migration ought to increase.

Figure 4.2 summarises the hypothetical internal and international migration flows from countries at different levels of average per capita income and draws our 'modified inverted U-curve'.[7] Whereas it can be expected for areas with a very high level of income that high-skilled international migration becomes quantitatively more important than low-skilled international migration, we assume that for essentially all countries internal migration remains the quantitatively most important form of mobility.

In this chapter, we do not aim to provide an econometric investigation of our 'modified inverted U-curve' hypothesis. In order to illustrate our point that the relation between emigration propensities and development

---

7. The initial work investigating an inverted U-curve relation between level of development and emigration is usually credited to Easterlin (1961). Åkerman (1976) was one of the first to present it as emerging from studies of time series of aggregate emigration rates for a number of countries. Recently, Faini and Venturini (1994) and Hatton and Williamson (1994) have taken up the idea and tested it within different contexts. Note that our modified inverted U-curve hypothesis of changing mobility patterns also shares features with Zelinsky's well known 'mobility transition' hypothesis (Zelinsky 1971).

Peter Fischer, Reiner Martin and Thomas Straubhaar

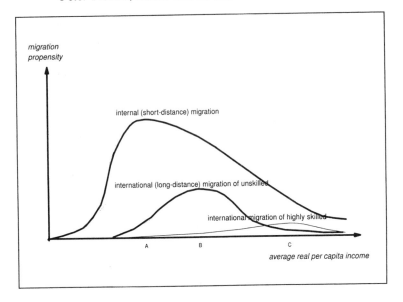

Source: Own illustration.

Figure 4.2 Migration and Development – the Modified Inverted U-Curve

is empirically non-linear, however, we have plotted international emigration rates from selected European countries from the second half of the nineteenth century to the 1990s in figure 4.3. It is remarkable that although the relationship is heavily distorted by historical influences, emigration intensities indeed usually have first increased, then peaked and decreased again.[8] So far, comparable longitudinal data are unfortunately available neither for internal migration nor separately for high-skilled migration.

Figure 4.3 illustrates that international migration reaches its peak when countries are at intermediate levels of per capita income. Germany reached this level well before the First World War, when its emigration rate was already declining. At present, the high levels of German out-migration can mainly be explained by Germany having become a major immigration country and emigration flows consisting mainly of previous immigrants returning back home. The Southern European countries Spain and Portugal reached the point where the emigration of their native-born population peaked later; Portuguese emigration peaked as

8. Note that there is a substantial gap in this series, namely from 1913 to 1960. During this time, however, economic development as well as migration flows were heavily distorted by the two World Wars and their aftermath.

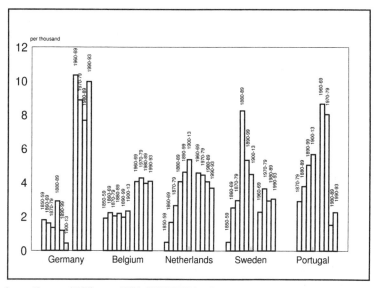

Source: Hatton and Williamson (1994), EUROSTAT (ann.).

Figure 4.3 Emigration from Selected European Countries

late as the 1960s. For Southern Europe similar patterns have been shown by Faini and Venturini (1994).

A recent study of the causes of mass emigration from Europe in the late nineteenth century has investigated the effects not only of wage increases in the sending countries but also of socio-demographic changes in Europe, as well as the stock of migrants abroad (Hatton and Williamson 1994). The results point towards the migration-increasing effects of industrialisation in Europe, the demographic transition process and the number of migrants already residing in the destination countries. Whereas the first two variables led to an increase in the labour supply on European labour markets, the third variable captured the risk- and cost-reducing effects of chain migration. (On this point compare chapter 3.) The impact of real-wage convergence between the 'old' and the 'new' world, however, reduced European mass emigration. Only 'as the demographic forces petered out, as the impact of industrialisation weakened, and as the emigrant stock abroad began to level out, real wage convergence increasingly dominated events' (Hatton and Williamson 1994: 556). From this point onwards, emigration rates declined from the peak level. The timing of this process differed significantly between the various emigration countries, reflecting the differences in the timing of the socio-economic changes taking place in the decades prior to the First World War.

Peter Fischer, Reiner Martin and Thomas Straubhaar

Summing up the discussion above, we assume that for most macro-level areas, regardless of their level of average per capita income:

4. *Internal migration remains quantitatively the most important form of migration.*
5. *Major changes in a country's position within the international migration system can occur. With increasing development, countries may suddenly become major migration-sending countries, but thereafter, with development proceeding further, emigration propensities are bound to decline again.*
6. *We expect each flow of migration separately first to increase and then to decrease with increasing economic wealth. Moreover, the effects of changes in relative income levels interact with changes of the socio-demographic situation.*

Which answers does this section on development and migration suggest for the 'guiding' questions of the book, namely 'why does migration start?' 'why do most people stay immobile?' and 'what are the dynamics of migration flows?'

Our hypothetical considerations have lent some support to the assumption that differences in development – approximated by international variations of per capita income – influence international migration patterns. An encompassing explanation of these patterns, however, together with an explanation for the immobility of most people, requires a much more sophisticated analysis based on micro-economic as well as non-economic approaches.

The third question, 'what are the dynamics of migration?', will be addressed in the next section, where we want to see whether migration has significant effects on the level of development. Provided these effects exist, they will in turn influence migration patterns, which would mean that the relationship between development and migration is of a two-sided dynamic nature.

Migration and Development

In the last section we argued that migration flows are largely specific to different forms of macro-economic organisation and the corresponding differences in per capita income. In what follows we will investigate whether these differences, which so far we took as exogenously determined, are not themselves partly dependent on migration.

Imagine first an economist, on a walking holiday in the Alps far away from his office and his books. You approach him, take him by surprise and ask him whether he would be in favour of more rather than less international migration. His intuitive answer (do not allow him too much time to think about it!) ought to be 'yes'. This positive answer results from one of the core propositions of traditional international economic theory, namely that economic integration increases the efficiency of international production, promotes economic wealth in all locations and stimulates economic convergence between the economic areas involved. In economic terms, however, international migration – the mobility of the production factor labour – improves economic integration and allows for a more efficient international allocation of labour.[9]

Now imagine meeting a blue-collar worker or a local politician in the German 'Ruhrpot' area. Unlike our prototype-economist they are bound to express concern about immigration-induced unemployment, wage reductions and a general deterioration of national welfare.

At first these differences look like a paradox, but the opposing attitudes result primarily from differences in their perspectives. While the economist's enthusiasm is based on a certain long-term, allocational efficiency school of thinking, the blue-collar worker's fears are based on a short-term, distribution-oriented perspective. In what follows, both points of view will be discussed.

There already exists a sizeable number of surveys looking at the links between migration and development. We used some of them as helpful starting points for our own analysis of the issue. To name just a few of them: Siebert (1993) and Grubel (1994) are comparatively short introductions, Giersch (1994) and Siebert (1994) are recent collections of papers with Siebert giving special reference to the European dimension of the problem. Straubhaar (1992 and 1994) provides an overview of the major issues. A very valuable and comparatively recent book combining case studies and theoretical insights is Papademetriou and Martin (1991). In chapter 5, Hermele takes up the issue from a more policy-making-oriented perspective.

The 'Balanced Growth' Convergence Point of View

Macro-economic theories analyse (economic) development within spatial economic entities. The starting point for this analysis is to look at the (changing) allocation of certain types of input factors and their most efficient use in terms of overall welfare. We usually distinguish between at least three factors, namely 'fixed resources' $(\overline{A})$, 'capital' (K) and

9. Under most of the theoretical assumptions usual in traditional models of international economics, international trade and international capital flows would be able to achieve similar results. Therefore, we did not want to allow our prototype economist too much time to think about whether he favours free migration. We will return to the relation between migration, trade and capital flows below.

'labour' (L).[10] Capital represents primarily stocks of (physical) investment goods (in later extensions also human skills) which, unlike for
example natural resources, can be accumulated over time. By means of
a set of available technologies, these inputs are transformed into output.
Questions related to the input-factor mix are called the *allocational*
aspects of economic activity whereas *distributional* aspects refer to the
distribution of the output between the different factors of production. In
economic terms development is roughly approximated by the (per
capita) output of the economic entity. (For a critique of this concept see
chapter 5.)

On the World of Neo-Classical Economics

Conclusions in neo-classical economics are usually derived on the basis
of a set of relatively rigid assumptions like the homogeneity of the
production factor labour (b) or the belief that markets normally clear and
reach a stable equilibrium (c). Box 4.1 summarises the most important
of these assumptions.

   (a) Different kinds of production factors are (imperfect) substitutes.

   (b) Migrants are a homogeneous group of working people (labour).

   (c) Labour markets are in equilibrium, there is no unemployment.

   (d) Transport and transaction costs are negligible.

   (e) Production technologies are identical and exogenously given
       across countries.

   (f) Production of goods and services takes place under constant
       economics of scale.

   (g) Markets are efficient and fully competitive.

   (h) Individual and collective interests are identical, there are no
       externalities of individual action.

Box 4.1 Neo-classical assumptions in macro-economic theory

10. In more formal terms, the relation between output produced and production factor
inputs can be specified in so-called 'production functions' like:

    (1) $Y = eT\,(\overline{A},K,L)$ or, more explicitly,

    (2) $Y_t = eT * K_t^{\alpha} L_t^{\beta}$, where $\alpha+\beta=1$ (constant economies of scale),

the so-called 'Cobb–Douglas'-specification.

    Y equals the total output produced with given quantities of the production factors
labour (L), capital (K) and (eventually exhaustible) resources that cannot be accumulated,
like land ($\overline{A}$). Y is produced on the basis of a certain technology (T) at an efficiency of e
(where $0<e<1$). In the Cobb–Douglas specification, the assumption of constant economies
of scale (see below) implies that $\alpha+\beta=1$ and the assumption of decreasing partial returns
to factor input equals the condition that both, α and β are smaller than 1.

The (rather realistic) assumption (a) states that different production factors can be partly, though not perfectly, substituted by each other. Suppose an economy produces only one good X using capital and labour in the proportion K/L^*. If our economy's natural endowment with capital at time t is $K/L_t < K/L^*$, production can not be efficient because labour has to act as (imperfect) substitute for capital. The relative scarcity of capital leads to a relatively high return for capital and relatively low wages for labour.

Neo-classical theories assume that technology spreads relatively fast across macro-level units. Technological information and production possibilities are therefore assumed to be similar in all countries or regions (e). Differences in efficiency are henceforth regarded as exogenous, capturing system-specific imperfections. In neo-classical terms the main differences between locations concern the *relative availability of production factors*; i.e. the relative scarcity of (different types of) labour, capital and natural resources. These differences in factor endowments explain disparities in wages, interest rates, prices and, last but not least, development. The more an economy is endowed with non-accumulatable resources and accumulatable capital per capita, the higher the output per person and hence economic development. Development will therefore be dependent on the savings behaviour, which in turn determines the available amount of capital per capita.

7. *Macro-economic theories analyse and explain 'development' in terms of the amounts of accumulatable factor inputs or fixed resources per capita, which in turn determines per capita output.*

A further important assumption (f) is that production takes place under constant economies of scale. This means that the double amount of all production factor inputs together is exactly double the output produced. Each single input, however, yields decreasing partial returns to scale, i.e. the more one increases the input of one single factor while leaving the other inputs constant, the less this factor's marginal return.

The subsequent relaxation of assumptions (b), (c) and (d) allows us to discuss most phenomena mentioned in discussions about the impacts of migration. Giving up assumptions (e), (f), (g) and (h) gives rise to the arguments of the divergence school presented in the second major subsection below.

Peter Fischer, Reiner Martin and Thomas Straubhaar

Convergence Effects of Migration – the Short- to Medium-Term Perspective

The impact of migration[11] on development is different in the short and in the long run. Figure 4.4 gives a schematic representation of different effects.

In the short to medium terms, migration affects wages in both emigration and immigration areas through the initial change in the relative availability of labour (*quantity effect*), through the altered (allocational) efficiency of production (*allocation effect*) and through the changes in the relative distribution of output produced *(distribution effect)*. Another channel to influence the short to medium term performance of the original destination economies is opened up by migrants who bring capital with them or send parts of their income to the country of destination (*remittances effect*). Migrants' additional contribution to the financing of public services in the country of immigration and the reduction of net tax income in the country of emigration causes *public transfer effects*. Finally, allocational effects of the changed availability of labour are bound to induce changes in the production structure and may alter the terms of trade[12] of both countries (*trade effects*).

Assume that labour is relatively abundant in the South and scarce in the North. What happens if people migrate from the South, where wages are relatively lower, to the 'North', where they are relatively higher? In the short run, the *quantity effect* of migration decreases wages in the North (labour becomes relatively less scarce) and increases them in the South (emigration decreases the relative availability of labour). Total employment *increases* in the North and *decreases* in the South.

Migration also improves the allocation of labour. In the medium term this allows an increased exploitation of the advantages of international specialisation, which in turn increases aggregate wealth and wages in both locations (*allocation effect* of migration on wages and development).

Migration also changes the relative distribution of output between labour (wages) and accumulatable input factors (return on capital). Labour in the South benefits from a relative income redistribution away from the owners of capital towards workers because emigration made labour more scarce in relation to the capital stock. The latter is assumed to be fixed in the short run. The total compensation for the production factor labour increases. The opposite effect takes place in the North

11. Unless otherwise specified the term 'migration' always refers to net migration, i.e. immigration minus emigration.
12. The terms of trade are defined as the value of export goods produced in terms of import goods.

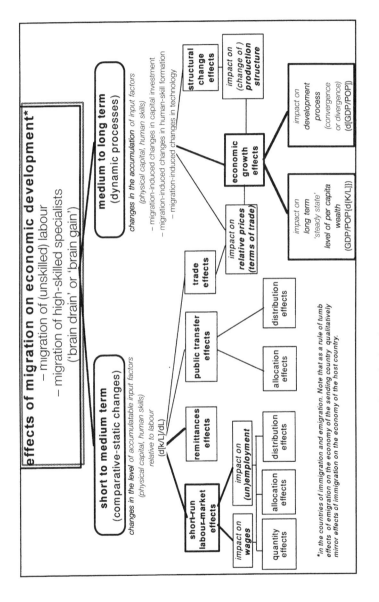

Figure 4.4 Effects of Migration on Economic Development – an Overview

where immigration makes labour relatively more abundant and induces a reduction in labour compensations relative to the returns on capital. This is the *distribution effect* in figure 4.4.

8. *If people migrate from where labour is relatively abundant and wages accordingly low to places where labour is relatively scarce and wages thus high, migration may be a strong force of macro-economic convergence. In the short run, the quantity effect of migration lowers wages in the immigration area and increases them in the emigration area.*[13] *Potential 'losers' of this convergence process may be wage earners in the North.*

9. *If in the medium term the allocation effect dominates the quantity effect, migration will induce wage increases in both emigration and immigration areas. But because in a neo-classical world wages will increase faster in the emigration than in the immigration area, migration will enhance wage convergence also in the medium term.*

Assumption (b), potential migrants are a homogeneous group of people, is now being dropped.

What the blue collar labour in the 'Ruhrpot' is afraid of is the short-term quantity effect of migration on wages. But the extent to which immigration really slows down the wage dynamics of native-born in the immigration country crucially depends on the substitutability of migrant and native-born labour. If immigrants substitute for native-born labour, the quantity effect of immigration unambiguously lowers native-born wages. But the more immigrants and native-born complement each other, the more important becomes the allocation effect of migration on native wages *vis-à-vis* the quantity effect.[14]

10. *In a neo-classical model that distinguishes between mobile and immobile labour as two production inputs that can partially*

---

13. This holds good only if our basic neo-classical assumptions apply and the development gap between the two locations is predominantly due to differences in factor endowments.

14. The working of a relationship between immigrants and native-born where both categories of labour do not perfectly substitute each other may be illustrated in terms of a neo-classical CRS-production function where mobile immigrant labour (*IM*) and immobile native workers (*IL*) are included as two seperate categories of production-input factors with partial substitution elasticities:

(3) $Y_t = eT \cdot K_t^{\alpha} \cdot IL_t^b \cdot ML_t^c$ where $\alpha+\beta+\chi=1$ (CRS).

substitute each other, the relation between mobile and immobile labour is similar to the situation between capital and labour discussed before. Their remuneration will depend on their relative scarcity. If mobile labour migrates more or less freely towards high-wage locations, the allocation and distribution effects are likely to dominate in the long run over the quantity (substitution) effect. However, since the allocation effect takes time, the negative quantity impact on employment of native-born may dominate in the short run.

The so-called 'brain-drain' discussion about the potentially deteriorating effects of migration on the development of emigration countries has been triggered by the observation that migrants from 'Southern' countries frequently belong to the most highly skilled of their societies.

In the traditional neo-classical model there is no distinction of skill levels but some economists use a simple 'trick' to analyse 'brain drain' within this framework. Bhagwati and Hamada (1974), for example, model the skills of migrants as capital which they carry with them. Emigration of such migrants thus has labour-market effects which are very different from those discussed above. Their immigration does not make labour in the country of immigration more abundant relative to capital, but more scarce. Henceforth, wages are lowered in the emigration country and increased in the immigration country. In this model 'brain drain' leads to short- to medium-term *divergence* effects.[15]

Alternatively, the neo-classical model can be slightly altered by accounting for human skills as a particular production input which is linked to the migrants. Given such a specification, output is produced under the usual neo-classical assumptions, but using at least three different kinds of production factors which may imperfectly substitute each other: 'simple labour' *(L)*, 'capital' *(K)* and 'human capital' *(HC)*. Human capital and capital can be accumulated. All factors get compensated according to their marginal profitability.[16] An individual migrant is thus compensated for her or his unskilled labour capacity as well as for her or his amount of human skills. 'Brain drain' reflects relative scarcities. Labour and skill both migrate from where they are

15. For a profound survey of the early 'brain-drain' literature see Bhagwati and Rodriguez (1975) and for an assessment of the 'brain drains' measurement and quantitative importance Galinski (1986).

16. The inclusion of human capital as an input factor on its own in the production function represents a change in the specification of the macroeconomic production function to (for example):

(4) $Y_t = eT \cdot K_t^\alpha \cdot L_t^\beta \cdot HC_t^\chi$ where $\alpha+\beta+\chi=1$ (CRS)

and total output (welfare) produced results from the input of capital (K), (unskilled) labour (L) and 'human capital' (HC).

more abundant to where they are more scarce, thereby balancing out relative endowment differences and *speeding up* development *convergence*. Note the different implications of 'brain drain' in the simple neo-classical model and the modified human capital model.

Neo-classical growth models have frequently been tested empirically. These tests usually demonstrate that absolute convergence (i.e. not conditional on any further exogenous explanatory variables) takes place, but at a (surprisingly) slow rate of about 2 to 3 per cent per annum (Barro 1990; Barro and Sala-i-Martin 1991, 1992). Especially on a regional level convergence depends on the structural features of the investigated group of macro-level units (Martin 1997). However, most of the development *growth* process cannot be explained by neo-classical convergence processes, but rather by (exogenously determined) changes in technology (total factor productivity) and the impact of other disequilibrating factors. Indeed, while one finds convergence within the group of Northern countries and the group of Southern countries, surprisingly little convergence takes place between South and North.

11. *In the simple two-factor neo-classical model 'brain drain' has a short-term negative effect on wages in the emigration country and increases labour compensation in the immigration country. This provides a first argument for the assumption that migration may cause divergence.*

12. *In a modified neo-classical model that distinguishes between skilled and unskilled labour, 'brain drain' will tend to enforce convergence between emigration and immigration countries, rather than hamper it.*[17]

Assumption (c), there is no unemployment, is now being dropped.

We will now drop the assumption of full employment. As much as emigration has traditionally been regarded as a suitable tool for the reduction of unemployment in sending countries, fears of unemployment in the receiving macro-level units have been arguments for the restriction of immigration. Whether immigration really increases native unemploy-

---

17. Admittedly, a drawback of the introduction of human capital into a neo-classical framework is that it implies that skills and human capital are more scarce in the 'North' than in the 'South'. It does not consider differences in technology and increasing economies of scale, features which are central to the divergence school.

ment depends firstly on the relative importance of the quantity effect *vis-à-vis* the allocation effect and secondly on the degree of substitutability between immigrants and native-born labour.

13. *If native-borns and migrants are perfect substitutes and if the quantity effect dominates the allocation effect, immigrants who are ready to work for lower wages will decrease the wage level in the immigration country and crowd native-borns out of the labour market. If immigration leads to strong demand effects or if immigrants complement native-born labour, however, they will create additional jobs and thus help to reduce native unemployment rather than augment it.*

To finish our discussion of the short- to medium-run effects of migration let us look briefly at *public transfers*.[18] Migrants contribute to the public household by paying taxes to the country of immigration, and they use social security and other public services. The difference between what they pay and what they get is called the absolute net public transfer. The difference between the net transfer of native-borns and of immigrants is usually called relative net transfer. Xenophobic calls for less immigration are often based on the 'argument' that immigrants are a drain on public resources. As in the case of the labour market, it should be kept in mind, though, that the composition of the immigrants has an important impact on their effect on public expenditure. Generally speaking, the younger and the better educated they are, the less likely it is that they are net recipients of public expenditures in the host countries. An especially favourable situation for the immigration country (and an especially problematic one for the state budget of the emigration country) comes about if migrants are predominantly high skilled, for example labour recruited in European countries during the 1960s and 1970s. As Borjas put it: 'After all, unskilled migrants are more likely to use many government services and pay lower taxes. In addition, there are economic reasons, arising mainly from the complementarity between capital and skills, that suggest that the immigration surplus might be larger when the immigration flow is composed exclusively of skilled workers' (Borjas 1995: 18–19).

It should be borne in mind that refugee movements are likely to have the opposite effect and constitute a drain on public resources.

---

18. Remittance effects are investigated in the survey of empirical studies below.

Peter Fischer, Reiner Martin and Thomas Straubhaar

In the Long-Run Neo-Classical Convergence Effects of Migration Matter Little

As illustrated in figure 4.4, direct economic growth effects (the main long-run effects of migration) and medium-term changes in production structure and relative prices (trade effects) can be distinguished. In fact, however, the two are closely linked. In the short run, migration leads to a change in the availability of labour relative to other production factors. In the long run, however, this effect will not last. If immigration makes labour relatively more abundant and capital more scarce, this initial change increases the return on capital investments and creates incentives to save and invest. In a neo-classical economy these incentives will last until the actual capital intensity equals the technologically determined optimal level where in the so-called 'steady state' markets and incentives are in equilibrium. But what determines this long-run 'steady-state' level of development?

Long-run development problems have been analysed in neo-classical growth theory, which started with Solow (1956) and has been largely extended since.[19] In these models, people allocate their share of output between instantaneous consumption and savings (investments). It is assumed that individuals prefer consumption now to consumption later. Henceforth this is called a 'discount' of future returns.[20]

Any technology defines factor returns and relative productivities or, in other words, people's return on saving. By deciding how much they will save, people define their steady-state level of wealth. But how much are they going to save? We can suppose that they are going to increase their savings (i.e. decrease present consumption) as long as the return on their investment (i.e. the interest rate which expresses the marginal productivity of capital) exceeds their preference for present consumption (i.e. is larger then their discount rate of future returns). Any given technology together with any determined discount rate of future returns therefore unambiguously defines an optimal capital intensity $K/L*$ where people just save enough to compensate for the reduction of the per capita capital stock through depreciation and population growth. Each optimal capital intensity determines a 'steady-state' level of per capita output and development where growth of per capita output just equals zero.

19. For an appraisal see Solow (1994). An up-to-date introduction to modelling and the empirical relevance of neo-classical growth theories is provided by Barro and Sala-i-Martin (1995), chapters 1–3.
20. Remember that in neo-classical models the partial marginal return to capital is decreasing. The higher the capital intensity K/L, the smaller the marginal return on investment (i.e. the interest rate).

People's intertemporal maximisation of income according to their time preference makes sure that in the long run – all other things being constant – the economy reaches the corresponding optimal capital intensity K/L^* and its 'steady-state' level of development. This level is therefore determined by the preferences of people for present consumption (incorporated in their discount rate), the available technology (profitability of investment), the discount rate of the capital stock and the population growth rate (defining the speed at which additional newborns endowed with no capital 'decrease' the average capital intensity). All determinants except the discount rate are assumed to be exogenous, which means that differences in income levels between countries reflect either differences in people's preference for the present or exogenously determined (temporary) departures from the long-run steady-state level of growth. Positive (or negative) growth rates of *per capita* wealth can only come about due to macro-economic adjustment processes, altered partial returns on capital or investment (technology or international integration or demand determined) or changed preferences for present consumption.[21]

Within this neo-classical model of per capita development migration may influence the long run 'steady state' only through a *constant* in- or outflow of people since this equals a change in the population growth rate. A temporary in- or outflow may help to bring an economy closer to its steady-state value. But alternatively that can as well be achieved by local saving and investment or international foreign direct investment. Temporary migration cannot alter the 'steady state' as such.

14. *In the long run it is not temporary migration, but rather the* intertemporal optimisation behaviour of individuals *that determines growth and development.*

15. *According to neo-classical theory economies converge to their long run 'steady state' of development anyway. Provided migrants do not fundamentally differ from the native-born population, they will not*

---

21. More formal, the condition for a 'steady state' may be described as:

$$(5) \quad s^*(i,\varphi) \cdot f\left(\frac{K}{L}\right)^* = (\delta+\eta) \cdot \left(\frac{K}{L}\right)^*,$$

where total gross investments being a fraction s^* of total output produced ($f[K/L]^*$) depend on the interest rate (i) and peoples discount rate φ of future consumption. Gross investment just equals the decrease in capital intensity through capital depreciation δ and population growth η: net investment equals zero.

This explanation of steady-state growth resulting from individual intertemporal optimisation behaviour corresponds to a more formal model originally formulated by Ramsey (1928) and developed by Koopmans (1965). For an introduction to its properties and modelling techniques see e.g. Barro and Sala-i-Martin (1995).

change this steady-state level. Migration is merely one possible instrument to speed up *the convergence process.*[22]

Imagine a world with two countries, two production factors and two goods. North is relatively well endowed with capital, South relatively well endowed with labour. Both have suboptimal factor endowments. Alternatively North can spend and South save until both reach the optimal capital intensity K/L^*, or North may invest in South, but these adjustments take time! Instead, people could migrate from South to North, but they may not like it or they may not be allowed to 'go'. The easiest and most efficient way to achieve an efficient factor allocation may therefore be *international trade*. North specialises in the product that is most efficiently produced by making relatively intensive use of capital, whereas South produces the labour-intensive product. If North and South now exchange (trade) their products until the product mix best suits their local demands they have an output at their disposal that closely matches the optimal output they could produce if they had an optimal aggregated factor proportion K/L^*. Henceforth, trade also allows for positive allocation effects.

Assumption (d), transport and transaction costs are negligible, is now being dropped.

Unfortunately assumption (d), that transport and transaction costs are negligible, is not normally satisfied. Trade alone is therefore usually unable to ensure the international equalisation of wages, returns on capital and wealth levels between trading countries.[23]

16. Theoretically, international trade is an efficient alternative mechanism to achieve internationally identical wealth levels. Due to

---

22. Unlike temporary flows, permanent migration can affect the steady-state level of an economy's development because it amounts to a change in the population-growth rates in the immigration and the emigration country. Provided that migrants do not carry any physical capital with them, the net migration rate (μ) will affect the per capita capital stock in a very similar way as the rate of domestic population growth (η)*. Total capital dilution per capita in the specification of our equation 4 now changes to $(\delta+\eta+\mu)(K/L)$. It decreases the immigrant country's steady-state level of development and increases it in the emigrant country, as long as population growth in both economies differs due to migration.

23. This key proposition has become famous in the economic literature as the so-called Heckscher–Ohlin–Samuelson factor-price-equalisation theorem.

transport costs and intervening obstacles this mechanism is not
normally sufficient, though.

17. *As a consequence, in a neo-classical world, trade, migration and
investment are likely to operate simultaneously in speeding up
development convergence, with the importance of each depending
on its relative costs and flexibility and the validity of our
assumptions above.*

In the next section we want to show that from a theoretical point of
view incentives for migration, capital accumulation and investment may
also lead to divergence rather than convergence.

The Divergence Point of View

Since Marx, Myrdal (1956 and 1957), Hirschman (1958) and Wallerstein
(1974) some scholars always argue that migration increases rather than
decreases development differences between regions or countries. These
divergence theorists usually combine different ideas derived from the
relaxation of at least one of the following neo-classical assumptions:
identical production technologies *(e)*, constant economies of scale in
production *(f)*, perfectly efficient markets *(g)* and the absence of positive
or negative externalities of production *(h)*. In what follows, we are going
to demonstrate these mechanisms by dropping, one after the other,
assumptions f to h from box 4.1 above.[24]

*Assumption (e), production technologies are identical across
countries, is now being dropped.*

A major characteristic of divergence theories is the argument that in
contrast to what we assumed previously, technological progress does *not*
spread from 'Northern' core locations to the periphery in the South. This
implies that we assume the North to use a superior technology or to have
an institutional framework that allows a more efficient use of production
input factors than in the South. If a given combination of input factors

24. Modifications of these neo-classical assumptions have in recent years led to the
emergence of new macro-economic sub-disciplines, often referred to as 'New Growth
Theory', 'New Trade Theory' and 'New Economic Geography'. For review articles on
New Growth Theory see e.g. Romer (1994), Grossmann and Helpman (1994), and Pack
(1994); on New Trade Theory see Krugman's introduction in Krugman and Smith (1994).
The pioneering work in 'New Economic Geography' is Krugman (1991). This is a very
valuable collection of fundamental ideas which is also accessible to non-economists.

produces a higher output in the North than in the South the input factors in the North will be better paid than those in the South.[25] If both factors (capital and labour) are mobile, it will pay for both of them to migrate to the North as long as factor proportions do not become too unfavourable in the North and as long as technology remains superior there.

18. *Migration does not induce convergence as long as absolute technological differences between locations persist. Wages and/or returns on investment will therefore remain lower in the disadvantaged region. The latter can only catch up by improving its technology and efficiency, which becomes more difficult once factors of production begin to leave. If in the extreme case all input factors were mobile, the disadvantaged location would in the long run face a total outflow of production factors, until 'the last turns off the light'.*

The radical solution of total impoverishment of a disadvantaged region may be replaced by a more realistic scenario, if we account for location-specific, fixed factors.[26] In such a situation, the technologically disadvantaged South has less output to compensate its three factors with. Given similar initial-factor proportions in both locations, it will pay for 'Southern' mobile factors to move to the North until they become so scarce relative to the location-specific, fixed factors that compensation of the mobile factors equalises in South and North, due to the compensation redistribution effect. This implies, however, that immobile, fixed factors will be compensated at correspondingly poor levels. Henceforth the incentives for potentially mobile factors to emigrate increases. To take location-specific, immobile factors into account thus explains equilibrium situations that do not require a total outflow of production factors, but it also derives two conclusions that may be critical for the development prospects of disadvantaged regions:

25. One can imagine situations in which, due to different relative scarcities of production factors, one factor may be better paid in the technologically inferior location. But the more mobile both factors are, the less stable such a situation will be. Over time, both factor payments will necessarily be smaller in the technologically inferior country than in the superior one.

26. Imagine, for example, 'South's' and 'North's' production being described by a production function that derive the usual neo-classical properties but where location-specific factors are incorporated as $\bar{A}^\chi$ and where eT in the 'South' is unambiguously smaller than eT in the 'North':

(6) $Y_t = eT * K_t^\alpha L_t^b \bar{A}^\chi$ where $\alpha+\beta+\chi=1$ (constant economies of scale, CRS)

19. *The more mobile production factors in a technologically disadvantaged location become, the higher are the incentives for so far immobile factors to emigrate as well (cumulative causation).*
20. *The more mobile factors of production in a technologically disadvantaged location are, the lower are the monetary incentives to invest in location-specific, immobile factors.*

Note that in the above macro-representation of an economy, development is still stable in the long run, due to the existence of immobile, location-specific factors and due to the assumption of constant economies of scale. Once the mobile factors have become scarce enough relative to immobile ones, compensations for the mobile factors will equalise internationally. In the medium run, however, North and South will be subject to diverging development, with the South potentially facing a 'poverty trap'.

Assumption (f), an economy produces under constant economies of scale, is now being dropped.

The above result of stable long-run growth prospects that persistently differ even in the presence of migration hinges crucially on the assumption of constant economies of scale. But is it realistic to assume constant economies of scale?

Theoretically, output expansion may happen at constant returns to scale (CRS), decreasing returns to scale (DRS) or increasing returns to scale (IRS). As far as IRS are concerned we can distinguish between

a. increasing returns to scale internal to the firm;
b. increasing returns to scale internal to the industry;
c. increasing returns to scale internal to the country or region.

IRS of type (a) make intuitive sense. Imagine a car plant. To set the plant up and to operate it requires huge fixed costs, for example the construction costs of the building. To produce 1,000 cars in this plant is therefore cheaper than to produce just 1, because one can divide the fixed per unit costs. Building 100,000 makes even more sense because it leads to increasing returns on scale internal to the firm.

If we transfer the IRS idea to the aggregate level of the economy (the macro-level unit), IRS implies that (given an efficient factor distribution) the larger the total amount of inputs, the higher their productivity.[27] What does that mean for migration? Imagine again two originally separate regions 'South' and 'North' which are identical in everything but the size of their economy. Due to the simple difference in economic output produced and the existence of IRS, the compensation of input factors in the bigger region (North) will be higher than in the South. If we now allow people to migrate from the South to the North where they get better compensation for their work, migration will no longer even out differences in factor payments but increase the scope for economies of scale in the 'Northern' economy even further. The process of widening wage and interest-rate gaps between area of emigration and area of immigration does not stop until scarce location-specific factors $\bar{A}^\chi$ in the area of immigration and corresponding redistribution effects eventually level out South to North differences in mobile factor's return to an extent that mobile factors no longer consider it worthwhile to move. Note that:

21. *If an economy faces increasing economies of scale, international mobility of production factors allows for their exploitation. This, however, widens the development gap between the economically more important area and the less important area.*
22. *Who benefits from economies of scale depends on what area is economically more important initially. Immigration into the initially bigger area strengthens its position as core economy, while the smaller economy loses competitiveness.*

While the example of a firm dividing fixed costs by a higher number of goods produced is intuitively convincing, the idea that West German labour and capital have become more efficient simply because there was a reunification of Eastern and Western Germany makes less intuitive sense. Generally speaking, the beneficial effects of economies of scale are limited by factors that decrease efficiency with growing scale, for example rising control and transaction costs. Increasing economies of scale internal to the firm may therefore determine the optimal size of a firm, but they rarely lead to sustainable divergence between macro-level units. Also, as far as increasing returns to scale internal to regions or countries are concerned, there are increasing transport, control, market access and transaction costs limiting the exploitation of IRS. But if an economy changes its institutional framework, integrates economically or faces technologically determined structural change, these changes ought

---

27. Technically, the idea of increasing economies of scale may be captured in a production function by setting the sum of the partial marginal productivities larger than 1:

(7) $Y_t = eT *K_t^\alpha L_t^b \bar{A}^\chi$ where $\alpha+\beta+\chi>1$ (increasing economies of scale, IRS).

to alter limiting factors as well. In such periods, there is therefore scope for further exploitation of additional economies of scale and the relation between migration and development is likely to evolve along the lines described here.

23. *The magnitude of economies of scale, constant, increasing or decreasing returns to scale, is likely to be dependent on the economic situation of the country. In (stable) equilibrium situations, scale economies will be constant at the margin. Technologically determined structural changes or economic integration of previously segmented markets, however, may well allow for an expanding exploitation of increasing economies of scale. In such phases, migration flows and their direction may be decisive in determining which macro-location becomes core and which periphery.*

The importance of increasing economies of scale and its interplay with migration may not only explain different development patterns of economies, it can also help us to understand what has been labelled 'economic geography' (Krugman 1991). On the one hand, firms will locate where there are concentrations of people who demand their products, where there are other producers and where a location offers particular scope for IRS. On the other hand, newly entering firms will 'pull' even more people into the location, thereby increasing the prospects for further output expansions and further economies of scale. This leads to a self-sustaining agglomeration process until economies of scale cease to increase or until agglomeration costs are too high for people to immigrate.

In short:

24. *The interplay between increasing economies of scale, people's willingness and ability to cluster in 'cores', and transport and transaction costs may explain the development of complex 'economic landscapes'. The mobility of people is therefore one of the potential determinants of core–periphery structures.*

Assumption (g), markets are efficient and fully competitive, and assumption (h), individual and collective interests are identical, there are no externalities of individual action, are now being dropped.

The assumption of increasing economies of scale implies that markets are no longer efficient in the classical sense because IRS precludes perfect competition between firms. Henceforth wages and interest rates will no longer correspond to the production factor's marginal return. Another potential reason for the inefficiency of market solutions is the existence of *externalities*. Positive externalities are the effects of subjects' actions that positively influence other subjects' actions without them having to do (or pay) anything for it and which are not internalised by the market. For the discussion of migration and development the alleged positive side effects of the total stock of 'human capital' on the productivity of all production-factor inputs are especially relevant.[28]

The basic argument is that the technology which determines the productivity of input factors is dependent on the available amount of 'human capital'. The higher the human capital stock, i.e. the total amount of (educated) knowledge, the higher the input factors' output production (given an efficient distribution of inputs). Input factors are assumed to exhibit constant private returns to scale and decreasing partial marginal productivities. They may substitute each other and are paid according to their marginal productivity. Given this set-up, however, markets fail, because they compensate people who invest in skills only for the partial marginal productivity of their human capital, not for the collective external effect of their skills on the technology. This is an important problem because, in such a situation, the accumulation of human capital may become an 'engine of growth' that explains persistent differences in growth paths.[29] Furthermore we may also derive important conclusions with respect to migration and growth:

25. *If technology depends on the locally available stock of human capital, then the 'skill content' of migration is of key importance for*

---

28. While neo-classical growth theories attribute changes in the total productivity of production factors to *exogenous* changes in technology, to assume positive human capital externalities is an attempt to explain such total factor productivity changes endogenously by changes in the total amount of (educated) knowledge accumulated in an economy. More formally, we may think of an aggregate production function:

(8) $Y_t = eT(HC)_t \cdot K_t^a L_t^b HC_t^x$ where $\alpha + \beta + \chi = 1$ (CRS)

where HC_t equals the total stock of human capital accumulated at time t. Given some further assumptions, this kind of growth model allows us to explain continuous growth paths endogenously. Such a model was first fully specified by Lucas (1988).

29. In fact, if we assume that the decrease in partial productivity of human capital in the production process is just compensated by the (external) effect of the increase in the stock of human capital on technology and on total factor productivity respectively, and if we find that the stock of human capital grows at a constant rate, then we have the Lucas (1988)-model explaining why economies may for a long time produce at constant growth rates.

development. Migration may induce positive or negative changes in the technology available in the immigration country.

26. In a situation where human capital determines technology, incentives for human capital will no longer correspond to the social return on skills.

27. In a world of the above kind, human capital is unlikely to flow to where it is most scarce. The higher an already existing stock of human capital is, the higher are the incentives for mobile factors to move there.[30]

Conclusions about the Potential Impact of Migration on Development

The above analysis of different macro-models of development and their implications for migration result in somewhat undetermined conclusions. They are undetermined in the sense that there is no clear answer to the question whether migration in general fosters convergence or divergence. There are sound theoretical concepts in favour of both views.

What applies to an actual situation depends on its macro-economic context and – more specifically – on the assumptions that apply to the nature of the production process. It is crucial whether economies are open or not, how market-oriented their systems are, to what extent immigration and emigration areas differ in their relative scarcity of production factors and their available technology. Development is not only directly dependent on production factor flows, it is also indirectly determined by the actual (development) policy in place. Policy influences what macro-economic model of analysis will best suit a given situation. This, however, opens up a policy debate that lies beyond the scope of this chapter.

In some situations migration contributes to a diverging development while in others it enforces convergence. Given the discussion above, it is most probable that there will be periods in the economic development of regions or countries when migration may induce divergence effects. They are likely to be followed by other periods when convergence effects dominate. Especially during periods of economic integration and structural change, migration may be important in shaping future convergence–divergence patterns. In many cases, however, migration will not matter that much, at least not for long-run growth and development processes. What actually applies to a concrete situation remains an

---

30. For a further discussion of models of sustainable growth and implications of the 'brain drain' see Findlay (1993) and Dolado (1994).

empirical question which in turn requires careful case-by-case studies, taking into account the micro-foundations of the migration process.

Empirical Studies on the Link between Migration and Development

In the last two sections we demonstrated that from a theoretical point of view, the overall influence of migration on development is ambiguous. In this section we therefore want to look at what empirical studies may tell us about the direction and strength of the link between migration and development. Studies that analyse simultaneously several effects of migration on development are summarised in table 4.2. Additional empirical material focusing on particular aspects of the migration–development link is referred to directly in what follows.

Most studies on the development effect of migration deal exclusively with short-term effects. This seems to be due to the obvious difficulties of isolating migration-induced long-term development effects. Although the sending and the receiving countries as well as the approach of the studies reviewed are very different, an overview suggests that the relationship between migration and development is rather 'settled' than unsettled, rather known than unknown, with respect to certain short-term effects.

Migration can help to even out the effects of (nation and region-specific) macro-economic shocks. This mechanism may be important in situations where other possible channels of adjustment are not sufficiently available. Blanchard and Katz (1992) show that for the United States, migration has in recent times played an important role in balancing out regional labour-market shocks within the country. For the European Union the evidence is much weaker due to a lack of interregional mobility in Europe (Neven and Gouyette 1994, Decressin and Fatas 1995).

With respect to the effects of migration on the wages of native-borns, the empirical evidence is rather mixed. Most authors find very direct labour-market effects of immigration on native wages in the host country (Gang and Rivera-Batiz 1994). The general picture is that direct effects depend heavily on the characteristics of immigrants. It seems that wage effects are the more positive the more skilled immigrants are. A small negative impact of immigration on low-skilled workers' real wages in the United States was found by Grossman (1982), Borjas (1990), and Borjas et al. (1992). Ekberg (1983) found the same for low-skilled wages in Sweden in the late 1970s. McDowell and Singell (1993), however, analysed the composition of US immigrants in more detail and found considerable variations in their characteristics. This in turn explained immigration-induced effects on regional wage variations rather well. Borjas et al. (1993) arrive at similar results.

As far as effects of migration on (un)employment are concerned, most empirical studies suggest that – despite the heated public debate of this topic – negative employment effects of migration are rare. Chapman et al. (1985) and Pope and Withers (1993), Simon (1989) and Mühleisen and Zimmermann (1994) all share the conclusion that native-borns do not have to fear unemployment due to competition from immigrants. In a comprehensive review of relevant empirical studies, Zimmermann (1993) also argues that negative effects of migration on wages and employment opportunities of native-borns are not normally identifiable. In a recent survey article this assumption is shared by Friedberg and Hunt (1995), looking specifically at immigration effects on the US labour market. Pischke and Velling (1994) and Smolny (1991), investigating immigration effects on the German labour market, also support that point. Smolny also emphasises the inflation-reducing effect arising from the relaxation of pressures on the German labour market. Despite some dissenting views, e.g. Winkelmann and Zimmermann (1993), DeNew and Zimmermann (1994), and Franz (1993), these articles also lend some support to the conclusion that immigrants are usually complements rather than substitutes. After all, even those scholars who arrive at somewhat more pessimistic conclusions do not find very strong negative effects for employment and remuneration of the native-borns.[31]

The effects of international migration on the employment situation in the area of emigration are generally perceived as positive. Some authors compare international migration with a safety valve for the sending countries' surplus labour. The flip side of the coin, however, is the absence of migration-induced structural changes in the labour markets. Migration essentially brings about short-term benefits rather than lasting development. In some cases there was evidence of labour shortages in certain sectors of the economy but none of the authors was too worried about brain-drain effects. The same applies to some studies looking specifically at the effects of brain drain on developing countries. Popoola (1988), looking at Nigerian high-skilled migrants in the United Kingdom, argues 'that [the] government should encourage free mobility of nationals especially when the skills of such persons are not directly required at the current level of our development' (Popoola 1988: 119).

Almost all the case studies assess the remittances effect of migration as positive on the micro- as well as on the macro-level. For the latter,

---

31. See also the review of effects on the European labour market by Zimmermann (1995).

Table 4.2 Conclusions of Empirical Studies on the Link between Migration and Development

NR.	Study	Sending Country	Receiving Country	Impact of Remittances	Labour-Market Effect	Impact of Return Migrants	General Impact on Development
1	Adler (1980)	Algeria	France	Positive effects but share of investment low.	Emigration as 'safety valve'.	Very little return migration due to lack of prospects.	'Fundamentally conservative impact' of migration. Some concern about brain drain but very positive assessment of emigration.
2	Burki (1991)	Pakistan	Middle East	Important positive effects of remittances.	Situation substantially eased due to emigration.		
3	Castano (1988)	Colombia	International	Positive short-term effects of remittances.		Very limited return migration due to lack of incentives.	Developing dependency on migration. No noticeable development effect, merely short-term solution.
4	Gilani (1988)	Pakistan	International	Social and regional income distribution improved. Investment share low.			Some concern about brain drain but positive overall assessment of development effect.
5	Gregory and Perez (1985)	Spain and Portugal	Western Europe	Positive effects at national level. Advanced regions benefit the most.	Some improvements.	Skills not normally useful after return.	No significant development impact.
6	Gitmez (1991)	Turkey	International	Important benefits but only in the short run.	Labour-market situation eased.	Limited due to different individual interests and skill limitations.	Short-run benefits but no significant development effects.
7	Habib (1985)	Bangladesh	International	Rise in consumption but no significant developmental effect.	Positive employment effects.	Skills gained abroad seem to be negligible.	Brain-drain effect likely to be minimal but no significant impact on development.

No.	Author (year)	Country	Destination	Economic / investment effects	Labour-market effects	Attitudes / behaviour	Overall development impact
8	Islam (1991)	Bangladesh	International	Negative due to inflationary pressure and the creation of absentee landlords.	In some segments manpower shortages due to migration.		No significant impact on development.
9	Martin (1993)	Philippines	International	Significant positive effects. Small-scale investments widespread.			No major promoter of change but 'safety net' for the economy.
10	Papademetriou and Martin (1991)	Greece	International	Investment potential largely unexploited.		Not exploited for lack of policy incentives.	Growth effects positive but smaller than expected.
11	Pongsapich (1988)	Thailand (Asia)	Persian Gulf	Despite positive effects productive potential not yet fully exploited.		Optimistic judgement but no detailed analysis	Significant positive changes in social attitudes.
12	South Pacific Commission (1987)	South Pacific	International	Positive but lack of productive investments.		In general conservative attitude.	No reduction of population pressure or significant development impact.
13	Stahl and Habib (1991)	South and Southeast Asia	International	Very little investment spending but positive effects of remittance-induced consumption.	Some labour shortages due to migration.	Little skill formation among emigrants. Returnees prefer small businesses to dependent employment.	Overall impact positive but no development effect because the structural problems, especially, for small countries, remain in place.
14	Straubhaar (1988)	Southern Europe	Northern Europe	Positive effect on standard of living but inflationary pressures.	Labour-market position eased in the short term only.	Few (unsuccessful) migrants returned; positive impact negligible.	Overall development effect positive during early stages of development; afterwards only marginal impact.

however, the effects are essentially short-run and consumptive with no major impact on the underlying socio-economic structure of the sending country. Remittances on their own are therefore unlikely to propel countries to a higher level of development. *Distributional aspects of remittances* have been investigated from a regional point of view in two of the case studies, namely Gilani (1988) and Gregory and Perez (1985). They arrive at more or less opposing conclusions. Whereas Gilani argues that remittances contribute to a reduction of regional imbalances, Gregory and Perez observed that the already advanced regions reaped most of the benefits from remittances. According to Lipton (1980) and Adams (1989), two studies which focused exclusively on the consequences of international migration on income equality and which were therefore not included in table 4.2, migration led to more inequality in income distribution because the well-off parts of communities are more likely to send migrants abroad. This is in line with our hypothesis that a very low level of development is likely to have a negative effect on total international migration but that the better-off part of the population is more likely to leave.

Most authors assume that by means of political and economic incentives the proportion of remittances employed for productive purposes can be increased (Chandavarkar 1980, Athukorala 1990, Mahmood 1991, Garson 1994). The use of, mandatory remittance requirements is usually disapproved of, whereas migrant-specific incentive schemes may result in more money being channelled into productive uses. Of crucial importance are stable macro-economic policies like realistic exchange rates and the existence of a functioning banking system in the remittance-receiving countries. These prerequisites illustrate the fact that the relationship between remittances and development is characterised by mutual dependence, albeit on a relatively low level. Remittances may support the process of economic development in the labour-sending countries but they also depend on the level of economic development and the quality of the countries' economic policy. After all, most migrants are not interested in investing their wages in a country where the potential benefits from these investments are slim.

Concerning the public transfer effect of immigrants, the empirical evidence does not suggest that immigrants are usually a drain on public resources. In effect, they are often larger per capita net contributors to public finances than native-borns. The actual pattern of net transfers depends very much on the demographic composition, qualifications and labour-market integration of the migrants (for a summary of empirical findings see Simon 1989 and 1994, Weber 1993, Table 1 in Straubhaar 1994).

The assessment of the impact of return migrants must come as a disappointment for more optimistic development economists. All but one (Pongsapich 1988) of the studies that addressed the issue argued that returnees are far from being 'agents of change'. In some cases their essentially conservative impact has been emphasised, in others it is simply the lack of demand and scope for the skills of potential returnees in their country of origin that prevents the dynamic and young from returning home as 'agents of change'.

The potential benefits of 'brain drain' for developing countries were already emphasised in the early 1980s (UNESCO 1984). Obia (1993) develops a framework for African countries to make use of their high-skilled nationals abroad. He argues that the link between 'brain drain' and development is a reciprocal one. High-skilled professionals can make a significant contribution to the development process, but there are at least two preconditions. Firstly, the country must be in a position to make use of the human capital, which usually requires the existence of certain location-specific assets, institutions and capital. The high unemployment rate of academics in many parts of the South shows that these requirements are not available.

A shortage of skilled personnel will of course make it more difficult to attract those factors necessary to activate the countries' human capital, but it is only one of many factors determining a location's attractiveness. Secondly, and this is often related to the first point, in order to keep high-skilled professionals or in order to attract those already abroad to come back a country must provide an attractive social and political system. The examples of China and South Korea show that 'brain drain' can become a problem for countries which experience fast economic growth and which are on their way to move onto a higher level of development (Chang and Deng 1992, Yoon 1992). To a lesser extent this problem is also experienced by other East and South-East Asian countries (Chang 1992). All of them are subject to rapid industrialisation and growth, which seems to be one of those phases in which international migration is indeed capable of influencing the development prospects of the sending country.

With respect to long-term convergence or divergence effects Barro and Sala-i-Martin (1995) analyse the influence of intra-national migration on growth in the United States since 1880, prefectures of Japan since 1930 and European countries since 1950. They find that migration has responded positively on initial levels of per capita income. Locations that enjoyed above-average development levels at the outset of the study period tended to report higher than average immigration rates (and slowing-down growth processes). These results were stronger for the United States and Japan than for Europe. But as far as the influence of net migration flows on convergence is concerned, Barro and

Sala-i-Martin's results are inconclusive. Migration seems to have had a minor influence on growth processes during this century.

Barro and Sala-i-Martin's results contrast sharply with the conclusions of research undertaken for the impact of migration on international convergence around the turn of the last century. In a recent paper Boyer et al. (1993) argued that the massive emigration from Ireland prior to the First World War contributed significantly to the convergence of real wages between Ireland, the United Kingdom and the United States. For Swedish emigration in the late nineteenth century, O'Rourke and Williamson (1995) find similar results. On a more global level Taylor and Williamson (1994) identified net migration as the major driving force of convergence between European countries and development in America and overseas at the end of the nineteenth century. Henceforth, it seems likely that migration has only had minor importance for twentieth-century growth processes, because very little migration took place and developments were driven by international trade and domestic factors, whereas the period prior to the First World War was a time of free migration.

In brief, most of the empirical studies agree that:

28. *For most countries the impact of international migration on development tends to be positive but essentially short-term. Especially labour-market and balance-of-payments problems are frequently eased, sometimes some growth effects due to increased consumption are noticeable. Convergence rather than divergence effects of migration on development are usually detected.*

29. *But migration rarely seems to be able to induce the far-reaching social and economic changes that are required to advance the developmental process in most countries of the South.*

The transfer of knowledge is rarely substantially improved nor are returning migrants agents of change. Migration can certainly support domestic development processes but it cannot replace or even induce them. On the other hand there are few noticeable negative effects of migration. The widely discussed 'brain drain' issue does not seem to be too problematic, with the exception of those countries experiencing periods of rapid economic transition. Such growth, however, will neither come about nor will it be prevented by international migration alone.

Conclusions

In order to answer the question whether migration is dependent on development or development on migration, macro(-economic) concepts of development have been introduced and analysed. We have found support for the hypothesis that migration depends on the level of economic development. But we have also come to the conclusion that migration can have a decisive impact on the direction and speed of macro-economic development, i.e. the convergence or divergence of macro-level units. The question is therefore not either–or, but both–and. A dynamic theory of migration and development has to consider a mutual interplay of both simultaneously, the impact of (initial) development on migration and the repercussion effects of migration on development. But such an integrated theory is still missing. To develop it, at least three things will be needed: (a) a better micro- and meso-foundation of macro-theories, (b) careful empirical research to determine contextual issues and (c) a more multidisciplinary character of theoretical approaches.

If we take development as exogenously determined, we can conclude that migration is linked to certain kinds of (economic) development. Our aim was not to explain the prevailing forms of economic organisation and the income levels of certain locations, nor did we try to determine why some countries remain stagnant while others pass through highly dynamic transformation processes. We merely wanted to see if there is an impact of development (approximated by per capita income) on migration and found a positive relation between development and immigration.

On the basis of previous attempts to introduce a general 'inverted U-curve' relation between development and emigration (Hatton and Williamson 1994, Faini and Venturini 1994), we suggested a modific-ation. We distinguish between different forms of emigration (internal and international, unskilled and skilled) and different stylised forms of economic organisation. In our 'modified inverted U-curve' hypothesis of migration, internal migration is prevalent in countries with traditional forms of production whereas at higher levels of development, first low-skilled and then high-skilled international migration gain importance. We suggest that these separate flows each follow an 'inverted U-curve' pattern. In the least-developed economies, there is only little internal migration, determined by resources and eventually conflicts. The necessary information and financial means for international migration are usually missing. With development proceeding, internal migration becomes a major characteristic of development, and economic progress also endows a highly skilled elite with the potential to migrate inter-nationally. In industrialising economies, internal migration initially increases even further, but loses importance eventually. More and more people are now able to consider international migration as a feasible alternative. Finally, in the wealthiest economies, the diversified and internationalised structure of the economy creates a high demand for internal and international highly skilled migration. But although highly skilled migrants may have greater incentives to migrate and are usually more mobile than low-skilled labour, migration demand is unlikely to match supply. The more developed an economy gets, the less people are willing to migrate. Migration is therefore likely to become a restricting factor for development.

With regard to South to North migration, our analysis of the development–migration relation leads us to expect future migratory flows to increase in magnitude, since more and more populous areas of the South approach a level of per capita income which makes international migration a feasible option for significant parts of the population.

Especially in the context of South to North migration, research has traditionally focused on the other side of the migration–development relationship, namely the impact of migration on development. We have therefore presented different 'grand' macro-theories, investigating whether migration tends to close or widen the gap between 'poor' and 'rich' macro-level units.

Classic economic theory of the so-called 'convergence school' expects emigration countries to obtain major benefits from migration, in turn promoting their development process. The 'divergence theory', however, argues that out-migration may in effect be an obstacle for the socio-economic development. Both arguments have been put forward in various forms and supported by various arguments. What we have shown in this chapter is how convergence and divergence arguments depend on underlying assumptions about an economy's macro-determinants of production relative to other locations of economic activity. In those cases where the differences mainly concern the relative endowment with production input factors like physical capital, location-specific factors and labour, migration is bound to contribute to development *convergence*. In those cases, however, where differences in technology, economies of scale and social externalities of human skills are important, migration is likely to enhance *diverging* development processes.

On the above grounds, we expect the impact of migration on development to change from convergence to divergence, and back to convergence again, several times in the course of complex development processes. Divergence impacts are likely to be characteristic for periods of enhanced development transformation with correspondingly fast structural change, as well as for periods following major technological innovation or market expansion.

The theoretical concepts introduced in this chapter are of value in assessing the impact of migration on development within actual case studies. If empirical case studies were to enable us to identify the macro-determinants of a certain process of development and economic integration, the theoretical macro-concepts discussed would allow us to foresee the potential convergence or divergence impact of migration. For the latter, however, careful empirical case-by-case analyses will be needed.

Especially in a divergence scenario, the direction and magnitude of initial migration may decide whether a certain location becomes 'core' or 'periphery'. On the grounds of the theoretical arguments discussed, there seem to be 'turning-points' in the development process of a country. At such points migration can become decisive, for example in a situation where the human capital required for realisation of full production potential is no longer available due to brain drain.

A cautious reservation has to be made with respect to the dependence of development on migration. While we demonstrate that there are sound theoretical reasons to attribute to migration a key importance for development in some situations, it must be emphasised that development in general is subject to much more complex determinants than just the mobility of people as well as of other production factors. In most situations, migration is likely to be of minor importance for development, although this may be partly due to the fact that migration usually occurs on a rather limited scale.

The empirical studies reviewed indicate that migration has had positive short-term effects for sending and receiving countries. With respect to the long-term effects, especially in terms of the development prospects for 'Southern' countries, the bulk of the empirical studies suggest that migration normally had little impact on the development process, and if anything, enhanced development convergence rather than divergence. A particular problem with this is, however, that long-term impacts of migration are extremely difficult to identify, due to the difficulty of constructing 'reference-scenarios' that determine macro-developments in the absence of migration.

Keeping in mind the complexity of the problem and the scarcity of suitable empirical material, it seems essential to work towards careful case-study analyses on the migration and development link. These analyses should be based on the country- or region-specific macro-conditions. After all, a uniform South does not exist nor can we expect the effects of migration on development to be uniform for all countries of the South. Ideally, though, such empirical work should strike a balance between, on the one hand, the macro-determinants of development at certain locations, the general theoretical mechanisms and predictions of the 'grand theories' presented above, *and* on the other, the micro- and meso-aspects of the migration process. In order to achieve this, the multidisciplinary character of the studies will have to be strengthened. It has been the purpose of this chapter to shed some light on the theoretical macro-relations between development and migration, migration and (or) development. The (empirical) linkages to the other micro- and meso-theories of migration presented in this book should be placed high on the agenda for research towards an integrated, multidisciplinary theory of migration and development.

–5–

The Discourse on Migration and Development
Kenneth Hermele

Introduction

The literature on migration and development contains two main strands of thought. The position that migration brings benefits to all, to emigrant as well as to immigrant countries, is widely publicised. In this tradition, the World Bank can summarise a discussion on migration simply by stating that 'Migration is usually beneficial to both sending and receiving countries' (World Bank 1995: 68). This mirrors the position adopted by the Social Democratic Brandt commission fifteen years ago, where assumed mutual interests between the North and the South was the leading idea. In a world of common North to South interests, of course, 'Migration has given benefits to all parties' (Brandt Commission 1980: 110).

A second line of argument sees migration as a simple reflection of the needs and strategies of transnational capital. Here, countries are less important, whether as winners or losers, and it does not matter whether they are emigration or immigration countries. The basic point is that there are no mutually beneficial relationships, and that the interests of the strongest economic actors define the rules of the game. The migration of labour which took place during 1945–75 can in this optic be described 'as a result' of 'the main economic strategy of large-scale capital' (Castles and Miller 1993: 65). Or in the words of a textbook which sets out to describe the foundations of the 'new international labour studies': 'the function of labour migration [. . .] is simply to produce a cheap and tractable labour force' (Munck 1988: 188).

In this chapter I take issue with both these positions. The first is far too general and disregards important differences in time as well as place at both ends of the migration process, while the second turns complex socio-economic–cultural relationships into a simple process of inter-nationalisation of production directed by transnational firms.

There also exists a third, rather ambivalent position, which says that the migration–development relationship is complicated, unresolved, unsettled, uncertain, critical, even unexplored(!), or both positive and negative for emigrant as well as for immigrant countries. This position, quite popular among researchers today (OECD 1979, Papademetriou and Martin 1991, Appleyard 1992a and b), goes back to economists of earlier periods. They argued that there were pros as well as cons regarding the impact of migration on development, normally ending up on an inconclusive note: migrants' remittances speed up development, while the emigration of skilled people hurts development in emigration countries (Lewis 1954a and b, Thomas 1961).

Although common in the economists' discourse, such an open stance among migration researchers in general is a rather new phenomenon. Until quite recently the customary position was to underline the negative impact of migration on emigration countries (Piore 1979, Böhning 1984). More recently, however, the ambivalent position has gained ground, which seems warranted judging from the mixed evidence of the migration–development issue which will be presented here.

Such changing opinions are not new to the migration debate. Already during colonial days, sharp divisions existed as to the impact of labour migration on African societies. Did the temporary, circular migration of labour harm the natural development of these societies? Or should migration rather be seen as an important means of ushering otherwise stationary societies into modernity (Freund 1988)? It is not far-fetched to assume that the positions of the researchers, politicians and colonial administrators engaged in that debate were influenced by their attitude to colonialism and European cultural superiority.

That similar connections between the migration debate and conjunctural factors exist in today's discussion will be shown, I hope, when we later in this chapter discuss three more recent migration–development issues: root causes, environmental refugees, and migration and security. A common characteristic of these three issues is the identification of the South as the active part in the migration process, and, hence, the part which must change or be made to change. The North, on the other hand, is depicted as a more or less passive recipient of migration flows. The South is frequently described as 'sender' or 'refugee producer', while the North is seen as an innocent 'receiver'. This active–passive dimension in the way migration is seen can be found in publications of international organisations, which are supposed to represent both Northern and Southern members, as well as in the publications of institutions and governments considered to be 'South-friendly' (Swedish Ministry of Labour 1990, ILO/UNHCR 1992, ILO/IOM/UNHCR 1994, Kane 1995).

The sender–receiver designations are important as they easily lead to self-righteous policy positions in the immigration countries. If the origin of unwanted migration movements is to be found in the 'sender' countries, the North may find itself morally and politically justified, even obliged, to intervene not only on behalf of its perceived self-interest, but also on behalf of the migrants who reluctantly have been pushed into migration by an incompetent sender state (cf. Loescher 1989). On the other hand, if the North is equally implicated in the processes creating migration as the South, the morally and politically permissible actions will be different and above all also include policies that directly address the migration production of the North itself.

Today's dominant position in the migration–development discourse – an open stance, 'it depends on the circumstances' – may appear neutral or uncommitted. But as Georges Tapinos (1993) has underlined with reference to the European Union, changing perspectives and needs have greatly influenced the way the migration–development relationship has been perceived and discussed after the Second World War. As long as Western Europe needed to import labour, migration was held to be beneficial to the development of the countries of origin. More recently, with a reduced need of migrant labour, emigrant countries are said to be able to develop without migration as increased aid and trade opportunities will substitute for the benefits that migration brought.

As a newcomer to the discourse on migration and development, I am struck by an absence of reflection regarding ecologically imposed limits to development. In the development literature in general, and certainly in the migration–development field, the great debates have centred upon the question what development policies to promote. But rarely has it been recognized that should the proposed policies be followed and – perhaps more unlikely – result in development, the ecological consequences may be dire, not only for the Southern countries concerned but for the whole world.

On a personal level we are normally aware of the existence of ecological limits to growth. We ask what would happen if the Chinese or Indians acquired 'developed' consumption patterns (refrigerators, cars, television sets, toilets, etc.). These questions are rhetorical because we think we know what the answer is: a globalisation of the life-style of the North would spell disaster for all of us.

Oddly enough, such thoughts do not colour the development debate. Here a strange similarity appears between otherwise opposed approaches. Although there exists a dramatic divide between a policy line in favour of an ever deeper integration into the world economy (e.g. Rostow 1960) and a line proposing delinking from that same world economy (e.g. Frank 1965, Amin 1970), both perspectives agree on the desirability of the South following their respective lead – and neither seems worried about the ecological consequences of success. In this way, the major developmental debate of the 1970s and 1980s avoided an issue which is fundamental: if ecological limits exist, what are the consequences for our argument on development in the South? To most development thinking, however, ecological considerations are still peripheral. With the exception of the eco-development strand, which argues in favour of a small-scale, sustainable development path, even 'alternative' development strategies of today – e.g. self-reliance, basic needs – assume that there is unlimited ecological space available (Hettne 1990, Griffin 1992). However, if there is in fact no such space available, the whole migration–development discourse will be seen in a different light.

Does Emigration Stimulate Development?

There are three distinct ways of answering this question.

Argument I: Emigration Hinders Development. It is not difficult to piece together a picture which unequivocally shows that migration hurts development in emigration countries. You can start by underlining that the emigration country loses qualified manpower that it needs for its own development. Such labour – 'the best and the brightest' in the words of Papademetriou and Martin (1991), the 'cream' according to a group of researchers directed by Charles Kindleberger (OECD 1979) – make a difference, we are led to believe. In this tradition, it is lamented that Africa by 1987 had lost one-third of its skilled workforce to Europe (UNDP 1992).

While abroad, migrants are held not to acquire new skills (Stahl 1989). For example, two-thirds of Thai migrants either work with the skills they already possessed before migrating, or in jobs that require fewer skills than they have. And Filipino migrants work as domestic maids although many of them have college degrees (Lim 1994b).

Not even remittances, whose importance in volume cannot be denied (see table 5.1), are considered to enhance development on this view. Remittances are not put to productive use, but mostly spent for unproductive purposes – housing, land purchases, transport, repayment of debt – or, to a smaller degree, wasted on conspicuous consumption, or simply saved as insurance and old-age pension funds.

Also, remittances cause inflation as demand is created without concomitant productive capacity. Furthermore, this demand, created by remittances, spills over and stimulates excessive imports, which hurts the balance of trade (Piore 1979, Birks and Sinclair 1980, Fergany 1982, Böhning 1984, Shah 1994b).

Table 5.1 Contribution of Workers' Remittances 1993 in Per Cent of Exports

	Remittances
	Merchandise exports
Asia	
Bangladesh	41
India	14
Pakistan	23
Sri Lanka	21
Yemen	53
Africa	
Algeria	9
Egypt	221
Morocco	48
Tunisia	15
Central America	
Dominican Republic	65
El Salvador	142
Guatemala	14
Europe	
Turkey	19

Source: World Bank 1995.

But the argument is even more pessimistic, as not even returned migrants are seen to constitute an alleviation. Firstly, as we have seen, they do not bring new skills since they have not acquired any. And if they by exception have managed to upgrade their knowledge and capacities, they do not encounter employment at home, at least not where they can take advantage of skills acquired. More frequently they stay unemployed waiting for a new spell abroad (Shah 1995). The returnees, although they originally may have come from rural settings, will not as a rule accept agricultural work. Thus, agriculture loses out not only once but twice: first when the emigrant deprived it of labour power, and then again when the returnee neither invests in agriculture, nor resumes agricultural activities (Piore 1979).

Underlying this view is an idealized vision of development as a gradual and slow transformation of the countryside and a regular and orderly growth of agricultural productivity at the same time as small scale industrial employment is created in towns and smaller cities. In this process, no major urbanization takes place, nor international migration.

Summing up this argument, one can say, with Böhning (1984: 186) that 'the gain-capital-abroad approach is a myth'. Instead of a boon to development and an injection of dynamism, the returnee means a return of failure, conservatism and retirement (Böhning 1984). Had the migrants not failed to establish themselves in the country of immigration, they would not have returned, the argument goes.

But a migrant's success is as damaging to development as failure. Not only would a successful migrant not return to employ his or her productive powers in the country of origin; a successful migrant would also gradually severe the links with this country and gradually reduce remittances and other transfers (Birks and Sinclair 1980).

The pessimistic line may seem a rather conclusive position, but a number of the arguments presented are quite contradictory. The UNDP (1992), for example, which regrets the *exodus* of skilled people from the South, simultaneously blames the North for *not letting in* more immigrants from the South. These barred would-be migrants, had they been allowed in, would have remitted over 200 billion US dollars annually, four times the global aid budget. In fact, it is this aborted migration, and hence the remittances forgone, which constitutes the major drawback the UNDP identifies in North to South relations. Here, migration suddenly appears as a positive force for emigration countries, in contradiction to the general position of the brain-drain argument which the UNDP simultaneously embraces.

Similarly, Kindleberger et al. (OECD 1979) simultaneously regret that migration means the emigration of 'cream' labour, and welcome the export of an 'unemployed and underemployed' surplus population. Also Piore (1979), who concludes that migration does not stimulate development, weakens his own conclusion by saying that the absence of investments in productive ventures may still be beneficial in the sense that returnees and remittances contribute to small-scale, informal activities, essential to support and service large-scale, formal industrial undertakings which thus are facilitated.

Argument II: Emigration Stimulates Development. In recent years, we have seen a growing trend in migration research to underline the positive impact of emigration on development, partly by simply interpreting the above facts in a different light. Thus, the emigration of skilled labour is a problem mostly in sub-Saharan Africa and in Central America and the Caribbean. (As far as Africa is concerned, this is not a unanimous position. Russel et al. (1990) claim that there has been an exaggerated preoccupation with lack of qualified labour in Africa, and that, excepting cases such as the Zambian brain drain, there normally exist sufficient qualified staff in the region). In South Asia and Latin America, however, there are enough trained workers for the jobs available. Obviously, emigration in those circumstances does not constitute a brake on development. Neither does the export of surplus labour, since the emigrants were not employed before they emigrated. For South Asian emigrants unemployment rates of 11–38 per cent before their departure have been reported (Shah 1995).

Likewise, a reinterpretation is possible with reference to skill acquisition. Although it is true that the majority of the migrants do not learn new trades or skills, an important minority do. Of Pakistani, Thai and Filipino migrants, 25–33 per cent are estimated to have acquired new skills abroad (Stahl and Habib 1991, Lim 1994).

The greatest shift in assessing the impact of migration has taken place with reference to remittances. It is now increasingly claimed that their impact is positive, even that they are put to productive uses. In sub-Saharan Africa remittances are invested in education or in agricultural equipment, such as water pumps, irrigation equipment, and tractors (Russel et al. 1990). Remittances may also enable the migrants' families to employ labour in their fields, while they themselves develop activities in urban settings.

The earlier preoccupation that remittances would only create inflation or spill over to imports is now seen as misreading the way the economies of the South function. On the contrary, remittances bring important secondary (so called multiplier) effects which create demand for local industry (Stahl 1989). Although a great share of the remittances is spent on consumption, each transaction has a series of secondary consequences: salaries are paid, new raw materials bought, new orders placed, etc. And if remittances are saved in banks or insurance companies, such institutions extend loans which also incentivate productive activities. Including such multiplier effects, the overall job-creating effect in Bangladesh of the remittances sent home by its 200,000 migrants – directly and indirectly – was estimated at 570,000 jobs (discounting import leakages) (Stahl and Habib 1991). To this positive impact of remittances should be added the (unknown) informal and unofficial remittances as well as remittances in kind (i.e. merchandise sent or brought home). Estimates figure such parallel remittances to be two to ten times as large as the official flows (Shah 1994b).

The significance of these figures can perhaps best be grasped by comparing official remittances to aid flows (see table 5.2). During the 1980s official remittances alone to the South amounted to between two-thirds and three-quarters of global aid flows.

Argument III: It Depends on the Time Perspective. So far we have looked at a negative and a positive interpretation of the impact of migration on development. There also exists a third approach which tries to bridge the other two. Papademetriou (1985) ventures the hypothesis that the use of remittances differs depending on whether the migrant remains abroad or is returning home. Unproductive use, especially in some forms of savings and in land acquisition, dominate while the migrant remains abroad. Once returned, however, the migrant will put

Table 5.2 Official Flows of Remittances and Aid between the South and the North, Billions of Current US Dollars

	Remittances	Aid	Remittances/Aid, %
1980	21	27	77
1985	21	29	72
1990	36	55	65

Sources: Russel 1992, World Bank 1995.

the remittances to work, either in construction or in business, with subsequent multiplier effects.

In other words, we have to distinguish between the short- and the long-term impact of migration. In the short term, negative factors dominate, while in the long term remittances, skill acquisition and higher agricultural productivity will stimulate development (Russel et al. 1990, Appleyard 1992b).

To sum up this rather inconclusive evidence regarding the impact of migration on development, a sort of circular argument has gained prominence: migration will stimulate development, if the emigration country is ready to be developed. In this vein, Appleyard (1992a: 263) 'firmly believe[s]' that 'the environment necessary for development must first be created' in order for migration to be able to stimulate development. What does this environment consist of? Nothing less than a diverse economic structure, an adequate supply of labour, a well-functioning financial system to channel remittances to productive uses, and productive flexibility that can respond to changed circumstances (Stahl 1989). In this enumeration we only lack 'the developmental state' in order to have a complete list of goodies that would satisfy any development planner. Consequently, if migration does not stimulate development, it is 'due largely to the structural features of under-development' (ibid. 380). The same kind of circular reasoning is also applied to policy recommendations to reduce emigration. For instance in a study on Caribbean migration we learn that 'economies that are more broadly diversified, that can generate adequate rates of economic growth, and that give sufficient attention to social objectives [. . .] can successfully reduce push factors usually associated with emigration' (Díaz-Briquets 1985: 55–6). In other words, economic growth alone will not reduce emigration unless accompanied by social and human development. We are left with a policy recommendation that is both too vague and too all-embracing to really guide us — or rather the emigration countries — in the difficult trade-offs between equally justifiable objectives. How would you, for example, advise an emigration country to balance growth and equity, a classic development policy contradiction, in order to limit emigration? The conclusions on this level boil down to next-to-meaningless statements: underdeveloped countries do not benefit from migration because they are underdeveloped. And those that do reap advantages from migration are diversified with adequate growth and sufficient social attention. A tall order for a typical emigration country.

Does Development Reduce Emigration?

It sounds almost self-evident: 'The best migration policy is development policy' (Körner 1987: 81). But underlying the statement is the assumption that underdevelopment stimulates migration, and that therefore development would reduce migration. This relationship is far from certain, as table 5.3 shows: there is no firm link between level of economic development (measured by per capita income) and relative emigration (measured by population). However, table 5.3 should not be used for analytical purposes as both measures, that of development as well as that of migration, are open to strong objections. The table merely demonstrates that simple statements of the relationship bear little relevance for explaining a complex reality. Thus, countries at totally different levels of development have the same relative emigration numbers: Pakistan and Sri Lanka, South Korea and Indonesia, Mexico and the Dominican Republic, Tunisia and Yemen.

Three lines of argument have been advanced to explain this missing link. Firstly, the view that development (i.e. economic growth) reduces migration has been refuted for being oversimplistic. True, development is necessary to stem migration, but it will not by itself greatly reduce migration movements. Equally necessary conditions are a fair distribution of the national income, political openness, a low rate of unemployment, a balanced economic base without one-sided dependencies with regard to export products or markets (Díaz-Briquets 1985).

Secondly, a short-run/long-run dimension is introduced. In the short run, development will encourage emigration. This is so for a number of reasons: people who had been considering emigrating, but who could not afford it, will have more money at their disposal as development takes place; development normally entails a process of urbanisation as well as great changes in social and economic structures which upset formerly more stable and slow-changing societies. All this stimulates migration, internal and external. However, as a country develops, the advantages of staying at home will overtake the benefits to be reaped through

Table 5.3 The Missing Links: Per Capita Income and Relative Emigration

Region	Per capita income, US dollars	Relative Emigration %
South Asia 1990		
Bangladesh	872	2
Pakistan	1,862	4
Sri Lanka	2,405	4
South East Asia 1990		
Indonesia	2,181	1
Philippines	2,303	2
Malaysia	6,140	1
South Korea	6,733	1
Thailand	3,986	1
Central America 1979		1980
Costa Rica	1,540	2
Guatemala	910	1
Mexico	1,290	3
Panama	1,290	4
Caribbean 1979		1980
Barbados	n.a.	17
Cuba	810	6
Dominican Republic	910	3
Haiti	260	2
Jamaica	1,110	13
Trinidad & Tobago	2,910	11
Africa South of the Sahara 1990		
Botswana	3,419	1
Burkina Faso	618	20
Lesotho	1,743	10
Senegal	1,248	4
Sudan	949	5
Swaziland	2,384	17
North Africa and West Asia 1990		
Algeria	3,100	5
Egypt	1,988	17
Jordan	3,869	44
Morocco	2,348	6
Tunisia	3,759	7
Yemen	1,562	7
Europe		
Turkey	4,652	4

Relative emigration: stock of emigrants as a share of the population of the country of origin.
Sources: Lattes and Rechini de Lattes (1994): table 4.5, World Bank 1979 and 1992, ILO/IOM/UNHCR 1994.

migration. Hence, development and reduced migration go together, but only after a certain point. Thus, the development–migration relationship can be described by an inverted U-curve with emigration on the y-axis and development on the x-axis (see figure 4.2, chapter 4).

The inverted U-curve states that the emigration–development relationship has two distinct phases. Starting out from a low level, emigration will increase as a country develops until a turning point is reached. Thus far, development stimulates emigration. But once the turning point has been reached, further development leads to less migration.

There are two critical issues here. The first is: at what level of development is the turning point located? Normally, the relationship is only assumed, e.g. by the US Commission for the Study of International Migration (1990), the most influential study embracing this argument. Here no specific turning point for Central America and the Caribbean is given.

However, one attempt has been made to fix the turning point based on migration figures for Southern Europe 1960–88 (Faini and Venturini 1994). This study concludes, as a first rough estimation, that a country needs to have achieved a GDP per capita of approximately 4,000 US dollars (at the price level of 1985) in order for further growth to reduce migration. Should this level be applied today, only a handful of Southern emigration countries would be on the other side of the hump of the U-curve, e.g. Mexico, Trinidad and Tobago and Oman.

A second issue relates to the time period needed for an emigration country to reach the turning point. Here it seems to be anybody's guess, and time periods are normally not given with more details than by the US Commission (1990: 3): 'Improved economic circumstances in migrant-sending countries may well increase emigration pressures for several decades.'

Similarly, it is guesswork when a study of Mexican emigration to the United States summarises its finding with a graph without stipulating the time frame (see figure 5.1). Here, we see the inverted U-curve, but no specific time perspective. Nevertheless, the study concludes that NAFTA would 'yield fewer total migrants to the United States than the alternative of continuing illegal immigration without free trade' (Cornelius and Martin 1993: 507).

There is also a third line of reasoning to explain the missing link. This argument takes as its point of departure the assumption that the number of immigrants to a certain country is decided not primarily by the country of origin but by the policy of the country of destination. This contradicts the study by Faini and Venturini (1994), which concludes that the origin of the changes in emigration from Southern Europe basically

Kenneth Hermele

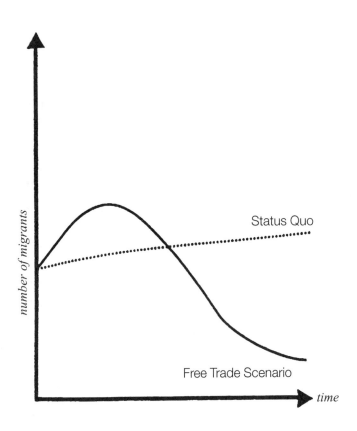

Source: Cornelius and Martin 1993.

Figure 5.1 Hypothesised Relationship between the Number of Mexican Migrants to the United States and Time with and without NAFTA

resides in domestic factors in the emigration countries themselves. Furthermore, according to this third argument, the country of destination is assumed to be more willing to receive immigrants as it develops. On the other hand, emigration from the country of origin is assumed to diminish as it develops (Appleyard 1992b). Hence we obtain the relationship depicted in figure 5.2 (although Appleyard himself only presents it in words).

Figure 5.2 presents a rather optimistic picture: as both Northern (immigration) and Southern (emigration) countries develop over time. The contradiction referring to migration movements seems to be dissolved. Potential immigration numbers will go up and potential emigration numbers down, until they reach an equilibrium. Against the background of figure 5.2 it is also possible to conceive of a lack of migrants, as the North may demand more immigrants than the South may be able to provide.

But figure 5.2 is based on a series of highly dubious assumptions. Firstly, the time dimension is undefined, and hence the period of imbalance between immigration and emigration needs may be quite extended. Secondly, the argument takes it for granted that there exists ecological space for the North and the South to grow simultaneously. (I shall return to this issue.) Thirdly, it assumes that the depicted relationships exist. But what if emigration does not decline with growing incomes (as is the case in a number of countries in table 5.3)? What if emigration increases with development as hypothesised by the inverted

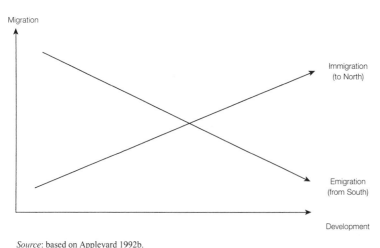

Source: based on Appleyard 1992b.

Figure 5.2 The Hypothesised Relationship betweeen Migration and Development

U-curve (see above)? And what if Northern countries will not accept more immigrants, although their economies are growing, as has been the case since the mid-1970s?

A Safe Bet: Emigration Will Continue

When analysts try to make sense of the contradictory evidence on the migration–development link, they come up with rather self-evident formulas, e.g. that development and emigration have 'coincided' when

> the basic ingredients for development predated the temporary emigration of labour. These ingredients include a large and diverse economy, a large and relatively modern agricultural sector which would not be starved for labor as a result of emigration, an already socially and politically mobilized population, a relatively effective system of private and public administration, a large and relatively modern infrastructure, and a financial system capable of channeling remittances to the private sector efficiently (Papademetriou and Martin 1991: 21).

Not many countries in the South meet such requirements. In fact, what the statement means is that only countries which already are rather well developed will benefit from migration. Or put in other words: migration from most countries may well continue without being hampered by development in the emigration country. But it is not only theoretical considerations which lead us to draw the conclusion that migration will continue. A series of circumstances point in the same direction.

Global Income Differences Increase

If income differences incentivate migration, then we seem to be stuck in a pattern that contributes to emigration. Such differences are of a scope that will take quite long periods of time to overcome, if indeed they will be overcome (and not increased, as is the tendency today, see table 5.4).

Table 5.4 Global Income Disparity 1960–91. Percentages of Global Income Attributed to Quintiles of World Population

	Poorest 20%	Richest 20%	Richest to poorest
1960	2.3	70.2	30:1
1970	2.3	73.9	32:1
1980	1.7	76.3	45:1
1991	1.4	84.7	60:1

Sources: UNDP 1992, 1994.

How long is the relevant time period here? In an exercise regarding income disparities between African emigration countries and European immigration countries, it was concluded that it would take in the best case more than fifty years, and in the worst case 450 years, for the emigration countries to reach the income levels that the immigration countries had in 1973. (Tapinos (1993) considering existing income gaps and average income growth rates of emigration countries 1960–73. Note that this exercise does not estimate when income parity is achieved, only how long it would take for emigration countries to reach a certain income level. In the meantime, the income of the immigration countries will also have grown.)

By updating these figures to existing income disparities in 1993, we learn that the gap has widened (see table 5.5).

Although income gaps by themselves, as we have seen, explain only a part of migration behaviour, it seems safe to assume that widening North to South disparities are likely to incentivate stronger emigration movements in the future. In other words: although an important explanation of actual migration flows in the past has been the existence or absence of control policies in immigration countries (see chapter 6), the widening global income gaps may be assumed to bring forth a growing number of would-be migrants. This conclusion also holds when we consider the measures now contemplated to reduce gaps and stimulate growth in the South. Such measures are either of doubtful value or of insignificant scope, at least to emigration countries.

Trade liberalisation, at least of the kind contemplated in the new GATT/WTO agreement, will primarily benefit the North and Southeast Asia. Calculations of what the new global trade agreement will spell in the beginning of the next century show that the major beneficiaries will be today's more dynamic trading areas. Hence, reductions of trade barriers will primarily benefit the OECD countries, which are estimated

Table 5.5 Income Disparities 1973 and 1993, Immigration Country/Emigration Country GNP/capita

Emigration country	Immigration country			
	UK-73	UK-93	CH-73	CH-93
Morocco	10	17	19	34
Algeria	5	10	11	20
Tunisia	7	11	13	21
Senegal	11	24	22	48
Mali	44	87	67	132

Note: the two immigration countries chosen – the United Kingdom and Switzerland – represent the low and high income end, respectively, of European immigration countries in the mid-1970s.
Sources: Tapinos 1993: table H.1 and World Bank 1995.

Kenneth Hermele

to reap two-thirds of the global increase in trade until the year 2002 (UNDP 1994). Other winners are the countries of Southeast Asia, including China. Losers, on the other hand, include Indonesia, Africa south of the Sahara, North Africa and many countries of Latin America/ Central America – all of which may be considered to be potential emigration countries.

Neither do foreign direct investments (FDIs) to the South show much hope. It is true that an upsurge in FDIs to the South has been noted since the beginning of the 1990s, but most of it passes the majority of emigration countries by. In 1989–92, ten countries – in descending order China, Mexico, Malaysia, Argentina, Thailand, Indonesia, Brazil, Nigeria, Venezuela, and South Korea – accounted for 72 per cent of the total FDIs going to the South (UNDP 1994).

Furthermore, foreign direct investments only employ less than 1 per cent of the labour force in the South (UNDP 1993). Thus it would be asking far too much to expect that foreign investments would contribute to resolving the economic problems of the South. Another way of reaching the same conclusion goes via a comparison of remittances and FDIs. While remittances, as we saw in table 5.1, are important for the emigration countries, FDIs mostly are not and would have to be increased a hundredfold in the cases of Bangladesh and Algeria to match remittances (see table 5.6). More modest but still impressive increases

Table 5.6 Foreign Direct Investments as a Share of Remittances 1993, %

	FDIs / Remittances
Asia	
Bangladesh	1
India	8
Pakistan	22
Sri Lanka	30
Africa	
Algeria	1
Egypt	9
Morocco	26
Tunisia	40
Central America	
Dominican Republic	50
El Salvador	2
Guatemala	74
Europe	
Turkey	21

Source: World Bank 1995.

– 148 –

are necessary for other emigration countries, ranging from a doubling to twenty-five times (cf. Ghosh 1992).

Also FDIs in the form of export-processing factories have proved to have only limited impact in comparison with the employment needs of emigration countries. Thus, the effect of FDIs in Northern Mexico may be seen as 'positive' although its employment effect is described as 'puny'. Consequently, FDIs will neither resolve Mexico's employment needs nor significantly reduce its emigration (Ibarra-Yunez and Stolp 1991).

It can further be questioned if FDIs in fact tend to reduce emigration in the so-called host countries, or if they on the contrary increase the likelihood of emigration. Here, the cultural contacts established through an investing transnational corporation may play an important role in establishing links to the 'home' country of the corporation (Sassen-Koob 1984).

In a similar line of argument, it is claimed that manufacturing employment in the foreseeable future will not absorb even 10 per cent of the labour-force growth in the Caribbean between 1988 and 2000 (Tucker 1991). The conclusion is straightforward: export promotion will not greatly change the employment situation – and hence will only marginally affect migration. Therefore, development policies must also include measures to stimulate agriculture, and industrial development cannot only focus on exports, but also needs a domestic market.

During the 1980s a *change in the dominating development doctrine* took place which contradicts some of the conclusions of such a balanced, inward-looking, labour-intensive strategy. This meant a neo-liberal shift, backed by the donor community, in favour of deregulation and international capital as vehicles of development.

This doctrine, known as Structural Adjustment Programmes, has so far led to growing social differentiation and increased poverty without sustained economic growth; in other words, the opposite of development for the majority of the populations affected (Stewart 1991). Furthermore, Structural Adjustment policies normally include drastic devaluations of (overvalued) local currencies. For the emigrants and their families at home, this means that the value of migrant wages and remittances is greatly increased, thus contributing to the attractiveness of migrating. Although some of these drawbacks of Structural Adjustment policies are recognised by the US Commission (1990), it nevertheless recommends the US government to make its aid conditional on whether recipient countries follow such policies. From the point of view of the objective of the Commission – to limit emigration from Central America and the Caribbean to the USA – this position is clearly counter-productive.

Complicating the picture is the prognosis that all over the world, in the North as well as in the South excepting Southeast Asia, *labour-force growth* will outstrip the increase in employment (see table 5.7). For emigration countries this means that growing numbers of people will not find employment at home.

But if unemployed workers from the South manage to emigrate to the North, they are likely to encounter a labour market that will suffer from high levels of unemployment. Not an enviable position for migrants looking for a job, certainly, but one of the few migration-reducing factors of the near future.

Table 5.7 also gives us an indication of the immigration countries of tomorrow. East and Southeast Asia is the only world region where employment is forecast to outgrow the available labour force. Consequently, we may expect a growing demand for labour here, and an increasing South to South migration to this part of the world in the near future.

To Prevent Migration: The 'Root Causes' Approach

Following the oil price hikes and the reduced rates of economic growth in the North during the mid-1970s, a major shift in the migration discourse occurred as the recruitment of foreign labour was brought to an end. From now on, the migration that took place was basically of two kinds: either family reunions, or political refugees. When refugee flows increased ten years later, the North redirected its attention to prevent the now unwanted migration movements. With a proactive policy it was stipulated to be possible to do away with the basic, underlying factors, the 'root causes' of emigration. Facilitating this shift was a redefinition of immigration as a form of menace or contagious disease, most eloquently expressed by the editor of a recent book on international migration, who compares the 'threat' to the North constituted by emigrants from the South to the 'spewing of nuclear waste and other hazardous materials' and 'the contamination of waterways'. Obviously, the North is justified if it wants to protect itself against such negative

Table 5.7 Projected Labour-Force and Employment Growth 1990–2000, Index 1990 = 100

	Labour force	Employment
Africa south of Sahara	138	127
Latin America	127	114
South Asia	122	116
East and Southeast Asia	117	137
OECD countries	105	104

Source: UNDP 1993, Figure 3.3.

factors, including intervening in the internal affairs of an emigration country since that country, just as any polluter, has 'internationalized its internal actions' (Weiner 1993: 25, quoted in Abiri 1995).

Migration policy thus moves into the security policy arena – the security of the North – in the guise of prevention. Leading immigration countries, such as West Germany and the United States, redefined the migration issue, stressing the unilateral interests of the North in reducing the flow of people across borders (Suhrke 1994).

To attack the 'root causes' of migration may seem attractive compared to efforts to hinder migration once it has been set in motion. For a number of reasons it is better to do away with the causes of migration, from simple humanitarian considerations to the fact that it is cheaper to stem and avert than to to deal with the consequences of unwelcome immigration, consequences ranging from immigrant reception costs in the North to refugee camps and violent conflicts in the South (Kane 1995, Myers and Kent 1995). Prevention is always to be preferred to relief.

Once a 'root-causes' approach is adopted, however, a number of issues arise. To begin with the origin of migration: what causes are to be considered roots of migration? Here, the discourse stresses internal conditions in the emigration countries: violation of human rights, authoritarian regimes, population growth (Loescher 1989, Widgren 1989). Very rarely is the widening North to South gap included in the discussion, and when it is alluded to (as in Widgren 1989) it does not lead to any concrete policy recommendation. The *real* root causes are always to be found in the South, with one exception: the protectionist trade policies of the United States and the European Union (US Commission 1990, Russel and Teitelbaum 1992).

The official Swedish positions illustrate this. In the Social Democratic government's first formulations on 'root causes', the gap in and between countries is mentioned as one of the factors that need to be considered (Swedish Ministry of Labour1990). In a subsequent government report, however, this global component has been done away with, and root causes are now to be found only in 'the countries of origin of the refugee movement' (SOU 1991: 1, 10, 109).

The way you define the 'root causes' of migration will of course influence what measures you find appropriate. In the Swedish case, both a parliamentary commission and a Social Democratic government bill frankly declare that 'root causes' can be tackled without any change in Swedish policy. The only thing that is needed is more of the policies already implemented by Sweden, and a better coordination between aid and foreign policy in order to stem migration flows (SOU 1991: 1, Swedish government 1990/1: 195).

A more recent Swedish governmental commission has opted for another approach. The global root causes are not denied, but described as 'complex', including aspects related to 'global structures of security, economy and population' (SOU 1995: 75,40). The statement is obscure, even in the Swedish original, and what is more important, it has no bearing on the policy recommendations that follow. Priority areas for Swedish policy, the report concludes, are to improve human rights in emigration countries and to make sure that refugees do not end up too far from their countries of origin, preferably not even outside their own borders. The lofty references to complex, global root causes are an adornment of the one-sided security interests of an immigration country and carry no weight when it comes down to money and real priorities.

When the South itself has a voice in discussing the root causes of migration, however, 'the structural problems of development' are introduced, including the colonial heritage and 'the critical economic situation of most of the developing countries, as reflected in particular in economic recession, balance-of-payments problems, deterioration of the terms of trade, indebtedness, inflation, etc' (UN 1986). Here, on the other hand, external factors, frequently shaped by the interests and policies of the North, are in the forefront at the expense of factors that the emigration countries themselves can influence. Through a process of compromises, the final text will then reflect both Northern and Southern positions, leaving the reader with a rather vague and unclear impression.

In the dominant 'root-causes' discourse, there are only two policy areas where change in the North is called for: an opening-up of markets; and an increase of the flow of aid and investments to the South, an echo of the Brandt Commission's call for a massive transfer of resources (Widgren 1989, Böhning and Schloeter-Paredes 1994). However, most analysts recognise that aid can only be a limited factor, a 'catalyst' at best (Breier 1994). Furthermore, the volume of aid may not be the central issue, but rather its orientation. The UNDP (1994) has proposed a 20/20 compact: the North should dedicate 20 per cent of its aid funds to human development purposes, such as basic health care, primary education, sanitation and safe drinking water. Simultaneously, the recipient countries should agree to spend 20 per cent of their budgets for the same purposes. Today the share of national budgets in the South going to human development is 13 per cent, whereas only 7 per cent of foreign aid has this focus.

Another problem with the resource-transfer approach is that it can be seen as contributing to migration rather than reducing it. A great deal of development aid is tailored to foster modernisation, which is hailed naively by many migration analysts as the resolution of the migration problem (Appleyard 1992b). But modernisation may be held responsible for millions of 'development refugees', especially in projects of dam construction, mining and irrigation. In India alone, the number of forced removals on account of such 'development' projects may total 20 million people (IOM/RPG 1992).

Focusing on what emigration countries ought to do, absolves the North. One can, perhaps, accept that 'industrialised countries do not want to reduce the pull factors of high wage jobs or safe havens; they want to maintain peace and prosperity' at home (Martin 1994: 243). In any case, this statement may reflect realism and *realpolitik*. But does it really leave us with only one option, that of 'reducing push forces' as 'the morally acceptable durable remedy for unwanted migration' (ibid.)?

What 'morally acceptable' should mean is not easy to say, nor whose morals we are discussing. In any case, the argument can be turned upside down, from a moral to an amoral argument. If we cannot trust the North's morals and sense of justice, if we cannot base our argument on 'ethical and humanitarian grounds' as the North closes its ears to such arguments, let us instead, as Susan George (1992) does, talk of the self-interest of the rich countries. Thus, if it can be shown that a certain policy of the North – in this case Structural adjustment policies in the indebted South – will cause an invasion of the North by millions of refugees, a simple argument can be made to change that policy – not because it is immoral or unjust, but simply because it would be in the interest of the North to do so.

A case in point is when the head of the Swedish International Development Agency (SIDA) argues in favour of protecting the aid allocations from budget cuts by underlining the 'common interest of development', in Sweden as well as in the South: 'Development Cooperation is an investment for the future.' What is at stake is 'our common future' (Göransson 1996).

Through an increased flow of resources to the South, the North will achieve two things. Firstly, it will gain leverage over emigration countries to 'stimulate the proper policy response' (Weintraub and Díaz-Briquets 1994: 140, see also US Commission 1990). This presupposes that Northern countries know 'the proper policy response' – a questionable assumption if we consider all the doubts and contradicting opinions regarding the migration–development relationship. But it is nevertheless not an uncommon position to see the North as a supplier of 'acceptable life-styles' and an exporter of 'the wherewithall for sustainable development' (Myers and Kent 1995: 13), the main provider of 'development packages' to stimulate 'economic growth and recon-struction' in Africa (Appleyard n.d.: 1). This stance, I believe, is fuelled

Kenneth Hermele

by the low weight that the 'root cause'-approach – in spite of its designation – gives to the contribution of the North in stimulating migration.

This contribution is but rarely recognised by governments in the North. To take one obvious example: arms sales are heavily concentrated in the hands of the five permanent members of the UN Security Council: of the arms officially supplied to the South in 1988–92, these five countries accounted for well over 80 per cent. With the dissolution of the Soviet Union the share of immigration countries has increased (although the total value of arms sales has declined considerably). In 1992, out of total arms exports of 18 billion US dollars, the following seven immigration countries accounted for 72 per cent: United States 46, Germany 10, France 6, United Kingdom 5, Netherlands 2, Italy 2 and Sweden 1 per cent (UNDP 1994). Out of the refugees that arrived in Sweden between 1983 and 1994, the Swedish peace movement has shown that 65 per cent came from warring countries where Sweden during the same period had supplied arms to one of the parties (Ångström et al. 1995).

But governments in the North close their eyes to such connections. In a position paper on migration and development, the US government could only come up with one 'pull factor' which attracted migrants to the North: the migrants' networks established in the immigration countries by already arrived migrants which made it easier for others to follow in their steps (USA 1992).

Likewise, the immigration countries rarely accept that they contribute to the brain drain, nor do they take any measures to stem it, although they may regret it in official speeches. But instead of financing return programmes for skilled labour and qualified professionals or stay-at-home packages for potential skilled emigrants, they frequently send their own nationals to staff their development projects (Pastor and Rogers 1985, Russel et al. 1990).

Underlying the feebleness of the 'root causes'-approach is a rather pessimistic tone regarding the possibilities of reducing migration. Not only is the South's capacity to formulate its own development visions and policies questioned (as we have seen in Appleyard n.d., the US Commission 1990 and Myers and Kent 1995), but doubts are also voiced as to the willingness of the North to stop stimulating migration (George 1992). This pessimism concerns the global economic and political world order (Zolberg 1992), as well as the likelihood of achieving a major transfer of resources to the South, at least sufficient to influence migration decisions to a considerable degree (Tapinos 1993).

Such pessimism may be completely warranted, and should perhaps rather be called realism. This may also explain why the 'root causes'-approach seems to be yielding to a security discourse. As it is realised that South to North migration will continue – the North will not change, the impact on the South of any realistic policy is 'puny' – the North now redefines the problem as one of security, i.e. the security of the immigration countries. It is only from such a Northern security perspective that it makes sense to argue in favour of safe havens for refugees – and refer to areas within emigration countries or in their neighbourhoods (see the various contributions in Böhning and Schloeter-Paredes 1994). To the refugees themselves, however, such 'havens' are less secure than asylum in the North (Abiri 1995).

Implications of Limited Ecological Space

Although the concept 'sustainable development' has been around for fifteen years and although it gained status as an unquestionable good with the publication of the Brundtland Report (1987), it has not been of central interest to the migration–development discourse. On the contrary, sustainability and ecological considerations are relocated to a subfield of the research area: environmental refugees.

However, ecological issues are absolutely crucial to any discussion of development. Without at least a preliminary understanding of the development–ecology links, any discussion of migration and development will lack an essential component. One way of establishing such a base is through the concept of ecological space.

Ecological space can be understood as the area occupied by a certain life-style. In a typical industrial country, that area totals 5 hectares, including an area to grow food, feed animals and absorb emissions (especially the hothouse gas CO_2). If areas where such ecological services can be performed were in unlimited supply, there would be no problem in visualising an unlimited number of people modelling their life-styles on the one reigning in the North. But since such areas are in fact restricted, and since the North is already occupying most of them, Rees and Wackernagel (1992) conclude that spreading the life-style of the North to the South would require two additional earths – a noun not frequently written in the plural – to provide ecological space for today's disadvantaged. Since there only exists one earth, say Rees and Wackernagel, the North is appropriating areas from the South. This means that development of the South requires a dramatic reduction in appropriated areas – and hence a drastic change, although not necessarily a deterioration in the concomitant life-style – of the North. Otherwise, any new demands on the common space would spell a further deterioration of the ecological situation.

Against this background we may assess the following statement. 'It is clear to us,' write Kindleberger et al., 'that if there is to be a solution to the 'migration problem' it lies ultimately in the narrowing of international disparities in opportunities. This means, primarily, the increase of growth rates in the developing countries' (OECD 1979: 32).

This may seem to be an inoffensive expression of the benefits that development (here called 'growth') would bring to the South. But the statement is unusual as it stresses the need to reduce 'international disparities in opportunities', a factor we have seen left out of most of the migration–development discourse.

Now, one may wonder if 'the increase of growth rates in the developing countries' would require any more profound changes in the life-style of the North. Not only are we confronted by an unequal distribution of ecological space, whose rectification by itself would require a major redistribution from the North to the South. We simultaneously have to prepare for a doubling of the earth's population in a time span of only two generations. With this twin challenge in mind – a redistribution of resources and space, a doubling of population – we can calculate what changes in life-style we have to contemplate as the North cedes ecological space to the South within the framework of global sustainable development. For the European Union, the following necessary reductions have been estimated.

Table 5.8 Reductions Required from Present Levels of Consumption in the European Union to Reach Long-Run Sustainable Levels, %

	Required Reductions, %
CO_2 emissions	77
Energy use	50
Non-renewable raw materials	85
Forestry products	15

Source: Friends of the Earth Europe (1995).

So, if space is limited, as I have argued, a real North to South contradiction exists, in spite of the wishful thinking of the Brandt and Brundtland Commissions. Development in the South of necessity entails a reduced availability of ecological space for the North. As Gunnar Myrdal (1973: 187) concluded more than twenty years ago, it is 'virtually impossible to believe in, and strive for, long-term development in underdeveloped countries without assuming a radical change downward of what we now in developed countries can count as incomes, investment, production and consumption'.

This is certainly an unequivocal position in recognition of the existence of limited ecological space. Now, compare Myrdal's stance with the statement by the former President of the United States, George Bush, who on the eve of the 1992 UN Conference on Environment and Development announced that the American way of life was not negotiable. What he really was saying was that the United States was not willing to give away any of the ecological space it today occupies. Now, if we assume that Bush's position in fact expresses the consensus of the North – our life-style is not negotiable – what then? Are we not forced to conclude that the South must not be allowed to develop, since development for the majority of the population of the world would, again of necessity, spell dramatically altered patterns of life for the North as the competition for the limited ecological space would grow ever more intense?

On the other hand, if the South will not be allowed to develop, as this would imply a redistribution of ecological space from the North to the South, the only way for the great majority of the population of the South to acquire a Northern life-style will be through migration. To limit the affluent life-style to the North may thus be assumed to stimulate migration.

There exists one way out. The ecological space appropriated by a certain life-style depends not only on the parameters of the life-style as such, but also on the number of people who enjoy (or suffer) that life-style. If we are pessimistic (realistic) as to the likelihood that the North will reform its life-style so that it can be accommodated within the limited ecological space available, one solution presents itself: to restrict the number of people who will live on this earth (Harrison 1992). With a smaller world population, the pressure for ecological space would not be as intense.

But it can be questioned whether the North has the capacity to stop the growth of the world's population: a doubling is next to certain since tomorrow's mothers already have been born. Likewise, the option of hindering traditional economic growth, with its concomitant ecological costs, in the dynamic economies of East and Southeast Asia, today's and tomorrow's main growth zones of the world, is hardly available to the North. Furthermore, the North is already dependent on this region for markets and, consequently, employment generation at home, which means that a consensus in the North to reduce economic growth in the South will not be easily achieved.

This more sober assessment of what the future will bring leaves the North with one choice: either to modify its life-style in order to create ecological space that the South may occupy; or to defend the ecological space it has appropriated. This latter option implies that a number of factors touched upon here will continue to produce emigration from the South to the North. A logical response, then, would be for the North to close its borders ever more in order to shut migrants out, and insist that the migration and refugee movements be halted before they cross the South to North divide. The attention given to migration as a security problem, coupled with the absence of global ecological considerations, indicate to me what road the North has chosen.

—6—

Exit, Voice and Citizenship
Ishtiaq Ahmed

Introduction

This chapter searches in the political science literature for answers to two central questions: why do people migrate/not migrate from the South to the North? And, how is migration related to the development process?

Some readers might wonder if political science could give any better answers than other disciplines which started focusing on migration much earlier and have made profound contributions to understanding this phenomenon. The fact of the matter is, however, that politics has almost invariably been involved in international population movements, which by definition involve the crossing of state borders. We shall here present some political science theories dealing with the central questions mentioned above. In doing this we shall also discuss why political science has been a latecomer in migration studies, and why its role has become central in the last decades.

The Evolution of the Modern Western State System and International Migration

In theories of international migration the role of the state has indeed been long neglected. One reason may be the nineteenth-century liberal idea (still broadly accepted as a utopia) that migration flows should not be interrupted. Only in emergencies should the state interfere in regulating migration flows. In modern Western history we find periods when migration regulation has been relaxed as well as those when it has been tightened (Öberg, N. 1994: 86–122). The gradual consolidation of political power around a central authority, in other words the emergence of the territorial state, was the precondition of regularised control of migration. In Europe the appearance of mercantilist ideas after the dissolution of feudalism provided impetus to the state to adopt measures to foster a commercial bourgeoisie which could promote exports. It was a period when the state began to protect the 'national interest' in a more determined manner *vis-à-vis* aliens. Population statistics began to be kept, travelling outside the state territory was discouraged, while immigration was encouraged from other parts of Europe. In particular, skilled workers and craftsmen were encouraged to settle (Hammar 1964: 7–11).

In the second half of the nineteenth century, the doctrine of free trade opened the borders for migration, although this lasted only for fifty years. Until 1914 there was virtually no restriction on travelling in Europe, and this was long remembered as the 'normal period' when no wars and economic disasters forced states to protect the domestic market. Already after the outbreak of the First World War, passports were requested (for travelling) and further restrictions were soon integrated in legal systems of immigration and alien control. No doubt, the state interfered strongly in cross-border migration. This trend continued during the Depression and lasted until the end of the Second World War (Öberg, N. 1994: 29).

The post-war economy based on Keynesian principles brought about the modern welfare state in Western Europe. However, the gigantic work of reconstruction, which greatly increased the need for labour, was compounded by the division of Europe as a result of the Cold War. Later, in the 1960s, foreign workers were recruited from Southern Europe by the advanced economies of the Northwest. The state tolerated this labour import, and in some cases even gave it a helping hand, but its terms were set by the market economy. A large part of this labour inflow was the spontaneous immigration of people who had not been recruited but who were individually seeking work (Hammar 1990).

The turning point came around 1974, when state after state decided that the recruitment of foreign labour had to stop, and that in the future only family reunion and refugee immigration were to be allowed. Still, even at that time, control of immigration was relatively relaxed. Rigid control systems were enforced only in the late 1980s when the number of asylum seekers started to increase drastically, as a result of the wars and civil wars in the Middle East, in Iran and Iraq, in other parts of Asia and in Africa, and also because the end of the Cold War led to new refugee flows from the East, especially to Germany.

It is no coincidence that political science during the last two decades showed an increasing interest in the study of international migration. It was in this period that states everywhere in the North began to stop unwanted immigration in protection of their territory, populations and welfare systems, etc.

Moreover, scholars studying international politics have in recent years begun to pay attention to international migration. Relations between states and also national security issues are involved when large-scale migration takes place. The implications of development for migration, and vice versa, have been discussed in Europe since the migration from Southern Europe and Turkey in the 1960s, but it is only during the 1990s that political leaders have expressed a desire for a comprehensive policy embracing migration, development assistance, foreign relations and security policy.

Political Science and International Migration

The core unit of analysis of political science is the so-called territorial nation-state and the *problématique* its smooth functioning both in the domestic sphere and as part of the international order. The conception of the modern state derives largely from the influential writings of Max Weber, who defined the state as a societal organisation which claims authority over a given population in a specific territory. It imposes its will through a system of administration and law modifiable by statute. The executive can legitimately use force on behalf of the state, within limits permitted or prescribed by its regulations (Weber 1978: 41). This definition of the state does not refer to the type or form of government prevailing in a state. Both democratic and autocratic governments are included. The right to exercise power and authority vested in the state is derived from the notion of sovereignty. It means that the state has the prerogative independently and freely to determine its internal and external policies, laws and societal ends. The state is thus entitled to exercise legitimate power and extract compliance to its will from the population living in its territory.

Modern political science and international law generally presume that the population which is permanently domiciled constitutes the nation. The nation in turn is understood as all those who are nominal citizens of the state, but because of international migration, some permanent residents are not citizens of the state. They are foreign citizens who have immigrated and taken up residence. Vice versa, there are also some citizens who have emigrated, settled in other countries and are therefore not permanent residents of the country where they are citizens. The terms population, nation and citizens must therefore be discussed and defined.

The Western way of conceptualising the nation derives from the democratic principles of the French Revolution, which converted the former subjects of the French king into citizens of a republic. It can be called the civic or statist conception of a nation. Underlying this modern concept of citizenship is the notion of consent: members (citizens) freely choose to obey the government, which is based on the rule of law. Rainer Bauböck (1994: 53–147) discusses at length the implications of consent for international migration. His thesis is that consent implies voluntary membership of the state in the sense that members can choose to emigrate to another state. It is, therefore, the foundational basis of the liberal state. However, while it entitles members to leave a state, it does not include the right to acquire membership of another. New members have to be accepted by the political community already organised in a separate state.

In the West there is, however, also another tradition of defining the nation. It derives from the German school, mainly headed by the Romantics, which has identified common culture and supposed descent as the only basis of nationhood. It can be described as the ethnicist or organic conception of nation (Brubaker 1992: 35–72; Ahmed 1996: 5–6). This latter view is also recognised by some contemporary social scientists, who emphasise that human groups based on ethno-cultural bonds have always existed and the nation is simply an extension of the same. Cultural groups confronted by dangers and threats to their existence begin to organise themselves politically into nations aspiring to some type of political self-rule (Shils 1957; Geertz 1963b). According to this view, a cultural nation can exist without a state of its own, or even organise itself in a single state. Pan-Slavic and Pan-German movements of the early twentieth century belong to the category of cultural nations. In the contemporary period Pan-Islamism, Pan-Arabism, and the most recently revived of all, Greater Serbian nationalism, are examples of cultural nationalism. Such an extra-state conception of the nation may in principle entitle individual members to enter the state on the basis of their cultural specificity, but the main goal may be territorial acquisition.

States committed to an ethnic or organic conception of the nation may exclude some indigenous individuals or groups on the basis of religion or race. The theocratic Islamic states such as Saudi Arabia, Iran, Pakistan and Sudan employ the religious notion of Umma to include only Muslims in the nation (Ahmed 1994: 43–4). Germany continues to observe the distinction between ethnic Germans and others (Brubaker 1992: 165–76). Ethnic Germans can seek entry into Germany as a birth right, while non-German residents of long standing are granted citizenship only on a very restrictive basis. In Israel the Law of Return qualifies Jews from any part of the world to come and settle in the country, but not the former Palestinian refugees who fled their homes and villages in the present territory of Israel during 1948 and afterwards.

Therefore to understand how the concepts of nation and nation-state are understood, the actual practice of specific states needs to be examined. Even in our times, there are many autocratic states, ruled by hereditary kings or other despots and dictators who continue to treat populations as subjects rather than citizens and exclude some parts of the population from what they call the nation. In other words, the presumption that the whole population of a state can be designated as the nation is far from established everywhere. The state–nation relationship obviously carries implications for the rights of immigrants and minorities to be admitted officially, to adjust, integrate or assimilate and be naturalised into the nation. For a democratic state the existence of a large, segregated and discriminated population of foreign citizens is not conducive to stability in the long run. Therefore it is in the interest of the host nation that within a reasonable period of time an opportunity be given to such a body of people to be incorporated into the nation through naturalisation. An alternative may be to grant foreign citizens who are long-term permanent residents (i.e. 'denizens'), but who do not want to change citizenship, substantial political rights and representation.

It is to be noted that the terms 'nationality' and 'citizenship' are sometimes used as synonyms, both meaning nominal membership of a state (referring to the passport-carrying person). A distinction, however, is made here between nominal and substantial citizenship, where the latter designates those rights that residents hold as permanent residents notwithstanding whether they are also nominal members. In this chapter, nationality is used only to indicate national or ethnic identity or identification, even if nationality in many countries simply means nominal citizenship, i.e. one is a national of the state whose passport one carries.

Now, the international political system recognised by the United Nations is constituted by sovereign states, the territories of which should not be changed by conquest, according to what has become a fundamental premiss of international praxis. The UN Charter (1945) recognises the general principle of self-determination, the state's sovereign rights over its territory and by that token over the people who live in it (Article 2–7). The system of representation in the General Assembly is also constituted primarily in terms of member states, while the people permanently residing in them are described as the nation. It should be noted, however, that no distinction is made between nominal citizens and permanently residing aliens. It is left to each state to make the rules for acquisition of citizenship, i.e. the laws of naturalisation, as well as to decide about the substantial rights which are to be granted to denizens.

While the Universal Declaration of Human Rights of 1948 takes an individualistic and not a group standpoint on human rights, the United Nations International Covenant on Economic, Social and Cultural Rights (1966: Article 1–1,2,3) and the United Nations International Covenant of Civil and Political Rights (1966: Article 1–1,2,3) explicitly recognise the right of self-determination of a people. Yet simultaneously the right of the 'nation-state' to ensure its survival, and by that token to prevent secession, is accorded primacy in the United Nations International Covenant on Civil and Political Rights (Article 4–1). Confusion has existed therefore in UN discussions and documents on the usage of the terms 'peoples' and 'nations'. Sometimes they were used interchangeably, but later 'peoples' came to be accepted as a wider term while 'nation' was used in a more reserved manner for political entities possessing a state of their own. Self-determination for peoples was understood in a positive sense of a right to exercise self-rule while for nations it applied negatively, in the sense of non-interference from outside powers. Such distinctions did not help facilitate the concrete application of such a right, once decolonisation had been achieved and it was demanded against an established state (Davidson 1993: 14–15).

It follows that most human beings are expected to pursue and promote their interests within the confines of the states they are born in. Thus while currently migration within the state is considered a human right (Universal Declaration Article 13-1), and states are not to prevent emigration (Article 13-2), there is no right to immigrate. In other words, there is no automatic right to enter a country of one's choice. Consequently various mechanisms to control and regulate the movement of population across borders are recognised in international law as an essential part of the sovereignty of the state.

It seems reasonable therefore to look for explanations of why relatively so few people migrate, and why many more stay in the states of their origin, in intervening political and legal mechanisms present at various levels, extending from the internal to the international political system. It can be proposed that the flow of migration occurs within the fluctuating parameters of control. Except for a situation in which a totalitarian state denies all routes of exit to migrants and this inflexibility is reciprocated by an equally rigid denial of entry at the receiving end, at least some migration can be expected.

The Welfare State, Migration and Control

Although economic change and demand for labour paved the way for immigration into Europe, important preconditions were changes in Western attitudes, particularly of the ruling elites, on the question of race, ethnicity and religion. Previously the most racist arguments were used to keep 'non-whites' out of Europe and North America. Nazi crimes against Jews and gypsies, however, proved a turning point in moral and political discourse. Henceforth openly racist arguments were generally the province of extremist forces on the right while mainstream political parties and democratic movements in principle accepted a non-racist, pluralist basis for politics. It was in these circumstances that war-ravaged labour-deficient Europe began to receive workers from Southern Europe. During the 1960s some Western European countries deliberately encouraged immigration from the the the former colonies (now independent states) in Asia and Africa. The United States and Canada also began to accept a yearly quota of Asians and Africans. Australia and New Zealand kept their borders virtually closed for non-whites, and only in the beginning of the 1970s gradually liberalised their immigration policy, accepting non-white immigrants.

Large-scale South to North migration has security implications. A strong argument for restricted migration may be that a massive influx of immigrants cannot easily be absorbed by the receiving country and therefore may virtually threaten its existence. Even short of such an invasion, a growing body of immigrants may worry politicians, governments and sections of the indigenous populations because of its anticipated cultural and social implications. Thus, for example, the early Afghan refugees, fleeing from the Soviet intervention in 1979, were at first warmly welcomed by the Pakistani people. However, in later years the Afghan presence was resented for the spread of drugs and illegal arms by Afghan *mafiosi*.

Myron Weiner (1993a) observes that the notion of security is a social construct which conveys different meanings to different societies and states. Reviewing various reasons why receiving countries accept or reject migration – in terms of absorptive capacity, economic situation, volume of inflow, and so on – he regards ethnic affinity as the 'most plausible explanation for the willingness of states to accept or reject migrants' (Weiner 1993b: 10). He writes further: 'A government and its citizens are likely to be receptive to those who share the same language, religion, or race, while it might regard as threatening those with whom such an identity is not shared' (ibid. 10). However, Weiner notes, 'ethnic affinity' is also a social construct. Nineteenth-century American Protestants did not regard Jews and Catholics 'as one of us' and many contemporary Europeans do not regard Muslims as 'one of us' (ibid. 10). Thus contemporary West Europeans regard East Europeans as fellow-Europeans, and therefore more acceptable as migrants, than people from North Africa. (Since Weiner wrote this, the situation may have changed. Even East Europeans are currently considered with some suspicion as many of them are trying to enter Western Europe under various pretexts.) It can reasonably be assumed that in the overall expected influx from the South migration of two sorts might be perceived as the most problematic; those from the so-called Islamic world and from sub-Saharan Africa. The cultural tension between Islam and the West, and the racial resentment against inflows from sub-Saharan Africa, make a great deal of sense in terms of Western cultural history. Regarding the so-called Islamic world, the great attention drawn by the article 'The Clash of Civilizations' written in the summer of 1993 by the prominent American political scientist Samuel P. Huntington gives some indication of the degree to which non-Western cultures and civilisations are being perceived as sources of challenge to the stability of Western civilisation. Both academic responses (Ajami 1993; Bartley 1993; Binyan 1993; Kirkpatrick 1993; Mahbubani 1993; Miller 1993) and extensive discussions in the press followed. The argument is rather simple, but sensational with the demise of the bipolar East–West ideological-political-economic-military confrontation, the world is no longer in the grip of a total struggle of mutually exclusive ideologies. The great vacuum now created is likely to be filled by a more deep-rooted clash of historical cultures or civilisations. Huntington candidly and explicitly mentions the Islamic and Confucianist civilisations as threats to Western civilisation; the former in particular for its alleged expansionist zeal and proclivity towards violence and warfare.

Considering that in the postwar period Muslims in large numbers have immigrated into the North – there are some 8 to 10 million in Western Europe and more than 8 million (including 3 million Black Muslims born in the United States, many of whom belong to US-based sects and religious cults) in North America – their presence is likely to be treated by some political forces with unease if not outright hostility (Karlsson 1994). Terrorist activity by Islamic extremists in Europe surely accentuates the worst fears of the people in general and their governments. This might imply that further influx from the Muslim world will be anticipated with great concern. In particular the countries with the greatest geographical proximity to the Muslim world would want to improve their control systems. Thus in one sense the 'front-line countries' in this 'new battle' – Portugal, Spain, France and Italy – would be the most likely to plug all inlets and pores through which legal or illegal migration might occur. This might be a most difficult control problem, not least for the time being, but even more difficult can be the control of the land route, for example via Bulgaria or other Eastern European countries.

Large inflows from sub-Saharan Africa do not seem to be currently impending, but the racial factor can be detected in how differently recent refugee inflows have been perceived in the West. In the United States for example, Cuban refugees of Spanish descent have been celebrated like heroes, while the mainly black Haitian refugees have been looked upon with dismay. This is not to deny that strong ideological or political considerations more than anything else might have influenced the attitudes towards immigration from these two Caribbean countries, but the racial factor must be recognised as another most important factor, fashioning US attitudes (Rystad 1990b: 205–20).

However, as the states in the North honour universalistic legal and welfare principles, they cannot easily adopt a specific policy to discriminate between immigrants. Therefore, in the coming years a very strict and explicit definition is likely to be adopted by all EU members of those who can enter the North with the intention of seeking refuge or work.

In any case, since control systems do exist, which ultimately are dependent upon the power and authority of the state and the international political system, it is quite clear that for security reasons the international political regime will, among many other things, also control the flows and movements of people across borders. A panic situation could arise suddenly if the control system were to break down or were to be flouted effectively. Thus earlier this decade, when Cuba decided to let go those who wanted to emigrate and thousands of Cubans headed for the United States, the general US policy of welcoming such exiles was quickly suspended.

Perspectives on Forced Migration

In our view, migration needs to be conceptualised as a continuum voluntary (see chapter 3) and forced migrations are ideal types, that in ordinary life often are mixed rather than pure cases of the one or the other. As soon as a decision to migrate involves getting permission, the element of free choice is modified. On the other hand, forced migration may include an element of rational choice of individuals sensing a threat to their well-being or security if they do not migrate. There are of course literally true cases of forced expulsion, where a state or some other powerful force in a society drives an individual or a group out of the country. Escape from natural calamities may also create situations of overwhelmingly forced migration. Forced migration can also be considered a process deriving its sustenance from the structure of the social or economic system rather than merely the result of any direct political or ideological violence or threat (Goodwin-Gill 1990: 22–9).

International Migration, Forced Movement of Labour and the Marxist Theory of the State

Although international migration is not a central concern of Marxism, its general conception of the predicament of the worker – it is assumed, namely, that a worker cannot store his capacity to work, which is thus a perishable commodity, and that consequently under capitalism he is forced to sell daily his physical capacity to work (called labour power in Marxist terminology) in order to ensure his physical survival – is useful for understanding migration of workers as forced activity (Adler 1977). According to this view, the worker does not choose between migration and immobility. Rather his painful and agonising uprooting is the result of the need to sell his labour power. International migration under capitalism is therefore an extension of the notion of forced labour (Cohen 1987).

In his theory of imperialism, Lenin discussed the misery of the migrant workers within Europe: how Italians, Poles and others migrants were doubly alienated in the Western European societies where they were settled. They were paid the lowest wages and given the hardest, low-status jobs (Lenin 1970). The bottom line of the Marxist argument on international migration is that the proletariat is not free to sell the products of its creative work. To sell its labour power it may even have to abandon hearth and home. As international capitalism expanded it would bring down cultural, social and legal barriers to the extraction of resources. Inevitably cheap labour would be drawn into the orbit of international capitalism. Therefore migration on the regional, national and international levels would occur, but on the terms of the capitalist hierarchy.

Also, with regard to understanding why so few persons undertake international migration, the Marxist theory of the state can provide some interesting clues. According to the orthodox Marxist tradition, the state perpetuates class society through repression as well as ideological manipulation (Engels 1970: 461–583). To achieve this result, a substantial part of the population must be available to produce the surplus as well as to defend the social order from internal and external threats. Thus ideology, generated by the ruling class, instils a false consciousness among the exploited classes (Marx and Engels 1976: 59). They acquire emotional attachment to the state and its symbols. The state-promoted nationalism aims at cultivating such an attachment among the exploited people to the otherwise iniquitous class society.

From the Marxist perspective it follows that people identify with the state, even if they are poor, neglected and deprived. A certain level of false consciousness therefore binds people to the state. Were it not so, rebellions and revolutions would have been routine in world history and killing and dying for the state a rarity. Since even the most inefficient and apparently weak states can survive for long periods of time, the significance of false consciousness in the state–society relationship can be presumed to be intrinsic to it (Engels 1970: 461–583; Marx and Engels 1976: 59). In other words, most people continue to stay on within the confines of the state because of ideological manipulation, economic dependence, and the ability of the state through outright force and even naked terror to ensure itself of the supply of cheap labour in the overall interest of the production and reproduction of the class society.

The question then arises if the working people are coerced and ideologically manipulated to remain loyal to the state, how does Marxism explain why some people emigrate? It can be asserted that from a Marxist perspective international migration occurs because of the dialectical contradictions between national and international capitalism: while the bulk of the population remains available as cheap labour for the national bourgeoisie, a portion of it may be available for export in the interest of the more advanced international capitalist order. Unemployed persons and unreliable ethnic minorities may belong to the category of people the state may want to send abroad.

The Marxist approach to international migration can be criticised for, among other things, not paying due regard to the non-economic reasons for migration. In particular, political and humanitarian refugees may flee to liberal democratic societies not for economic reasons but for the democratic freedoms and religious toleration proffered by them. Significant numbers of South to North migrants belong to the category of refugees. The contrast between lack of democratic freedoms in their countries of origin and those they settle in is so great and the conditions for any change back at home so few that many become permanent residents; a decision they perhaps did not take when originally exiting. In any case, international migration is not a central concern of Marxist theory, but it has influenced the radical approach on international migration which sees it as an effect of the unequal relations between the strong and the weak societies involved in the global division of labour (see Castles and Kosack 1973; Adler 1977).

Dependency Theory

The Marxist conception of international migration has influenced dependency theory, which proceeds on the assumption that a single capitalist economy pervades the whole world, that it has a centre (or core) where all power is concentrated, and a periphery which is dependent and vulnerable to the will and interests of the centre. The North is the centre, while the South is the periphery. The argument in its most extreme form was put forth by Andre Gunder Frank (1970), who theorised that the structure of the world economy was such that surplus produced in the periphery was appropriated by the centre. The ties of dependence of the periphery *vis-à-vis* the centre did not allow genuine self-perpetuating development in the periphery. Rather, it allowed an inverse relationship between development in the centre and underdevelopment in the periphery the more the periphery was integrated into the centre, the more it was underdeveloped.

Dependency theory did not explain the phenomenon of non-migration, but maintained that labour migration was the result of the dictates of the centre. The flow, extent and direction of migration was determined by structural changes in the global economy. Thus in the initial phases of the formation of the world capitalist system in the sixteenth century the centre was able to transplant its own surplus population in the periphery through conquest. Additionally the slave trade of the seventeenth and eighteenth centuries transported Africans to the Americas. Where the centre managed to penetrate most deeply, as was the case in Latin America, the local population was decimated (Frank 1970).

Migration from Southern to Northern Europe in the first post-war period has been described in similar terms as a continuation of the power of the centre to impose its interests on the periphery (Castles and Kosack 1973). This depiction applies even more strongly to South to North migration from Algeria to France in the 1960s. Dependency theorists point out that brain-drain from South to North adversely affects the development of the former. A well-educated and skilled elite, which might be most valuable to the periphery, is lost to the centre. As regards the economic benefits accruing to the periphery from its policy of exporting labour force to the North – a policy which helps rid the economy of labour it cannot exploit efficiently and which brings in remittances – dependency theorists point out that such remittances are rarely invested in production. Most such capital goes into the purchase of houses in the cities and expansion of consumer life-styles. It is argued that such change does not contribute to real development. On the contrary it compounds the difficulties of a weak economy because inflation rises and the differentials in income are increased (see chapter 5). Furthermore, the centre can politically exploit the presence of these workers to exert influence on the periphery (Adler 1977: 36–7). For example, the United States gained great political capital from Cuban and Nicaraguan economic migrants and political refugees to build up an armed resistance against these states.

Some of the more complicated political implications of contemporary South to North migration seem to have escaped the attention of the dependency theorists, however. For example, large diaspora groups settled in the West can use their position to carry out agitation, prop-aganda, and other legal and illegal services on behalf of their separatist movements. For examples Sikhs, Tamils and Muslims from Pakistani-administered Kashmir are settled in sizeable numbers in Britain. These diaspora groups have been noted to render help to their co-ethnics in

South Asia, who have been engaged in protracted armed struggles against the states in the region in a bid to carve out their own separate states (Ahmed 1996). Another powerful diaspora force in Europe is the large Kurdish population. The Kurds have been lobbying governments and human-rights groups for support for their right of self-determination, which can range from cultural autonomy to complete independence depending which faction one is talking to. Thus a cultural group marginalised in the South can strive to enhance its political position and influence by its emplacement in the North.

On the other hand, a large diaspora community may have a disturbing impact on the political affairs of the centre. The Algerian civil war has e.g. caused considerable political and social tension in France, including several acts of violence and terror. Thus the problems of the South are internationalised to a point that the North is included in the ambit of the struggle in the South.

The full implications of such developments is neglected in the dependency approach, which concentrates primarily on the economic asymmetry between South and North. A more balanced understanding of the phenomenon of international migration may be that it creates some sort of interdependence working to some costs and some benefits of both sending and recipient countries. The incomes being remitted by foreign workers may at least help to take care of the educational and health needs of the family members back home, and they may also have a more general economic impact through multiplier effects. Without such help some people would be without any support. There is, however, no doubt that the interdependent relationship remains massively in favour of the centre.

Refugee Movements: The Epitome of Forced Migration

The dramatic growth in the number of people claiming refugee status since the mid-1970s is an almost unprecedented phenomenon. Some 150 million people have at least for some time sought refuge outside their country of origin. The 1951 UN Convention Relating to the Status of Refugees and its expansion in 1967 define refugees as persons who have fled their country of citizenship and are unable or unwilling to return to their country of origin because of a 'well-founded fear of being persecuted for reasons of race, religion, nationality or political opinion'. Refugees have the right to apply for asylum and to demonstrate the political nature of their situation, according to recognised international criteria for securing refugee status. In the meantime, they are to be assisted by the authorities in maintaining themselves physically, psychologically and socially. It is laid down that refugees should not be compelled to go to states where they are in danger of persecution (Loescher 1989: 8–9). However, there is no individual right to be granted asylum under the present international law. Rather, the right to grant asylum is a right of the state: it may or may not grant it. In recent years, however, the right to asylum has been interpreted in favour of the refugee by the UN General Assembly, albeit in moral rather than legal terms (Dacyl 1992: 59–60), while at the same time a restrictive interpretation of the UN Refugee Convention has spread among almost all countries of the North.

It is important to note that the above definition does not include among refugees the main body of migrants: those who emigrate/leave/ escape a country because of economic hardship or ecological and human catastrophes. As emphasised, often the motives for going are intrinsically mixed economic and political at the same time. Given the blatant economic inequalities and political and cultural tensions prevailing in most developing states, it is not surprising that some people want to migrate to the North. Sometimes the political regime of a state is only partially in control of its territory. Sometimes the regime is unable to secure just and safe living conditions or even to provide the water and food needed for daily life. Many people want to leave a country because of poverty and unemployment. However, these life situations are not considered reasons for being granted admission into a country and a permit to stay and work. The ultimate decision to let aliens in is at the discretion of the states.

International refugee regimes have existed since the inter-war period. In 1949 the UN High Commission for Refugees (UNHCR) succeeded the International Refugee Organisation (established 1943). The leading donor countries in Europe, North America, Japan and Australia have exercised a considerable influence on its working. Although attempts have been made, there is no coordinated policy of tackling the growing refugee problem. Many states, and especially the great powers, have allowed foreign-policy goals to colour their positions on different refugee cases or flows. Among countries of the North, the United States have openly exploited their refugee policy. As already mentioned, Cuban and Nicaraguan refugees were recruited by the United States to fight the socialist regimes in their countries. Also in other countries ethnicity, economic interests and regional security concerns weigh heavily in the refugee policies (Loescher 1989: 7–33). It can be mentioned that the former Soviet Union and other Eastern European communist countries did not participate in the working of the UNHCR, but during the Cold War received students from the South and other trouble-ridden areas. Efforts are now being made to make the successor states join the UNHCR.

Violence and Refugees

Zolberg, Suhrke and Aguayo (1989: 33) define refugees as persons whose presence abroad is attributable to a well-founded fear of violence, as might be established by impartial experts. The authors emphasise the central role played by violence in causing refugee flows. On the basis of their findings the authors present three categories of refugees:activists (opponents within the political elite, dissenters and rebels), targets (individuals belonging to special groups singled out for violent action) and victims (those caught up randomly in the cross-fire or exposed to generalised violence respectively) (ibid. 269). Proceeding in a historical framework (ibid. 5–18), they identify the emergence of the refugee problems in the modern period to widespread religious persecutions prevalent in Europe during the sixteenth and seventeen centuries. Many people emigrated to North America. Later came refugees from the convulsions of revolutions of the eighteenth, nineteenth and early twentieth centuries. The political opposition, including both the displaced ruling elites as well as breakaway factions within the revolutionary movements, had to flee when those who captured state power proceeded to consolidate their power. It required considerable repression to crush the challenging forces. A third phase in refugee migration occurred in the nineteenth and first half of the twentieth centuries as the huge land-based multi-confessional and multilinguistic Austro-Hungarian and Ottoman empires collapsed and were succeeded by territorial states based on the idea of ethnic homogeneity and nation-state. This reorganisation of Europe was painful for those ethnic minorities who could not fit into the new norm of the nation-state. Jews, Armenians and gypsies were the main groups to suffer genocide and forced expulsion.

The authors note that unrestricted entry of aliens has been more of an exception than a rule in international affairs in the twentieth century. The receiving countries have imposed prohibitions and restrictions. Fascist Italy and Portugal (as late as the 1960s), and the Soviet Union and the other East bloc countries did not permit easy exit to their nationals partly because of the need for labour and partly out of concern that mass emigration might reflect badly on their claims of popular support.

As regards post-war refugee flows from the South to the North, Zolberg, Suhrke and Aguayo (1989) point to similar reasons. Religious differences, ethnic tensions, conflicting standpoints on nationalism and the efforts of the state to cull out a coherent nation – all such factors may result in conflict, violence and refugee flows. In addition the material and cultural achievements of the North serve as an attraction to displaced, uprooted and persecuted people. They head towards the North both in search of protection and to improve their standard of living.

Migrations are therefore always mixed, both political and economic, voluntary and forced. A dilemma for liberal Western states in the contemporary era is that while they have long denounced restrictions on exit from the former Soviet Union, now that the Berlin Wall has fallen they deplore the appearance of large-scale refugee movements. Thus, in one sense, in their subsequent actions they seem to approve of those repressive measures of the sending countries to prevent exit which they previously condemned.

This observation is confirmed by Janina W. Dacyl (1992), who has studied the responses of Thailand, China, the United States, Indonesia and Malaysia to Vietnamese refugees as an expression of ambivalence 'between compassion and realpolitik' (title of her book). According to her, it was in the final analysis *realpolitik* that determined refugee policies, and the receiving states employed various legal and coercive means, including forced expulsion, to rid themselves of asylum seekers they did not want on their territory. No doubt in recent years the search for strategy and policy to stem refugee flows has been uppermost in state planning (see also Rystad 1990).

The arguments put forth by Zolberg, Suhrke and Aguayo identify the role played by violence in accentuating migration flows. They demonstrate the need for a new refugee convention, suitable for the post-Cold War period and the new flows of mass migration resulting from efforts to escape from intolerable and life-threatening violence. What is lacking in their survey-like account is a theoretical argument which can identify the linkages between social, cultural, economic and political factors at the various micro-, meso- and macro-levels which constitute situations that produce migration as well as explain why most people – often among them persons persecuted by the regimes – remain within state borders.

Voice-Exit and Migration – Non-Migration

Albert O. Hirschman's seminal work, *Exit, Voice and Loyalty* (1970), provides an interesting micro-level theoretical framework for analysing the relationship between migration and non-migration (chapter 7). His theory focuses on individual choice and purports to explain primarily the behaviour of economic organisations and their members, within a competitive market framework. However it can also be extended to analyse a wide variety of other relationships of a social and political nature. The general argument is that an organisation, for a number of reasons, can fail to meet the expectations of members at some point in time. Members' dissatisfaction may be expressed either in terms of *exit* (some may stop buying its products) or *voice* (they may protest in the hope of influencing management). Exit is the predominant form of protest in economic matters, while voice is the more normal type of political protest.

Now, member dissatisfaction does not imply that an organisation collapses forthwith. Organisations such as human societies and states can withstand considerable inefficiency and deterioration. This happens because they produce a surplus which suffices to sustain them even when a general deterioration and fatigue is discernible in their functioning. This gives them a chance to recuperate and revive.

Hirschman introduces the idea of *loyalty* to explain why members are not willing easily to abandon an organisation. Members, particularly those concerned with quality, generally develop confidence in an organisation and its products and therefore can be won back. For this to happen the organisation in question (business firm, political party, even state) has to pay heed to voice and respond to criticism. Such measures discourage exit. However, ties of loyalty are tenuous. Loyalty can change into disloyalty, if a member is being denied effective voice. If, instead, the exercise of effective voice is allowed this can pre-empt exit, but in certain circumstances exit may be the only alternative for a member to exercise his voice. Thus exit and voice are not necessarily mutually exclusive options, but rather complementary to each other: both are expressions of the will of members.

Roger Ko-Chih Tung (1981) applied a modified model of exit–voice to analyse the relationship between migration and political participation. Instead of loyalty, which he found an unsatisfactory concept for explaining inaction, Tung introduced the notion of *autism* or self-adjustment to the environment. Thus when a dissonance occurs between an individual and his environment three types of responses are possible. Firstly, the member strives for self-adjustment (autism), in other words, rather than trying to change his environment, the individual tries to adjust to the environment. It is a subjective change of mind and not an act of manifest outward behaviour. It seeks equilibrium and the result is inaction. Secondly, he attempts mobility between environments. It means exit from one environment and entry into another. It occurs when an individual cannot resolve a conflict between himself and his environment. Under repressive regimes that leave no freedom to express voice, exit is often the only choice left for the persecuted persons. Migration across borders may be the expression of such a response. The third response is an effort to change the environment. It means exercise of voice in terms of participation and representation. Democratic states based on multiparty systems and sustained by welfare provisions provide avenues for voice. These might therefore be assumed to be least prone to unleash a wave of migration.

Tung's concept of autism improves upon loyalty. It has more power to explain immobility in that it gives a sophisticated and nuanced understanding of inaction or immobility. As a concept loyalty is too vague to capture inaction. Many people may not have a strong sense of loyalty, but may still display no signs of dissenting behaviour such as exit or voice. Self-adjustment may be the only way to survive in an apathetic external socio-political environment. Ethnic minorities, low castes and aliens are typical categories of people who may feel no sense of belonging to the larger society and have little sense of loyalty to the state.

It can be said in criticism that Tung's concept of autism is meant to explain the state of affairs among minorities and marginalised groups. The problem is that not only Hirschman but also Tung exaggerate the consensus basis of the political system, which presumes that most people stay put because voice can be exercised and necessary corrections can be demanded of the system. It can be argued that in many countries, and not least in the South, not just the minorities, but the large mass of the population remain inactive. They neither exercise voice nor exit. Instead of the idea of autism, which connotes self-adjustment and by that token some sort of reconciliation; a better expression of their plight is *despondence*. In the South, structural poverty and stigma compounded by cultural parochialism, social particularism and repressive political control render them despondent and thus inactive. Despondence, however, need not be seen as a permanent feature inherent in the nature of the oppressed. In the case of a breakdown of the state or successful social revolution the oppressed strata can suddenly be animated to considerable activity; unfortunately sometimes even to extreme acts of cruelty against victims identified as former oppressors.

More interesting in the international context of the voice–exit relationship is that it only indicates the potentiality of exit; it does not mean that it can be exercised in reality. The international control system can block any such exit.

Legitimacy and the Consensus Perspective on Migration

Following Talcott Parsons's notion that the basis of a social system is consensus and not conflict, Easton (1965) describes a political system as a 'set of interactions through which valued things are authoritatively allocated to a society' (1965: 153). According to Easton a political system is also a means of resolving differences, and it is a set of inter-actions through which demands are processed into outputs. Additionally it is 'a means through which the resources and energies of society are mobilized and oriented to the pursuit of goals' (ibid. 153). For the political system to manage stress and to function it must support its members. Extreme indications of the absence of support might be revolution or emigration or separatism, but riots, demonstrations and law-breaking may also indicate a decline of support. The support given by members is produced and in the long run reproduced by political socialisation. Ties of affinity are cultivated through the educational system and participation in the political process. Such socialisation invests the political system with legitimacy. Easton puts it succinctly: 'No system could endure, at least for very long, without the presence of some moderate belief in its legitimacy' (ibid. 278). While support for a government or a regime may weaken and be withheld, people may still persist in supporting the political community with which they identify emotionally. However, if the community rejects them they might have to opt for exit (the classical example is that of many – but far from all – German and French Jews who left their states of origin rejected, persecuted and threatened with death, but at that time not recognised as political refugees).

The idea of support and legitimacy is not far from the concept of loyalty put forth by Hirschman. The process of socialisation begins at home, continues in school, and is augmented by religious, cultural and other factors which foster emotional and sentimental ties between individuals and the community, and by that token to the state. For immigrants, the process of creating and developing emotional ties to the new country takes time. It involves a process of resocialisation. While millions of immigrants are integrated into the economy, they are not granted the right to participate in the affairs of the polity. Citizenship and voting rights are usually reserved for full citizens, although conferring citizenship and voting rights on immigrant non-citizens also might be the most effective means of resocialisation (Tung 1981: 7).

The main criticism of the consensus perspective, and particularly of the idea of legitimacy, is that unless the society as a whole is free from marked differences in living standards and social status, it cannot be assumed that inaction is a result of routine identification with the community. Such a perspective ignores the role of structural poverty, religious, ethnic and political divisions, social degradation, political alienation and exclusion, as well as an outright fear of the state that instils among the underclass such despondence and resignation that it renders both voice and exit meaningless. The system can sustain the democratic process of elections, political parties and a free press without conceding too much to this underclass. Voice of the subordinate sections can be ignored with impunity and protest put down brutally. This applies particularly to multi-ethnic societies in which the state can rely on the mainstream society for reproduction of the social and political order. Many states in the South adhering to some sort of quasi-democratic system routinely ignore the wishes of the underclass constituted by the abject poor among whom ethnic minorities, lower castes and other depressed unemployed, marginalised sections of society form a large portion. Multicultural and multi-ethnic democracies such as India and the United States can get away with considerable disregard for the voice of the poor and weak. At any rate, to consider lack of protest (that is, despondence) a proof of legitimacy is an unwarranted methodological deduction. Large numbers of people just do not have anywhere to go and therefore remain apparently immobile.

It can be assumed that while, on the one hand, for reasons just mentioned the poorest sections of society have little opportunity to exit, on the other hand, the upper classes from the mainstream society have little reason to do so. Rather, the middle strata may be the most mobile on the international level. Individuals who possess a strong sense of group belonging and solidarity and who belong to the group which is not the victim of institutionalised discrimination or persecution and violence may be less prone to migrate than those who individually or as part of a group feel threatened. Whatever the initial reason for migration, however, once it has begun among people conscious of group loyalty and obligation it tends to, assume a chain character, arranging for the movement of members between, for instance, South and North, within the political parameters of the country of exit and the country of entry.

Towards a Political Understanding of Migration

A macro-theoretical perspective suggesting that migration is inherent in the anarchical nature of the global political system underlies my argument. This anarchical nature stems from the existence of, on the one hand, an economy which pervades the whole world and is constantly penetrating more deeply into the peripheral economies of the South. Such a change entails considerable wear and tear as the indigenous production processes disintegrate (see chapter 5). On the other hand, while the breakdown of indigenous production processes is under way at an increasing rate, the indigenous social, cultural, religious and ethical systems tend to put up considerable resistance to the cultural homo-genisation processes concomitant with the global market economy. One can assert that since economic disintegration hits many people hard and rewards only a few, social tensions are exacerbated. A sense of deprivation and alienation may find expression in cultural, religious and ethical forms. Very often such cumulative experiences give birth to nationalist protests and agitation. Thus the functioning of the global economic system is mediated by the international political system of sovereign states, and by nationalism, ethnicity, cultural particularism, militarism and other non-economic factors. As a result not only political and legal systems but also social, cultural, religious and ethnical systems impact on international migration (see chapter 2), both as triggers to various types of international migration and as obstacles and controls.

The Control Mechanisms in the South and International Migration

In the contemporary world, each society, in a routine sense, functions within the precincts of the state. The society itself comprises various smaller units such as the individual, family, tribe, caste group, religious community, linguistic group and nationality, and so on. Cultural groups such as clans, tribes, sects and so on, exert pressure to keep members within the group (see chapter 8). Together they function to produce and reproduce a more or less stable membership, which in turn functions as the support base of the state. It is no wonder, therefore, that the act of migration remains an exceptional one. Also individuals often attach great emotional value to their social and cultural ties.

Finally, obstacles to international migration might derive their ultimate sanction from religious and ethical convictions. Thus, for example, both Islam and Hinduism do not encourage the pious to go outside their own civilisational spheres. Traditionally high-caste Hindus were not supposed to cross the sea and abandon India. Similarly Islam divided the world into the Dar-ul-Islam (abode of peace where Muslims were in power) and the Dar-ul-Harb (abode of war, where the enemies of Islam held power). Yet, migration did take place in the post-war period and Hindus and Muslims, among other cultural groups of the South, are currently found in substantial numbers in the 'Christian North'. It is important to note, however, that unmarried young men and women – those least tied in a relationship of direct obligation – mostly undertake long-distance migration.

Nevertheless, the fact remains that poverty, illiteracy and hierarchical social stratification act as control mechanisms discouraging migration among the lowest sections of the population. The punitive and repressive apparatuses of the state are used to make a domestic labour force available for routine production and reproduction of the social order. In other words, social structure, culture and the state reinforce non-migration.

Sometimes states may promote emigration in the hope of reducing unemployment, or to gain new skills and above all to raise their capital holdings through foreign reserves. Equally, states may force political opponents and unreliable or suspect ethnic minorities to emigrate so as to rid themselves of internal threats. Also, even if states may restrict emigration through control of passports, widespread corruption in the police and bureaucracy can enable some people to exit. Migration may tend to grow when the interface between the social, cultural and political systems is no longer functioning complementarily and the society is in flux and transition.

The Nation-State Project and Migration

The development processes set in motion by states in the South, most of which are post-colonial, can be characterised by one main political concept: the nation-state project. Various economic, social, educational, industrial and political inputs are made by the state, in order to improve the standards of living and thereby to foster a stronger linkage between the state and the larger society. However, the risk of failure cannot be discounted, although this may not mean that the state entirely fails to harness society to its will. It may simply mean that the processes of gaining greater penetration are resisted by various sections of society; in some cases resistance may be quite strong and threatening.

Such complications are inherent in the anatomy of most Asian and African states: they have been bequeathed outstanding disputes over borders and territories and the distribution of populations by the former colonial powers. Therefore, the interface between state and society is weak, particularly between the state and atypical cultural units such as religious minorities, linguistic nationalities, etc. The multi-ethnic population therefore poses considerable problems for national consolidation (Smith 1983). Regional tensions and big-power interference exacerbate the sense of insecurity of the state. Governments therefore strive to establish a structure of obedience among the people calculated to ensure their survival. Whereas the state exists formally, the nation has yet to be consolidated from among the disparate population (Ahmed 1996).

The objectives of the nation-state project may be said to be the establishment and consolidation of an exclusive political-military control of the state over a certain territory, the building up of a defence structure to thwart external threats to such territory, and the creation of political legitimacy, material welfare and a degree of cultural homogeneity (Hettne 1993: 77–8). The successful implementation of such a process is calculated to enhance and consolidate the control of the state over society. However, the project can end in failure. The absence of democratic practices and institutions usually compounds the implementation of the nation-state project. In this connection elite competition and widespread corruption among the ruling circles tend to erode the consolidation of national unity and the social peace. Whatever strategy a state adopts to create a nation, the survival of the state itself against internal and external dangers is a paramount consideration (Buzan 1991).

The question of collective identity is significant. The social groups which share a common ethnic identity with the ruling elite are rather easily convinced that a common destiny binds them together. They all depend on the survival of the state. Thus Punjabi Muslims, upper-caste Hindus, Turks, Sunni Arabs, Alawite Arabs, Wahabis and so on are groups from among whom the ruling elites of Pakistan, India, Turkey, Iraq, Syria and Saudi Arabia have emerged. The states treat protests and other forms of moderate employment of voice among such groups differently from that taking place among ethnic minorities. Cultural groups which are different from mainstream society or the dominant cultural group in a marked sense, for example in religion, may be viewed with suspicion in the nation-state project. Not necessarily in an ideological sense, but in a political one. For example, Muslims in India are treated with suspicion because their recognised leaders opposed the unity of India and created Pakistan. Kurds are treated with suspicion by Iraq, Iran and Turkey where they constitute substantial ethnic minorities living along the international borders, because of the presence of strong separatist tendencies among them.

Although no systematic study seems to have been made of this, a hypothesis comes to mind in this regard, namely that members of the mainstream ethnic group are likely to employ voice to express their preference to stay on while those who belong to alienated ethnic minorities may under some conditions exit and then only later in the North use voice, hoping to influence politics at home or to facilitate exit of their members. Needless to say, the different forms of action signifying protest of one kind or another pertain mostly to those individuals who are no longer tied down by crushing poverty.

Contradictions in the Nation-State Project

Although we may assume that the state treats protest actions emanating among cultural groups differently, depending on their ethnic origins, the state cannot ignore the need to consolidate a strong support base in society. Potential loyalty and support have to be consolidated with material incentives. Moreover, cultural groups which are different from the state elite may also have to be won over and assimilated into the nation. Indeed, official definitions of nations are usually universal or at least not explicitly particularistic. To enlarge the support base in the wider society may therefore be part of the nation-building strategy of states. Nationalism and patriotism are virtues relevant essentially in connection with the external interests of a state, particularly security concerns. Thus a grand variety of material and cultural measures are undertaken by the state with the intention of instilling a sense of belonging, identification and loyalty (Easton 1965; Hirschman 1970).

However, the various educational and socio-economic inputs undertaken as means of modernisation and development do not necessarily follow the requirements of centralised planning. A sharp increase in population compounded by mass uprooting from a subsistence economy and the production of a modern-educated intelligentsia is known from most agrarian Third World societies. A growing pool of potential migrants and emigrants may be the result. Moreover, it is in the nature of new multi-ethnic, multicultural states that nation-building does alienate sections of the population. The national identity is woven out of the patronage and selection of popular myths, symbols, emblems, and a variety of other rites and rituals which are calculated to forge closer links between the political establishment and society. Creating a coherent nation therefore requires ideological propaganda and political policy as well as the more general efforts at economic and political development which are expected to facilitate the expansion of equal opportunities to all citizens. Both these processes proceed in the context of existing cultural heritage, class structure, internal power distribution and external linkages of the various groups present in society. This means that the allocation of resources, employment opportunities and influence over the state will hardly be even and just for all groups, classes and people (Ahmed 1996: 39–66).

This unevenness may actually be even more noticeable in the ideological sphere of nation-building. Language, race (ethnic group) and religion are identity markers that historically have played an important role in shaping large-scale collective identity. Language plays an important role in communication and its importance in nation-building cannot be ignored (Gellner 1964: 147–78). In a purely technical sense a language is a neutral medium which facilitates communication between human beings. A language, however, is also a cultural factor. It is the chief outlet for expression of emotions, feelings, views, serious thought and the whole range of social relations. Neither the production of the material needs of a society nor its other multifarious functions can be performed without regular and systematised communication. Most states give preference to one language out of many. It is usually the one which marks off the cultural identity of the nation. Also, it facilitates an efficient utilisation of skills of the intelligentsia over the whole length and breadth of the country (ibid.). This fact has a direct bearing on the ability of people to seek employment: those whose language is chosen for official use have an obvious advantage. Separatist nationalism is often an attractive proposition for groups whose language does not enjoy state patronage. But there is, of course, the hope that the state may be able to assimilate linguistic minorities in the nation through the educational system and economic incentives.

Similarly, ethnic or racial minorities which are discriminated against will be prone to exit, and would use it if an opportunity arrived. Likewise in a multi-religious or multi-sectarian society, if the state adopts the religion or sectarian faith of any one group as official ideology and embarks upon a policy of discrimination or is unable to prevent the majority community from persecuting the minorities, this surely strengthens separatism among the minorities. These may either fight or seek exit. The Kurds and Sri Lankan Tamils represent the first tendency, while the Bahai of Iran and the Ahmadiyya of Pakistan the second one.

The fact remains that, notwithstanding the various strains and tensions which are inherent in the nation-state project, the aim of the state is to maintain control over its territory and population. The international political regime is in principle supportive of such a control, although regional and global actors work against the interests of specific states. Unless a complete systemic breakdown takes place, the state will continue to ensure that it can control its territory and population (Ahmed 1996).

Conclusion

To return to the chief puzzle this chapter sought to solve – why do people migrate or not migrate, and why do so few actually migrate from the South to the North? – it can be asserted that some important political clues have been identified in the political science literature. These are as follows:

(1) Given the primacy in the global political system of the territorial state, which is conceived as sovereign and the legitimate holder of organised power, one key determinant of the size and scope of South to North immigration remains the state in the North. Some amount of illegal immigration will always be possible, but the modern state can legally equip itself with ever more effective controls. As pointed out earlier, while the right of emigration is considered a human right under international law, immigration is not.

As regards the politics of control in the North, it can be asserted that some categories of people are not desired (and have to be excluded). Among them can be included especially those cultural groups who at that moment in time are considered to be 'not one of us'. Moreover, even when state policy to exclude some people is not geared to the larger questions of nation and nation-building, they may not be admitted because the labour market and the economy does not need them. During periods of economic downturn, which bring unemployment, racism, xenophobia and security concerns, controlling further immigration gains currency in society and inevitably affects political debate and the political process.

(2) State control in the North has several aspects. Besides regulating visits and business trips the state determines the terms of the labour market, social welfare entitlements, treats applications for permanent residence and settlement as well as for nominal citizenship. Thus complete prohibition of all immigration is not possible and persons who have been residing for a long period of time tend to get their claim to citizenship accepted. Exceptions are states like Germany where gaining citizenship is extremely tedious.

(3) On the one hand, international law requires that political refugees shall be allowed to seek asylum. On the other hand, it is a right of the state to give asylum. This works to the disadvantage of the asylum seeker. The problem is that there are no clear-cut criteria for determining who is a genuine political refugee and who is not. As mentioned earlier, voluntary and forced migration are ideal types: they should be seen as a continuum rather than a dichotomy. In most cases of both political and economic migration a mix of both is present. Political and academic discussion about the UN Refugee Convention and the UNHCR agrees that the present definition of a refugee, based on the political situation of the Cold War in 1951, is outdated and does not suit the present 'mass-refugee' crisis such as in Africa (Rwanda), Asia (Afghanistan) or Europe (Yugoslavia). The Northern states, however, apply strict definitions of refugees because they do not want to be overburdened with all those refugees to whom other states deny asylum. In this connection one can also consider if the Marxist concept of 'forced labour' or 'forced migration' resulting from the devastating impact of international capitalism does not require serious thought. The neo-liberal offensive of international capitalism has in recent years brought about mass unemployment in many parts of the South. Should not people who are starving to death be given asylum?

(4) The exit–voice discussion shows that a mixture of motives result in immigration. The main line of thought developed here is that exit and voice are not two exclusive alternatives. Most people stay although economic, political and other reasons do exist which commend exit. They do it out of loyalty or support for the regime, because of socialisation and the influence of the nation-building process. However, among the subordinate classes and ethnic groups the ability to exit is severely limited. Thus autism or despondence may better capture their state of resignation to the hostile environment around them. Those who exit may do so temporarily, at least in their planning.

(5) The migration potential in the South is also a product of the overall impact of the nation-state project. The various inputs from the state to stimulate economic development tend to uproot more people than can be absorbed by the economy. Although the state aims that a sufficient workforce remains available, it seldom prohibits all emigration. As the crisis sharpens the intelligentsia strive to emigrate, and if the opportunities are available, a chain of migration can begin (persons who may share a strong group feeling can build up a flow of migration).

(6) The problems of security faced by countries in the South also play a role in fomenting migration. Minority ethnic and religious groups may be treated with suspicion by the state. In some cases the state may force them to flee. Thus alienated minorities tend to produce a higher degree of refugees than persons belonging to mainstream society. In any case, in the North belonging to a persecuted minority is more readily accepted as a ground for granting asylum.

(7) Thus, although political science has in the past neglected international migration, it is now being discussed widely in the discipline with regard to both control and integration policy in the North. This also demands that the overall development policy and population policy be brought into a comprehensive approach to international migration. In this connection seeking international co-operation on questions of democracy and human rights may be necessary.

The Crucial Meso-Level
Thomas Faist[1]

Lacunae in Sociological Theories of International Migration

Sociological approaches have presented an impressive array of plausible arguments as to why people move from one place to another, especially across the borders of nation-states. However, these theories have not directly addressed the question of why so few people migrate from so few communities and why so many return. Firstly, the total migrant population in the world is estimated to about 2 per cent of the world's population. Secondly, return migration constitutes an important fact. The social ties between movers and stayers are not automatically ruptured. For example, between 1960 and 1993 out of an estimated total of 12 million labour migrants and dependants from the Mediterranean countries of Southern Europe and North Africa, 9.3 million returned to their countries of origin from Germany (own calculations, based upon Statistisches Bundesamt 1955–95). Nevertheless, the immigrant population in Germany increased as a result of family reunification during the later 1970s and 1980s after the ending of guestworker recruitment.

In short, any theoretical attempt should therefore not focus on movers only, but on both movers and stayers, and also on how stayers who once make a move shuttle back and forth, or become stayers again, be it in the countries of origin or destination.

Most theoretical efforts have mostly focused either on global structural factors inducing migration and refugee movements (macro-theories) or on factors motivating individuals to move (micro-theories). This review and partial reconstruction of theories about international

1. The author would like to thank his collaborators in the 'Migration and Development' project for fruitful comments. Thanks also go to the author's colleagues at the centre for Social Policy Research and at the Institute for Intercultural and International Studies at the University of Bremen. Moreover, various individuals contributed stimulating criticism that sometimes differs vigorously from the positions taken by the author: Hartmut Esser, Jutta Gatter, Jürgen Gerdes, Hans-Joachim, Hoffmann-Nowotny, Stefan Leibfried, Bernhard Peters, Stefan Sandbrink, Charles Tilly, Madeleine Tress and Carsten G. Ullrich.

South to North migration emphasises the *meso-level* between what are usually called the micro- and the macro-levels, the level of analysis between individuals and larger structures such as the nation-state. It does so in focusing on social relations (social ties) between individuals in kinship groups (e.g. families), households, neighbourhoods, friendship circles and formal organisations.

Two strands of literature have paid attention to the meso-level. Firstly, in recent years the processes of immigrant incorporation have been studied in economic sociology (Portes 1995). However, so far little has been said about the costs and benefits involved in transferring human capital abroad or about the mediating role of resources inherent in social relations (social capital) in the decision-making process. Secondly, there is a huge and impressive empirical literature on migrant networks (Massey et al. 1993). There are also plausible arguments as to why these migrant networks embedded in migration systems (Kritz and Zlotnik 1992) are crucial elements in explaining international migration. Yet this literature is more successful in explaining the *direction* (e.g. from former colonies to the European and North American core) than the *volume* of international movement. In particular, it is not clear what exactly happens in networks and collectives that induces people to stay, move and return.

The specific characteristics of social capital are important in explaining the low volume of international movement, chain migration and often high rates of return migration. It is very difficult to transfer social capital abroad; even harder than the transfer of human capital. However, once pioneer migrants have moved abroad, relatives, friends and acquaintances can draw upon social capital and processes of 'chain migration' develop. Nevertheless, social ties of movers and stayers do not simply vanish in the course of international migration. This is why many movers return to the countries of origin.

The following discussion evaluates micro-level rational choice theory and macro-level migration systems theories. Secondly, it introduces three levels of analysis – the structural (political-economic-cultural factors in the sending and receiving countries and at the international level), the relational (social ties of movers and stayers) and the individual (degrees of freedom of potential movers). Thirdly, the decision-making processes and the dynamics of migration are partially reconstructed. Two crucial categories are used as a point of departure: social ties and social capital in social networks and collectives.

Dominant Theories of International Migration

This section appraises micro- and macro-level theories about the volume and dynamics of South to North movement. The idea is not to evaluate these theories as such but what they say about decision making and the dynamics of international migration. Theoretical and empirical work started with Sir Ernest George Ravenstein (1885 and 1889). He perceptively analysed relations between distance and propensity to move, developing seven 'laws' of migration.

The laws are: (1) The majority migrate only short distances and thus establish 'currents of migration' towards larger centres. (2) This causes displacement and development processes in connection with populations in sending and destination regions. (3) The processes of dispersion and absorption correspond to each other. (4) Migration chains develop over time. (5) Migration chains lead to exit movements towards centres of commerce and industry. (6) Urban residents are less prone to migrate than rural people. (7) This is also true for the female population.

These observations are a useful starting point as empirical rules of thumb that may apply to certain regions of the world at specific time periods. Ravenstein himself found abundant evidence for these 'laws' in mid-nineteenth-century internal English migration. However, his generalisations and later those of Everett Lee (1964) must be placed into more general sociological frameworks if we want to know whether and *why* their rules of thumb are true or not. Rational choice and systems theories may provide such frameworks.

The Rational Choice Approach: Between Preferences and Opportunities

The basic instrumental statement is: In choosing between at least two alternative courses of action, a person is apt to choose the one for which the perceived value of the result is the greater. It is assumed that the actor is able to make rational decisions on the basis of a set of tastes or preference orderings.

Some sociological rational choice theories take as the basic component not only the *values* (goals, preferences) but also the *expectancies* (subjective probabilities) a potential mover holds (DeJong and Fawcett 1981; see also chapter 3).

The basic value-expectancy model is straightforward:

$$MM = S(i) \, P(i) \, E(i)$$

where 'MM' is the strength of the motivation to migrate, 'P' is the preferred outcome, 'E' is the expectancy that migration will lead to the desired outcome, and 'i' refers to the specific preferences (values) potential movers hold.

The preferences may be most diverse. They may be related to improving and securing: wealth (e.g. income), status (e.g. prestigious job), comfort (e.g. better working and living conditions), stimulation (e.g. experience, adventure and pleasure), autonomy (e.g. high degree of personal freedom), affiliation (e.g. joining friends or family), exit from oppression of all kinds (e.g. refugees), meaningful life (e.g. improving society), better life for one's children, and morality (e.g. leading a virtuous life for religious reasons). In this view the potential migrant might not only be a worker, a member of a household or a kinship group, but also a voter, a member of ethnic, linguistic, religious and political groups, a member of a persecuted minority, or also, among many other things, a devotee of arts or sports.

In addition to values (preferences) and expectancies Hartmut Esser explicitly adds a third important element, opportunities and constraints. Therefore, his approach can be called *structural individualism*.

We could restate the above equation to read:

$$MM = S(i) \ V(i) \ P(i), \text{ depending on O/C}$$

'O/C' is the set of external opportunities and constraints encountered by a potential migrant.

Esser's theoretical approach deals with assimilation and acculturation of immigrants in the receiving country. Yet Esser's premises could be used to deal with decision making in the sending countries as well. His first fundamental hypothesis (1980: 210–11) could be restated as follows: The more intense the motives of a migrant are regarding a specific goal, the stronger the expectation that she can fulfil her goals by (temporary) territorial exit, the higher the propensity to attribute a high preference (value) to exit and the fewer the constraints working against exit, the more likely a potential mover will choose the exit option. These constraints and opportunities could include factors such as societal and cultural norms (e.g. gender roles), state policies (admission policies of the receiving countries) and economic differentials related to income or employment.

In addition to opportunity structures *information* plays a decisive role for migration decision making. Depending on the availability of inform-ation on transport and opportunities for jobs and housing, potential migrants can optimise their benefits. Such information may flow along various communication channels, such as mass media and friends who migrated before but also pioneer migrants outside the inner circle of relatives and friends.

An important prerequisite of immobility then is that a potential mover has sufficient information as to what goals can be better accomplished in the sending or the receiving country. If a potential migrant decides to be mobile, the question arises whether the necessary resources can be transferred abroad. The territorial restriction of certain assets has been termed *'location specific capital'* (DaVanzo 1981: 116). It is a widespread phenomenon that highly educated and trained movers, especially refugees, cannot enter at the same occupational level in the receiving country. For example, lawyers, physicians and engineers may not get accredited to practise law, medicine and mechanics and may have to look for work outside their field. Information about these and other limitations may prohibit international movements although they would not discourage the internal movement of migrants. In these cases it is more likely that internal and not international migration occurs.

Rational choice accounts certainly are a powerful tool with which to model migration decision making and action. Yet, we have to examine what is meant by opportunities and constraints in order to understand more clearly the decision-making process. Sociological and anthropological studies have frequently found that migration decisions are taken in social units such as the family, extended families or even whole communities. These social units use available resources in their perceived self-interest. Often, in patriarchal systems, the male head decides at the expense of females and younger members of the family.

This problem of defining a supra-individual decision-making unit is partly remedied by the 'new economics of migration' (Stark 1991), whose theorists do not prejudge the sole social unit of decision making to be the individual actor but try to aggregate the utilities of the individuals involved, especially in the case of rural economies. Yet, by considering family utility in aggregate terms, these theorists have ignored or simplified the relations between family members, the social ties that bind or separate family or household members. If basic social relations are disregarded in this way, we do not get a good idea of power and authority relations, (mis)trust and solidarity. For example, who decides which member of a social unit such as a household migrates and what is the legitimation of the decision maker?

Even if we specify the structural opportunities and constraints, we should still explain how they relate to individual rationality. Rational choice approaches to migration do not specify *how* structural opportunities are translated into individual action and vice versa. In essence, we encounter the problem of linking macro- and micro-levels of analysis: 'For example, a sophisticated individual might be aware of the level and nature of foreign investment in his or her country, but would still be unlikely to perceive it as immediately affecting a residence desire and possible decision to move' (Gardner 1981: 73). To make this link we need to complement micro-level approaches with more elaborate concepts of social relations and social ties.

Thomas Faist

The Migration-Systems Approach: Between the World System and Networks

While rational choice theories of migration have evolved from the micro-level to consider macro-level factors also (structural individualism), systems theorists have come full circle: They were at first exclusively concerned with the macro-level (migration systems), but have gradually come to introduce lower-level concepts such as migrant networks.

The most elaborate effort at developing a fully-fledged system-theoretic analysis is Hoffmann-Nowotny's concept, encompassing four levels, the individual, national subsystems, national societies and the international society (1970 and 1973). Hoffmann-Nowotny applies general social systems theory to the phenomenon of international migration. He starts with the fundamental relation between power and prestige in a society. In his conceptual universe 'prestige' legitimises 'power'. Hoffmann-Nowotny posits that in any society there exists some sort of consensus about the value attributed to material and immaterial goods (e.g. education). Power and prestige in a social system are determined by the position and by the status attributed to their positions. 'Structural tensions' arise from inequalities and status inconsistencies in the sending country. These structural tensions may generate 'anomic tendencies', i.e. an imbalance between power and status. Action directed to resolve these tensions may take forms such as social mobility, giving up the social position held or emigration to a country where status aspirations can be attained (Hoffmann-Nowotny 1973: 11–14). In essence, for Hoffmann-Nowotny (international) migration constitutes an 'interaction between societal systems geared to transfer tensions and thus balancing power and prestige' (1973: 19; translation T. F).

Later migration-systems approaches have four main characteristics. Firstly, migration-system theories assume that migration systems pose the context in which movement occurs and that it influences actions on whether to stay or to move. An analysis of trade and security linkages and colonial ties helps to explain the *origin* and *direction* of international movement. Basically, a migration system is here defined as two or more places (most often nation-states) connected to each other by flows and counterflows of people (see Faist 1995). Secondly, using dependency-theory and world-systems approaches, systems theories have stressed the existence of *linkages between countries* other than people, such as trade and security alliances, colonial ties and flows of goods, services, information and ideas (Portes and Walton 1981). These linkages often have existed before migration flows occurred. For example, in the case of European receiving countries (e.g. France, Netherlands and Great Britain) most movers come from former colonies.

Thirdly, migration systems theory focuses on *processes within migration systems*. Movement is not regarded as a one-time event but rather as a dynamic process consisting of a sequence of events across time (Boyd 1989: 641). Already Mabogunje suggests in his programmatic article on rural-urban migration in Africa that migration needs to be studied as 'a circular, interdependent, progressively complex and self-modifying system' (1970: 4). Theorising the dynamics of migration has thus moved from a consideration of movement as a linear, unidirectional, push-and-pull, cause-effect movement to notions that emphasise migration as circular, interdependent, progressively complex and self-modifying systems in which the effect of changes in one part can be traced through the entire system. For example, once it has started, international migration turns into a self-feeding process. Petersen assumed that pioneer migrants or groups set examples that can develop into a stream of what he called 'mass migration' (1958: 263–4). This helps to explain international movement as a self-feeding process that gains in momentum as networks reduce both the direct monetary costs of movement and the opportunity costs (that is, the earnings forgone while moving, searching for work and housing, learning new skills), and also decrease the psychological costs of adjustment to a new environment in the receiving country. Movers and stayers are regarded as active decision makers (Fawcett 1989).

Fourthly, within the context of important factors such as economic inequalities within and between nation-states and the admission policies of the receiving states, individuals, households and families develop strategies to cope with stay-or-go alternatives. Lately, systems theorists have started to apply social network theory vigorously. The main assumption is aptly summarised in Charles Tilly's provocative phrase that it is 'not people who migrate but networks' (1990: 75). In other words, migrants are not 'atomistic flies' (Cohen 1987). *Social networks* consist of more or less homogeneous sets of ties between three or more actors. Network patterns of social ties comprise economic, political networks of interaction, as well as collectives such as groups (e.g. families, communities) and (public) associations. 'Network theory builds its explanations from patterns of relations. It captures causal factors in the social structural bedrock of society, bypassing the spuriously significant attributes of people temporarily occupying particular positions in social structure' (Burt 1986: 106). *Migrant networks*, then, are sets of interpersonal ties that connect movers, former movers and non-movers in countries of origin and destination through social ties, be they relations of kinship, friendship or weak social ties (see Choldin 1973). In international migration, networks may be even more important than in domestic migration because there are more barriers to overcome, e.g. exit and entry permits, and if not available, costs for illegal border crossing.

Concerning migration and non-migration, a system-theoretic perspective emphasises that *predisposing factors* of very different kinds can enhance migration (e.g. wage differentials between countries, population growth, civil wars) when embedded in the context of historically grown political, economic and cultural linkages between senders and receivers, while other macro-factors may lead to non-migration, such as very restrictive exit and entry policies. *Precipitating events* (e.g. economic crises in sending countries) and *intervening factors* (e.g. migrant networks) are then thought to enhance migration. An important insight is that migration processes are accompanied by feedback effects affecting decisions to stay or go. For example, earlier internal migrations may lead to international migration or pioneer migrants may serve as role models for other potential migrants.

In sum, migration-systems theories constitute a great advance in the explanation of the dynamics of international movements. Yet, the real significance of social and political units between the micro- and macro-levels remains blurred. Contrary to what is claimed, we get no clear understanding of the *mechanisms* by which macro-factors shape micro-level decision making. To posit the relevance of intermediate structures such as the family, household and migrant networks is not sufficient to establish a meso-level. It begs the question as to how intermediate structures systematically pattern decision making, and are shaped both by the actions of potential and actual movers and by larger social structures.

Both rational choice and migration-systems theories have started to place more emphasis on processes linking the micro- and macro-levels: Rational choice theories have come to consider social units such as families and migration-systems theories emphasise networks. But both show a decisive weakness in conceptualising the social ties of movers and stayers within families or households and networks. Processes within these social units and relations between them and larger aggregates (e.g. state institutions) have to be brought into this analysis. One of the crucial factors is the lack of an appropriate conceptual framework. The following exposition of a social relational approach is therefore not meant to substitute but rather to enrich the rational choice and migration-systems approaches to international migration by paying more systematic attention to the meso-level.

Three Levels of Analysis: Macro-Structural, Relational and Individual

In its most general form spatial movement can be understood as a transfer not only from one place to another but also from one social unit or neighbourhood to another. This transfer may strain, rupture, change or reinforce previous social ties. In a sociological analysis of international migration three levels are relevant: (1) political-economic-cultural structures on the level of the international system, the country of origin and the country of destination (structural level), (2) density, strength and content of social relations between stayers and movers within units in the areas of origin and destination (relational level), and (3) the degree of freedom or autonomy of a potential mover (individual level), i.e. the degree to which he or she has the ability to decide on moving or staying.

(1) *Political-economic-cultural structures* denote an array of factors in the sending and receiving countries and in the international political and economic system of nation-states. The nation-states differ in the political realm as political and administrative units. For example, sending countries may vary with respect to political stability. This has consequences for the emergence of refugee flows. The admission and integration policies of sending countries also vary. Nation-states also differ along characteristics such as living standards, jobs and working conditions, unemployment rates and wages in the sending and receiving countries. Such differentials are important prerequisites for migration to occur between nation-states. Finally, in the cultural realm there are differences in normative expectations and collective identity. For example, in some areas of the world, 'cultures of migration' have developed (e.g. Caribbean islands and the Indian island of Goa). International norms and organisations also have an impact on the mobility of persons (e.g. international convenants on human and social rights by the International Labour Organisation and the Geneva Convention on refugees and asylum seekers).

Research into structural opportunities has been abundant, especially into the history of international labour migration. Hatton and Williamson (1994) summarise their findings on transatlantic migrations from Europe to America around the turn of the century, saying that demographic growth in the sending regions and income gaps between home and overseas destinations were both important, while industrialisation (independent of its influence on real wages) made a modest contribution. Frank Thistlethwaite argued in his précis on earlier transatlantic migrations that 'the inner secrets of emigration are to be sought in the working of those two revolutions which are so interconnected, the demographic and the industrial' (1991: 236–7).

With respect to political refugees, however, large refugee flows have been caused by international wars, especially the Second World War, but also the Cold War. Many more recent refugee flows have originated as a by-product of the formation of new states in the South, or as a result of social transformations (e.g. revolutions) and ethnic conflicts in both old and new states. External intervention in less developed countries has also been a common cause of refugee flows, for example in the South (Zolberg et al. 1989). Also, the very formation of territorially bounded states in the South after decolonisation resulted in migration and refugee flows. Moreover, in processes of state formation and the rebuilding of states the persecution and expulsion of minority groups can achieve a high priority.

(2) The social ties of the movers and stayers vary with respect to *density, strength and content*. These ties may go to the receiving or the sending countries or to both at the same time. They can range from a dense network of social ties to the country of origin to a total break, i.e. no social relations anymore and a reorientation to the country of destination in the process of settlement. Yet even in the case of permanent settlement abroad, social ties can be established or reinforced both in the country of origin and in the receiving country. Therefore, permanent settlement in the receiving country does not necessarily mean fewer social ties to the area of origin. If these social ties are systematically patterned in networks and collectives, we can link the relational to the structural level.

(3) On the individual level international movements can be characterised by a continuum along the *degrees of freedom* for potential movers. At one end, in some instances – for example, slaves, convicts, some refugees, contract workers, sometimes children and spouses – the essential decision maker is not the migrant him- or herself. At the other end, there are individuals with a high degree of autonomy, based on resources such as money, information and connections. The degree of freedom or autonomy is circumscribed in a context in which the main sets of parties involved in migration decision making and the dynamics of migration are: (1) individuals in the place of origin; (2) collectives and social networks of potential and actual movers and stayers such as families, households, friendship and kinship circles, neighbourhoods, ethnic, religious and professional associations, but also (3) interested collective actors in the countries of origin and destination (e.g. Non-Governmental Organisations, supra-national organisations such as UNHCR, sending and receiving country governments, political parties, unions and employer organisations).

Characteristics of a Meso-Level Approach

Firstly, emphasis needs to be placed on how decisions on moving and staying are made in and between groups of people (e.g. families and various forms of larger territorial and extra-territorial communities) rather than by isolated individuals or groups where economic-political-cultural structures only come in as external constraints and opportunities. A processual account will help us to specify the mechanisms causing changes in social relations. In this *interpersonal* and *inter-group* perspective decisions over moving and staying may be taken on different levels – for example, by individuals and differently sized groups – or imposed upon these groups by outside collective actors such as governments of nation-states. The basic assumption is that potential migrants and groups always relate to other social structures along a continuum of degrees of freedom. Particular units such as households or families therefore deserve special attention. Empirical studies muster abundant evidence that these units have figured most prominently not only in earlier transatlantic migrations from Europe to the white-settler colonies (Bodnar 1985), but also do so in contemporary movements from the South to the North, especially from rural areas in the South (Hugo 1995). It would be naive to conceptualise all social units such as households as single-interest decision-making bodies. There is too much evidence on the importance of diverging interests and of power relations within these units, for example expressed in hierarchical and patriarchal decision making.

Secondly, the *internal dynamics* of migration can indeed be described as self-feeding processes of cumulative causation, usually in ways that reinforce existing staying/moving patterns. Historically, waves of international moving and staying usually had a clearly discernible beginning, a climax and an end – with dynamics somewhat independent even from economic and political conditions in the receiving and sending countries once migration started (Thomas 1973). A relational analysis tries to capture the dynamics of migration by a close analysis of collectives (e.g. families or households) and networks. This implies that international migration is not simply seen as a straight line, only interrupted by external factors that may or may not capture 'mass migration'. Instead, movers and stayers take advantage of the opportunities offered by macro-level constraints such as demographic, economic and political developments.

A Pioneering Exemplar: The Polish Peasant in Europe and America

One exemplar that implicitly sketches theoretical considerations and empirical evidence along these lines is Thomas's and Znaniecki's acknowledged masterpiece on *The Polish Peasant in Europe and America* (1918–20). It deals with transatlantic migration of peasants from Russian Congress Poland to the United States. According to

Thomas and Znaniecki, the decisions of movers and stayers can be described by reference to the breakup of traditional society, and particularly of its extended-family system due to the marketisation of economic life in the areas of origin. The breakup of the peasant family was said to create new possibilities, especially through the 'growing assertion of the personality' (ibid. 2: 217). This evolutionary determinism may be criticised, but the shift from affectual to purposive and rational forms of action is the most relevant aspect of *The Polish Peasant* for the study of the causes and dynamics of migration. Importantly, Thomas and Znaniecki argued that this development of more abstract, complex and cognitive levels of social reorganisation did not entail the disappearance of primary-group attitudes and values but was largely constituted out of them.

Newer research has focused on migration not as an expression of societal disorganisation but as an active strategy to diversify income in rural households dependent on crops, etc. Yet what may be needed most for a comprehensive interpersonal and processual account is a focus on migration that includes processes of both societal organisation and disorganisation. Clearly, the focus of these two authors on household, communal and other ties remains valuable because it helps to construct the meso-level, whether we focus on disorganisation (e.g. persecution of political refugees) or organisation (e.g. migration as a household strategy for economic survival or even advancement).

Thomas and Znaniecki observed that potential migrants can reorganise both in the country of origin *and* in the new country of settlement. In the former country examples of co-operative collective action included education of peasants through the press and the emergence of co-operative institutions, such as co-operative shops, loan and savings banks, and agricultural improvement societies (ibid. 4: 178–304). We could add forms of political voice such as peasant protests (see Scott 1976). Indeed, there were alternatives to moving in improving the life situation in the country of origin. In the main country of destination, the United States, Polish immigrants came to be members of various forms of communal life, ranging from mutual aid societies and parishes to cultural organisations. Typically, immigrants such as Poles used their investment in family, ethnicity and religion as resources to redefine their situation, as workers, citizens, and members of household and religious groups. A parallel story could be told about political refugees. Although the root causes may differ and options to stay without endangering their lives may be minimal for refugees at the time of flight, the same principles of social analysis could be applied.

The Decision-Making Process

Social Ties and Social Capital

Social relations in collectives and social networks constitute distinct sets of intermediate structures on the meso-level. It is via these social relations that the resources of individuals are related to opportunity structures (figure 7.1). According to rational choice approaches decisions to move or to stay are inevitably made by individual or collective actors who weigh the costs and benefits involved. What migration-systems theories emphasise is that these decisions are always made within specific economic, political and cultural contexts that are determined by larger opportunity structures – reflected in the family, neighbourhood, workplace and community.

The macro- and micro-levels of analysis can be connected by the concepts of social ties and social capital. Movers and stayers are embedded in a social-relational context characterised by *social ties*, a continuing series of interpersonal *transactions* to which participants attach shared interests, obligations, understandings, memories and fore-casts. *Strong ties* are characterised by direct, face-to-face transactions between the actors involved. They are durable and involve obligations and substantial emotions. They are most widespread in small, well-defined groups such as families, kinship and communal organisations. By contrast, *weak ties* are defined by indirect relationships. They involve no direct or only fleeting contact. Weak ties refer to a more narrow set of transactions. Transactions among 'friends of friends' is an apt shorthand for weak social ties.

Social capital are those resources inherent in patterned social ties that allow individuals to co-operate in networks and collectives, and/or that allow individuals to pursue their goals.[2] Such resources include information on jobs in a potential destination country, knowledge on means of transport, or loans to finance a journey to the country of destination. Social capital also serves to connect individuals to networks and collectives through affiliations. Social capital thus has a dual thrust: it facilitates co-operation between individual (and group) actors in creating trust and links individuals to social structures. Furthermore, social capital serves to mobilise financial, human, cultural and political capital. (For other and differing definitions of social capital, see Bourdieu 1983 and Portes 1995).

Social capital is not simply an attribute of individual actors. The

2. 'Social capital ... is created when the relations between persons change in ways that facilitate action' (Coleman 1990: 304).

MACRO-LEVEL: STRUCTURAL	MESO-LEVEL: RELATIONAL	MICRO-LEVEL: INDIVIDUAL
opportunity structures	collectives and social networks	values, expectancies and resources
(political-economic-cultural structure)	(social relations)	(degrees of freedom)
economics: — income and unemployment differentials; access to capital *politics:* — regulation of spatial mobility (nation-states and international regimes); — political repression, ethnic and religious conflicts — interdependence in international system of states *cultural setting:* — dominant norms and discourses *demography and ecology:* — population growth; — availability of arable land — level of technology	*social ties:* — strong ties: families and households; — weak ties: networks of potential movers, brokers and stayers; — symbolic ties: ethnic and religious organisations *social capital:* resources available to potential movers and stayers by participation in networks and collectives through weak, strong and symbolic social ties	*individual values* (goals, preferences and *expectancies*) — improving and securing survival, wealth, status, comfort, stimulation, autonomy, affiliation and morality *individual resources:* — financial capital — human capital: educational credentials; professional skills — cultural capital: common worldviews, forecasts, memories, symbols — political capital: voice

Figure 7.1 Three Levels of Migration Analysis

amount of social capital eventually available to individuals depends on the extent of the network of social ties that can be mobilised and the amount of financial, cultural and political capital that members of collectives or network participants can muster. In short, social capital is created and accumulated in social relations, but can be used by individuals as a resource. Social capital is thus primarily a meso-level category.

The primary question concerning the meso-level is how social capital is created, accumulated and mobilised by collectives and networks, given certain macro-conditions. Moreover, how is this capital made available to individuals, members and non-members of these collectives? How does it serve to mobilise other forms of capital such as financial, cultural and political capital? It certainly makes a difference whether we deal with first-time movers, return movers or non-movers. For the sake of simplicity this section deals exclusively with first-time movers while the section on the dynamics of migration takes up the issue of return movers and their influence on decision making.

Analytically, we can distinguish three different macro-level dimensions for this relational analysis: functional considerations, normative expectations and collective identity (distinction based on Peters 1993; see also Habermas 1981). On the level of potential movers and stayers we can then make an ideal-typical distinction between interest-related, norm-oriented, and expressive behaviour and action. Along this typology we are then able to chart various forms of social capital that facilitate decision making in collectives and networks – exchange, reciprocity and solidarity (figure 7.2).

The first context in which social capital figures prominently is *exchange* relationships. This is the classical case analysed by rational-choice approaches. Accordingly, migrants move when they expect that they can reap higher benefits in another location. Persons who are involved in aiding these movers (facilitators) can also expect to benefit through material (e.g. money) and immaterial (e.g. social status) gains. Favours, information, approval and other valued items are given and received in transactions between movers and facilitators (e.g. pioneer movers who return to the place of origin). In the course of social interaction the movers, stayers and facilitators involved accumulate deposits based on previous favours by others, backed by the norm of reciprocity.

Reciprocity does not imply that favours given and received must be of the same value or identical. For example, in many cases the head of the family is responsible for the flow of the household income. Yet this

macro-level dimensions	functional considerations	normative expectations	collective identity
orientation of movers and stayers	interest-related	norm-oriented	expressive
forms of social capital	exchange	reciprocity	solidarity

Figure 7.2 The Meso-Level: Three Forms of Social Capital in Interpersonal Relations

does not mean that the head moves himself or herself in order to supply cash. Reciprocity is a form of social capital when at least two norms are adhered to: Firstly, persons help those who have helped them, and secondly, persons should not harm those who helped them before (Gouldner 1960). Reciprocity may serve to increase the financial capital available in collectives such as families or households. Migrant labour is a means to get much-needed cash to supplement income earned through crops. In case of crop failure income through labour migration can even act as a temporary substitute. In this case reciprocity would mean that, on the one hand, the moving family members remain loyal and actually send money back home and, on the other hand, the remaining family members work in the fields. *Trust* between members of relevant collectives such as families or households is a very valuable resource upholding reciprocity. This norm-related aspect of reciprocal transactions also refers to the third type of social capital, solidarity.

Solidarity is based on a group identity ('we') that refers to a unity of wanting and action. It is an expressive dimension to be distinguished from interest-based and norm-oriented behaviour. The group's self- and other-definition makes it meaningful to talk about the importance for potential movers that membership of a collective and participation in a network have.

Usually, transactions of the exchange type are characterised by weak social ties, while reciprocity and solidarity require strong social ties (Sahlins 1965). Yet norms of solidarity go with weak social ties, when individual or collective actors feel closely bound to ethnic, religious and national identities. Movers and recipients may be connected through *symbolic ties*, characterised by transactions based on shared worldviews, understandings, forecasts and memories. For example, in many African countries borders of nation-states are the result of drawing-board exercises by the former colonial powers, and arbitrarily cut across ethnic and linguistic groups. Refugees who cross international borders are often more generously received by groups with whom they share strong ethnic and linguistic affinities. The existence of symbolic ties across nation-states and the fact that most refugees in the South are movers with few resources explain why many refugees, especially in Africa, end up in countries adjoining the state of origin, and why only a minority ever moves on to countries in the North.

Taking Talcott Parson's distinction between *self-orientation and collectivity-orientation* as a point of departure (Parsons 1951: 60), we can further distinguish between migration decision making that is oriented towards the self and towards relevant collectives. Tensions can arise between, for example, occupational self-fulfilment and the expectation to contribute to the sustenance of the family in the country of origin, as Thomas and Znaniecki have amply demonstrated. For example, movers at the onset of political persecution could decide further to support their family (collectivity orientation) although imminent danger of being singled out as a target of violence strongly suggests that they move immediately, albeit individually. To complicate matters even further, potential movers are not only members of families but also citizens of a nation-state, members of religious or ethnic groups, etc. In short, they occupy several *roles*, i.e. there are *cross-cutting ties*.

The Difficult Transfer of Social Capital

In order to say what contributes to migration or enhances immobility, we have to start from the fundamental insight that many resources are *local assets* and transferring them to foreign countries would involve high *transferral costs*. This does not apply only to the transfer of human capital discussed earlier. Networks of social ties connect migrants to other migrants and natives in the receiving country (who hold various amounts of human, financial and political capital). It takes social capital to build such networks and substantial resources are required. It is quite time- and energy-consuming to construct or join new networks in the receiving country, especially in those cases where it is not the whole family that is moving. It is even more difficult to establish and join new collectives. Also, if a mover leaves behind family, friends and other important persons – relationships that are characterised by strong and affective social ties – it involves high costs to maintain these ties while abroad, for example economic costs (return trips) and psychological costs of adjustment to a new environment. Costs are especially high for pioneer migrants who cannot rely on established networks of movers to guide and facilitate their migration. Only if expected gains in transferring various forms of capital exceed perceived costs are potential migrants seriously encouraged to move. In sum, local assets that are undergirded by financial, human, political and social capital can lead a potential mover to prefer *in situ* adjustment in the sending country to adjustment abroad because transferral costs are high.

Secondly, *social capital is often a prerequisite for the accumulation and mobilisation of human, financial, cultural and political capital*. New social ties in the receiving countries have to be well established, before migrants can make use of their financial and human capital or that available to other migrants who may help them in finding work and housing. If there is no access to social capital, it is extremely difficult to invest resources such as money and skills in a beneficial way. This is especially true when there are no pioneer migrants and brokers who act as intermediaries for scarce resources. Moreover, without social capital there is no basis for a rich cultural life in migrant communities; for example, no religious institutions will be established. Similar things can be said about political participation. If migrants do not engage in collective action to voice their interests, they will probably face more discrimination in the receiving countries. For political voice, they need to form associations.

Therefore, we would expect that potential migrants prefer those forms of movement that allow them to keep their social ties intact (circular migration), to interrupt them only briefly (seasonal migration) or to transfer the whole set of important social ties abroad (e.g. family migration in the context of chain migration).

The First-Time Decision-Making Process

We may now conceptualise decision making and dynamics of movement in various networks and collectives. The most relevant units constituting meso-levels are households and families, groups of kinship, the reference community, but also friends and acquaintances in the work-place, and groupings such as ethnic, religious and political associations. Interest-guided survival strategies, normative obligations of family members to each other and expressions of collective identity are not mutually exclusive realms, the first relating to hard-core purposive (economic) action, the second to the soft fringe of social and the third to the even softer fringe of cultural action. We must analyse the set of social relations that structures decision making and the dynamics of migration, the social connectivity itself, the direct and indirect connections between actors. Here, we have to measure the density, strength, symmetry, range, and so on, of the ties that bind and the transaction and conversion costs and gains of various forms of capital. Furthermore, we must study the cultural content of functional imperatives and normative expectations.

Using the threefold typology developed earlier, we can hypothesise that exchange relationships, albeit asymmetrical regarding power and authority, may explain why family or household members engage in a division of labour and migration. Thanks to reciprocity as a form of social capital, household members can count on a fair division of burdens and benefits. As a subsistence and socialising unit, the house-hold allocates economic roles and assigns tasks according to age, sex and kinship ties. It may give incentives to household members – both at home and abroad – to forgo more immediate satisfactions and carry burdens in the expectation that migratory arrangements serve the household and its members in the long run through factors such as acquisition of land, durable consumer goods and improved human capital. Also, reciprocity could lead movers to continue sending remittances home although they do not intend to return. In cases of refugee flows social ties with actors in the country of origin are likely to be severed quite abruptly. Family members are often separated for long time periods. In these situations solidarity between family members really needs a basis in past practices and family bonds, including both reciprocity and solidarity as forms of social capital.

On a cautionary note it should always be remembered that families or households are defined by different economic, political, cultural, demographic and ecological settings and are not social units with universal behaviour (see chapter 8). For example, it certainly makes a difference whether we analyse movement from Africa to Europe or from Latin America to the United States as well as from various communities, regions or countries within these continents. Factors such as household size and expectations directed towards family members are likely to differ, not to speak of the variations pertaining to historical links between sending and receiving regions, current exit and admission policies, income, wage and unemployment differentials between sending and receiving countries.

The Dynamics of International Migration

So far, the main question has been why potential migrants decide either to stay or to go. If we consider the dynamics of moving, questions then arise as to what happens after the migrants have moved and why they return to the country of origin or stay in the receiving country. After an analysis of first-time decisions on moving or staying we shall now specify the causal mechanisms that allow us to follow subsequent developments in the flow of choice processes over time.

All the previous conceptual considerations on migration decision making at the different levels of households, kinship relations (e.g. families), friends and even larger groups suggest that there is a continuum along the definiteness of the break of social ties with the origin. Return migration is one case in which strong social ties between sending and receiving regions matter.

Historical evidence of earlier transatlantic migrations also attests to this thesis: While estimates vary and although most records of immigration are imprecise, return rates probably ranged from 25 to 60 per cent for European immigrants in the United States in the late nineteenth and early twentieth centuries (Piore 1979: 110). Sometimes, even permanent migrants retained strong ties with their rural regions of origin; they maintained their location-specific human and social capital, e.g. bought land, built houses, and contributed to village and city projects.

Furthermore, leaving and returning may not be decisions taken only once. Empirical research suggests that they occur repeatedly over the life course of a mover. This suggests that space in international migration is inadequately described by focusing solely on countries of origin and destination (see chapter 2). Rather, as international migration proceeds, transnational spaces unfold that cross-cut nation-states. A flow of people, goods, capital and services emerges. In sum, in addition to the interpersonal and inter-group dimension, all these aspects concern the intertemporal dimension of international migration.

Three questions have to be addressed: Firstly, how do networks of movers and stayers come into existence? Secondly, how do migration flows turn into 'chain migration' – migration as an established pattern that may depart from its original incentive? Thirdly, are there discernible patterns concerning the feedback effects on the sending side?

How Transnational Networks are Formed and Function

Exchange relationships partly account for network formation. Clearly, cost–benefit calculations could lead the actors involved to intensify social contacts. Migrant and refugee networks and organisations facilitate social and individual action in reducing information and transport costs as well as costs of integration in the country of destination. For example, migrants may get information about prospective employment by mail or telephone, and for refugees information about reception centres in potential destination countries may be a valuable resource. Also, exchange relations decrease the risk of not finding a job and income in the country of destination. Very often, movers know who awaits them and many probably already know their prospective employer.

For the brokers facilitating international migration, migrant networks can provide a lucrative business. Brokers can be pioneer migrants or refugees who capitalise on their experience, professionals in organisations concerned with labour recruitment, or respected individuals in the sending or receiving communities who facilitate or enable contacts of potential and actual migrants to employers and legal authorities. These brokers or gatekeepers thus turn into transnational entrepreneurs. They benefit through money or social debts incurred to them in the process of migration (exchange). Yet they are themselves constrained by social norms to respond to legitimate claims for assistance (reciprocity transactions). Exchange relationships can also be applied for sending-community strategies chosen. For example, inhabitants in some Mexican villages can best expect to reap results from international migration if they all agree to sponsor selected individuals for graduate studies in the

United States (Pries 1996). The individualised strategy would be illegal entry in the country of destination.

Reciprocity is another source of network formation. For example, when migrants arrive in the country of destination on prepaid tickets, they are expected to pay back the expenses defrayed beforehand. Often only informal agreements and not legal contracts undergird these kinds of transactions between movers and intermediaries. Solidarity may be a prime resource when the actors living and working abroad send back remittances or arrange for their family members to join them in the country of destination.

Access to migrant networks tends to be selective. Usually, it is not open for all members of a sending community. Access is governed by available information and financial resources, but also by (in)formal norms of reciprocity and solidarity. For potential movers to get access to migrant networks does not necessarily require everyday social inter-action and direct acquaintance within a community. Indirect social contacts maintained over large geographical distances may also work. Although there is no empirical evidence yet, we can draw on the 'strength of weak ties' (Granovetter 1973). The argument here is that weak ties may break more easily, but also transmit distant information on migration opportunities more efficiently under certain circumstances. For example, potential movers may remember persons in destination and sending countries with whom some kind of contact existed in the past, or who know friends who know migrants. These persons then serve as brokers of information or even gatekeepers for entry into the receiving countries, and access to jobs and housing. Those to whom potential movers are weakly tied are more likely to move in circles different from theirs and will thus have access to resources such as information different from that of the community of origin.

The value of networks for international movers and stayers differs, among other things, by the amount of human, financial, cultural and political capital available to the participants. We may hypothesise that if the amount of financial, human and cultural capital held by individuals or collectives forming a network is very low, networks may act to retard the adjustment of movers into the receiving nation-state (see also Pohjola 1991). The reason is that the capacity to employ social capital crucially depends on the amount of other forms of capital the respective network participants can muster. For example, a comparative study on Colombian and Dominican immigrants in New York City during the 1980s found that movers with higher amounts of human and financial capital were found to be less likely to rely on kin at the place of destination, while movers who had lower amounts of capital depended more on kinship networks to get established (Gilbertson and Gurak 1992). Among others, the latter group relied more heavily on relatives to assist them with housing upon arrival. They received assistance in seeking employment. The immigrants who reported heavy assistance from family networks when they arrived were also found to be culturally and socially much less integrated in New York. They had less language ability and held lower-status jobs.

Not only individuals can participate in networks but also collectives such as households, kinship groups or organisations (figure 7.3). Networks with strong ties may constitute secure environments that not only supply valuable information and provide emotional encouragement (or the opposite!) but often arrange for the subsequent move of members from various collectives. Once migrants have arrived at their destination, these collectives lend valuable assistance in adjusting to the new environment, especially in finding housing and employment. Also, the migrant networks in which collectives participate need not only consist of migrants themselves. Often, patron–client relationships emerge in the employment field between natives and newcomers.

Finally, the strongest form of regularization of social interaction is found in various organisations in the field of international migration, which for their purposes apply institutional rules and resources. These may be transnational companies sending personnel abroad (e.g. management and/or construction workers), labour-recruitment agencies (often supervised or even run by state institutions in Asian sending countries), or human-rights organisations in the countries of origin and destination which extend shelter. The most regularised forms of migrant selection

Networks of Movers and Stayers	Organisations
– sending networks: aid with travel arrangements, financial support, etc. – illegal intermediaries (e.g. smugglers)	– elite institutional networks (e.g. transnational corporations) – legal/extra-legal agencies (e.g. recruitment bureaus) – state labour recruitment (e.g. national labour offices) – refugee-aid organisations (e.g. UNHCR and privately sponsored associations)
– receiving networks: aid with legal systems, housing, jobs, schooling, capital for enterprises, language training	– support associations in the receiving country (e.g. human-rights organisations)

Figure 7.3 Networks of Movers and Stayers and Organisations in International Migration

are labour recruitment directly performed by the receiving country in the sending countries (e.g. German labour-office authorities in Turkey during the 1960s), or the selection of refugees in camps near the region of origin (e.g. Canadian government in Africa since the 1980s).

Chain Migration and Relative Deprivation

At some point in migration processes, networks sustain population flows in ways that are less dependent on objective economic-political conditions in the areas of origin and destination (for example, see Shah 1994a: 34). The hypothesis would be that, once the number of network connections reaches a certain level, international movements become self-perpetuating because they create the social structure necessary to sustain them. In other words, it is likely that networks of circular migration – a regular circuit in which migrants retain claims and contacts and routinely return home – transform themselves into *chain migration* – the following of related individuals or households ('friends and relatives effect'). The processes can be described as a 'snowball' effect: The more immigrants of a given place and state in the destination region, the more want to come. It takes time to develop the chain and this is the reason why we see it fully-fledged only in later phases of international migration. When the accumulated capital finds better opportunities for investment and exchange in the countries of destination, and brokers and gatekeepers find worthwhile benefits in advising and channelling movers (exchange relationships), when norms of reciprocity can be enforced (e.g. money remitted to family) and when forms of mutual aid among migrants create broad commitments to other migrants (solidarity), networks of movers and stayers begin to flourish.

For this to occur, those not yet migrating need to receive information from earlier migrants, or even to see the concrete results of the ventures of those who migrated before. Therefore, (pioneer) return migrants play an important role in spreading information on opportunities regarding where to go, work and live.

However, this does not answer the question of how the process of chain migration starts, given favourable macro-conditions. To name norms, motives, preferences and various forms of capital that guide the behaviour of potential movers does not suffice to account for a phenomenon such as chain migration. We might compare places of origin that are very similar regarding both people's preferences to move or stay and the opportunity structures they are faced with. Yet it has been repeatedly observed that the number of people moving abroad from two most similar villages in this regard is not seldom vastly different. In this virtually unexplored area, *threshold* models of collective behaviour could be used to give situation-specific explanations of moving and staying that do not explain outcomes solely in terms of structures, goals and expectancies of actors before the movement begins (Granovetter 1978). Only when we view decisions on moving and staying as being also dependent upon the number or proportion of other potential movers, who must make the decision before another stayer does so, can we start to understand the process of chain migration. The cost-benefit calculations involved in threshold behaviour are easiest to follow in the case of strong, symbolic and affective social ties, for example when all family members move to live together abroad.

Migration may bring about more migration by changes in social status and income distribution. *Relative deprivation* theory posits that individual and household satisfaction arise not only from improvements in absolute economic status but also through comparison with other actors in the reference community. If a potential migrant's level of income is low, the level of motivation to exit will also be low as long as incomes are low across the board. However, if some actors in the reference community experience an increase, then a poor actor will feel relatively deprived. This can be a direct effect of migration. When household members migrate abroad for work, they earn higher incomes than those available locally, and when they send money home, they increase the amount of income available at the top of the income distribution in the country of origin. This may lead to more international migration. Relative deprivation need not necessarily relate only to income but also to ways of life. For example, in a way that is poorly understood, cultural norms of potential migrants have evolved in the Caribbean to form a veritable 'culture-of-migration' (Marshall 1982).

One of the key elements introduced by economists into the analysis has been the so-called '*inverted U-curve*' thesis: development often first enhances and thereafter reduces the scope and incentives for migration (see chapter 4). This inverted U-curve depends upon external factors such as the level of income (economic development). In addition, we could also speculate about an '*s-shaped curve*' concerning the social diversity of migration (figure 7.4). An s-shaped curve would depend upon factors that arise from the very process of migration itself, i.e. that are internal to migration processes.

Massey et al. (1994) found in research on Mexico–US migration that social diversity was low in the initial stages of migration, increased dramatically during the intermediate stages, and then stayed constant or fell slightly as a level of mass migration was reached. In this view migration begins with a narrow range of each community's socio-economic structure, but over time broadens to incorporate other social groups. How could we explain this s-shaped pattern?

The Crucial Meso-Level

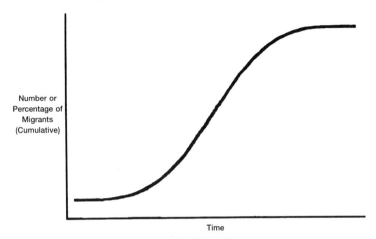

Figure 7.4 A Stylised S-Shaped Migration Curve

In an initial period, migration turns into a self-feeding process that gradually encompasses more and more groups and social classes from a local community because of declining costs. In a second period, the movement becomes somewhat independent of economic conditions in the host country as immigrants acquire social benefits in the receiving country and as family reunification and marriage migration quicken due to guaranteed civil rights and the establishment of immigrant communities. This contributes both to rising numbers of migrants and to less selectivity as to social class. At this stage even children and older kin migrate in growing numbers. There could be spill-over effects even to relatives and friends in other communities in the same country of origin. In a third phase, migration may become more selective again; this time in favour of groups that have been underrepresented in the beginning (e.g. members of lower-class or lower-status groups from remote parts of the sending regions). Finally, in a fourth period, as migration has captured virtually all groups and classes, the value of migration declines for potential migrants. Those who could not migrate are not only relatively but also absolutely deprived and even socially and economically marginalised in the community. Yet all those who could participate in migration had a chance trying to overcome their sense of relative deprivation *vis-à-vis* the early movers. As the migrant potential is gradually exhausted in the sending communities, some migrants settle in the country of destination, some return to the country of origin for good — and others, probably a minority, may continue to move back and forth for extended periods of time. Eventually, the volume declines again.

Thomas Faist

Cumulative Causation: Feedback Effects in the Sending Regions

Some of the feedback effects of migration that lead to further migration are part of a process called *cumulative causation*, dating back to Gunnar Myrdal's use of the term. As is clearly seen by the 'new economics of migration', temporary migration may be a strategy of risk diversification in rural households. Foreign wages sometimes lead farmers to farm their land less intensively than before or even let it lie fallow. If these migrants buy land, the outcome might be that there is less land under intensive cultivation in the community, that local food production is reduced, the price of staple crops raised and the demand for labour decreased. These consequences may give incentives to the remaining members of the community to move, too.

Also, if land is more intensively cultivated, as farmer migrants can now afford more capital, this could lead to more out-movement because less manual labour is needed (Massey 1990). However, remittances spent on agriculture could actually increase agricultural profits. In some Mexican villages, for example, the money from 'El Norte' has helped to develop productivity and output, and migrant farmers have even been able to keep marginal land under production (Cornelius 1991: 108). In this latter case we could not expect economic feedback effects to encourage further migration.

Even very high and increasing levels of migration do not necessarily imply the exodus of virtually all potential movers or the settlement of all movers in the receiving country. Assets and capital may be location-specific and the transferral costs of social and other capitals may keep the volume lower than expected.

As to return rates, movers may maintain social ties with the sending region and build new ones in the receiving country. Caces and others have tried to capture the first phenomenon on the household or family level by using the concept of the *shadow household*. It includes 'all individuals whose principal commitments and obligations are to a particular household but who are not presently residing in that household' (Caces et al. 1985: 8). The intensity of their commitments or obligations can be operationalised as indicators of household affiliation. Of course, they may differ from one culture to another, and depend on the closeness of kinship and other social or symbolic ties that keep the family or household together.

Therefore, decisions over moving or staying made by families and individuals not only influence later decisions made by other individuals and households but also the long-term social and economic arrangements within the families, households and the sending communities. Furthermore, changes in the networks and collectives in the country of origin could be expected during the absence of movers and upon their return. For example, migration may entail the reallocation of responsibilities which ultimately impact on the roles and status of household members. In the absence of male adult members of the household, the gendered division of labour may change, as women may take over additional roles, or vice versa. Female contract workers from Indonesia in the oil-exporting countries of the Gulf have often spent months away from their families, and special arrangements have been made for the care of their children. In addition, there is empirical evidence that the traditional division of labour along gender lines has broken down as women have taken pride in autonomy and competence in handling family affairs in the absence of their husbands, or as men have taken more responsibility in childrearing during the overseas employment of their wives or as women have increased their involvement in financial affairs upon returning home (Hugo 1995).

Women more than men may be willing to settle in the receiving countries. For example, male and female migrants from a Mexican village in the United States in the late 1980s differed strongly in their responses to whether they planned to return to Mexico on a relatively permanent basis. In general, women looked much less favourably than men on the idea of returning to live in Mexico. It could be that women may not get a job on the formal labour market there, and that women's housework in the Mexican countryside generally involves more drudgery than it does in US cities. For men, however, rural Mexico represents a place where tradition is adhered to and men can be men through either work or leisure activities, while the United States remain the place of work, proletarian and spatial discipline, and diminished male authority (Goldring 1995).

On the community level in the country of origin the feedback effects can be conceptualised as virtuous and vicious cycles: In some cases a *virtuous cycle* evolves because migration eases the pressure on land and labour. Remittances enable subsistence. However, one also has to consider that the dependence on harvests or crop price is replaced by one on urban wages. Moreover, not only economically, but also politically, this may strengthen the voice option. This is especially the case when members of groups opposing the political regime in the country of origin move back and forth between the two regions. Even political campaigning may take place in the country of destination, e.g. Dominicans in New York City and Algerians in France. Refugees in the country of destination may stay in contact with political activists in the sending country. Sikh secessionists in the United Kingdom and Kurdish activists in Germany constitute clear-cut examples of this.

It is equally plausible that a *vicious cycle* evolves. When labour migration grows in importance, this works against economic and political co-operation at the village level. Financially, external links might become the most significant and the nexus of social pressures and economic imperatives that held a subsistence-oriented village together could weaken. Here, new forms of solidarity and reciprocity may arise – as described by Thomas and Znaniecki (1918–20). If efforts to build mutually beneficial arrangements of exchange, reciprocity and solidarity fail, however, social disorganisation may ensue that rules out the mutuality and the shared poverty, replacing it with involution and mutual hostility. What Edward Banfield has termed 'amoral familism' in Southern Italy is perhaps the accumulation of migration feedback effects in a village that became economically marginal. According to Banfield this effect has been produced by three factors acting in unison: a high death rate – and important for our context – certain land tenure conditions and the absence of the institution of the extended family (Banfield 1958: 10).

The Importance of Change and *Stability*

One hypothesis is: the stronger the commitment of migrants to social units in the country of origin (not only in terms of strength of social ties – weak and strong – but also regarding the content – reciprocity and solidarity), the more likely it is that return migration of successful migrants takes place. In turn, the higher the rate of this kind of return migration, the greater the likelihood that positive economic feedback effects occur.

To determine the rates of return, we have to ask to what degree the goals of the actual movers could be fulfilled while living abroad and whether a change in their preferences has taken place in the course of their absence from the sending place. Firstly, high rates of return migration may attest to the fact of the successful achievement of some goals involved (e.g. transfer of remittances and skills). Or, alternatively, it could be an indicator that the goals aspired to could not be achieved, a sign of failure. Secondly, return may also indicate the existence, maintenance and further development of social ties that bind movers to those left behind, sometimes despite the strains and changes created by international mobility. It would indeed be unwarranted to assume that potential and actual movers can only maintain social ties to either side, the sending or the receiving country. Therefore, it is feasible to assume that migrants use social capital to retransfer various other forms of capital.

In an age of increasing international migration we can also observe that migrants not only cultivate social ties to the area of origin but, simultaneously, also in the country of destination. At first sight, this is somewhat counterintuitive. There is a continuum regarding social ties between temporary commuting and circulation, on the one hand, and permanent emigration and immigration, on the other hand. Commuting and circulation are terms that denote a great variety of movement, usually short-term, repetitive or cyclical in nature, but all having in common the lack of any declared intention of a permanent or long-lasting change in residence. They imply few breaks of links with the place of origin and little distance regarding the political, economic and cultural sphere. At the other end of the continuum, permanent emigration and thus immigration are more likely to change significantly the character of social ties and involve greater economic, political and cultural distances. Regarding short-term movements we would expect a higher degree of a sojourning orientation (e.g. towards seasonal and cyclical movement) than in the case of permanent settlement in the country of destination (Tilly 1978).

The intentions of migrants to stay are relatively clear-cut, if we differentiate between those who intend to stay permanently and those who come temporarily. However, there are labour migrants or refugees who did not come to stay permanently, but eventually settle and still indicate that they wish to return to their homeland. This phenomenon has often been referred to as the *'illusion' of return*. In these cases we must look not only at the social ties of migrants to persons in the sending countries, but also at the symbolic ties, namely the set of collective representations (e.g. religious symbols), memories, forecasts and worldviews that migrants perceive to have in common with those in the sending countries. The prevalence of symbolic ties, a basis for cultural capital, is one important element in the explanation of actual settlement and declared return.

In short, it is the differential strength and the content of social and symbolic ties of movers to the place of origin as well as destination that can be used to classify different types of spatial mobility on the domestic and international level across different administrative units such as nation-states. However, transnational social spaces suggest that even more permanent settlement in the receiving country does not necessarily imply a complete rupture of social ties and other forms of linkages.

The existence of *transnational social spaces* attests to the ability of movers creatively to pattern their occupational and personal experience. In this perspective it would often seem appropriate to talk of transnational migrants instead of emigrants and immigrants. We need to develop concepts that can not only be applied in either the sending or the receiving regions but can also refer to emerging transnational social linkages, such as those between Algeria and France, India and the United

Kingdom, Turkey and Germany, and Mexico and the Caribbean and the United States. Glick-Schiller and her associates give a vivid picture of social ties in transnational spaces:

> Whether the transnational activity is sending the barbecue to Haiti, dried fruits and fabric back home to Trinidad so these goods can be prepared for a wedding in New York, or using the special tax status of Balikbayan boxes to send expensive goods from the United States to families back home in the Philippines, the constant and various flows of such goods and activities have embedded within them relationships between people. These social relations take on meaning within the flow and fabric of daily life, as linkages between different societies are maintained, renewed, and reconstituted in the context of families, of institutions, of economic investments, business, and finance and of political organizations and structures including nation-states. (Glick-Schiller et al. 1992: 11)

Towards a Meso-level in International Migration

This analysis suggests that answers to pressing issues of international migration can be found in supplementing the dominant micro- and macro-sociological theories and including an explicit social relational perspective. Conceptual meso-levels introduce a distinct layer of analysis to the already rich empirical literature working on this level. Ironically, the study that comes closest to the social relational concepts advanced in this appraisal is the one that stood at the beginning of the sociology of international movement, namely William I. Thomas's and Florian Znaniecki's theoretical-empirical study on *The Polish Peasant in Europe and America*. These authors have posed the core questions of staying or moving and the feedback effects in a way that also deserves much more attention than it has received lately. Looking at moving and staying as both an interpersonal and an intertemporal process, we can analyse first-time moves, repeated migration and return migration with the same conceptual tools.

Using these tools we come to realise not only that territorial exit is one of several possible strategies to respond to declining or increasing opportunities. *In situ* adjustment and change have to be considered as well. We also pay more attention to the importance of local assets, high transaction costs for social capital and the difficulties involved in converting various forms of social capital because they do not seem to be traded in a common 'currency'. Also, the analysis of transnational social spaces developing within migration systems offers a way to study the transfer and retransfer of various forms of capital.

Moreover, various forms of migration and economic mobility always have to be complemented by the possibility for voice. Sometimes voice is directly or indirectly one of the immediate causes for moving, as in the case of persecution. And even in the case of labour migrants the feedback effects of migration on opportunities to express voice can be important. For example, political activists move between and within both the sending and receiving countries. The current conflicts surrounding the political role of Islam in West European and North American countries is a vivid case in point. One of the questions to be addressed is to what degree these conflicts are transferred from the sending to the receiving country, and to what extent these politicisation processes are outcomes of migrant adjustment to new centres of work and life.

—8—

Gender and Reproduction
Gunilla Bjerén

Anthropology, Migration and Development

The favoured objects of study in the early days of academic social anthropology were small-scale communities in distant places in the parts of the world that in this book are subsumed under the heading 'South'. The picture drawn of these communities was often timeless and bounded; as if they had changed little since time immemorial and had had as little contact with the outside world. It is only from the 1960s on that anthropology in earnest has turned some of its attention to urban centres and so-called 'complex societies' and to the dynamics of change and interaction in rural areas.

The reasons for this new focus of interest were linked to migration. Rural–urban migration in the South brought anthropologists to towns and cities along with their informants; in Europe labour migration and refugees from Southern countries landed the informants on the anthropologists' own doorsteps (Hannerz 1980: 1). But even though rural–urban and international migration played an increasing role in anthropological studies, the discipline developed few theoretical notions of migration as such. 'Modern' migration was regarded as part and parcel of what was called 'social change'. Theoretical interest was rather focused on 'social change' as such, a phenomenon which in retrospect greatly resembles the process that in this book figures as 'development'.

'Development', in the loose sense of an improvement in material condition and general well-being in an entire population, is often seen either as the result of a process of economic, social and cultural globalisation whereby local societies and economies are brought into and integrated with the world economic system, or as that process itself. However, the 'globalisation' process might result in an increase in GNP for the national economy[1] while at the same time causing havoc in local

---

1. The conventional measure of 'development', also used in this book.

economies. There are many examples of loss of autonomy and livelihood opportunities due to the ravages of the 'development' process on local scenes or for particular segments of the population (Tinker 1990).

The contentious, fragmented and contradictory character of development and the dependence of migration on it are partial reasons why anthropology offers no grand theories of migration and development despite the large number of empirical studies focusing on migration and development in the discipline (Eades 1985, Kearney 1986). Other reasons are based on the reluctance of many anthropologists to formulate any kind of theories divorced from actual contexts, a reluctance based on anthropological research practice which will be discussed later in this chapter.

In anthropological migration research, there have been frequent references to the distinction between 'rate' and 'incidence' of migration (after Mitchell 1959). The rate of migration would be determined by structural aspects of a historical situation, which form the 'necessary conditions for migration' in Mitchell's vocabulary. The rate of migration is measured on the 'macro'-level of society and is the focus of interest for several of the other chapters in this book.

In contrast, the incidence of migration – who actually moves and who stays – can be thought to belong to the 'meso'-level of society (chapter 7). This is the societal level where most anthropological migration research is carried out. At this level migration, and immobility, can be understood as the spatial aspect of relations between individuals and groups in the flow of time. Such relations are informed by culture-specific rules that apply to groups of people sharing the same culture;[2] they are further elaborated on a sub-cultural or ethnic level by smaller groups sharing more specific identities. The cultural rules, or 'script', that generate and order social relations are a major topic of study for social and cultural anthropologists, although admittedly the spatial aspects of cultural scripts have not been a major focus so far.

The metaphor of a cultural 'script' is used to describe dynamic processes. Cultural scripts are not given once and for all; they are continuously revised and rewritten. New lines are borrowed, changed and amalgamated to existing ones. Migration from areas dominated by one cultural syndrome to others, for instance, induces cultural innovation and elaboration. 'Culture' is neither uniform in a given population, nor

---

2. I use 'culture' as a term for the cosmology, norms, values and practices that are shared by a (relatively) bounded collective at a given time. See also the discussion about culture-specific social rules above. The idea of 'sharing the same culture', however, is not as self-evident in contemporary anthropology as it used to be (Hannerz 1992, Appadurai 1991).

are individuals inevitably bound by the scripts of the culture they are raised in. The culture of a group affects its migration patterns in many different ways. Some of these ways will become apparent through the examples given in the rest of this chapter.

The chapter is organised around three aspects of the question 'Why do, and why don't, people move from South to North?'. The first aspect relates to 'people' and draws attention to the fact that migration is a *gendered process*, which means that the different positions of women and men in society are reflected in international migration. The second aspect relates to 'why do, and why don't' and focuses on the spatial consequences of *human reproduction* and on the culture-specific character of the social organisation surrounding reproduction. The third aspect also deals with the 'why do, and why don't' question and hints at complications in the spatial aspects of *the search for livelihood*. But first of all, some comments on the anthropological scientific endeavour.

Anthropological Thinking and Practice

Social anthropology prides itself on taking a *holistic* view of societies and social processes. An anthropological approach requires an explicit understanding of how the process under study is related to other vital processes and phenomena. One might say that anthropology is the antithesis of disciplines which base their arguments on *ceteris paribus*[3] conditions. In anthropological thinking 'other conditions' can never be assumed to be equal or irrelevant.

A preoccupation with the context of social and cultural phenomena is related to the holistic ambition of anthropology. In relation to the possibility of general theories of cultures and societies, two positions are discernible within the discipline. One is that social processes cannot be understood severed from the historical, economic, cultural, etc. context within which the processes occur, and that general theories about a process such as 'migration' therefore are not possible. The other position is that there are cross-contextual regularities in social processes that allow for conclusions with applicability beyond the singular context (Harris 1968).

The source of the contextual knowledge imperative for anthropological analyses comes primarily from *ethnographic fieldwork*. The essence of fieldwork in anthropology is that the researcher herself is present in 'the field' for extended periods of time, acquiring the cultural and social competence necessary to communicate with the persons around her, gradually coming to an understanding of their points of view

3. 'all other conditions being equal'.

and eventually reaching a point at which she is able to gather information of many different kinds to account for the core phenomenon under study. Understanding and attempting to present the *standpoint of the 'other'*, the person under study, is an ambition close to the heart of the anthropological research venture. Cross-cultural *comparison* is another cornerstone of the discipline.

'Migration' as a topic for academic study cross-cuts all social science disciplines; there is consequently considerable interdisciplinary borrowing of concepts and ideas. Nevertheless, the accustomed division of labour between disciplines means that all disciplines inevitably engage in 'black-boxing' – ignoring conditions on some level while focusing on another. Making analytical detours around some black boxes is necessary to allow for in-depth analysis of whatever subject matter constitutes the *tour de force* of a given discipline. The assumption is that if the black box were to be opened for inspection, the earlier analysis would not be invalidated.

The way in which research is conducted sets boundaries for what can – and cannot – be learnt in social science. Through fieldwork, the anthropologist has the possibility of achieving a (for social scientists[4]) exceptional understanding of the processes at work in the community under study. By being able to observe, the researcher avoids the exclusive reliance on spoken, or written, accounts that mar most social science practices. Since the researcher, as a person, interacts with real people, relations between variables is not in focus in most anthropological investigations, although findings often include statements about such relations.

On the other hand, the dominant mode of empirical research in the social sciences, through large-scale surveys,[5] is entirely focused on the uncovering of relations between variables. All the same, inference about thinking and behaviour of people is often made from the very slim empirical base of surveys and censuses.[6]

Large-scale social surveys are certainly necessary in migration research since it is only through such studies that the relative (quantitative) importance of different phenomena, the distribution of characteristics and the relationship between variables can be ascertained. However, the limitations imposed by the method of investigation must be respected for the results to be valid. The same holds true for detailed studies of social

---

4. Extended fieldwork and participant observation belong to the methodological tools of other disciplines as well; in social anthropology they are a *sine qua non* for the aspiring scholar.

5. With little or no contact between researcher and researched.

6. It may seem strange to describe large-scale data as forming 'slim' empirical bases. However, there is always a trade-off between depth and numbers. Uncovering meaning, motivation and reasoning requires depth and context.

contexts, where the fascination of the complexity of life may make it difficult for the researcher to step back and free herself from the idiosyncrasies of an individual setting or situation. The challenge for the anthropologist is to comprehend the logic of a situation which will allow for statements of a more general kind, while not falling into the trap of undue generalisations based on the knowledge of a limited number of cases.

Where It Really Happens: Gender, Reproduction and the Search for a Livelihood

The Gender Aspect of Migration was Neglected for a Long Time

One area where the anthropological contribution to migration research has been particularly influential is in contributing to a focus on *gender* in empirical migration studies.

Gender was for a long time an ignored social relation in general migration research. The visible migrant in social research was a man, a young man, just as he had been in Dorothy Swaine Thomas's findings in the 1920s. However, conditions have changed, and women make up an increasing proportion of many international migration streams. Migration researchers in general were slow to wake up to this fact, but there now exists a considerable body of literature relating to women in migration.[7] The body of findings focusing on gender in South to North migration have come up with the following general conclusions:

> that women form a large part of many migration streams, but not all;
> that women are also *labour migrants,* that is, they move
> independently with the aim of finding economic opportunities for
> themselves, but their opportunities are very different from those
> of men;
> that women move in many different ways, one of which is to
> move as dependants (wives, daughters, mothers);
> that *men* also can be found among migrants who migrate because
> of marriage;
> that on the whole, the migration of women and men *differs* in
> many dimensions.
> The inevitable conclusion is that migration is *a gender-
> differentiated process* and must be understood as such.

---

7. For contributions to and reviews of some of this literature see Phizacklea (1983), Morokvasic (1983), Kearney (1986), Pedraza (1991), Tienda and Booth (1991), Chant and Radcliffe (1992), Buijs (1993).

Gunilla Bjerén

These conclusions have cast a dour shadow over the large number of empirical studies and theoretical arguments that have not taken gender into account. If migration is seen as a gender-differentiated process, it follows that all descriptions and analyses that do not take gender into account give faulty pictures and lead to doubtful conclusions. Since women and men have different migration patterns, a description that merges data for women and men catches the characteristics of neither. However, despite the bulk of research proving the 'gendered' character of migration, and the long time – twenty years and more – that such studies have been available, a consistent gender perspective is still not the rule.[8] Gender awareness travels within and between disciplines slowly. Consider, for instance, the following quotation: 'Migration research, like much of social research, is only beginning to redress a severe imbalance that is the legacy of the male domination of the profession . . . Most books and articles purporting to deal with the migration of people in fact focus on the migration of men' (Gugler and Ludwar-Ene 1995: 257).

Josef Gugler, a prolific writer on African migration since the end of the 1960s, has, in his own words, actively contributed to the neglect of women in migration. He is in no way typical in his recanting of old sins; many prominent researchers have not yet discovered the fundamental importance of gender differentiation and gender relations in the causes, forms and effects of migration, international or otherwise.

How is it possible, then, for a researcher like Gugler to write about the migration of 'people' for such a long time without discovering the importance of gender? What is concealed in the black box of 'male dominance in the social research profession'? Let me briefly point to two related aspects.

The first has to do with the relative status of women in society, a status which in most instances has been described as lower than that of men. Although current ideas about the uniformity and shape of women's subordination leaves room for considerable variation and complexity, there is no denying that in many aspects women are underprivileged in relation to men. The status of women in society is reflected in the status of 'women-related' topics in research. Gender is such a women-related topic. Because of the low importance accorded this and similar topics, literature in the area is little referred to outside the circle of involved researchers, who most often are women themselves. The 'state of the art' is then that a majority of male authors write about migration in mainstream literature as if gender did not matter, while many women

8. Evidence of this is that *all* the references in note 7 include phrases about the neglect of gender relations in migration research in general.

authors deliver fatal criticism of main(male!)stream research from a gender perspective but are little read outside their own circle and their criticism makes little impact on the main body of knowledge.

The second aspect deals with the mechanisms by which mainstream migration researchers have failed to appreciate the significance of gender in their own work. The following are some of the most obvious:[9]

Men are still seen as the most significant migrants. This misconception is based on a time lag combined with a 'majority bias'. Women make up an increasingly higher proportion of migration flows. In explanations of migrations dynamics, however, 'mostly men then' often translates into 'all men now'. Zlotnik points out (in 1995!) that the gender aspect of migration has been ignored to the extent that available statistics still make it difficult to distinguish the balance between men and women in individual migration streams. She concludes all the same that the participation of women in the international migration directed to developed nations is of major importance. In several migration streams, women outnumber men, and where they do not, the dominant trend is towards more balanced sex ratios. 'International migration from South to North cannot be understood unless women become visible both in terms of statistics and as major actors in the migration process' (Zlotnik 1995: 252).

Men are thought of as 'breadwinners' and women as 'dependants' – which makes men 'primary' migrants (and decision makers) and women (and children) passive joiners. The migration of 'everybody' can then supposedly be explained by the conditions surrounding the migration of men. The perception of women as passive dependants, in addition, might have serious policy consequences for women's opportunities to make a living for themselves in Northern countries (Boyd 1995).

There is a close relation between migration research and policy which has put a premium on the study of *labour* migration, thereby excluding all actors who have been thought to be marginal to the formal, regular labour market. Despite the fact that (legal) labour immigration to Europe, for instance, has virtually ceased, male labour migration still forms the framework for many migration theories (Morokvasic 1984). The identification of labour migration with *male* labour also means that the significant labour migration of women has been ignored.

What is a 'Gender Aspect' and How Does Gender Affect Migration?

So far I have written as if 'gender' were a concept that needed no further explanation and as if the content of 'gender relations' were self-

9. Cf. Zlotnik 1995: 229.

explanatory. However, these concepts are still the subject of discussion within the social sciences. What follows is but a brief presentation of a concept of considerable complexity.

The term 'gender' was introduced into the social sciences by anthropologists in the 1970s to underline the difference between biologically and socially determined sex (Rubin 1975). Biologically, most persons can be unambiguously identified as either male or female. This fact, however, has no cultural or social meaning in itself. Whatever else is genetically implied by the biological differences between women and men, the plasticity of the human being is such that the meaning of being a woman or a man, and the roles and characteristics pertaining to each, is largely constructed by the culture into which the new-born is enculturated.[10] The resulting woman or man is a cultural interpretation of a biological difference.

> [G]ender ... designates a set of categories to which we can give the same label cross-linguistically, or cross-culturally, because they have some connections to sex differences. These categories are, however, conventional or arbitrary insofar as they are not reducible to, or directly derivative of, natural, biological facts; they vary from one language to another, one culture to another, in the way in which they order experience and action. (Shapiro 1981: 449, quoted in Yanagisako and Collier 1987: 33)

The gender concept is valid beyond the individual, although it is a considerable leap to think of gender as being also a property of collectivities, institutions and historical processes (Connell 1987: 139). For example, migration can be seen as a process that is fundamentally influenced by the gender differentiation of social, cultural and economic life and which therefore must be considered a 'gendered' process.

Despite the fact that 'gender' is a relational concept – the one gender being construed in relation to the other – 'gender research' has often centred on women. During the last few years attention has finally been directed also towards men (Connell 1995). In the final analysis, however, the actions and intentions of men as well as of women are based on the *relations* between genders, and these relations are omnipresent, in all areas of human life and in all human organisations. *The migration of men as well as of women is predicated on the time/space strategies of persons of the other sex.* That is why the neglect of women in migration research has been so fatal; not only because women make up a large number of the migrants but because the mobility of men will be misunderstood if not seen in relation to the mobility of women.

10. Enculturation: the transmission of socio-cultural traits from one generation to the next by means of learning (Harris 1971: 632). In other social science disciplines often referred to as 'socialisation'.

The idea of a 'correct' gender order is an integrated part of the worldview of any culture and has therefore a strong ideological backing. The gender order is maintained through social practices which reproduce and embody ideas about how men and women are, and what men and women should do, in people's daily lives and life-long biographies.

Migration, the 'Household' and the 'Family'

Integral to the idea of any gender order are firm beliefs about how human reproduction should take place. Just as social anthropology has played a major role in exploring the variability in gender relations between and within cultures, variation in the social organisation of reproduction has been a prominent theme in anthropological research (Robertson 1991). Gender differentiation in migration patterns is often the result of the different roles, responsibilities and power that women and men have in relation to reproduction.

This is because there is a definite relationship between the reproductive process and mobility. For one thing, there is an existential relationship between migration and reproduction in that human beings are born into space and time; all our actions leave traces in space as well as time.[11] There are other, more immediate, ways in which migration is implied in reproductive processes and relations. I shall discuss two such implications, namely (1) the spatial consequences of the social organisation of reproduction; (2) migrants as members of households and families.

Migration and the Social Organisation of Reproduction

Reproduction is a dynamic process covering several generations. This process is at the heart of social life. It is a process embedded in culture as rules to govern reproduction have evolved in all societies, rules that form the basis of kinship systems, caste systems, rules that control the distribution of land and other property, that regulate the size and growth rate of populations, etc. *ad infinitum*. There is great variation in the rules that direct reproduction in different cultural settings, rules that themselves continue to change and evolve.

'Reproduction', however, is not a unidimensional concept. The concept can be used to refer to at least two analytically distinct processes: the reproduction of people as physical beings, and the social reproduction of people with identities and characteristics prescribed by a given social and cultural context (Moore 1994: 89).

---

11. Creating in the process the life trajectories mentioned in chapter 2.

Gunilla Bjerén

Reproducing People: Demographic Migrations

The reproduction of people is governed by cultural rules and norms in all societies. These rules indicate at what time and with whom culturally accepted mating should take place, where and with whom people should live, who should be responsible for the care of the young and the aged and so on. These rules have been called the 'procedural norms'[12] of a given culture (Robertson 1991: 19). Many of these norms prescribe geographical moves for the individuals involved, as residential rules do, for instance. Figure 8.1 depicts the *dynamic character* of reproductive units, how they develop as the constituent members are born, mature, age and die.

Figure 8.1 Stages in the development of a compact household (after Robertson 1991: 12). Points in time where a move is likely to occur are marked by a ♣.

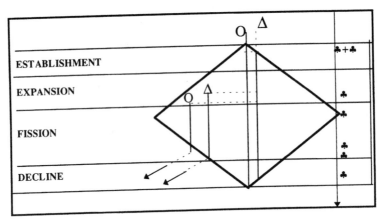

Comments: The figure shows the development of an ideal type compact family/household through *establishment* when a woman (O) and a man (Δ) form a conjugal couple, *expansion* when a daughter and a son are born, *fission* when the children leave the family/household and *decline* when the original spouses die.

The points at which geographical moves are likely to occur in this particular case are at marriage (because of a residence rule prescribing e.g. neolocality*), at the consecutive births of children (because of ideals of space and separation of family members), at the maturation of children (because of ideals about independence between generations) and at old age (the points are marked with ♣ in the diagram above).

* Neolocal: 'Residence of a couple after marriage in a new household not linked spatially to that of the groom or the bride' (Keesing 1976: 562).

12. '"Procedural norms" of domestic developments measure off a household's progress through the different stages and exert strong social pressure urging individuals along in their domestic careers (Robertson 1991: 19). Needless to say, these procedural norms have a heavy gender content since they prescribe appropriate behaviour of people according to their gender.

Mobility that is caused by transitions during the reproductive careers of individuals and households is termed *demographic mobility* by geographers and demographers. Demographic mobility is assumed to be over relatively short distances (Warnes 1992: 175ff).

However, international migration streams challenge such assumptions. Marriage migration is one case in point (Watts 1983). Many 'ethnic' groups[13] maintain strong endogamic preferences[14] also when residing far away from the main concentrations of culturally preferred marriage partners. The combination of group members residing in different international territories and endogamy rules will produce a traffic in grooms and brides – in both directions, as the diaspora community[15] looks homeward for properly enculturated marriage partners and as a returnee will find himself/herself more highly valued on the marital market at home than in the community residing abroad.

From a cross-cultural perspective, demographic migration includes two distinct components. One is the *life-course* component: the development over time of a reproductive unit in a given cultural setting. The other is the *normative* component: the fact that reproductive rules vary from one cultural group to another which means that the timing and contents of demographic migration vary between groups.

The norms surrounding reproduction are, however, neither immutable nor too 'cultural' to be used for a combination of reasons. For example, Anita Böcker found in her research on a Turkish group in the Netherlands that the marriage rules affected migration from Turkey to Nijmegen and that the migration process in turn changed some basic conceptions relating to marriage. In the Turkish group, marriage between close kin (cousins) was the rule. That meant that the persons who were able to enter the Netherlands as spouses-to-be of resident persons were frequently related to the party already there, which consolidated the kinship group in the Netherlands, and strengthened the social field[16] encompassing the two countries. If non-kin were party to the marriages, they had to compensate the lack of kin relations with an extra large bride

13. Ethnic group: minority group distinguished primarily on the basis of cultural characteristics.
14. 'Endogamy: the practice of selecting spouses from a single group of which ego is a member' (Harris 1971: 632).
15. Diaspora: originally referring to Jewish religious communities living dispersed among peoples with other religions. In current usage, the term is used to refer to culturally distinct minority groups of external origin that maintain links to one another and to a homeland (Clifford 1994).
16. Social field: social relations stretching across geographic territories that may not be contiguous, in a 'seamless fabric made up of the original home, the new home, the people left behind, people encountered . . ., as well as all the ramifications of a move upon all parties' (Nelson 1992: 109).

Gunilla Bjerén

price or costly bridal gifts. The Turkish gender order was such that it was primarily young men who were willing and able to marry themselves into the Netherlands. By using the marriage rules for migration these young men incidentally defied another cultural rule concerning marriage, namely that the young couple should live patrilocally[17] (Böcker 1995: 161–3).

In other instances, marriage migration is brought about not because of endogamic marriage rules, but because of a continued preference for 'home girls' because they are expected to have the 'correct' norms, values and expectations of marriage. Summerfield reports from south London that Bangladeshi parents keep bringing over young women as brides for their sons since only such girls will behave as 'proper' daughters-in-law. What is expected of a young wife is that she should willingly wait on her mother-in-law, that she should be willing to live patrilocally, that she should give up all of her salary to her husband and his kin, if she works for wages, that she should refrain from using contraceptives and that she should accept corporal punishment (Summerfield 1993: 87).

Another form of marriage migration is for women to marry nationals from other countries, in South to North streams. The women of these unions may not be able to marry locally for a variety of reasons, they may be seeking to avoid the kind of marital conditions that await Bangladeshi brides for example, or they may simply be using the marital opportunity instrumentally to improve their life chances (cf. Thadani and Todaro 1984, cited in Hugo 1995). At the moment, important flows of marriage mobility go from Thailand and the Philippines to Australia (Hugo 1995: 201), Northern Europe and North America, but there are many others. The reasons why men in these countries look for women so far away is not much discussed in the literature. Hugo reports that the Filipino wives in Australia primarily move to areas where the ratio of women to men is low. A qualified guess would be that the 'importing' husbands, as their 'imported' wives, have problems finding mates locally, but for different reasons. More sinister motives can easily be imagined, as the traffic in wives slides into traffic in women, in sex workers and 'entertainers'.

What is typical of demographic migration is that it is concentrated in specific periods in the life-course[18] of the individual and of the

17. Patrilocal residence: in the same dwelling as the husband's parents.
18. The 'life-cycle' concept has been replaced by the 'life-course' concept in social science literature to make clear that social and economic change can and do occur between cohorts meaning that the life-course events, timing and experience of one cohort will not necessarily be repeated by a later cohort, as was implied by the 'life-cycle' idea (Warnes 1992: 179ff).

household to which she/he belongs, the most obvious being the period when the young leave the residential unit of childhood and early youth. The length of the period when mobility is possible and desired varies culturally but would in most instances be longer for men than for women. During this period early in life when mobility is possible and perhaps expected, mobility may be set in motion by other mechanisms than those related to reproduction; the necessary condition is nevertheless that the potential migrant is not locked into a reproductive process that prescribes presence in a specific location.

Reproducing Social Identities: Cultural Migration

Producing babies is not the same as reproducing cultures. To produce a 'proper person' in the sense of a given culture, the new individual must be enculturated into his/her appropriate identity in a large number of dimensions. To begin with, this is a job for the person/s who take care of the young person in infancy, but soon it will be a concern of many more actors. In the Bangladeshi group referred to earlier the importance of adequate enculturation encourages parents to send their young girls 'home' to be brought up in a way that will give them the right social identity and therefore success on the marital market later on. The upbringing of the child will be left to the father's relatives, local schools, religious institutions, etc. In some instances reported by Summerfield, a man might have a wife living permanently in Bangladesh; she becomes pregnant on her husband's visit and she will join her husband with the baby soon after delivery to ensure the child's future residence rights in Britain. Once this is achieved, mother and child returns to Bangladesh.[19] Also among the Somali in south London, there was an established pattern of infancy in Britain, childhood and adolescence in Somalia, and adulthood in Britain, before the collapse of Somalia in 1991 (Summerfield 1993).

For West Indian communities[20] straddling Caribbean islands and metropolitan areas in the United States and the United Kingdom, the practice of fostering children 'at home' is the very basis for relationships that link home and host communities:

> To either leave or send one's child to a surrogate parent communicates the desire of the absent parent to maintain links with the home community, links which represent a desire to return in the future and become an active participant in the community. For the persons who do the fostering the activity puts

19. According to Summerfield (1993), British immigration authorities have a term for these women – 'carrier wives'.
20. Particularly, English-, French- and Dutch-speaking. The Spanish-speaking Caribbean communities also practise extensive child fostering, but the gender orders differ and that leads to another meaning for a similar practice (Soto 1987).

them in touch with happenings in the host society and in a position of prestige *vis-à-vis* the biological parent(s) and children. From the children's perspective, the residential shifts between home and host countries . . . ensure that they become acquainted with their kindred and the community with whom they are expected to acquire life long responsibilities . . . In sum, fostering is an activity which results in the redistribution of wealth, resources and services across international boundaries. (Soto 1987: 133)

The fear of 'losing it' – the cultural and social identity of the original homeland – has for some groups led to a traffic in women, or traffic in children, or both. Additional 'mobility points' along the life-course appear – the time when children start school, or should begin to receive religious education, for example. The permeability of the 'household' and the insufficiency of individual care givers when it comes to successful enculturation give rise to North to South migration in order to ensure social reproduction of identities and culture, while the promise of improved life chances under the protection of established kin groups stimulates migration in the other direction.

Migrants from different cultures value the maintenance of the social identities of the original culture differently. Group ambitions change and develop with time. Each group develops its own strategy of how to maintain a distinct culture with a distinct repertoire of social identities; within groups there is variation as well. Concerns about social reproduction are the engine for considerable migration in both directions and provide some of the glue that prevents those first established abroad in a kin group to cut loose from the source of identity back home.

'Social Ties' and Reproductive Units

The most visible aspect of human reproduction is its *social organisation*, the constitution of kinship-based groups. In contemporary migration literature, these groups have been given a great deal of attention as the loci for migration decision making as well as for overall reproductive and livelihood strategies (see e.g. chapter 7). Kinship groups have been the focus for anthropological investigation since the emergence of the discipline. The anthropological literature on the problematic of the cross-cultural use of 'household' and 'family' contributes to a deeper understanding of the cultural nuances in 'household' and 'family' formation, particularly from a gender perspective.

Migrants as Members of 'Households'

In attempting to understand the household context in which the 'new migrant' is placed by current migration literature, it is important to distinguish between 'family' and 'household' – two concepts that are often used as synonyms in Northern contexts. The family concept should be reserved for kinship relations; the household is a potentially different group and defined through its *functions*. What the functions defining a household should be is an open question. In the literature co-residence seems to be the minimalist definition.[21] Other defining functions are 'domestic functions',[22] the care for and enculturation of children, and having a joint economy.

Migration research has shifted emphasis from the migrant as an individual mover and decision maker, to the migrant as part and parcel of households. These imaginary households were for some time presented as unproblematic co-operating, resource-pooling units. Research focusing on women has, however, undermined the view of households as the safe haven (for everybody) from a competitive and ruthless outside world. In the new conception, the household is seen as an arena of social relations organised along generational, gender and kinship lines. The relations generate and are reinforced by structures of power, ideological meanings, and sentiments which contribute to hierarchy and inequity within the household. Conflict and struggle among members to control and change the lines and terms of power and authority over decision making, the division of labour, and household resources are, in this view, an integral part of household dynamics (Pessar 1988: 196–7, Robertson 1991: 41).[23]

At the same time as previous perceptions of relations within 'households' have been questioned, the cross-cultural validity of the household concept itself is rejected by many anthropologists (Yanagisako 1979; Bjerén et al. 1981; Moore 1994). The rejection of 'households' as a meaningful concept across cultures is founded in comparative anthropological research, which has stigmatised the household concept as hopelessly ethnocentric.[24]

At the heart of the anthropological project is the endeavour to understand and describe 'other cultures' on their own merits, not in an ethnocentric manner. This is difficult at all times, but particularly difficult when anthropologists perceive a phenomenon in a culture different from their own that looks familiar and appears to fulfil the same functions as in their own culture. This is precisely one of the problems of

21. This is echoed in census and survey questions where co-residence and commensality often are used to define households.
22. Relating to everyday life, such as cooking joint meals, eating together, washing clothes, etc.
23. Cf. the entire Dwyer and Bruce volume (1988).
24. Ethnocentrism: the belief that one's own socio-cultural practices and values are invariably better and more natural than the practices and values found in other societies.

households.[25] Already Malinowski admonished against the attribution of European characteristics to non-European families without adequate investigation of details of actual family relationships (Malinowski 1963 (1913), cited in Yanagisako 1979: 161).[26]

When it comes to studying gender or 'households' anthropologists approach areas where all cultures carry heavy emotional investment and where consequently there are firm beliefs about what is 'normal' or 'human'. A good example of this is the fact that social science students, including anthropology students, well into the 1960s were taught that the 'nuclear family' was the cornerstone of *all* human societies despite the fact that 'there is no scientific basis for the application of our Euro-American concepts of family, house, home, or household to the entire known spectrum of human domestic arrangements' (Harris 1971: 266).

One reason for the ethnocentric bias in the evaluation of what seemed to be 'straightforward' household units in non-Euro-American societies studied was its basis in *implicit* comparisons between a (supposedly) familiar household model, and a (seemingly) similar form. Such implicit comparisons are always at work, when people are confronted with culturally alien forms of social organisation. One of the problems of implicit comparisons, however, is that the point of reference, perceptions of conditions in the anthropologist's society, is not based on empirical knowledge, 'facts', but on perceptions that may be dated, normative or simply wrong. By not knowing exactly what we are comparing with in our own cultures, anthropologists, along with others who compare, run the risk of making erroneous assumptions about the concepts of other people, based on comparisons with erroneous assumptions about the simplicity or homogeneity of our own cultural concepts (Yanagisako and Collier 1987: 17, after Bloch and Bloch 1980: 125).

For example, Robertson has coined the phrase 'apical family norm' for the prevalent idea of the 'normal family' in any culture. This norm is 'an essentially static image of the household at the peak of its achievements, a little portrait of the happy, fulfilled family at its most expanded and extended stage' (Robertson 1991: 18). In figure 8.1 this would be the expansion stage in household/family development, in Euro-America often concretely imagined as a married man and woman, with two children of their own, a boy and a girl, living in their own house. In analysing the 'families' and 'households' in other societies, Euro-American

25. As it is also the problem of gender.
26. Bronislaw Malinowski (1884–1942), one of the founding fathers of modern social anthropology, famous for his advocacy of long-term fieldwork and participant observation in the study of culture and society.

anthropologists run the risk of confusion because they are comparing, however implicitly, with this apical family norm of 'home'.

Against this we should pose the complicated family/household situations of many persons in North America and Europe today, characterised by sequences of cohabitations/marriages. As a consequence, the family/household unity can no longer be assumed to be universal; 'family' = kin and 'household' = co-resident unit often diverge and there is a large variation in space/time solutions and a fast turnover of situations. Some 'households' do not have the same composition over the week or the month, as 'my' children move between myself and my ex-partner and 'your' children move between you and your ex-partner, with 'grandparents' of different pedigrees stepping in to fill in the gaps (Bjerén 1984). In addition, what at one time were thought to be self-evident 'domestic functions' (pertaining to the household, that is) change and the location for these functions moves. The family/household functions are unravelling, as many small children are brought back and forth to and from day nurseries, several household members have one – maybe their main – meal outside the house and the changing daily time/space schedules of individuals lead to a process of 'breakfastification'[27] of the evening meal. In addition, the apical family norm suffers from its lack of dynamics; even a highly conventional family will resemble the norm momentarily only as the life-course of the family/household moves on inexorably.

Anthropologists have given up the attempt to find a cross-culturally valid definition of 'household', even though the term keeps on being used as an 'odd-job' word for descriptive statements (Yanagisako 1979). *What functions are performed by which group of people, related how, must be approached as empirical questions, to be answered for each particular context.* No two functions can be assumed to go together; not even the mother–child unit can be assumed to be invariant in all cultural contexts (ibid.). Least of all is it possible to assume congruence with the normative image of Euro-American family/households, which is not accurate as a description even of the indigenous households themselves.

Anthropological doubts about 'household' as a cross-culturally valid concept have made little impact on other disciplines. The perception of 'households' as complex units, the 'locus of competing interests, rights, obligations and resources, where household members are often involved in bargaining, negotiation and possibly even conflict' (Moore 1994: 87), has won more widespread acceptance, largely through the interdisciplinary work of feminist scholars. The 'household' in migration

27. Meaning members of the family will grab a bite to eat at their own convenience, rather than sit down for a joint family dinner.

Gunilla Bjerén

literature is often invoked when it comes to discussing who is actually taking the decision to migrate. Here anthropologists should ask if it is not the kinship network rather than the 'household' which is at issue – and also put the whole idea of the one decision about migration under scrutiny. Let us have a look at the 'family'.

'Families' and Migration

If 'households' are conceptualised on the basis of their functions, then 'families' are thought of in terms of kinship relations. Kinship may appear as a less ambiguous way of determining membership than the amorphous 'household functions' discussed above.

From the beginning of modern anthropology the description and analysis of 'kinship systems' have been a major concern. The variation and complexity of people's ways of reckoning kin relations have been studied and described in detail. The kinship systems were thought of as mental maps of significant relations and also firm guidelines for actual behaviour.

As the discipline matured, the fit between the idealised kinship system and what was actually going on turned out to be less accurate than the rules prescribed. One conclusion has been that kinship rules are to be seen as ideologies that can be manipulated to serve a variety of goals (Keesing 1976: 270). Because of the overwhelming importance of the social relations of reproduction in people's lives, the rhetoric of family relations is powerful as an explanatory device and as a means to justify one's own and other people's actions. But who is thought to be 'family' and what that implies varies – between groups, individuals and contexts.

Look at this description from a conversation with Olive, a Barbadian at the time of the interview living in Britain, and her son Jasper.

Olive . . . had been brought up, in her mother's absence (in Trinidad), by her maternal grandmother and great-grandmother. Lola, her great-grandmother, had also raised Olive's mother (whose father was away in Cuba and whose mother had to work). When Olive migrated to Britain in 1956, she left three of her four children in the care of her mother, and the forth, her son Jasper, in the care of her grandmother whom, Jasper recalls, 'I loved . . . dearly . . . she was so much a part of me . . . I sometimes believe that my great-grandmother is still looking after me' 'Our family', Olive insists, 'was very, very close'. 'A big, happy family', according to Jasper, in which family identity was the primary loyalty and where 'family meant something. The family relationship was very strong . . . My grandfather had about three women . . . and this all became part of the family . . . because we all belonged to one person . . . my grandfather . . . The outside family and the inside family, all were family'. (Chamberlain 1994: 122)

Or reflect on the family situation of some Somali and Bangladeshi migrants in Britain, referred to earlier. Both groups are Muslim and polygynous and adhere to Muslim law with regard to marriage, dowry and divorce. Women of both groups

> are expected to live amongst their husband's kin, and both are expected to defer to their husbands privately and publicly. In both societies domestic violence is regulated rather than prohibited and in Somali society is used as a ritualised expression of male dominance. A Somali husband is expected to beat his wife on her wedding night with a ritual whip . . . Somali women are also fully circumcised, with clitoris and vulva excised . . . (Summerfield 1993: 97)

The Bangladeshi women, on the other hand, are kept, as far as possible, physically separate from men. Whereas the Somali women can and do go out to work, learn English, support one another, keep contact with their own kin and divorce when they so desire, the Bangladeshi women do piecework at home, do not mingle with other women, do not learn English, see their own kin rarely and are expected to obey their mother-in-law in all things, and are more severely and more often beaten by their husbands. For both groups, some children are sent 'home' to be brought up, by husbands' kin (in Bangladesh) or by co-wives (for the Somali) (Summerfield 1993).

How could one possibly fit these three groups of women – Barbadian, Bangladeshi and Somali – into a common 'family' frame of reference?

Anthropological research has shown that 'household' and 'family' as analytical concepts are not applicable in cross-cultural contexts. Nevertheless, South to North migration does take place in networks based on kinship or pseudo-kinship, which I would call *effective*[28] kinship links between people localised within social fields encompassing two or several countries (Gurak and Caces 1992). The image I want to use is of effective kinship networks crossing at 'residential nodes'. Such a residential node could be a grandmother/grandchild 'household' in a 'home' country, dependent on remittances sent by the grandmother's adult children, one of whom would be the grandchild's mother living in a residential node of a 'host' country.[29] The residential nodes have life-courses of their own, dynamics that are premised on demographic events in the life-courses of individuals who make up the networks crossing at the node but also on changes in composition following a logic other than

---

28. 'Pseudo-kinship' could be relations based on friendship or co-ethnicity, for instance.

29. The 'home'–'host' distinction is borrowed from Caribbean migration studies (Soto 1987 and others). Another typology has been 'parent'–'daughter' communities (Kearney 1986).

the demographic. For instance, as the grandmother ages and the grandchild grows up in the example above, there comes a time when the child will be fetched by her parent and incorporated in a residential node in the host country. Eventually, the aged grandparent might be brought to live with her daughter abroad, or the daughter/parent will return to the home community and take care of the old grandparent. The composition, consistency and duration of residential nodes depends on the social organisation of home communities, conditions for individuals in the network and contingencies for the network as a whole.

Kearney has suggested the term 'articulatory migrant network' for the migration network described here (Kearney 1986: 353). 'Articulatory' may be taken to stand for the 'joining together' – of distinct communities, and economies, but also of one type of economic activity to another – and 'giving expression to' – economic relations in kinship terms, for example (Foster-Carter 1978: 215). Kearney thinks of the articulatory migrant network as having a developmental cycle of its own. It is to be seen as 'a vascular system through which flow persons, information, goods, service and economic value' (Kearney 1986: 354).

Kearney's metaphor points to the material base for migration networks: the activity that brings them into existence and helps to maintain them – the search for livelihoods.

The Search for Livelihoods

For a long time economistic explanations have dominated the thinking about migration. There are many reasons for this, such as the concentration of research on labour migration (which is economic by definition), the close relation between policy and migration research with a focus on present and future economic consequences of migration, the exclusion of women from the research agenda and the ascent of economics as a meta-discipline in the social sciences.

It is true that migration researchers from all disciplines agree that the skewed spatial distribution of economic power and resources between states and continents sets the stage for intercontinental migration from poor to rich regions of the world. On that stage, however, the movements of people are caused by many different mechanisms. To imagine that economic motives would always dominate when individuals move about would be to commit the common fallacy of inferring 'motives from a study of objective structural determinants, and then to impute these motives to the migrants' (Willis 1974: 59). The 'objective determinants' in large-scale migration studies are of necessity the ones that can be observed and measured easily, such as geographical distance, size of places, average incomes and rate of unemployment. Their relation to people's motivations and perceptions is an entirely open question.

Even when there appears to be a distinct economic incentive to move, this may not be sufficient to explain why the person in question actually migrates. Economic gain is rarely an end in itself; to understand the mechanisms behind migration one must question the reason *why* finding more money is vital. The *because* is likely to point also to reproductive processes – like the need to support one's children – which in turn may be linked to cultural demands – like the need to accumulate dowry to marry. Furthermore, one can pose questions about why a particular 'need' must be/can be met by international migration and why the actual migrant is the person to do it – questions that are likely to be answered with reference to the local/regional versus the international opportunity structure, the gender order and other aspects of social organisation.

For whatever reason, however, it is clear that the possibility of finding a livelihood that is decent in the eyes of the concerned does play a significant role in international migration. What constitutes a 'decent livelihood' varies with who is looking, from the trained Southern professional who might be part of a South to North brain-drain, to the landless farm labourer who is looking for seasonal work.

Despite formal barriers, there may be opportunities for highly qualified migrants in the upper echelon of the formal sector, particularly when there is a labour shortage. From the point of view of professionals in the South, some occupations stretch over national boundaries to a virtually 'deterritorialised' spatial hierarchy.[30] Highly desired training opportunities overseas give a Southern person qualifications with high value at home but, once returned there, also a potential return ticket to the country of training. As a matter of fact, the creation of a core of indigenous professionals in the colonies, potential national leaders but in all other aspects beholden to the metropolitan country, was part of the colonial strategy.[31] The post-colonial training of academics from the South in Northern countries can be seen, however inadvertently, as a continuation of the colonial policy; it has at any rate created anchor points for future immigration to the training country. The hierarchical structure of deterritorialised occupational fields must not be forgotten; it is no option for a Northern professional to gear her career towards openings in the South. She – or more likely he – might still fall for the temptation to take up a well-paid temporary position in some rich Southern country on a lower level of the professional hierarchy, as for

---

30. Cf. Appadurai 1991: 192–3 on deterritorialisation.

31. 'We must do our best to form a class who may be interpreters between us and the millions whom we govern; a class of persons, Indian in blood and colour, but English in taste, in opinion, in morals, and in intellect' – Lord Macaulay, 'Minutes on Education' relating to the nineteenth-century Raj, quoted in Hannerz 1992: 296 n.11.

instance in the Northern trek to Saudi Arabian health and other institutions. However, there is a professional price to be paid for such an excursion, since it might render little professional credit in later career steps in the North.

In the middle ranges of the formal sector, where migrants compete with local persons for the available openings, there are few opportunities. The largest number of openings can be found in the lowest echelons of the formal sector, typically vacated by local persons because of seasonality, insecurity, low pay, poor working conditions and no possibility of advancement. Even so, there is a further division of this low-status domain into a male and a female arena. The formal sector can be seen to encompass several labour markets where most will be out of reach for immigrants who for a variety of reasons, one being outright discrimination, cannot compete with local job applicants. The division into a male and female immigrant labour market reflects the gendered division of the labour market as a whole.

As an alternative to formal employment some immigrants will work as small-scale entrepreneurs in activities that straddle the three sectors – some activities open for inspection in the formal (tax- and fee-paying, regulation-abiding) sector, some in the informal sector (not open to inspection, untaxed money circulating), and some in the domestic sector (outside the elementary logic of monetary rewards). The farther away one moves from the 'open' labour market of the formal sector, the more individuals will depend on their networks to find livelihood opportunities.

The difference between male and female migration patterns depends partly on the difference in available opportunities at home and abroad, but also on the organisation of reproduction and domestic work in the home communities, and on the relative autonomy of women there (Chant 1992: 197–8).

During a period after the Second World War, there was a need for unskilled manual labour that could not be met by the available persons in many industrial countries of the North. This was the time of the labour migrant – the male worker who came to work for a time and who was expected (not least by himself) and often obliged to return to enjoy the fruits of his work at home. The decline of manual work in industry marks the decline of male labour migration.

Women migrants, who became numerically significant much later than men, have not had access to the same range of opportunities as men, and the remuneration and conditions of their opportunities differ from men. Chant and Radcliffe (1992b) distinguish the following major livelihood opportunities for the majority of women in contemporary South to North migration streams:

Domestic service is the most common economic activity overall, particularly for female international migrants from East and South Asia to Singapore, Hong Kong and the Middle East, from Mexico and the Caribbean to the United States;

Garment factoring in sweatshops (to the United States, Europe and Australia).

Marriage – 'often only a thin veil for cheap domestic and sexual services' (particularly from the Philippines to the United States, Japan and Europe);

(Chant and Radcliffe 1992b: 8–9)

Health services is another area of employment for many women migrants from the South.

The Search for Livelihoods in Context

From an anthropological perspective, relative South to North mobility, its direction, content and dynamic is formed by the outcome of coalescing influences ranging from historic events and relations between states and continents to relative opportunities and gender differentiation. I shall now turn to some examples of how contexts form actual migration as people search for livelihoods on the stage set by the global economic order of today.

Organised Migration into Domestic Life: Maids to the Gulf States   The first example is the contractual recruitment of women from Sri Lanka to the Gulf states[32] from the late 1970s on.[33]

The oil-based boom in the states around the Arabian Gulf from 1973 led to the rapid initiation of extensive investment programmes. The labour demand created by these new programmes could not be met locally and workers were engaged from abroad. When Asian workers started coming – often to work in construction – Gulf labour policies had the form of strict guest-worker programmes. The workers were only allowed to stay in the host country for the duration of their contracts. They were physically controlled, often required to live near the work sites, and were not allowed to bring in their families (Brochmann 1993: 45). As time went on, an increasing proportion of the citizens of the Gulf states gained affluence and acquired life-styles which included domestic help of different kinds. Because of low wages and their presence in the region, Asian women, particularly women from Sri Lanka, became the preferred domestic workers. In 1993, 1.2 million persons in the Gulf states were estimated to be maids (ibid. 46).

32. Kuwait, Bahrain, Qatar, the United Arab Emirates, Oman and Saudi Arabia.
33. The following account is based on Brochmann (1993).

During the boom period in the Gulf states, the economic situation in Sri Lanka deteriorated. Some of the adverse conditions on the home front could be met by male labour migration. During the 1980s, however, fewer men were recruited while opportunities for female labour migration increased.

The dominant gender order in Sri Lanka is described as being 'patriarchal', implying strict male authority over women, and of older kinsmen over younger. Division of labour in the poor segment of the population before female labour migration began was, typically, that the men brought in whatever monetary income could be found, and the women did everything else. Women's work outside their homes for wages was not common. This was not considered appropriate; there were few local labour markets for female workers.

Seen from the outside, the likelihood of large-scale independent labour migration of married women from Sri Lanka seemed small indeed. Nevertheless, it came about. How was it possible?

Research from societies with similar gender orders as the Sri Lankan has shown that actual gender regimes may vary in different segments of the society. An 'inverted U-curve' has been described, where the poor and the rich comply less rigidly with cultural norms than the middle classes when it comes to women's participation in extra-domestic economic activities (Mårtensson 1976). The poor cannot afford the luxury of female seclusion, and the rich may transcend the local gender order in their identification with more cosmopolitan ways of life.

The 'Middle East Avenue' in fact developed in ways that could accommodate a patriarchal gender order. The women who left were fairly young, often married and with young children. Their migration can be seen as an extension of their motherly and wifely responsibilities, since they went to enhance the well-being of their children, husbands and other close kin. Their absence did not mean that they launched projects of their own. Instead, they were as controlled in their capacities as domestic maids as they would be at home, sometimes more. Broch-mann's respondents, who were returned maids, reported that they were never allowed out of their employers' houses on their own. Furthermore, their husbands were not required to cross the gendered division of labour in their wives' absence since childcare and other domestic tasks were taken over by female kin. Finally, it appears that the husbands (or more often fathers if the women were not married) retained considerable control over the proceeds from the migrants' work periods.[34]

---

34. That the money sent home is spent in an appropriate manner is a problem for all contract workers, not only women. In the Filipino expatriate group in Saudi Arabia stories circulate about the misuse by women of husbands' and brothers' remittances back home.

Labour migration between Sri Lanka and the Gulf so far has not formed the basis of a multi-local social field, nor has it yet resulted in noticeable social or economic change in the communities where the migrants come from. These are slow processes. Until now, it appears that female migration to the Gulf supports the established way of life, including the prevailing gender order, while reproducing the causes for migration. The latter comes about because female labour migration improves material conditions in the affected households in a way which can only be upheld through further migration.

Migration into the Informal Sector: Street Peddling in Italy   The second example is the spontaneous migration of middle-class young men from Senegal to Southern Italy.[35] The young men who arrive in Southern Italy imagine themselves to have gone to a universally wealthy 'Europe' – instead they find themselves in a region with a 20 per cent official unemployment rate which, in their eyes, in many ways compares unfavourably with the Dakar they have left behind.

Their emigration is based on an illusion, feeding on the image of 'power' and 'wealth' linked with Europe and the United States. The migrants hold a more coherent vision of Europe than Europeans have ever had, a view that does not recognise the different conditions between regions and nations. The illusion further feeds on mass-media representation of Europe and the United States and, maybe most importantly, on the inaccurate reports of previous migrants who – for fear of losing face – do not want people back home to know how they are actually faring.

Why male migrants and not female? Going to work in Europe is a way for young men, both single and married, to break off from authority exercised by older (male) kin and religious leaders. They are apparently not integrated in a reproductive system that obliges them to serve the interests of others. Instead, for them to form a credible adult male identity entails travelling and the acquisition of knowledge. 'Like the "Grand Tour" of old, travel in Europe seems to be becoming *de rigueur* for the young Senegalese man's position back home' (Zinn 1994: 59). For young women, travelling would do nothing to enhance their identity formation – on the contrary, even moving independently to other urban centres in West Africa might lead to accusations of prostitution (cf. Olurode 1995).

Most of the Senegalese who land in Southern Italy come from the middle class in their homeland and expect to land well-paying jobs that are simply not there. Rather than work in highly controlled, low paying

---

35. The following account is based on Zinn (1994).

jobs they earn their living as *ambulanti*, itinerant street vendors, working the cities of the Mezzogiorno or the small-town markets and festivals. The rationale for doing this kind of work is that if they are to make miserable earnings with long hours and no insurance at another job, they might as well be self-employed, unsupervised peddlers, even though they consider this kind of work to be below their dignity. The profits are small; even if they want to, there is nothing to remit back home. Nevertheless, many remain for a long time and newcomers keep on arriving. Finding their presumptive careers as labour migrants ended before they began, some plan for further travels, to 'do' all the countries of Europe.

> The corner of Europe in which these Senegalese immigrants find themselves . . . is not at the end of a line segment drawn from Dakar. It is a dot on the circumference of the four-dimensional transnational migration circuit, a Grand Tour realm composed of home, stop-overs, lay-overs, seasonal moves, places heard of and territories dreamt of, all in constant motion. (Zinn 1994: 65)

Concluding Discussion

Let me conclude this excursion into different areas of anthropological thinking about migration by pointing to the implications of this academic journey for the three questions guiding the inquiry of this book.

How Does a Migration Process Start?

In all examples presented in this chapter, international relations of long or short duration have preceded contemporary South to North migration. In some instances, the relation is founded on slavery, as in the case of the Caribbean connection with Britain and the United States. The Caribbean migration to the United States began when some plantation owners moved their operations to the Southern United States in anticipation of emancipation (in 1834). After emancipation, Afro-Caribbeans continued moving north as free men (Chaney 1987: 7). In other cases the relationship was that of colonisation, as between Pakistan, Bangladesh, Somalia and Britain, and between France (and therefore Europe) and Senegal. In some instances, the international relation is migration itself. This is true for Turkey and Germany (and from there the Netherlands) and for Sri Lanka and the Gulf states. Here the background is active labour recruitment by the richer country, seeking temporary contract labour. In these particular examples, links are of much shorter duration, from the 1960s and the 1970s respectively. Whatever the type, however, relations between countries preceded and were part of migratory relations. All migration processes are embedded in historical processes. Migration is a consequence of historical events, and shapes future events as they unfold through migration.

The influence of migration processes on what comes to pass stems from the frequently made observation that 'the migration that was initially propelled by an external, structural dynamic and logic increasingly acquires an internal dynamic and logic of its own' (Pedraza 1991: 308). This 'internal dynamic and logic' can be interpreted as the continuation of the social organisation and reproductive processes of the migrant's home base but in a new environment, an environment that is neither 'here' nor 'there' but constituted by the new social field encompassing both 'home' and 'host' communities. As I have argued in this chapter, the internal dynamic and logic of international migration streams are set by the coordinates of gender, reproduction and the search for livelihood, and played out in a whirlpool of thresholds and loopholes, opportunities and booby traps rigged and structured by forces beyond the reach and maybe even the vision of the individual migrant. The migrant herself is moved through a migrant network with a biography of its own, from the first landing of the first mover down to today, a network that changes, evolves and matures as mobility itself acquires new meaning for new network members through the passage of time and changes in conditions.

Seen in this way, the individual woman's or man's migration path can only make sense in the light of what went before – family mobility history, network biography – and what goes on simultaneously – the division of duties and tasks at different locations between genders and generations. The individual move in a person's life trajectory in turn must be related to her or his accumulated migration history to be understood and seen together with, intertwined or separate as they may be, the trajectories of kin and other meaningful relations.[36]

How is Migration Related to the Development Process?

However frustrating, the only possible answer to this question from an anthropological perspective is that it 'depends'. It depends on the kind of 'development' process and how that process affects regions and groups within regions in the South. The same process of economic, political and social change might make some segments of the population

---

36. This approach to migration has relatives in other disciplines. Hägerstrand's time geography runs in the same vein and Skeldon notes that the biographical approach to the study of migration is promoted as standard procedure by the ESCAP National Migration Survey manuals from 1980 to 1984, inspired by 'ethnographic style holistic approaches' (Skeldon 1995: 91).

affluent and lead them into international tourism, study and business travel with residence abroad as a possible consequence, like the Senegalese young men in Italy. Other segments might become 'development refugees' within the country – displaced by dam constructions or modern forestry practices. For others again, development of mass transportation in combination with economic changes abroad might open Middle East or New York avenues – as has been the case for many women from Sri Lanka and the Caribbean. At the 'meso'-level where anthropological studies are concentrated – it all depends.

Why Do, and Why Don't, People Move from South to North?

One of the main points of this chapter has been to show the gender differences of 'people'. Women and men stay – and move – for different, or similar, reasons, but because of the gender differences in their relations to others and conditions of life, the form of their mobility and the consequences of their staying or moving might be quite different.

Mobility is the consequence of other processes, such as reproduction or the need to find a livelihood, which take place in spatially defined social and cultural contexts. If a man or a woman in the South belongs to a network in a social field encompassing several countries, international mobility might be an expected ingredient of the life-course, a consequence simply of growing up, finding a livelihood and growing old. Such a 'new' migrant is perhaps not a settler but a long-term commuter, or 'transmigrant' (Glick-Schiller et al. 1992: 1).

For other groups in the South, or persons belonging to networks with different spatial coordinates, the same processes of reproduction and economic activity will not lead to international migration.

From Common Questions to Common Concepts
Thomas Faist

Common Questions and Common Concepts

The questions raised in the previous chapters were: firstly, why do some people migrate? Secondly, why do most people stay in their country and why do many emigrants return? Thirdly, how is international migration related to development? Does development spur international migration and/or does migration enhance development? This chapter summarises major findings of the disciplinary contributions in a comparative view and develops selected conclusions a step further.

The results of our multidisciplinary venture call for *common or integrative concepts*. Three main ideas emerge in most chapters that may be called migratory space, local assets and cumulative causation.

Firstly, migration occurs in what could be called a *migratory space* that not only consists of one or several spatial locations but also of politically, economically and culturally relevant ties and institutions. Migratory space is the sum total of personal projects, perceptions and images, on the one hand, and the structure of opportunities available to potential migrants, on the other, linked by intermediate mechanisms such as networks and collectives. In economic terms we may say that individuals and collectives try to maximise their individual or collective utilities, i.e. their quality of life. It is crucial to analyse the manifold projects potential migrants have in the region of origin; varying by factors such as the stage in their life course, the number of projects, the character of the kinship groups and the community they are involved in and the strength of manifold ties and material linkages. The relevant decision making can proceed on an individual basis, in small units such as the family, but is also enabled and constrained by larger aggregates that impact on the decisions, such as kinship networks, companies, international relief organisations or government policies.

Secondly, regarding relative immobility and high rates of return, it has indeed proved fruitful to consider location-specific or *local assets* and non-transferable information in the sending communities and countries that translate into insider advantages of potential migrants. Local assets may refer to economic capital (e.g. financial assets), cultural capital (e.g. collective identity), human or educational capital (e.g. degrees, professional skills) and social capital (i.e. transactions between individuals that facilitate social action). The question comes up under which conditions local assets are transferable and under which they are not, and therefore rather contribute to relative immobility.

Thirdly, it is of utmost importance to conceptualise the impact of migration on the sending regions once international movement has started. This can be done through highlighting various aspects of *cumulative causation*, the idea that rising emigration sets off structural changes that make additional migration more likely. In turn, additional migration and return migration affect various aspects of economic *development* and social, political and cultural life. While the feedback effects of migration on economic development have received most attention in the research and the literature at large, the migration process itself and, increasingly, social, cultural and political change figure prominently among issues that demand our attention. Examples include the alteration of family and gender relations, a 'culture of migration' and migrants voicing their political dissent abroad.

The following discussion summarises how the contribution of each of the disciplines involved approaches the three questions asked and the resulting focus of theoretical analysis. According to the results of the individual disciplinary chapters the three integrative concepts are: migratory space, local assets, and the principle of cumulative causation in connection with development and change. In the sections on decision making and on the process of international migration theories and concepts are ordered along three analytical levels – micro, meso and macro. Some implications of this research for normative reasoning are listed. Finally, this summary of theoretical concepts concludes with crucial questions, meant to guide further empirical research.

In proceeding this way, the discussion introduces 'migratory space' as a new term to summarise the findings pertaining to the causes of migration. The terms local assets and cumulative causation have been elaborated in more detail in the disciplinary chapters. Furthermore, this conclusion makes reference to concepts not discussed extensively in this book, yet prominent in the literature, e.g. migration-systems theory. At times, these conclusions also go beyond the findings and speculate about further steps to be taken. Although this part synthesises our findings and thus uses results simultaneously, references to the individual chapters are meant to direct the reader to a more detailed discussion of underlying key concepts and ideas. Finally, the questions for further research emerge out of our common work.

Disciplinary Approaches in Geography, Micro- and Macro-Economics, Development Economics, Political Science, Sociology and Anthropology

In order to present systematically the commonalities and differences regarding theories of migration of the disciplines, we need to review briefly two dimensions: (1) the approach taken to study migration decision making and the dynamics of migration; and (2) the disciplinary questions asked within the confines of the three general questions.

The capacity to integrate a host of factors is most obvious in the *geographical* approach to migration that focuses on the implications of spatial differentiation in a temporal perspective. Migration as well as other forms of spatial mobility are central themes. The geographical approach has moved far beyond a preoccupation with physical barriers and carriers to migration and now places a premium on (socially 'constructed') space and time. Seen from a micro-perspective space consists of the projects people are engaged in and the values they adhere to. Time is seen as embedded in larger social structures. The projects and events have a time duration, which sometimes is flexible but often is given, e.g. the individual life course or the migration cycle. The main question asked is thus: How are movements of people in temporal space limited by various opportunities and restrictions? Migration is thus seen as a special instance of *time-space resolution*. This emphasis on a life-path perspective strongly overlaps with sociological life-course analysis of migration and with the premium anthropology places upon the cultural causes of population movements (chapter 2).

The *micro-level economic* approach to migration decision making in the neo-classical tradition may be characterised as the most ambitious among all the disciplines gathered here, and it has the most coherent theoretical framework. It is based on a rather stringent set of analytical assumptions. As with other topics, it starts from the general assumption that 'people are rational and that they try to *maximise their individual utility* or, put in another way, *their individual quality of life*'. The potential mover (migrant) is conceived as a *utility maximiser*. In its traditional form, this micro-economic (neo-classical) approach is more powerful in explaining why migration starts and changes, than in explaining the levels (volume) of migration and non-migration. The argument is that the micro-economic decision-making framework may also offer a suitable tool to analyse and explain the more compli-cated questions on migration versus non-migration, once stringent

Thomas Faist

assumptions are relaxed and more realistic ones are introduced. These assumptions concern costs and risks of international migration, information to reduce uncertainty, the rationality of decision makers, the homogeneity of people in a group, and the interdependence of the decision makers (chapter 3).

The *macro-economic* chapter 4 deals with the question: does development enhance migration and/or does international migration trigger economic development? Migration is primarily conceptualised as a problem of the *allocation of resources* for economic development. It starts from the well-known assumption that international migration is at least partly dependent on differences in income and development between the sending and receiving countries involved. This is a crucial question to ask because the literature has been basically dominated by two rival views. The Firstly, grounded in neo-classical economics in the vein of Lewis (1954a/1978) and Thomas (1973), argues that international migration really functions as an equilibrating mechanism. It reallocates labour from relatively unproductive to relatively productive areas so that aggregate output is increased. This implies the enhancement of economic welfare in both the sending and receiving countries. The second and opposing view holds that the disproportionate concentration of human and economic capital, other resources and political power implies concentration in the sending and receiving areas – a view that is emphasised in the chapter on development economics. Therefore, international migration would exacerbate rural–urban and international economic inequalities (chapter 4).

The *development economics* chapter 5 also grounded in a macro-level view, focuses more on the discourse on migration and economic development than on settling the dispute between the two rival macro-economic views. International migration is intimately tied to how the principal collective actors such as receiving country governments encourage but more often constrain international migration. International migration and its regulation affects the *distribution of resources* between the South and the North, but also among the non-monolithic South and inside the Southern nation-states. Prominent is the meta-question: In what ways has the changing political discourse on migration also influenced the way in which the migration–development relationship is discussed in economics and the social sciences? This discussion is complemented by an assessment of the global ecological implications of the Western economic development model (chapter 5).

Political science was a relative latecomer in the field of international migration. Nevertheless, over the past decades social scientists have increasingly realised the saliency as well as the capacity of the nation-state to control international migration. In this perspective migration is

– 250 –

seen as a problem for both *state sovereignty* and *conflict and consensus* on the level of nation-state political systems. The main questions asked are: How does the territorial division of the world into nation-states affect international migration? What causes refugee flows and how are these movements connected to the possibility of political voice in the sending countries? What are the implications for membership viz. citizenship in the receiving countries, both for the newcomers and for the settled population (chapter 6)?

The *sociological* contribution presented here has been situated as a meso-level between the micro- and macro-levels of analysis. This approach deals with the study of decision making and the dynamics of migration as an enterprise emphasising the strength and the content of social ties in networks and collectives, groups and institutions. It sees migration primarily as a *social structural* phenomenon of interacting individuals, groups and institutions. The main question asked is: How does the structure of social interaction shape migration decision making? This approach deals with migration decision making, migration networks and migration as cumulative causation. It depends heavily on network-theoretic approaches (social ties) and general sociological theory (dimensions of social integration and the notion of social capital). So far, among all the disciplines concerned, sociology has been the one most concerned with the dynamic aspect of migration: How can migration processes be understood as taking on a life of their own, once started (chapter 7)?

The *anthropological* approach to migration and the method used are intricately interlinked, even more than in all the other social science disciplines. Migrants are conceived as *culturally contextualised* and *gendered* beings. This disciplinary understanding is tied to a specific method. Ethnographic fieldwork forms the solid base for such an undertaking. The researcher spends extended periods of time in the field, acquiring the cultural and social competence in order to grasp the standpoint of the 'other'. It is open to a social relational and structural approach that emphasises the close links persons form in their immediate living sphere. This discipline is therefore particularly attentive to phenomena in small groups and networks of groups. The main question asked is: How do interpersonal cultural and social relations, gender relations in particular, impact upon the incidence of migration (chapter 8)?

These various disciplinary approaches broadly fall into two categories of explanatory modes, namely causal and processual. Firstly, *causal* explanations concentrate on what starts the process of international migration and typically derive their concepts from the origins. Macro-level world-systems theories or micro-level motivational and utility-maximiser theories are of that kind.

Secondly, *processual* approaches concentrate on what happens as the process of international migration unfolds or where it comes to a halt: as migrants follow pioneer migrants to destination countries through either individualised planning, formal channels (e.g. recruitment bureaux), or by means of migrant networks; as migrants return to the countries of origin and change the economic setup in investing in houses, consumer products, agriculture or services; as return migrants enhance or change kinship relations and the gendered division of labour in households. In short, processual accounts specify the causal mechanisms producing alterations in social, political and economic structures.

Determinants of Mobility and Immobility: The Migratory Space

The first question of our study has been: Why do or do not some people migrate? The intellectual project ahead is very much one of filling a theoretical space which we could call a *migratory space* (see figure 9.1). Following the lead set by geographers, space not only refers to physical features, but also to larger opportunity structures, the social life and the subjective images, values and meanings that the specific and limited place represents to potential migrants. On a micro-level this has to be seen in conjunction with the use of time to form particular time-space strategies of potential migrants. Viewed as a meso-level, the context of decision making is constituted by the potential migrants themselves in interacting with significant others, for example in kinship groups. Larger structural factors such as economic and political opportunities constitute a more remote, albeit an enabling and constraining context in which individuals, collectives and networks operate.

The Micro-Level: Migrant Decision Making

Temporary or permanent territorial exit are part of a variety of strategies of individuals to deal with stress and strain, to search for security and collective identity, to voice political dissent or to enlarge options in various markets. In order to account for a potential migrant's decision, three main dimensions are of special relevance: the costs and benefits of migration, the uncertainty and risks involved in the migration decision, and the time-space situation characterised by the local ties of migrants and the period in their life course.

Firstly, various *cost factors* involved constitute a variable to be considered, e.g. costs of getting adequate information, costs of exit and transportation, search for jobs and housing in the country of destination but also psychological costs of adapting to a new environment, the

Level	Micro	Meso	Macro
Focus	individual decision making	social relational context of choice	structural opportunities and constraints
Key terms and issues	– insider advantages – costs and benefits of staying and going – uncertainty and risk-reducing information – time-space resolution: stage in life course – location-specific capital and assets	– social ties of potential migrants with migratory space – capital specificity, especially of social capital – cultural variation in structure and role of meso-level units	– political (in)stability in sending countries – specific migration systems of nation-states within global politico-economic systems – levels of economic development in sending and receiving countries

Figure 9.1 Levels of Analysis in Migration-Decision Making

time and energy involved in forging new social relationships and maintaining and rebuilding the existing social ties to the country of origin (chapter 3).

In general, potential migrants weigh perceived costs and benefits, comparing conditions in the sending and receiving countries. As the micro-economic analysis shows, not only wage differences matter for migration decisions, but also factors such as the likelihood of getting unemployed or finding a new job in one country relative to the other. Ideally, a potential migrant weighs all kind of utility differences between countries by the probability of realising different outcomes. Furthermore, sociological value-expectancy analyses have introduced other factors that are less easily quantified, such as status, comfort, stimulation, autonomy, exit from oppression of all kinds, better life for one's children and morality. In sum, the net increase in utilities has to outweigh the benefits of staying relatively immobile and the perceived costs of migration. Migrants' decisions can be conceptualised as *place utility* that embraces the conditions in a specific location (chapter 2).

Secondly, potential migrants face *uncertainty*, the degree to which a number of alternatives are perceived with respect to the occurrence of successfully adapting to a new environment in the case of migration (e.g. finding a job and housing in the country of destination) or non-migration (e.g. economic future or safety of life in the sending country) and the relative probabilities of these alternatives. The degree of uncertainty or risk can be reduced by an individual by obtaining *information*. The availability of information may depend upon various factors such as level of education or social ties to other persons. Interestingly, while potential migrants may have too little information to make the 'right' decision, they may also have too much information, a sort of information overload. Both situations may result in second-best decisions that could result in remigration because the perceptions of the conditions in the receiving country are not accurate and result in disappointment (chapter 3). However, return migration may also be a part of a conscious life-course strategy as the analysis of the following dimension suggests. Potential migrants can be said to have *mental maps* or *cognitive maps*, i.e. knowledge, images and attitudes of near or remote environments (chapter 2).

Thirdly, the *time-space situation* has to be considered. Analytically, two aspects can be distinguished, the various ties potential movers have to local space and the stage in their life course. The stage of the individual in his or her life course and earlier decisions crucially affect the decision to stay or to go (chapter 2).

As to *local ties*, they arise in the course of an individual's involvement in and attachment to specific places. One of the main constituents of potential migrants' local projects are local ties. These local ties are reflected in transactions called social ties. Viewed from an exchange perspective, potential migrants have invested in relations with significant others and reap continuous interests from their past investments. This is called insider advantages that are non-transferable: A decision to migrate leads to their partial or complete loss. The crucial point here is that some assets, such as experience and social ties, but also skills, educational and vocational diplomas and other credentials, may only be used in a circumscribed local context, often smaller than the nation-state. Seen from a reciprocity perspective, an important prerequisite for business and personal life such as *trust* as a form of social capital can only arise in local contexts, mutually recognised by all participants involved. Belonging to an ethnic, religious or national group may give a person some sense of ontological security and a feeling of solidarity. Local ties may both hinder or spur migration of potential migrants, depending upon the perceptions of migrants about preferences and expectations at a specific time in space. On the one hand, local ties may hinder migration when capital cannot be transferred. On the other hand, once pioneer migrants have established themselves in receiving countries, local ties are transnationalised and may indeed even induce migration.

In order to understand how local ties enter decision making, it is helpful to distinguish between location and place. While *location* refers to the physical environment and the social life surrounding a potential migrant, *space* is more holistic encompassing both the physical and social environment on the one side and the subjective images, values and meanings the location represents to people. Local ties are thus embedded in places that signify a 'whole' to the potential migrant. Individual life projects are tied to specific places. It is plausible to assume that the more strongly persons are engaged in local projects such as reproduction, community, work, religion, and politics, the less likely they are to migrate for long periods of time (chapter 2).

Specific time-space resolutions may thus encourage some important ties and projects to be local rather than transnational. Yet this does not necessarily imply that all communal ties are organised into spatially defined entities. We will take up this point later when discussing transnational social spaces emerging from migration. Furthermore, long-distance ties can be maintained even without modern communication and transportation, as long as such ties are structurally embedded in kinship systems or common local origins. Geographical mobility in times of distance-reducing communication also encourages the maintenance and construction of weaker social ties that extend beyond closely knit local collectives. In sum, micro-level theories are best in accounting for individual decision making.

The Meso-Level: The Migrant's Social Context

Many micro-level theories are predicated upon the assumption that potential migrants react to macro-level differences such as wages or rights. Yet migration decisions are made in a context constituted by the intensity and type of engagement in a localised set of ties and projects. Stated in a radical way, meso-level analysis does not start from individual potential migrants but from the fact that these individuals maintain strong, weak or symbolic social ties with others. Information, norms and interests are channelled across these ties. It looks at the pattern of relationships between the relevant sets of individual and collective actors.

The meso-level analysis assumes that the mutual transactions of individual actors are one of the most crucial facts of cultural, political and economic life. They thus constitute the starting point for any analysis. This approach concentrates on how the very structure and content of social ties between individual and collective actors shapes their behaviour. In this perspective migration decision making is analysed by looking at membership in collectives (e.g. groups and institutions), participation in a network (e.g. people who know each other but have no authoritative spokesperson) or the coordination of several collectives (e.g. how organisations relate to each other). *Social capital* exists if social action is facilitated within and between collectives, institutions or networks through mutual trust, the norm of reciprocity, and solidarity (chapter 7).

We could start with the proposition that individuals are members of economic units, such as co-residing kinship groups. Such a group may seek to diversify the risk to its economic well-being by sending members to work in different labour markets, one of which could be located abroad. The goals pursued could be as diverse as the education of children or the purchase of a house and of consumer goods. The actual decision made (stay or move or a combination of both), the strategies pursued after moving (relocate temporarily, return home after recurrent stays or settle abroad) or staying (exploiting local assets or voicing dissatisfaction) would depend very much on specific gendered social ties in units such as households. It would also depend upon decisions on reproduction and work over the life course (chapter 8). Yet it is not enough to assume that small groups of kin or other relations instead of individuals optimise or maximise certain utilities. Furthermore, interesting questions arise, such as: Who decides on who migrates and who stays in household or family with a specific social structure of authority and power?

Anthropologists have pointed to the prominence of gender and household relations in shaping the causes, forms and consequences of migration. Nevertheless, they have also insisted as a sort of corollary that gender relations and household dynamics vary widely between cultural groups and over time, and are in themselves the result of cultural rules played out in specific economic and political contexts (chapter 8). The social-relational concept has the advantage that it can operationalise social ties, among others, in terms of their strength (weak and strong), their content (e.g. exchange, reciprocity, solidarity) and the centrality of actors (e.g. power and authority).

Not only local ties in their various forms but also *symbolic ties* that transcend local communities and relate to symbolic (or 'imagined') communities of religion, ethnicity or nation are visible (chapter 7). For example, there were about 18 million international refugees in the early 1990s, while approximately 24 million were internally displaced. Of course, we have to consider the fact that a fair share of those internally displaced would have no recourse to move abroad in the first place due to a lack of resources to overcome barriers of transportation (despondence, see chapter 6). Moreover, we would expect that many of the 18 millions abroad are close to their homelands, especially in Africa.

Nevertheless, this ratio of internally displaced to refugees and asylum seekers abroad attests to the plausibility of the hypothesis that symbolic ties in the form of common ethnicity may be operative across nation-state borders. Most borders in Africa are the legacy of European colonial powers and cut across linguistic and religious lines.

We may now enquire about the most likely *stay-or-go strategies* of potential migrants involved, which depend on the stage in their life course and their position within relevant decision-making units as part of a time-space strategy. The range of options for potential movers who do not fear persecution seems to be clearest. When a decision-making kinship group is growing and children are young, we would expect, *ceteris paribus*, either no migration or temporary or recurrent migration to take place as favoured options. In contrast, settlement in the receiving country of families migrating with young children would tend to be a rather prolonged process and thus not as likely. Also, as the European post-war experience teaches, there are often legal restrictions to bringing the family along in the beginning, e.g. only single male or female workers were allowed in on guestworker schemes. Again, all other conditions being equal, we would expect this latter strategy to be chosen by single men or women, or recently married couples without children. Among other things, the age of children is a key factor in determining decisions to migrate and to return. A possible time scheme could look like this: We would expect that a child of up to 6 years of age is mostly socialised in the family. This poses few obstacles for a family living abroad. Yet in the 7–12 years bracket school starts and, if parents emphasise learning of the mother tongue, language training may induce return. In the following age group, the 12–16 year-olds, gender roles are taught and in some cultures, parents may prefer their daughters to return in order to be married. If the children are between 16 and 20 years old, it may be too late to return for the childrens' sake because they may want to stay because they have been (partly) socialised and educated in the receiving country.

Using a social-relational and structural approach, we can derive two hypotheses about the role of the social organisation of reproduction and gender relations. Firstly, human reproduction is inherently culturally embedded. For instance, culture-specific norms organise not only when and where children are born, and to whom they are related kinship-wise. These norms also have immediate relevance for mobility since they also influence where the new reproductive units should reside, and where and how children should be brought up in order to ensure cultural 'literacy' Secondly, connecting meso- and macro-levels, it depends on the recruitment policies of the receiving countries whether men or women are hired as migrant labour. Thus, changes in the global division of labour could cause a shift in the gendered division of labour migrants with subsequent repercussions on those parts of kinship or friendship networks that may be left behind (chapter 8).

In sum, a meso-level approach is best in explaining the local character of many assets as a result of the social embeddedness of various forms of capital.

The Macro-Context: The Structural Causes and the Direction of Migration

Macro-level structural factors indicate that there may be very different contexts (settings) that shape geographical mobility and immobility. It is safe to assume, and it has been shown repeatedly, that specific structural conditions (e.g. political conditions such as revolutions and civil wars, or economic inequalities and immigration policies) have caused, prohibited, directed and accelerated migration and refugee flows at key historical junctures. Approaches concentrating on economic, political and cultural factors have placed the causes of emigration in a global perspective. World-systems theory, developed by historical sociologists, views migration as part of worldwide and long-term processes of politico-economic competition between core and periphery, North and South. While some versions of world-systems theory have focused on the uneven development of capitalism as a driving force of global strat-ification, others have emphasised the strategic interactions of political collectives such as nation-states. One could extend arguments that the cultural linkages between colonial powers and their (former) dependencies have been conducive to international movement. The application of this approach to international migration and inputs from general systems theory have led to more specific theories that have conceptualised migration as taking place in a system of sending and receiving counties, emphasising the manifold linkages between senders and receivers.

There are also more partial macro-structural theories for explanations taken up here. For example, economists have made the convincing argument that differentials in income, capital, employment opportunities, etc. between sending and receiving countries are among the key pre-requisites that drive movers. (On the micro-level this approach posits that potential migrants observe these wage differentials between sending and receiving countries and respond to expected positive returns on foreign employment.) Alternatively, some theorists have concentrated on receiving-country factors: migrants may be recruited by foreign employers seeking to import workers for specific tasks. This latter approach seems to be best applicable to specific historical periods and countries, mainly guestworker recruitments into Northwestern Europe from the Mediterranean during the 1960s. Nevertheless, it is one of the few undisputed findings of international migration research that virtually all labour-migration flows have been originally initiated by the receiving countries in the North.

Apart from these politico-economic explanations, disciplines such as geography have favored the eco-demographic approach, i.e. the impact of physical environment and of population growth on migration. A crucial idea is that population growth and environmental deterioration trigger migration, although the causal links are not entirely clear.

This latter insight suggests that the *control policies* of the countries in the North decisively shape the onset, the direction and the selection of migrants. One of the most crucial facts of state control of international flows of people is the fact that the nation-states in the North largely control entry. It is evident that migration within a nation-state is considered to be a human right and states are not allowed to prevent emigration. However, there is no corresponding right to immigration under international law. Immigration is regarded as an issue of nation-state sovereignty. This state of affairs is an expression of the undisputed *sovereignty of nation-states* in the global political order (or anarchy when seen from a 'realist's' point of view) to control borders and regulate which category of people is or is not admitted and what the specific conditions of entry are concerning legal status, access to work, housing and social services. If temporary migrants turn into permanent settlers questions of access to rights and membership in the polity come up. What civil, social, political or even cultural rights are attached to a particular legal status of an immigrant? Under what conditions are immigrants and refugees 'naturalised' and do thus gain access to *citizenship*? The latter issue is of utmost importance because it defines the parameters of political participation and belonging in the receiving nation-states (chapter 6).

Until recently, political scientists and legal scholars have over-emphasised the analysis of labour migration to the detriment of refugee movements. Looking for the causes of refugee movements, political scientists have started to focus upon the breakup of societal consensus, reflected in political conflicts in the state, such as social class, ethnic and religious strife. People may flee for many reasons, for example because they fear for their physical safety, want to practise their religion, escape from political, racial or ethnic oppression, or even from environmental disaster (e.g. Saharan Africa).

Regarding the international political system, there is a partial international regime that regulates the admission of refugees. The basic expression of this partial regime is the Geneva Convention. International law stipulates that political refugees are allowed to seek asylum. Yet, again, it is the prerogative of sovereign nation-states to grant asylum. It is not a right an individual can claim *vis-à-vis* the nation-state. Therefore, the admission of refugees is plagued by the fact that there are no clear-cut criteria of who is a refugee and who is not (chapter 6).

An analysis of refugee movements can start with the efforts of state builders to establish and consolidate *nation-state projects* by instilling a sense of collective identity, loyalty and cultural homogeneity. Among the more common measures taken are inducing people to speak a common language and implementing a universal educational system. However, as the fledgling nation-states in many parts of the world show, it is not a foregone conclusion that these projects succeed in the ambitious goal of homogenising the population, and in the even more fundamental one of maintaining control over the territory. Although the international system of nation-states usually supports state sovereignty, there are manifold constellations that induce or even produce refugee flows. For example, members of ethnic minority groups may seek to widen their political influence over domestic affairs by relocating abroad, especially if their political activities are restricted. In more dramatic cases, civil war may ensue, the nation-state project may collapse and widespread flight is usually one of the consequences (chapter 6).

It is not enough simply to distinguish between labour migration and refugee flows, and develop separate analytical tools to deal with these distinct movements of people. The very fact of separation largely hinges upon the decision to make a distinction between involuntary and voluntary forms of movement; sometimes thought to be a continuum from forced movement in the midst of political persecution at one end of the scale, to a conscious decision to move abroad in the face of obvious attractions in the receiving countries, on the other. This distinction is only plausible if we reject a commonly held assumption about the nature of political and economic factors. Involuntary migration is often associated with political persecution while voluntary migration is tied to economic motivations of the movers. This is fallacious because, among other things, economic crises that induce movements can also be interpreted in some instances as an outcome of political choices concerning economic policy. There are many instances of ruinous economic policies that drove nation-states to the brink of disaster. In addition, involuntary flight might be caused by many factors other than political ones. For instance, ecological disasters have ravaged Saharan Africa during the past decades.

By and large, macro-structural theories are particularly useful in explaining the underlying *structural causes* and the *direction* of inter-national migration. The direction of the three great waves of international migration – from Europe to the colonised world, from Europe to the

white-settler colonies and from South to North – can all be explained by
the stark extent of economic inequality, imbalance of political power
and, perhaps, the cultural divergence (e.g. more attractive life-style)
between sending and receiving countries. Macro-structural theories
thus give us an idea as to where migration is most likely to occur and
even a first hint as to group selection and admission. However, these
questions can only be answered in a more comprehensive way if we
take into account the motives and resources of individual actors,
the stage in their life course and the social relations among the actors
themselves as points of departure for our analysis of the particular
migratory space.

The Volume of International South-to-North Migration: Limited by Local Assets

The second main question of this book has been: Why do most potential
migrants stay in their home countries? Why is relative immobility
so prevalent? Immobility is relative when we consider international
migration but not internal migration within the respective nation-state.

First of all, one plausible explanation for relative immobility is that
internal migration may constitute a viable alternative. In other words,
there are a *variety of time-space strategies* available to potential
migrants. Internal circulation and internal migration (rural–rural, rural–
urban, urban–urban, urban–rural) are often well-established strategies.
Yet, much international movement is due to 'artificial' nation-state
borders, for example in Africa. Most borders are the legacy of European
colonial powers. Modern-day borders therefore cut across old internal
migration flows, and have turned them into international ones. Also,
internal migration could function to restrict international migration but
could also be a first step towards long-distance migration across nation-
state borders.

Secondly, there are alternatives to geographical exit, for example
political voice. Territorial exit is often anteceded, accompanied and
followed by political voice. The general idea is that political organisations such as nation-states may fail to meet the demands of their
members. Members' dissatisfaction may be expressed in terms of exit or
voice. *Exit* can mean a variety of strategies of geographical mobility.
Voice means political expression and action in the place of origin or in
the receiving country. The options of potential migrants to exercise exit
and/or voice strategies are constrained by nation-state policies and
international policies. Importantly, exit and voice are not exclusive
alternatives. Instead, they can be used in a sequence (e.g. migration and
political voice upon return), or at the same time (e.g. political activities

in the receiving state, influencing domestic politics in the sending country).

The concept of *loyalty* has been taken two steps further. In a first step, the idea of self-adjustment (autism) is an alternative to exit and voice. Rather than trying to change the environment, the individual adjusts to it. Inaction, in our case more specifically, non-exit and non-voice, is the result. However, this would also mean to exaggerate the consensus basis of many political regimes in the South. Therefore, in a second step, the term *despondence* takes this into account, saying that the masses in the South completely lack resources for exit and/or voice, and are in a state of resignation to a hostile environment around them (chapter 6). Because of severe structural constraints, these persons cannot be considered to be potential migrants anymore.

Thirdly, many assets available to potential migrants, be they economic, political or social, are tied to certain spaces. A certain part of the abilities and assets of individuals and groups are *location-specific*, because they can only be used in a specific place and are not readily transferable to other places of residence, especially when viewed in an international perspective (chapter 3). This points to the fact that there are problems involved in transferring financial and human capital. According to this approach, individual actors weigh the costs and benefits of transferring capital. For example, potential migrants could decide to stay or to move in the country of origin because they are not able adequately to deploy their educational and professional assets abroad. The value of relative immobility then could be a result of strategies chosen by potential migrants to accumulate their advantages. This insider advantage allows potential migrants to reap the rewards of staying relatively immobile. Economists so far have mainly focused on advantages from being an insider in a certain firm and therefore earning more. While these production-side advantages have been explored more often, consumption-side benefits are less explored.

Language skills are a prime example of an asset that constitutes an insider advantage. Of course, language is an indispensable means of communication in getting to all kinds of resources. Migrating to another country may incur costs of learning another language. Unless a migrant is proficient in this other language, there are usually serious obstacles to 'good' jobs, self-employment and even housing.

The personal projects, ties and various linkages to important persons in specific places or geographical units can be an important explanation as to why potential migrants prefer to stay in the place of origin despite the economic advantages (e.g. labour migrants) or despite actual or potential harm to life (e.g. refugees). The question then is which sort of ties potential migrants value the most.

Local and non-transferable assets may pertain to many areas of life. Human capital such as specific vocational qualifications is certainly but one example. Furthermore, social ties can be seen as the basis for social capital. Not only individual characteristics but also forms of social capital, such as trust, the norm of reciprocity and solidarity, facilitate social interaction. Social capital can only arise in social transactions between and among individual and collective actors. In this perspective the transferability of local assets abroad is extended to the social ties and social capital. For example, there are not only transferral costs in moving human capital abroad. It is also evident that social capital is not easily transferred internationally. This is an important insight because other forms of capital need a basis in social capital to be deployed. The enhanced concept of rationality means that one of the main reasons for relative immobility is that various forms of assets are difficult to transfer abroad (chapter 7). Furthermore, although our analytical tools do not allow for a systematic analysis of all the ties potential migrants attach to specific places, it is plausible to assume that emotional attachments to persons and physical features can also constitute an important factor favouring relative immobility. Should we perhaps also speak of emotional assets?

A very fruitful yet so far undertheorised approach that can bring in elements of analysis on all three levels is migration-systems analysis (chapters 2, 6 and 7). The migration-systems approach has three main characteristics. However, this approach has so far suffered from its lacking micro-foundation and, to the extent that it has not specified what makes networks function, a specified meso-level.

Firstly, the migration-systems approach assumes that migration systems pose the context in which movement occurs and that it influences actions on whether to stay or to move. Basically, this approach has at its most basic concept a migration system, defined as two or more locations (most often nation-states) connected to each other by flows and counterflows of people. It does not simply distinguish between regions of suppliers and receivers. In particular, the control policies of the sending and receiving states regulating exit, entry, residence and rights are of special importance. Also, international migrations cause counterstreams, e.g. remigration, that have to be considered. On the basis of the results of our analysis, migration systems could be conceptualised as *multi-tiered migratory spaces* that are defined by both inter- and transnational elements.

Secondly, systems theories have stressed the existence of *linkages* between countries *other than people*, such as trade and security alliances, colonial ties and flows of goods, services, information and ideas.

Thirdly, movement is not regarded as a static or one-time event, but rather as a *dynamic process* consisting of a sequence of events across time. Given the context of important factors such as economic inequalities within and between nation-states and the admission policies of the receiving states, individuals, households and families develop strategies to cope with stay-or-go alternatives. In short, self-feeding and feedback processes develop within migration systems. Theorising the dynamics of migration has thus moved from a consideration of movement as a linear, unidirectional, push-and-pull, cause-effect movement, to notions that emphasise migration as circular, interdependent, progressively complex and self-modifying systems in which the effect of changes in one part can be traced through the whole of the system. It helps to explain international movement as a self-feeding process that gains in momentum as networks reduce the direct monetary costs of movement and the opportunity costs (that is, the earnings forgone while moving, searching for work and housing, learning new skills), and decrease the psychological costs of adjustment to a new environment in the receiving country. Yet, as our results show, the overemphasis of systems analysis on the flow and direction of migration has to be rectified by introducing the specific nature of various forms of personal and collective projects and local assets.

Migration Processes: Cumulative Causation, Development and Change

The question following why potential migrants may or may not migrate is: What are the initial dynamics of migration? Basically, migration can be seen as a self-feeding process with a strong internal momentum that over time reinforces itself. Migration is also thought to have feedback effects upon development in the sending countries. The master concept with many integrative functions for the analysis of the migration process after first-time decision making is *cumulative causation*: Rising out-migration sets off structural changes that make additional migration more likely and that accelerate changes in the economic, political, social and cultural context. Here, the notion of cumulative causation is being extended beyond the realm of its impact on the migration process itself and economic development, highlighting the feedbacks on processes of social, cultural and political changes in the sending countries.

Following the distinction of analytical levels made earlier, we can separate the changes of values or preferences of individual movers and stayers (micro), the internal social relational or structural momentum of migration (meso) and the larger factors impacting upon and affected by migration (macro) (see figure 9.2). The corresponding questions therefore are:

analytical	**MICRO** **individuals' motives** **and access to basic** **resources**	**MESO** **interactive uses** **of capital and** **time**	**MACRO** **structural** **oppprtunities**
key concepts	rising expectations and relative deprivation	chain migration: migrant networks; 'S-shaped curve'	development and change; 'inverted U-curve'
explains primarily what?	value (preference) change among stayers and movers	internal dynamics of the migration process	effects upon economic development, social, political and cultural change

Figure 9.2 Levels of Analysis in the Process of Migration

1. How do the preferences, desires, values of movers and stayers develop once migration is underway? What are the dynamics of the process of rising expectations?
2. How do migrants overcome the 'barriers' of migration by means of informal (e.g. networks) or formal (e.g. recruitment agencies) 'carriers'? How do they solve the problem of providing migrant networks? How do collective actors try to regulate the relations between organisations and networks?
3. Does migration impact on economic development, social, political and cultural change, or vice versa? If yes, how? What are the long-run consequences of development fostered by migration?

The Micro-Level: Information and Relative Deprivation

Once migration has been triggered, swift changes follow regarding the ease of moving abroad. Here, *brokers and pioneer migrants* fulfil an important role. Brokers can trigger migration through recruiting pioneer migrants. The early migrants follow the footsteps of the pioneer migrants: Past migration increases information available for actual decision makers on the advantages and disadvantages of certain locations. Provided pioneer migrants are relatively successful, past migration accelerates further decisions to 'go' because it increases the level of information for later migrants which in turn reduces the risks associated with a decision to migrate. As a consequence, chain migration is likely to develop. Failure of pioneer migrants to establish themselves has the opposite effect. As networks develop and as brokers gain a foothold in various locations in the receiving country it can be assumed that a certain degree of geographical spread ensues. Networks, especially kinship networks, can also have a sort of insurance function. The utility of networks is likely to be greatest where migration risks are very high in general and information on job and housing opportunities are rare and costly (chapter 3).

Once migration movements have started, changes in preferences and desires may be expected among stayers and movers. This is a reaction to opportunity structures that may become more favourable to the migrants thanks to changes in the admission policies of receiving countries and the conditions in the countries of origin. As migration flows develop, the desires of the potential migrants to move could expand. For this to occur, information flows via media and personal contacts (e.g. return migrants) are prerequisites, given the strong tendencies towards relative immobility postulated earlier. Information travels easily through migrant networks. Yet the basic idea is that, as opportunities for migration increase, frustration increases even faster. This is a special instance of *relative deprivation*. Large gains with limited migration opportunities, i.e. guestworker recruitment in Europe or the Bracero Program in the United States, ultimately lead to frustration of those who could not migrate, and even to illegal (unauthorised) migration. Thus, migration as a self-sustaining process depends not only on decreasing information costs through expanding networks of migration, but also on transformation of preferences and expectations of the stayers who feel the feedback effects – such as growing scarcity of land that may be bought by return migrants and lower social status associated with not migrating abroad (chapter 7). In other words, the mental or cognitive maps of migrants change as the migration process gets underway (chapter 2).

A similar yet distinct process could apply to refugees. However, in their case it would not be so much admission policies but internal persecution or discrimination that set off chains of events leading to flight and more flight. In the absence of direct persecution and repression, minority groups in nation-states could perhaps come to favour a relocation abroad to escape and even change the oppressive political regime.

The ultimate preference change would be the settlement of migrants in the receiving countries. However, the changes in individuals' preferences, initiated and spurred by macro-conditions and opportunities, take place within the boundaries of collectives and networks.

The Meso-Level: The S-Shaped Curve

The very process of international migration tends to affect individual motivations, social structures and cultural milieux in ways that can enhance migration but also limit it. As such, international migration tends to increase in volume and tends to become socially more diverse before it slows again. These changes accumulate over time and change the situation in which migration occurs. They also have repercussions on admission policies in the receiving countries that become more restrictive when, for example, perceived 'overforeignisation' and competition for jobs, housing and social services, or threats to an alleged cultural homogeneity, are connected to undesired immigrants and turned into political issues. However, in the initial stages of the migration process, when information about international migration accumulates and network connections to the receiving countries intensify, the risks and costs associated with international movement tend to decrease. This induces more people to move abroad. When the supply of potential migrants is exhausted, the migration volume falls. In sum, international migration may tend to turn into a self-feeding process and acquire an internal momentum of its own. Gradually, it may become increasingly independent of the conditions that originally caused it.

We could also speculate about an s-shaped curve concerning the geographic diversity of migration. In this view migration begins with a narrow range of each community's socio-economic structure, but over time usually broadens to incorporate other social groups, and then slows again. If we cumulatively plot this development, we arrive at an s-shaped curve. In the course of events, especially during the expanding phase, it becomes easier for migrants to gather more accurate information and to transfer their assets such as financial, human and social capital abroad. This is made possible in large part by the enabling structures such as networks and support groups that embed individual migrants in relations of trust and contribute to reciprocity and solidarity. All these aspects help to reduce individual uncertainty and the transferability of assets (chapter 7).

Regarding *return migration*, it is likely that each type of migration has a differential impact on the propensity to go back to the country of origin, depending on whether it be permanent migration, recurrent migration or temporary migration. These types of movement involve widely differing levels of commitment on the part of the mover to origin and destination. In the case of temporary migration, the relatively short time of absence can work to leave social ties to the country of origin basically unchanged. This could also apply to recurrent migration, even though the absence from the sending unit is somewhat institutionalised. In the case of permanent migration, we would expect that ties and linkages, of both a material and symbolic nature, gradually decline as time passes. In the second generation we would expect these ties to the communities and countries of origin to be much less prevalent than among the first generation. Yet, it is an open question for empirical investigation whether facilitated means of transportation and exchange of information and goods could prolong the period in which strong and symbolic social ties are maintained to the country of origin. Furthermore, there are no pure types of migration. For example, temporary migration may turn into permanent migration and vice versa.

This type of reasoning could be used to get a clearer understanding of which groups are most likely to return. Studies of the feedback effects of migration have tended to focus on the individual migrant, on the one hand, and large aggregates of individuals, on the other. It is plausible, however, that much of the feedback is felt by social units such as families and communities involved in the organisation of daily life. One hypothesis would be: The stronger the commitment of the migrants to social units in the country of origin in terms of ties and material linkages (e.g. investment of remittances in the sending country), the more likely it is that return migration of successful migrants takes place. In turn, the higher the rate of this kind of return migration, the greater the likelihood that positive economic feedback effects occur in the sending communities. This functions as a complement to the hypothesis that some return migrants move back to the sending region because they have failed to establish themselves economically in the receiving country, or did not find the new environment suitable for their desires. Moreover, the whole catalogue of possible motives mentioned for first-time movers could be applied to return migration. Extrapolating from earlier considerations on the importance of local assets, two factors seem to be decisive. Firstly, to what extent is it possible for migrants to retransfer local assets to the original sending country? Secondly, and related to this first aspect, is it possible for return migrants to pick up local ties established before departure that they have perhaps maintained during their absence?

So far, the basic thrust of the asset concept used here has been to suggest some ways in which networks facilitate access to scarce resources such as information, jobs and housing for individuals and small social units in first-time, recurrent or return migration. If we extend the meaning of networks to include not only individual migrants but also collective actors such as nation-state governments and NGOs, we also get yet another view, not only on how migration dynamics unfold but on their longer-term impact.

The Macro-Level (1): Migration and Economic Development

The relationship between migration and economic development is twofold, depending on whether we analyse the effect of levels of economic development on migration potential and behaviour, or whether we are interested in the consequences of international migration for economic development. Firstly, the question is to what extent emigration depends not only upon the differences between the development in the emigration and immigration country but also upon the absolute level of development in the sending country. Secondly, analysts mostly agree that many individual migrants derive significant net welfare benefits from migration, but the net impact of their moves on the communities and regions the migrants leave and the areas they settle in are less clear, not to speak of the effects on economies on a national and international scale.

As to the first set of questions concerning the impact of development on migration, one of the crucial hypotheses is that the *absolute level of development* matters. Net immigration and the net stock of foreigners residing in a country are in some way positively related to its level of development. When seen over decades in the late nineteenth and throughout the twentieth century this relationship seems to hold even considering the strong influence of other factors, such as immigration control policies (chapter 4).

One of the key elements is the so-called '*inverted U-curve*' thesis: it says that development often first enhances and thereafter reduces the scope and incentives for migration. In more detail, the argument is that countries at some intermediate level of development (measured as per capita income) are the most likely emigration countries. While at a lower level of development, initial monetary costs of migration represent serious obstacles to moving internationally, income differentials matter most as incentives for migration at intermediate levels of development. To the degree that the sending countries develop modern economies, the opportunities structuring migration decisions alter and broaden. Migration rapidly increases at this stage and reaches a hub. Yet, increasing levels of economic development, integration and the growing importance of insider-specific advantages bound to a certain location make potential migrants less likely to migrate. The sequencing of enhancement and reduction of migratory flows (the location of the U-curve's hub) would, among other things, very much depend on the distance involved in migration (e.g. internal short-distance migration, international long-distance migration) and on certain characteristics of migrants (e.g. financial, human and social capital).

Secondly, there is the large question about the impact of migration on the level and direction of development. The effects of migration on the sending and receiving countries basically depend upon the type of differences between them. From a classical economic point of view, *convergence* between the two countries will eventually result when countries mainly differ in their relative endowment with production factors (capital and labour) but are otherwise relatively equal. The effect of migration will be to enhance the welfare in both countries and will speed up the convergence process. In this case migration between these two countries will only be a very temporary phenomenon; it will proceed until the endowment with production factors has evened out.

From a *divergence* point of view it can be argued that countries may differ because there is a variation in the technology they use and in their production structure. Furthermore, it is assumed that economies of scale can be realised. In a situation where these differences between countries matter, migration can become a crucial factor shaping centre–periphery patterns. If economies of scale stay important and/or if the differences in technologies available persist, migration would allow the front-runners at least temporarily to secure and even enhance their lead. In this case migration could contribute to widening instead of narrowing the gap. However, in this view divergence would still be a temporary phenomenon because, in the long run, the diffusion of technologies is thought to restrict the scope for reaping scale economies and for maintaining technological leads.

While these considerations imply that economic development is usually important for migration flows, the consequences of migration for development are much less clear-cut. As shown, there are plausible theoretical arguments to expect migration to contribute to development under particular circumstances; yet it is equally plausible to argue that development in general is subject to much more complex determinants than migration. Therefore, in many situations, migration is likely to be of minor importance for economic development, although this may be partly due to the usually rather limited scale of international migration that actually occurs (chapter 4).

These considerations are of vital importance when evaluating policies of nation-states in the North, aimed to curb international migration flows by helping sending countries to develop economically. One example is the so-called '*root-causes*' approach. Although governments and analysts cannot agree on what exactly the root causes of international migration are, a complex set of policy recommendations is geared towards improving the human-rights situation in sending countries, making sure that refugees receive help not too far from their countries of origin, and varied forms of aid to economic development. However, if these forms of aid include humanitarian viz. military intervention and development projects displacing populations from their residential space, these policies could even contribute to more migration (chapter 5). In other words, it is not clear whether policies can really modify the development–migration nexus without inducing and producing even more migration and thus even more hardship.

The very premise underlying economic development in the sending countries is open to question. In general, migration research has mentioned *ecological issues* only in regard to environmental refugees. Yet, behind the migration–development discourse held by academic researchers loom unresolved questions of a larger kind. Often, it is assumed that migration is *one* of the means, albeit not the most crucial, to reduce disparities of opportunities between people in the South and the North by resettlement in the North but above all by economic development in the South. This would require steep advances in economic development (measured in growth rates such as GDP) in the countries of the South. Immediately, given limited ecological space, this raises the problem of ecological overload in the South, especially in the light of continuing population growth rates (chapter 5).

The Macro-Level (2): Social, Political and Cultural Change

Social change: Migration is often associated with a separation of the kinship groups. This could mean a widening of the roles of those group members who stay behind, especially women. Migrant women can be expected to increase their autonomy in, for instance, financial affairs. During their absence, it would certainly depend on the specific situation whether tasks are appropriated by women who stay, or taken over by other male members of extended households. Gender-role alterations could thus occur upon the return of male or female migrants who have gathered experience abroad. Or, those left behind could take over new roles in the absence of those migrating. However, we could also imagine situations in which the migration of women is organised in ways that accommodate a patriarchal order and thus stabilise a way of life in the sending communities. The direction of social change would seem to depend very much on the *gendered power and authority relations* in the narrow and wider kinship groups (chapters 7 and 8).

Political change: Very similar to the question raised by economists concerning the relationship between migration and economic development is the problem of migration and political change and the stability of political regimes (chapter 6). This is a plausible link to be pursued in further research. In many nation-states in the South we cannot discern a continuous curve representing incremental alterations at the margins. Rather, the formation of new nation-states and the accommodation of social and political groupings have often resulted in building pressures that have not only erupted in social revolutions, domestic warfare and political persecution, but have also been visible in more subtle forms of minority discrimination. Therefore, theories of flight that regard ethnic and social class conflicts in newly formed states in Africa and Asia as a prime producer of international refugees would fit very well into such a *non-incremental view of political change.*

The other side of the coin is the question of how refugee flows impact upon further political development in the sending countries. Large numbers of refugees abroad do indeed form political pressure groups to influence the political process. They sometimes exert influence also upon the governments of their host countries (e.g. Kurds in Germany or Sikhs in the United Kingdom). Also, there are political return migrants (e.g. Namibia). This is certainly an instance of transnational political spaces.

Cultural change: As mentioned above, processes of cumulative caus-ation work to reinforce migration in a self-generating way, contributing to more migration. One of the impacts of ongoing international migration on culture could be that a *culture of migration* develops where migration is understood to be an accepted and desirable way to achieve social and economic mobility, more income or a life-style that could not be sustained by dependence on local resources only. On the receiving side, issues of language and religion have figured prominently in the process of politicisation of immigration. Large numbers of immigrants often raise the fear among the native and settled populations that the newcomers will not learn the mainstream language and will practise religious beliefs that are alien to believers of the respective mainstream religions. For example, fears over Spanish getting a foothold as a permanent second language have been prominent in the United States, while in Europe Islamist tendencies have served as a rallying term to denote allegedly illiberal practices. Often, these dangers are evoked to implement immigration controls of unwelcome groups.

Many of the issues raised for social, political and cultural change converge in the concept of *transnational social space* (chapter 7). These spaces can be defined as relatively permanent flows of people, goods and services across international borders that tie stayers and movers in both areas. Both regions are sending and receiving at the same time. This concept could be seen as an extension of the concept of migratory space introduced earlier. Transnational social spaces suggest that even more permanent settlement in the receiving country does not necessarily imply a complete rupture of social ties and other forms of linkages. Because there is a constant circular flow of people, it could even be argued that it may be useful in certain cases to talk of transnational migrants instead of emigrants and immigrants.

Transnational social spaces can plausibly be expected to require a flourishing transnational exchange of goods, ideas and persons that is hardly imaginable without a multitude of strong, weak and symbolic ties between the sending and receiving communities and regions. And local assets come in again: While this concept helps to explain immobility (first-time decision making), migration (once the process is underway), return migration and decline of migration flows, transnational social spaces seem to depend on *twofold local assets* that are located both in the sending and in the receiving countries. If such transnational spaces exist for longer periods of time, e.g. longer than the first generation of migrants, effects are expected to be seen not only on the level of exchange but also on the level of collective identity.

Exit policies of the sending countries and entry and integration policies of the receiving nation-states exert a significant influence on the shape transnational migrant communities take. These policies circum- scribe two extremes on a continuum of transnational social spaces. At the one end, if the option of return is cut off for various reasons including nation-state policies, we would expect transnational communities to turn into *diasporas*, i.e. communities with a distinct cultural and social life over long periods of time. The members of diasporas refer to a common homeland they long to return to. Globally, before the establishment of the state of Israel, the Jewish diaspora was a prime example. If, at the other end, the migrants were easily to adapt culturally and socially to the receiving groups, transnational communities would rapidly dissolve and the migrants would *assimilate*, based on ethnic or religious common- alities with the majority of the receiving population. Most members of the sending communities would try to join the pioneer movers, often accompanied by generous receiving-state policies. The return of ethnic Germans from Eastern Europe to the Federal Republic of Germany after the Second World War would be a good example. Most South to North transnational communities could be expected to be situated in between these two polar opposites.

Coming Full Circle: Common Questions Revisited and Expanded

The partial answers to the three questions which guided our project have been dealt with under the headings of three common concepts. Our results suggest that the disciplinary findings have indeed converged significantly. Despite largely differing disciplinary foci, methods and intellectual traditions, many concepts used can be fruitfully extended for multidisciplinary purposes. A number of conceptual tools flow like a thread through various chapters and could be extended to virtually all disciplines involved: the enhanced rationality concept with relaxed assumptions about individual utility maximisers who engage in personal and collective projects, the primacy of place, local ties and local assets, the transferability of various forms of assets, especially capital, the gendered structures of power and authority, the options of exit, voice, self-adjustment and despondence, and the inverted U-curve. Nevertheless, our common work has also made more obvious glaring deficiencies that need more theoretical attention. One of the most obvious examples is the concept of refugee. Despite numerous attempts to typologise international movement, it has not been possible to discuss labour migration and refugee movements under a common roof. Our analyses have presented some ideas that could be helpful along the way, such as attention to the genesis of these flows in nation-state projects and complex issues of economic development.

This comparative summary now allows us to specify better and more detailed questions for further research. Ultimately, the value of our effort can only be seen when subjecting the common concepts and hypotheses on the causes of migration, relative immobility and cumulative causation to thorough empirical testing. The following items are a selected list of problems and questions arising from our theoretical considerations that should be submitted to empirical investigation.

(1) Migration-Decision Making: Migratory Space

Conceptualising migration: How can we conceptualise migration as including various forms of migration hitherto thought to be opposites, e.g. economically motivated labour migration and forced refugee movement?

Time horizons: What determines the time horizon of potential migrants? How do potential migrants or groups select and process information?

Iteration: Does the decision-making process itself impact upon the decision to stay or go, i.e. how much more or less likely is a potential migrant to say 'yes, I go' or 'no, I stay' in his/her n-th consideration than in the first?

Life course: How do specific life-course trajectories of potential migrants (including time horizons of individuals and collectives) vary by age, gender, education, etc.? How do institutional factors and decisions in life courses shape individual migration trajectories?

Uncertainty and risk: How are problems of uncertainty managed by channelling information to reduce risks? What channels of communication are most important for what kind of migration and migrant (e.g. social ties versus publicly available information)?

Decision-making units: Under what circumstances are individuals or small social units (e.g. kinship groups) decision makers? What kind of authority and power relations condition the decision-making process?

(2) Explanations of Immobility: Local Assets

Local assets: To what extent and under what conditions are abilities and assets of potential migrants location-specific?

Transferability: What determines the transferability of migrants' capital and assets?

Alternatives to migration: Under what circumstances do internal migration or internal circulation present a first step or an alternative to international migration?

(3) The Dynamics of Migration: Cumulative Causation

Structural initiation of migration and refugee flows: How do migration dynamics differ depending on the factors that triggered them (e.g. civil wars or recruitment on the part of receiving countries)? How does the role of supporting networks and collectives vary in these cases?

Selectivity and functioning of migrant networks: Who gains access to migrant networks via which communication channels? How is the problem of providing the collective good of reducing migration costs solved in migrant networks?

Rate of adopting migration strategies: Why do we find in some places within the same sending country or region that migration rapidly reaches a state of chain migration while others develop more slowly and achieve only modest rates of emigration or none at all?

Self-feeding processes and information: Are mass-media channels more effective in creating knowledge of countries to go to than inter-personal channels? Are social ties more effective than the mass media in forming and changing attitudes towards the very idea of exiting, and thus in influencing the decision to stay or to go?

Economic development: Has international South to North migration enhanced development convergence rather than divergence?

Social change: Under what circumstances do return migrants change the division of labour in families or households and under what con-ditions does it stay the same? How does international migration impact upon the composition of domestic groups?

Political change: How do non-movers organise collectively to combine strategies such as recurrent and temporary migration, on the one hand, and improving the quality of life through associations in the region of origin, on the other? What role does political 'voice' play in this process? How do sending-country governments intervene in issues concerning their (former) citizens in the receiving countries?

Cultural change and continuity: How do 'cultures of migration' develop over generations in specific regions of the world?

Transnational social spaces: Is it true, as often claimed, that immigrants today increasingly migrate between two spatial locations, moving back and forth? Under what circumstances do transnational social spaces evolve? What implications does the possible existence of transnational social spaces have for our notions of emigrants and immigrants, migration and remigration? Do forms of recurrent migration between sending and receiving countries evolve that are stable over a long period of time, possibly over generations?

References

Abiri, E. (1995) *Human Rights or Security: Perceptions of Migration,* mimeo, PADRIGU, Gothenburg University.

Adams, R. H. (1989) 'Workers Remittances and Inequality in Rural Egypt', *Economic Migration and Cultural Change,* vol. 38, pp. 45–71.

Adepoju, A. and Hammar, T. (1996) eds. *International Migration In and From Africa: Dimensions, Challenges and Prospects,* PHRDA/CEIFO, Dakar, Senegal.

Adepoju, A. (1995) 'The Dynamics of Emigration: Sub-Saharan Africa', in *Causes of Migration,* Proceedings of a Workshop, Luxemburg Dec. 1994. Eurostat.

Adler, S. (1977) *International Migration and Dependence,* Gower, Farnborough.

—— (1980) *Swallows' Children: Emigration and Development in Algeria,* International Labour Office, International Migration for Employment Branch, Geneva.

Ahmed, I. (1994) 'Western and Muslim Perceptions of Universal Human Rights', *Afrika Focus,* vol. 10, no. 1–2.

—— (1996) *State, Nation and Ethnicity in Contemporary South Asia,* Pinter, London and New York.

Ajami, F. (1993) 'The Summoning: "But They Said, We Will Not Hearken"', *Foreign Affairs,* vol. 72, no. 4, Sept.–Oct, pp. 2–9.

Åkerman, S. (1976) 'Theories and Methods of Migration Research', in Runblom, H. and Norman, H. eds. *From Sweden to America,* University of Minnesota Press, Minneapolis.

Albrecht, G. (1972) *Soziologie der geographischen Mobilität,* Ferdinand Enke, Stuttgart.

Allardt, E. (1975) *About Dimensions of Welfare: An Exploratory Analysis of a Comparative Scandinavian Survey,* Research Group for Comparative Sociology, University of Helsinki.

Amano, M. (1983) 'On the Harris–Todaro Model with Intersectoral Migration of Labour', *Economica,* vol. 50, pp. 311–23.

Amin, S. (1970) *L'Accumulation à l'échelle mondiale,* Anthropos, Dakar.

—— (1974) 'Introduction', in Amin ed. *Modern Migrations in Western Africa,* Oxford University Press for International African Institute,

References

Oxford, pp. 65–124.
Ångström, L., Jiborn, M. and Westander, H. (1995) 'Escape from Swedish Guns', *Dagens Nyheter*, May 26 (in Swedish).
Appadurai, A. (1991) 'Global Ethnoscapes: Notes and Queries for a Transnational Anthropology', in Fox, R.G. ed. *Recapturing Anthropology. Working in the Present*, School of American Research Press, Santa Fé, New Mexico, pp. 191–210.
Appleyard, R. (1992a) 'International Migration and Development – An Unresolved Relationship', *International Migration*, vol. XXX, nos. 3–4, pp. 251–66.
—— (1992b) 'Migration and Development: A Critical Relationship', *Asian and Pacific Migration Journal*, vol. 1, no. 1, pp. 1–19.
—— (n.d.) *International Migration: The African Experience*, mimeo, Third African Population Conference, Dakar, IOM.
Åquist, A.-C. (1992) *Tidsgeografi i samspel med samhällsteori*, Meddelanden från Lunds universitets geografiska institutioner, Avhandlingar nr 115.
Arensberg, C.M. and Kimball, S.T. (1940) *Family and Community in Ireland*, Harvard University Press, Cambridge, Mass.
Asian and Pacific Migration Journal (1995) Special Issue 'Migration and the Family', vol. 4, nos. 2–3.
Athukorala, P. (1990) *The Use of Migrant Remittances in Development: Lessons from the Asian Experience,* Department of Economics, Discussion Paper 23/90, La Trobe University.
Banfield, E. (1958) *The Moral Basis of a Backward Society,* The Free Press, Glencoe, Ill.
Barro, R.J. (1990) 'Government Spending in a Simple Model of Endogenous Growth', *Journal of Political Economy*, vol. 98, pp. 103–25.
Barro, R.J. and Sala-i-Martin, X. (1991) 'Convergence Across States and Regions', *Brookings Papers on Economic Activity*, vol. 1, pp. 107–82.
—— (1992) 'Convergence', *Journal of Political Economy*, vol. 100(2), pp. 223–51.
—— (1995) *Economic Growth,* McGraw-Hill Advanced Series in Economics, McGraw-Hill, New York.
Bartley, R.L. (1993) 'The Case for Optimism: The West Should Believe in Itself', *Foreign Affairs*, vol. 72, no. 4, Sept.–Oct, pp. 15–18.
Basch, L., Glick-Schiller, N. and Szanton-Blanc, C. (1994) *Nations Unbound: Transnational Projects, Postcolonial Predicaments, and Deterritorialized Nation-States*, Gordon and Breach, Langhorne, PA.
Bauböck, R. (1994) *Transnational Citizenship: Membership and Rights in International Migration*, Edward Elgar, Aldershot.
Becker, G. (1962) 'Investment in Human Capital: a Theoretical

Analysis', *Journal of Economics*, vol. 70, pp. 9–49.

—— (1964) *Human Capital : A Theoretical and Empirical Analysis with Special Reference to Education*, New York and London.

Benmayor, Skotnes, R. and Skotnes A. (1994) eds. *Migration and Identity*, International Yearbook of Oral History and Life Stories, Oxford University Press, Oxford, vol. 3.

Berninghaus, S. and Seifert-Vogt, H.-G. (1987) 'International Migration under Incomplete Information', *Schweizerische Zeitschrift für Volkswirtschaft und Statistik*, vol. 123, pp. 199–218.

—— (1992) 'A Microeconomic Model of Migration', in Zimmermann, K.F. ed., *Migration and Economic Development*, Edition Springer, Berlin.

Bhagwati, J.N. and Hamada, K. (1974) 'The Brain Drain, International Integration of Markets for Professionals and Unemployment', *Journal of Development Economics*, vol. 1, no. 1, pp. 19–42.

Bhagwati, J.N. and Rodriguez, C. (1975) 'Welfare – Theoretical Analyses of the Brain Drain', *Journal of Development Economics*, vol. 2, pp. 91–100.

Bhagwati, J.N. and Srinivasan, T.N. (1974) 'On Reanalyzing the Harris–Todaro Model: Policy Rankings in the Case of Sector-Specific Sticky Wages', *American Economic Review*, vol. 64, pp. 502–8.

—— (1975) 'Alternative Policy Rankings in a Large Open Economy with Sector-Specific, Minimum Wages', *Journal of Economic Theory*, vol. 11, pp. 356–71.

Bhagwati, J.N. and Wilson, J.D. (1989) *Income Taxation and International Mobility*, Cambridge and London.

Bhattacharyya, B. (1985) 'The Role of Family Decision in Internal Migration – The Case of India', *Journal of Development Economics*, vol. 18, pp. 51–66.

Binyan, L. (1993) 'Civilization Grafting: No Culture is an Islam', *Foreign Affairs*, vol. 72, no. 4, Sept.–Oct, pp. 19–21.

Birks, J.S. and Sinclair, C.A. (1980) *International Migration and Development in the Arab Region*, ILO.

Bjerén, G. (1984) 'Familj i Sverige: Några tankar om släktskap och samliv', in Andersson, B.-E., ed., *Familjebilder: myter, verklighet, visioner* ('Family in Sweden: Some Reflections on Kinship and Cohabitation', in Swedish) Liber, Stockholm.

Bjerén, G. et al. (1981) 'Women: Work and Household Systems', special issue of *Antropologiska Studier*, nos. 30–1.

Blanchard, O. and Katz, L. (1992) 'Regional Evolutions', *Brookings Papers on Economic Activity*, vol. 1, pp. 1–75.

Bloch, M. and Bloch, J.H. (1980) 'Woman and the Dialectics of Nature in Eighteenth Century French Thought', in MacCormack, C. and

References

Strathern, M. eds, *Nature, Culture and Gender*, Cambridge University Press, Cambridge.

Böcker, A. (1995) 'Migration Networks: Turkish Migration to Western Europe', in *Causes of International Migration,* Proceedings of a Workshop, Eurostat, Luxembourg, 15–16 December 1994, pp. 151–72.

Bodnar, J. (1985) *The Transplanted: A History of Immigrants in Urban America*, Indiana University Press, Bloomington.

Böhning, W.R. (1984) *Studies in International Labour Migration*, Macmillan, London.

Böhning, W.R. and Schloeter-Paredes, M.-L. (1994) eds. *Aid in Place of Migration?,* ILO.

Borjas, G. J. (1985) 'Assimilation, Changes in Cohort Quality, and the Earnings of Immigrants', *Journal of Labour Economics*, vol. 3, pp. 463–89.

—— (1987) 'Self-Selection and the Earnings of Immigrants', *American Economic Review*, vol. 77, pp. 531–53.

—— (1990) *Friends or Strangers? The Impact of Immigrants on the US Economy*, Basic Books, New York.

—— (1991) 'Immigrants in the US Labor Market 1940–80', *American Economic Review*, vol. 81, pp. 287–91.

—— (1994) 'The Economics of Immigration', *Journal of Economic Literature*, vol. 32, pp. 1667–1717.

—— (1995) 'The Economic Benefits from Immigration', *Journal of Economic Perspectives*, vol. 9, no. 2, pp. 3–22.

Borjas, G.J., Freeman, R.B. and Katz, L.F. (1992) 'On the Labour Market Effect of Immigration and Trade', in *Immigration and the Workforce: Economic Consequences for the United States and Source Areas*, A NBER Project Report, University of Chicago Press, Chicago and London.

Boserup, E. (1965) *The Conditions of Agricultural Growth: The Economics of Agrarian Change under Population Pressure*, Allen and Unwin, London.

Bourdieu, P. (1983) 'Ökonomisches Kapital, kulturelles Kapital, soziales Kapital', in Kreckel, R. ed., *Soziale Ungleichheiten* (Soziale Welt, Sonderheft 2), Otto Schwartz and Co., Göttingen, pp. 183–98.

Boyd, M. (1989) 'Family and Personal Networks in International Migration: Recent Developments and New Agendas', *International Migration Review*, vol. 23, no. 3, pp. 638–70.

—— (1995) 'Migration Regulations and Sex Selective Outcomes in Developed Countries', in *International Migration Policies and the Status of Female Migrants*, Proceedings of the United Nations Expert Group Meeting on International Migration Policies and the Status of

Female Migrants, San Miniato, Italy, 28–31 March 1990, pp. 83–98.

Boyer, G.R. et al. (1993) *The Impact of Emigration on Real Wages in Ireland 1850–1914*, CEPR Discussion Paper 854, London.

Brandell, I. (1991) ed. *Workers in Third-World Industrialization*, Macmillan, London.

Brandt Commission (1980) *North–South: A Programme for Survival*, Pan, London.

Breier, H. (1994) 'Development and Migration: The Role of Aid and Co-operation', in OECD (1994).

Briody, E. (1987) 'Patterns of Household Immigration into South Texas', *International Migration Review*, vol. 21, pp. 27–47.

Brochmann, G. (1993) *Middle East Avenue: Female Migration from Sri Lanka to the Gulf*, Westview, Boulder, CO.

Brown, L. and Sanders, R. (1981) 'Toward a Development Paradigm of Migration with Particular Reference to the Third World', in DeJong and Gardner (1981b).

Brubaker, R. (1992) *Citizenship and Nationhood in France and Germany*, Harvard University Press, Cambridge, Mass.

Brundtland Report (1987) *Our Common Future*, Oxford University Press, Oxford.

Buijs, G. (1993) ed. *Migrant Women: Crossing Boundaries and Changing Identities*, Berg Cross-Cultural Perspectives on Women, Oxford/Providence, vol. 7.

Burda, M.C. (1995) *Migration and the Option Value of Waiting*, Seminar Paper No. 597, Institute for International Economic Studies, Stockholm University, Stockholm.

Burki, S.J. (1991) 'Migration from Pakistan to the Middle East', in Papademetriou and Martin, *The Unsettled Relationship,* pp. 139–62.

Burt, R.S. (1986) 'Comment', in Lindenberg, S., Coleman, J. and Nowak, S. eds. *Approaches to Social Theory,* Russell Sage Foundation, New York, pp. 105–7.

Buttimer, A. (1971) *Society and Milieu in French Geographical Tradition*, Chicago.

Buzan, B. (1991) *People, States and Fear*, Harvester Wheatsheaf, London.

Caballero, R.I. and Lyons, R.K. (1990) 'Internal versus External Economies in European Industry', *European Economic Review*, vol. 34, pp. 803–26.

Cadwallader, M. (1989) 'A Conceptual Framework for Analysing Migration Behaviour in the Developed World', *Progress in Human Geography*, vol. 13, pp. 494–511.

—— (1992) *Migration and Residential Mobility: Macro and Micro Approaches*, University of Wisconsin Press, Madison.

References

Caces, F., Arnold, F., Fawcett, J. T. and Gardner, R. W. (1985) 'Shadow Households and Competing Auspices', *Journal of Development Economics,* vol. 17, no. 1, pp. 5–25.

Castano, G.M. (1988) 'Effects of Emigration and Return on Sending Countries: The Case of Colombia', in Stahl, Ch. ed., pp. 191–203.

Castells, M. (1989) *The Informational City; Information Technology, Economic Restructuring and the Urban-Regional Process*, Basil Blackwell, Oxford.

Castles, S. and Miller, M. (1993) *The Age of Migration: International Population Movements in the Modern World*, Macmillan, London.

Castles, S. and Kosack, G. (1973) *Immigrant workers and class structure in Western Europe*, Oxford University Press, London.

Chamberlain, M. (1994) 'Family and Identity: Barbadian Migrants to Britain', in Benmayor, Skotnes, R. and Skotnes A. eds. *Migration and Identity,* pp. 119–35.

Champion, T. and Fielding, T. (1991) eds. *Migration Processes and Patterns*, Research Progress and Prospects, vol. 1, Belhaven, London.

Chandavarkar, A.G. (1980) '"Use of Migrants" Remittances in Labour-Exporting Countries', *Finance and Development*, June 1980, pp. 36–9.

Chaney, E.M. (1987) 'The Context of Caribbean Migration', in Sutton, C.R. and Chaney, E.M. eds. *Caribbean Life in New York City: Sociocultural Dimensions*, Center for Migration Studies, New York, pp. 1–14.

Chang, P. and Deng, Z. (1992) 'The Chinese Brain Drain and Policy Options', *Studies in Comparative International Development*, vol. 27, no. 1, Spring, pp. 44–60.

Chang, S.L. (1992) 'Causes of Brain Drain and Solutions: The Taiwanese Experience', *Studies in Comparative International Development*, vol. 27, no. 1, Spring, pp. 27–43.

Chant, S. (1992) 'Conclusion: Towards a Framework for the Analysis of Gender-Selective Migration', in Chant S. and Radcliffe S.A. eds. *Gender and Migration in Developing Countries*, pp. 197–206.

Chant, S. and Radcliffe, S.A. (1992a) eds. *Gender and Migration in Developing Countries*, Belhaven, London and New York.

—— (1992b) 'Migration and Development: The Importance of Gender', in Chant, S. and Radcliffe, S.A. eds. *Gender and Migration in Developing Countries*, pp. 1–29.

Chapman, M. and Prothero, R.M. (1983) 'Themes on Circulation in the Third World', *International Migration Review*, vol. 17, pp. 597–632.

Chapman, M., Pope, D. and Withers, G. (1985) *Immigration and the Labour Market*, Centre for Economic Policy Research Discussion Paper 184, Australian National University, Canberra.

References

Chayanov, A. (1966) *Theory of Peasant Economy*, Richard D. Irwin, Homewood.

Chiswick, B.R. (1978) 'The Effect of Americanization on the Earnings of Foreign-Born Men', *Journal of Political Economy*, vol. 86, pp. 897–921.

—— (1986a) 'Human Capital and the Labor Market Adjustment of Immigrants', in Stark, O. ed. *Migration, Human Capital and Development*, pp. 1–26.

—— (1986b) 'Is the New Immigration Less Skilled Than the Old?', *Journal of Labour Economics*, vol. 4, pp. 168–92.

—— (1992) *The Performance of Immigrants in the Labor Market: A Review Essay*, Hebrew University of Jerusalem, Jerusalem.

Choldin, H.M. (1973) 'Kinship Networks in the Migration Process', *International Migration Review*, vol. 7, no. 2, pp. 163–76.

Clammer, J. (1978a) 'Concepts and Objects in Economic Anthropology', in Clammer, J. ed. *The New Economic Anthropology*, pp. 1–20.

—— (1978b) ed. *The New Economic Anthropology*, Macmillan Press, London.

Clark, W. (1981) 'Residential Mobility and Behavioural Geography', in Cox. K. and Golledge, R. ed. *Behavioural Problems in Geography Revisited*.

Clifford, J. (1994) 'Diasporas', *Cultural Anthropology*, vol. 9, no. 3, pp. 301–38.

Cohen, R. (1986) 'Some Theories of Migration: A Synopsis and Comment', in *Themes and Theories in Migration Research*, Proceedings from an International Seminar on Migration Research, September, Danish Social Science Research Council, Rungstedgaard.

—— (1987) *The New Helots: Migrants in the International Division of Labor*, Avebury, Aldershot.

Coleman, J.S. (1988) 'Social Capital in the Creation of Human Capital', *American Journal of Sociology*, vol. 94, pp. 95–121.

—— (1990) *Foundations of Social Theory*, The Belknap Press of Harvard University Press, Cambridge, MA.

Collier, J.F. and Yanagisako, S.J. (1987) eds. *Gender and Kinship: Essays Toward a Unified Analysis*, Stanford University Press, Stanford.

Connell, R.W. (1987) *Gender and Power*, Polity Press, Cambridge.

—— (1995) *Masculinities*, Polity Press, Cambridge.

Corden, W.M. (1974) *Trade Policy and Economic Welfare*, Clarendon Press, Oxford.

Corden, W.M. and Findlay, R. (1975) 'Urban Unemployment, Inter-Sectoral Capital Mobility and Development Policy', *Economica*, vol. 42, pp. 59–78.

References

Cornelius, W.A. (1991) 'Labor Migration to the United States: Development Outcomes and Alternatives to Mexican Sending Communities', in Díaz-Briquets, S. and Weintraub, S. eds. *Regional and Sectoral Development in Mexico as Alternatives to Migration*, vol. II.

Cornelius, W.A. and Martin, Ph. L. (1993) 'The Uncertain Connection: Free Trade and Rural Mexican Migration to the United States', *International Migration Review*, vol. XXVII, no. 3, pp. 484–512.

Courgeau, D. (1995) 'Migration Theories and Behavioural Models', *International Journal of Population Geography*, vol. 1, pp. 19–27.

Cox, K. and Golledge, R. (1981) eds. *Behavioural Problems in Geography Revisited*, Methuen, New York.

Dacyl, J.W. (1992) *Between Compassion and Realpolitik*, University of Stockholm, Stockholm.

DaVanzo, J. (1981) 'Microeconomic Approaches to Studying Migration Decisions', in DeJong, G. F. and Gardner, R.W. eds. *Migration Decision Making*, pp. 90–129.

Davidson, S. (1993) *Human Rights: Law and Political Change*, Open University Press, Buckingham.

Davis, K. (1989) 'Social Science Approaches to International Migration', in Teitelbaum, M.S. and Winter, J.M. eds. *Population and Resources in Western Intellectual Tradition, Population and Development Review*, Supplement, pp. 245–61.

De New, J.P. and Zimmermann, K.F. (1994) 'Native Wage Impacts of Foreign Labour: A Random Effects Panel Analysis', *Journal of Population Economics*, vol. 7, pp. 177–92.

Decressin, J. and Fatas, A. (1995) 'Regional Labour Market Dynamics in Europe', *European Economic Review*, vol. 39, no. 9, pp. 1627–55.

DeJong, G.F. et al. (1983) 'International and Internal Migration Decision Making: A Value-Expectancy Based Analytical Framework of Intentions to Move from a Rural Philippine Province', *International Migration Review*, vol. 17, no. 3, Fall, pp. 470–84.

—— (1986) 'Migration Intentions and Behavior: Decision Making in a Rural Philippine Province', *Population and Environment*, vol. 8, pp. 41–62.

DeJong, G. F. and Fawcett, J. T. (1981) 'Motivations for Migration: An Assessment and a Value-Expectancy Research Model', in DeJong, G. F. and Gardner, R.W. eds. *Migration Decision Making*, pp. 13–58.

DeJong, G.F. and Gardner, R.W. (1981a) 'Introduction and Overview', in DeJong, G.F. and Gardner, R.W. eds. *Migration Decision Making*, pp. 1–12.

—— (1981b) eds. *Migration Decision Making: Multidisciplinary Approaches to Microlevel Studies in Developed and Developing*

Countries, Pergamon Press, New York.

Delbrück, C. and Raffelhüschen, B. (1993) *Die Theorie der Migration*, Diskussionsbeiträge aus dem Institut für Finanzwissenschaft und Regionalpolitik der Christian-Albrechts-Universität zu Kiel 42, Kiel.

DeNew, J.P. and Zimmermann, K.F. (1994) 'Native Wage Impacts of Foreign Labor: A Random Effects Panel Analysis', *Journal of Population Economics*, vol. 7, pp. 193–215.

Díaz-Briquets, S. (1985) 'Impact of Alternative Development Strategies on Migration: A Comparative Analysis', in Pastor, R.A. ed. *Migration and Development in the Caribbean*.

Díaz-Briquets, S. and Weintraub, S. (1991) eds. *Migration Impacts of Trade and Foreign Investment: Mexico and the Caribbean Basin Countries*, vol. III, Westview, Boulder.

Dolado, J.J. et al. (1994) 'The Growth Effects of Migration in the Host Country', *Journal of Population Economics*, vol. 7, pp. 133–56.

Dorigo, G. and Tobler, W. (1983) 'Push-Pull Migration Laws', *Annals of the Association of American Geographers*, vol. 73, no. 1. pp. 1–17.

Downs, R. (1981) 'Cognitive Mapping', in Cox. K. and Golledge R. eds. *Behavioural Problems in Geography Revisited*, pp. 95–122.

Dustmann, C. (1992) Migration, savings and uncertainty, Department of Economics, European University Institute, Firenze, Italy.

Dwyer, D. and Bruce, J. (1988) eds. *A Home Divided. Women and Income in the Third World*, Stanford University Press, Stanford.

Eades, J. (1987a) 'Anthropologists and Migrants: Changing Models and Realities', in Eades, J. ed. *Migrants, Workers, and the Social Order*.

—— (1987b) ed. *Migrants, Workers, and the Social Order*, ASA Monograph 26, Tavistock, London and New York.

Easton, D. (1965) *A Systems Analysis of Political Life*, John Wiley and Sons Inc, New York etc.

Eisenstadt, S.N. (1954) *The Absorption of Immigrants. A Comparative Study Based Mainly on the Jewish Community in Palestine and the State of Israel*, Routledge, London.

Ekberg, J. (1983) *Inkomsteffekter av invandring* (with English Summary), Acta Wexionensia, Tryck and Skrivservice Växjö.

Engels, F. (1970) 'The Origin of the Family, Private Property and the State', in *Marx and Engels: Selected Works*, Progress Publishers, Moscow.

Entrikin, N. (1991) *The Betweenness of Place*, John Hopkins University, Baltimore.

Esser, H. (1980) *Aspekte der Wanderungssoziologie. Assimilation und Integration von Wanderern, ethnischen Gruppen und Minderheiten*, Luchterhand, Darmstadt and Neuwied.

Ethier, W.J. (1985) 'International Trade and Labor Migration', *American*

Economic Review, vol. 75, pp. 691–707.

EUROSTAT (ann.) *Migration Statistics*, Eurostat Publications, Luxembourg.

Faini, R. and Venturini, A. (1994) *Migration and Growth: The Experience of Southern Europe*, CEPR Discussion Paper 964, London.

Fairchild, H.P. (1925) *Immigration: A World Movement and its American Significance*. Putnam, New York.

Faist, T. (1995) *A Preliminary Analysis of Political-Institutional Aspects of International Migration: Internationalization, Transnationalization and Internal Globalization*. Bremen, Centre for Social Policy Research, ZeS-Arbeitspapier Nr. 10/95.

Fawcett, J.T., (1989) 'Networks, Linkages, and Migration Systems', *International Migration Review*, vol. 23, no. 3, pp. 671–80.

Fergany, N. (1982) 'The Impact of Emigration on National Development in the Arab Region: The Case of the Yemen Arab Republic', *International Migration Review*, vol. XVI, no. 4, pp. 757–80.

Fielding, A. (1993) 'Mass Migration and Economic Restructuring', in King, R. ed. *Mass Migration in Europe*, pp. 7–18.

Fields, G.S. (1975) 'Rural–Urban Migration, Urban Unemployment and Underemployment and Job-Search Activity in LDCs', *Journal of Development Economics*, vol. 2, pp. 165–87.

—— (1976) 'Labor Force Migration, Unemployment and Job Turnover', *Review of Economics and Statistics*, vol. 58, pp. 407–15.

—— (1979) 'Place to Place Migration: Some New Evidence', *Review of Economics and Statistics*, vol. 61, pp. 21–32.

Findlay, A.M. (1993) 'New Technology, High-Level Labour Movements and the Concept of the Brain Drain', in OECD, pp. 149–59.

Fischer, P.A. (1991) 'Migration, its Determinants and Integration, Some Presumptions about the Nordic Experience', in Korkiasaari, J. and Söderling, I. eds. *Migrationen och det framtida Norden*, Nordisk Ministerråd/Institute of Migration: Copenhagen and Turku.

Fischer, P.A. and Straubhaar, Th. (1996) *Migration and Economic Integration in the Nordic Common Labour Market*, Nord Series, Nordic Council of Ministers, Copenhagen.

Foster-Carter (1978) 'Can We Articulate "Articulation"?', in Clammer, J. ed. *The New Economic Anthropology*, pp. 210–49.

Fotheringham, S. (1991) 'Migration and Spatial Structures: The Development of Competing Destinations Model', in Stillwell J. and Congdon P. eds. *Migration Models*.

Frank, A.G. (1965) *Capitalism and Underdevelopment in Latin America*.

—— (1970) 'The Development of Underdevelopment', in Rhodes, R. I. ed. *Imperialism and Underdevelopment*, Monthly Review Press, New York.

Franz, W. (1993) *Zur ökonomischen Bedeutung von Wanderungen und den Möglichkeiten und Grenzen einer Einwanderungspolitik*, CILE Diskussionspapier 3, Fakultät für Wirtschaftswissenschaften und Statistik, Universität Konstanz, Constance.

Freeman, R.B. (1993) 'Labour Markets and Institutions in Economic Development', *American Economic Review*, vol. 62, no. 3, pp. 403–8, papers and proceedings.

Freund, B. (1988) *The African Worker*, Cambridge University Press, Cambridge.

Frey, B.S. (1990) *International Political Economics*, Blackwell, 2nd edition, Oxford.

Friedberg, R.M. and Hunt, J. (1995) 'The Impact of Immigrants on Host Country Wages, Employment and Growth', *Journal of Economic Perspectives*, vol. 9, no. 2, pp. 23–44.

Friends of the Earth Europe (1995) *Towards Sustainable Europe*, Brussels.

Gabriel, S. and Levy, D. (1988) 'Expectations, Information and Migration: The Case of the West Bank and Gaza', *Applied Economics*, vol. 20, pp. 1–13.

Galinski, D. (1986) *Brain Drain aus Entwicklungsländern, Theoretische Grundlagen und entwicklungspolitische Konsequenzen*, in *Europäische Hochschulschriften*, Reihe V, Peter Lang, Frankfurt.

Galor, O. (1986) 'Time Preference and International Labour Migration', *Journal of Economic Theory*, vol. 38, pp. 1–20.

Gang, I.N. and Rivera-Batiz, F.L. (1994) 'Labour Market Effects of Immigration in the United States and Europe (Substitution versus Complementarity)', *Journal of Population Economics*, vol. 7, pp. 157–75.

Gardner, R.W. (1981) 'Macro-Level Influences on the Decision-Making Process', in DeJong, G.F. and Gardner, R.W. eds. *Migration Decision Making*, pp. 59–89.

Garson, J.-P. (1994) 'The Implications for the Maghreb Countries of Financial Transfers from Emigrants', in OECD, *Migration and Development*, pp. 275–87.

Geertz, C. (1963a) *Agricultural Involution: The Process of Ecological Change in Indonesia*, Los Angeles.

—— (1963b) 'The Integrative Revolution', in Geertz, C. ed. *Old Societies and New States*, The Free Press, New York.

Gellner, E. (1964) *Thought and Change*, Weidenfeld and Nicolson, London.

George, S. (1992) *The Debt Boomerang: How Third World Debt Harms Us All*, Pluto, London.

Ghatak, S., Levine, P. and Wheatley Price S. (1996) 'Migration Theories and Evidence: An Assessment', *Journal of economic surveys*, vol. 10, no. 2, pp. 159–98.

Ghosh, B. (1992) 'Migration, Trade and International Economic Cooperation: Do the Inter-Linkages Work?', *International Migration*, vol. XXX, nos. 3–4, pp. 377–98.

Giersch, H. (1994) ed. *Economic Aspects of International Migration*, Springer Verlag, Berlin.

Gilani, I.S. (1988) 'Effects of Emigration and Return on Sending Countries: The Case of Pakistan', in UNESCO, *International Migration Today*, pp. 204–16.

Gilbert, A. and Gugler, J. (1981) *Cities, Poverty and Development: Urbanization in the Third World*, Oxford University Press, New York.

Gilbertson, G. and Gourak, D. T. (1992) 'Household Transitions in the Migrations of Dominicans and Colombians to New York', *International Migration Review*, vol. 26, no. 1, pp. 22–45.

Gitmez, A.S. (1991) 'Migration Without Development: The Case of Turkey', in Papademetriou, D.G. and Martin, Ph. L. eds. *The Unsettlement Relationship*, pp. 115–34.

—— (1988) 'The Socio-Economic Reintegration of Returned Workers: The Case of Turkey', in UNESCO, *International Migration Today*, pp. 217–33.

Glick-Schiller, N., Basch, L. and Blanc-Szanton, C. (1992) 'Transnationalism. A New Analytic Framework for Understanding Migration', in Glick-Schiller, N., Basch, L. and Blanc-Szanton, C. eds. *Towards a Transnational Perspective on Migration: Race, Class, Ethnicity, and Nationalism Reconsidered*, Annals of the New York Academy of Sciences, New York, vol. 645, pp. 1–24.

Gmelch, G. (1980) 'Return Migration', *Annual Review of Anthropology*, vol. 9, pp. 135–59.

Goldring, L. (1995) 'Gendered Memory: Reconstructions of Rurality Among Mexican Transnational Migrants', in DuPuis, M. and Vandergeest, P. eds. *Creating the Countryside: The Politics of Rural and Environmental Discourse*, Temple University Press, Philadelphia.

Goldscheider, C. (1971) *Population, Modernization, and Social Structure*, Little, Brown, and Company, Boston.

Goodwin-Gill, G.S. (1990) 'Different Types of Forced Migration Movements as an International And National Problem', in Rystad, G. ed. *The Uprooted*, pp. 15–46.

Goos, J. and Lindquist, B. (1995) 'Conceptualizing International Migration: A Structural Perspective', *International Migration Review*, vol. XXIX, no. 3.

Goss, E.P. and Paul, C. (1986) 'Age and Work Experience in the Decision to Migrate', *The Journal of Human Resources*, vol. 21, pp.

397–405.

Göransson, B. (1996) 'Irrational to Reduce Development Aid', *Dagens Nyheter*, April 18 (in Swedish).

Gould, P. and White, P. (1986) *Mental maps*, Allen and Unwin, 2nd ed., Boston.

Gouldner, A.W. (1960) 'The Norm of Reciprocity: A Preliminary Statement', *American Sociological Review*, vol. 25, no. 2, pp. 161–78.

Granovetter, M.S. (1985) 'Economic Action and Social Structure: The Problem of Embeddedness', *American Journal of Sociology*, vol. 91, no. 3, pp. 481–510.

—— (1978) 'Threshold Models of Collective Behavior', *American Journal of Sociology*, vol. 83, no. 6, pp. 1420–43.

—— (1973) 'The Strength of Weak Ties', *American Journal of Sociology*, vol. 78, no. 6, pp. 1360–80.

Graves, P.E. and Linnemann, P.D. (1979) 'Household Migration: Theoretical and Empirical Results', *Journal of Urban Economics*, vol. 6, pp. 383–404.

Greenwood, M.J. (1993) 'Migration: A Review', *Regional Studies*, vol. 27, pp. 295–383.

—— (1985) 'Human Migration; Theory, Models and Empirical Evidence', *Journal of Regional Science*, vol. 25, pp. 521–44.

—— (1975) 'Research on International Migration in the U.S.: A Survey', *Journal of Economic Literature*, vol. 13, pp. 397–433.

Greenwood, M.J. and McDowell, J.M. (1991) 'Differential Economic Opportunity, Transferability of Skills and Immigration to the United States and Canada', *Review of Economics and Statistics*, vol. 73, pp. 612–23.

Gregory, D. and Perez, J. (1985) 'Intra-European Migration and Regional Development: Spain and Portugal', in Rogers, R. ed. *Guests Come to Stay*, Westview, Boulder, pp. 231–62.

Griffin, K. (1992) 'Suggestions for an International Development Strategy for the 1990s', in Dutt, A.K. and Jameson, K.P. eds. *New Directions in Development Economics*, Edward Elgar.

Grigg, D. (1980) 'Migration and Overpopulation', in White, P. and Woods, R. eds. *The Geographical Impact of Migration*, pp. 60–83.

Grossman, G.M. (1982) 'The substitutability of natives and immigrants in production', *Review of Economics and Statistics*, 64, pp. 596–603.

Grossman, G.M. and Helpman, E. (1994) 'Endogenous Innovation in the Theory of Growth', *Journal of Economic Perspectives*, vol. 8, no. 1, pp. 23–44.

Grubel, H.G. (1994) 'The Economics of International Labor and Capital Flows', in Giersch ed. *Economic Aspects of International Migration*, pp. 75–92.

Gugler, J. (1988a) 'Overurbanization Reconsidered', in Gugler, J. ed. *The Urbanization of the Third World*, Oxford, Oxford University Press, pp. 74–92.

—— (1988b) ed. *The Urbanization of the Third World,* Oxford University Press, New York.

Gugler, J. and Ludwar-Ene (1995) 'Gender and Migration in Africa South of the Sahara', in Jonathan Baker and Tade Akin Ain (eds), *The Migration Experience in Africa,* The Nordic Africa Institute, Uppsala.

Gurak, D. and Caces, F. (1992) 'Migration Networks and the Shaping of Migration Systems', in Kritz, M., Lim, L. and Zlotnik, H. eds. *International Migration Systems: A Global Approach*, Clarendon Press, Oxford, pp. 150–76.

Habermas, J. (1981) *Theorie des kommunikativen Handelns*, 2 vols, Suhrkamp, Frankfurt.

Habib, A. (1985) *Economic Consequences of International Migration for Sending Countries – Review of Evidence from Bangladesh*, Dissertation, University of Newcastle.

Hägerstrand, T. (1963) 'Geographic Measurements of Migration: Swedish Data', in *Les déplacements humains. Entretiens de Monaco en sciences humaines,* Première session 1962.

—— (1975a) 'On the Definition of Migration', in Jones, E. ed. *Readings in Social Geography*, Oxford University Press, London, pp. 200–10, also in *Scandinavian Population Studies*, vol. 1, 1969.

—— (1975b) 'Space, Time and Human Conditions', in Karlqvist, A. ed. *Dynamic Allocation of Urban Space,* Farnborough.

—— (1993) *Om tidens vidd och tingens ordning*, Liber.

Haggett, P. (1965) *Locational Analysis in Human Geography*, London.

Halfacree, K. (1995) 'Household Migration and the Structuration of Patriarchy: Evidence from the USA', *Progress in Human Geography,* vol. 19, no. 2, pp. 159–82.

Halfacree, K. and Boyle, P. (1993) 'The Challenge Facing Migration Research: The Case for a Biographical Approach', *Progress in Human Geography,* vol. 17, no. 3, pp. 333–48.

Hammar, T. (1964) *Sverige åt svenskarna*, Tomas Hammar, Stockholm.

—— (1990a) *Democracy and the Nation State: Aliens, Denizens and Citizens in a World of International Migration*, Avebury.

—— (1990b) 'The Integration or Non-Integration of Refugee Immigrants: Historical Experiences in Sweden', in Rystad, G. ed. *The Uprooted*, pp. 179–92.

—— (1993) 'The Democratic Nation-State and the Challenge of Migration', in *Migration: The Politics of Contemporary Population Movements,* papers presented at Sam. pol. konferansen 1993 at Bergen University.

—— (1995) 'Development and Immobility: Why have not Many More Emigrants Left the South?', in EUROSTAT ed., *Causes of International Migration*, pp. 173–86, Luxembourg.

Hannerz, U. (1992) *Cultural Complexity: Studies in the Social Organization of Meaning*, Columbia University Press, New York.

—— (1980) *Exploring the City: Inquiries Toward and Urban Anthropology*, Columbia University Press, New York.

Harbison, S.F. (1981) 'Family Structure and Family Strategy in Migration Decision Making', in DeJong, G.F. and Gardner, R.W. eds. *Migration Decision Making*, pp. 225–51.

Harris, M. (1968) *The Rise of Anthropological Theory: A History of Theories of Culture*, Thomas Y. Crowell Co., New York.

—— (1971) *Culture, Man, and Nature: An Introduction to General Anthropology*, Thomas Y. Crowell Co., New York.

Harris, J.R. and Todaro, M.P. (1970) 'Migration, Unemployment and Development: A Two-Sector Analysis', *American Economic Review*, vol. 60, pp. 126–42.

Harrison, P. (1992) *The Third Revolution*, Penguin, Harmondsworth.

Harvey, D. (1969) *Explanation in Geography*, Edward Arnold, London.

Hatton, T.J. and Williamson, J.G. (1994) 'What Drove the Mass Migrations from Europe in the Late Nineteenth Century?', *Population and Development Review*, vol. 20, no. 3, pp. 533–59.

Hayfron, J.E. (1993) *The Earnings of Third World Migrants in the Norwegian Labor Market*, University of Bergen, mimeo.

Haynes, K. and Fotheringham, S. (1984) *Gravity and Spatial Interaction Models*, Sage, Beverly Hills.

Hazari, B.R. (1993) *An Analysis of the Impact of Outmigration on Unemployment, Welfare and Structural Change*, Graduate School of Management Working Papers 9302, Deakin University, Canada.

Helou, M. (1993) *Politics of Multinational Brain Drain System Evolution, Policy Implications. The Case of Lebanon, 1975–1991*, Working Paper 4, Department of Marketing, University of Western Sydney, Nepean.

Herzog, Schlottmann, and Boehm (1993) 'Migration as Spatial Job-Search: A Survey of Empirical Findings', *Regional Studies*, vol. 27, pp. 327–340.

Hettne, B. (1993) 'Dynamics of Ethnic Conflict', in Lindholm, H. ed. *Ethnicity and Nationalism: Formation of Identity and Dynamics of Conflict in the 1990s*, Nordnes, Göteborg.

—— (1990) *Development Theory and the Three Worlds*, Longmans.

Hicks, J. (1932) *The Theory of Wages*, Macmillan, London.

Hirschman, A.O. (1970) *Exit, Voice, and Loyalty: Responses to Decline in Firms, Organizations, and States,* Harvard University Press,

References

Cambridge Mass. etc.

—— (1958) *The Strategy of Economic Development*, Yale University Press, New Haven.

Hoffmann-Nowotny, H.-J. (1970) *Migration: Ein Beitrag zu einer soziologischen Erklärung*, Ferdinand Enke, Stuttgart.

—— (1973) *Soziologie des Fremdarbeiterproblems*, Ferdinand Enke, Stuttgart.

—— (1995) 'Soziologische Aspekte internationaler Migration', *Geographische Rundschau*, vol. 47, nos. 7–8, pp. 410–14.

Holm, E., Mäkilä, K. and Öberg, S. (1989) *Tidsgeografisk handlingsteori – Att bilda betingade biografier,* GERUM 8, Geografiska institutionen, Umeå universitet.

Hugo, G.J. (1981) 'Village-community ties, village norms and ethnic and social networks: a review of evidence from Third World', in DeJong, G.F. and Gardner, R.W. eds. *Migration Decision Making.*

—— (1982) 'Circular Migration in Indonesia', *Population and Development Review*, vol. 8, no. 1, pp. 59–83.

—— (1990) 'The Migration of Asian Women to Australia', in *International Migration Policies and the Status of Female Migrants*, Proceedings of the United Nations Expert Group Meeting on International Migration Policies and the Status of Female Migrants, San Miniato, Italy, 28–31 March 1990, pp. 192–220.

—— (1995) 'International Labor Migration and the Family: Some Observations from Indonesia', *Asian and Pacific Migration Journal,* vol. 4, nos. 2–3, pp. 273–302.

Hunt, J.C. and Kau, J.B. (1985) 'Migration and Wage Growth: A Human Capital Approach', *Southern Economic Journal*, vol. 51, pp. 697–710.

Huntington, S.P. (1993) 'The Clash of Civilizations?', *Foreign Affairs*, vol. 72, no. 3, Summer, pp. 22–48.

Ibarra-Yunez, A. and Stolp, Ch. (1991) 'Exports and Employment Generation in Mexico', in Díaz-Briquets, S. and Weintraub, S. eds. *Migration Impacts of Trade and Foreign Investment,* pp. 193–223.

ILO/IOM/UNHCR (1994) *Migrants, Refugees and International Cooperation*, Geneva.

ILO/UNHCR (1992) *Informal Summary Record*, Joint ILO/UNHCR Meeting on International Aid as a Means to Reduce the Need for Emigration, mimeo, Geneva.

IOM/RPG (1992) *Migration and the Environment*, June.

Islam, M.M. (1991) 'Labour Migration and Development: A Case Study of a Rural Community in Bangladesh', *Bangladesh Journal of Political Economy*, vol. 11, pp. 570–87.

Jackson, P. and Penrose, J. (1993) 'Placing "Race" and Nation', in

Jackson P. and Penrose J. eds. *Construction of Race, Place and Nation*, UCL Press, London.

Kane, H. (1995) 'Leaving Home', in World Watch Institute, *State of the World '95*, Norton.

Karlsson, I. (1994) *Islam och Europa*, Wahlström and Widstrand, Stockholm.

Katz, C. and Monk, J. (1993a) eds. *Full Circles: Geographies of Women over the Life Course*, Routledge, London.

—— (1993b) 'When in the World are Women', in Katz, C. and Monk, J. eds. *Full Circles*.

Katz, E. and Stark, O. (1986b) *Mobility and Information*, Discussion Paper no. 27, Migration and Development Program Harvard University, December.

—— (1986a) 'Labour Migration and Risk Aversion in Less Developed Countries', *Journal of Labour Economics*, vol. 4, pp. 131–49.

Kearney, M. (1986) 'From Invisible Hand to Visible Feet: Anthropological Studies of Migration and Development', *Annual Review of Anthropology*, vol. 15, pp. 331–61.

Keesing, R.M. (1976) *Cultural Anthropology: A Contemporary Perspective*, Holt, Rinehart and Winston, New York etc.

King, M. (1990) 'Health is a Sustainable State', *The Lancet*, vol. 336, Sept. 15, pp 664–7.

King, R. (1993) ed. *Mass Migration in Europe: The Legacy and the Future*, Belhaven, London.

King, R. and Öberg, S. (1993) 'Europe and the Future of Mass Migration', in King, R. ed. *Mass Migration in Europe*.

Kirkpatrick, J.J. (1993) 'The Modernizing Imperative: Tradition and Change', *Foreign Affairs*, vol. 72, no. 4, Sept.–Oct, pp. 22–6.

Koopmans, T.C. (1965) 'On the Concept of Optimal Economic Growth', in *The Econometric Approach to Development Planning*, North Holland, Amsterdam.

Kritz, M.M., Lim, L.L. and Zlotnik, H. (1992) eds. *International Migration Systems: A Global Approach*, Clarendon Press, Oxford.

Kritz, M.M. and Zlotnik, H. (1992) 'Global Interactions: Migration Systems, Process and Policies', in Kritz, M.M., Lim, L.L. and Zlotnik, H. eds. *International Migration Systems*, pp. 1–18.

Krugman, P.R. (1991) *Geography and Trade*, Leuven University Press, Leuven.

Krugman, P.R. and Smith, A. (1994) *Empirical Studies of Strategic Trade Policy*, National Bureau of Economic Research, University of Chicago Press, Chicago.

Kuper, A. and Kuper, J. (1985) eds. *The Social Science Enyclopedia*, Routledge and Kegan Paul, London, pp. 524–8.

Körner, H. (1991) 'Future Trends in International Migration', *Intereconomics*, vol. 26(1), pp. 41–4.

—— (1987) 'The Experience in the Main Geographical OECD Areas: European Sending Countries', in OECD, *The Future of Migration.*

Lattes, A. and Recchini de Lattes, Z. (1994) 'International Migration in Latin America: Patterns, Determinants and Policies', in Macura, M. and Coleman, D. eds. *International Migration.*

Lauby, J. and Stark, O. (1988) 'Individual Migration as a Family Strategy: Young Women in the Philippines', *Population Studies*, vol. 42, pp. 473–86.

Layton-Henry, Z. (1990) ed. *Political Rights of Migrant Workers in Western Europe*, Sage, London.

Lee, E.S. (1966) 'A Theory of Migration', *Demography*, vol. 3, pp. 47–57.

Lenin, V.I. (1970) *Imperialism: The Highest Stage of Capitalism,* Progress Publishers, Moscow.

Lewis, W.A. (1954a) 'Economic Development with Unlimited Supplies of Labour', *The Manchester School of Economic and Social Studies*, vol. 22.

—— (1954b) *Theory of Economic Growth*, Unwin, London.

—— (1978) *Growth and Fluctuation, 1870–1913*, George Allen and Unwin, London.

Lien, D.-H.D. (1993) 'Asymmetric Information and the Brain Drain', *Journal of Population Economics*, vol. 6, pp. 169–80.

Lim, L.L. (1994a) 'Growing Economic Interdependence and its Implications for International Migration', *Population Distribution and Migration*, UN 1994.

—— (1994b) 'International Labour Migration in Asia', in Macura, M. and Coleman, D. eds. *International Migration.*

Lipman, B.L. (1993) *Information Processing and Bounded Rationality: A Survey*, Queen's University Discussion Paper Nr. 872, January.

Lipton, M. (1980) 'Migration from Rural Areas of Poor Countries: The Impact on Rural Productivity and Income Distribution', *World Development*, vol. 8, no. 1, pp. 1–24.

Loescher, G. (1989) 'Introduction: Refugee Issues in International Relations', in Loescher, G. and Monahan, L. eds. *Refugees and International Relations*, pp. 1–34.

Loescher, G. and Monahan, L. (1989) eds. *Refugees and International Relations*, Oxford University Press, Oxford.

Lucas, R.E. (1988) 'On the Mechanics of Economic Development', *Journal of Monetary Economics*, vol. 22, no. 1, pp. 3–42.

—— (1983) 'International Migration: Economic Causes, Consequences and Evaluation', in Kritz, M., Keely, Ch.B., Tomassi, M., eds. *Global*

References

Trends in Migration: Theory and Research on International Population Movements, Center for Migration Studies, New York.

Mabogunje, A.L. (1970) 'Systems Approach to a Theory of Rural–Urban Migration', *Geographical Analysis,* vol. 2, pp. 1–17.

Macura, M. and Coleman, D. (1994) eds. *International Migration: Regional Processes and Responses*, UNECE/UNPF.

Mahbubani, K. (1993) 'The Dangers of Decadence: What the Rest Can Teach the West', *Foreign Affairs*, vol. 72, no. 4, Sept.–Oct, pp. 10–14.

Mahmood, R.A. (1991) 'International Migration, Remittances and Development: Untapped Potentials for Bangladesh', *BIISS Journal*, vol. 12, no. 4, pp. 526–57.

Maier, G. (1985) 'Cumulative Causation and Selectivity in Labour Market Oriented Migration Caused by Imperfect Information', *Regional Studies*, vol. 19, pp. 231–41.

Malinowski, B. (1963) *The Family among the Australian Aborigines: A Sociological Study,* Schocken, New York, originally published in 1913.

Mankiw, N.G., Romer, D. and Weil, D.N. (1992) 'A Contribution to the Empirics of Economic Growth', *The Quarterly Journal of Economics*, vol. 107, pp. 407–37.

Marshall, D. (1982) 'The History of Caribbean Migration', *Caribbean Review,* vol. 11, no. 1, pp. 6–9 and 52–3.

Mårtensson, M. (1976) 'Decision Making between Spouses in Rabat', unpublished fil. lic. dissertation, in Swedish, Department of Sociology, Stockholm.

Martin, Ph. (1994) 'Reducing Emigration Pressure: What Role Can Foreign Aid Play?', in Böhning, W. R. and Schloeter-Paredes, M. L. eds. *Aid in Place of Migration?*, pp. 241–52.

—— (1993) *Migration and Trade: The Case of the Philippines*, A Conference Report.

Martin, R. (1997) *Regional Convergence in the EU: The Importance of Macro-Economic Policies and Regional Policy Variables*, HWWA – Discussion Paper, no. 43, HWWA, Hamburg.

Marx, K. (1977) *Der achtzehnte Brumaire des Louis Bonaparte, Ausgewählte Schriften in zwei Bänden*, Dietz, Berlin.

Marx, K. and Engels, F. (1976) *Collected Works, vol. 5*, Progress Publishers, Moscow.

Maslow, A.H. (1972) *Motivation and Personality*, Harper and Row, New York.

Massey, D.S. (1986) 'The Settlement Process among Mexican Migrants to the United States', *American Sociological Review*, vol. 51, pp. 670–85.

—— (1990) 'Social Structure, Household Strategies, and the Cumulative Causation of Migration', *Population Index,* vol. 56, no. 1, pp. 3–26.

Massey, D.S., Alacron, R., Durond, J. and Gonzalez, H. (1987) *Return to Aztlan: The Social Process of International Migration from Western Mexico*, University of California Press, Berkeley.

Massey, D.S., Goldring, L. and Durand, J. (1994) 'Continuities in Transnational Migration: An Analysis of Nineteen Mexican Communities', *American Journal of Sociology,* vol. 99, no. 6, pp. 1492–533.

Massey, D.S., Arango, J., Hugo, G., Kouaouci, A., Pellegrino, A. and Taylor, E. (1993) 'Theories of International Migration: A Review and Appraisal', *Population and Development Review*, vol. 19, no. 3, pp. 431–66.

McCall, B.P. and McCall, J.J. (1987) 'A Sequential Study of Migration and Job Search', *Journal of Labor Economics*, vol. 5, pp. 452–76.

McDowell, J.M. and Singell, L.D. (1993) 'An Assessmant of the Human Capital Content of International Migrants: An Application to US immigration', *Regional Studies*, vol. 27, pp. 351–63.

Migdal, J.S. (1983) 'Studying the Politics of Development and Change: The State of the Art', in Finifter, A. ed. *Political Science: The State of the Discipline*, American Political Science Association, Washington D.C., pp. 309–38.

Miller, J. (1993) 'The Challenge of Radical Islam', *Foreign Affairs*, vol. 72, no. 4, Sept.–Oct.

Mincer, J. (1978) 'Family Migration Decisions', *Journal of Political Economy*, vol. 86, pp. 749–73.

Mitchell, C.J. (1959) 'The Causes of Labour Migration', *Bulletin of the Inter-African Labour Institute,* vol. 6, pp. 12–46.

Molho, I. (1986a) 'The Migration Decisions of Young Men in Great Britain', *Applied Economics*, vol. 18, pp. 221–43.

—— (1986b) 'Theories of Migration: A Review', *Scottish Journal of Political Economy*, vol. 33, pp. 396–419.

Molle, W.T.M. and van Mourik, A. (1988) 'International Movements of Labour under Conditions of Economic Integration: The Case of Western Europe', *Journal of Common Market Studies*, vol. 26, pp. 317–39.

Moon, B. (1995) 'Paradigms in Migration Research: Exploring "Moorings" as a Schema', *Progress in Human Geography.* vol. 19, no. 4, pp. 504–24.

Moore, H.L. (1994) *A Passion for Difference,* Polity, Cambridge.

Morawska, E. (1990) 'Labor Migration of Poles in the Atlantic World Economy, 1880–1914', *Comparative Studies in Society and History,* vol. 31, no. 3, pp. 237–72.

References

Morokvasic, M. (1984) 'Birds of Passage are also Women', *International Migration Review*, vol. 18, no. 4, pp. 886–906.

—— (1983) 'Women in Migration: Beyond the Reductionist Outlook', in Phizacklea, A. ed. *One Way Ticket.*

Morrison, A.R. (1994) 'Capital Market Imperfections, Labor Market Disequilibrium and Migration: A Theoretical and Empirical Analysis', *Economic Inquiry*, vol. 32, pp. 290–302.

Muhleisen, M. and Zimmermann, K.F. (1994) 'A Panel Analysis of Job Changes and Unemployment', *European Economic Review*, vol. 38, pp. 793–801.

Mulder, C.H. (1993) *Migration Dynamics: A Life Course Approach*, PDOD Thesis Publishers, Amsterdam.

Munck, R. (1988) *The New International Labour Studies*, Zed Books, London.

Muus, Ph. (1993) 'South-to-North Migration', draft version of paper presented at *the UN Expert Meeting on Population Distribution and Migration*, Santa Cruz, Bolivia, 18–22 Jan. 1993.

Myers, N. and Kent, J. (1995) *Environmental Exodus: An Emergent Crisis in the Global Arena*, Climate Institute.

Myrdal, G. (1956) *An International Economy*, Harper and Row, New York.

—— (1957) *Rich Lands and Poor*, Harper and Row, New York.

—— (1973) *Against the Stream. Critical Essays on Economics*, Pantheon, New York.

Neary, P.J. (1981) 'On the Harris–Todaro Model with Intersectoral Capital Mobility', *Economica*, vol. 48, pp. 219–34.

Nelson, N. (1992) 'The Women Who Have Left and Those Who Have Stayed Behind: Rural–Urban Migration in Central and Western Kenya', in Chant, S. and Radcliffe, S.A. eds. *Gender and Migration in Developing Countries*, pp.109–38.

Neven, D.J. and Gouyette, C. (1994) 'Regional Convergence in the European Community', *Journal of Common Market Studies*, vol. 33, no. 1, pp. 47–65.

North, D.C. (1981) *Structure and Change in Economic History*, W.W. Norton, New York.

Öberg, N. (1994) *Gränslös rättvisa eller rättvisa inom gränser?*, Acta Universitatis Upsalienis, Uppsala.

Öberg, S. (1994) 'Spatial and Economic Factors in Future South to North Migration', in Lutz, W. ed. *The Future Population of the World: What Can We Assume Today?* IIASA, Earthscan. London.

Obia, G.C. (1993) 'Brain Drain and African Development: A Descriptive Framework for Deriving Indirect Benefits', *Journal of Third World Studies*, vol. X, no. 2, pp. 74–95.

OECD (1979) *Migration, Growth and Development*, Paris.

—— (1993a) *The Changing Course of International Migration*, Paris.

—— (1993b) *Trends in International Migration: Annual Report 1992*, Continuous Reporting System on Migration/SOPEMI, OECD, Paris.

—— (1994) *Migration and Development; New Partnerships for Co-operation*, Paris.

Olsson, G. (1965) *Distance and Human Interaction: A Review and a Bibliography,* Regional Science Research Institute, Philadelphia.

O'Rourke, K.H. and Williamson, J.G. (1995) 'Open Economy Forces and Late 19th Century Swedish Catch-Up: A Quantitative Accounting', *Scandinavian Economic History Review*, vol. 43, pp. 171–203.

Pack, H. (1994) 'Endogenous Growth Theory: Intellectual Appeal and Empirical Shortcomings', *Journal of Economic Perspectives*, vol. 8, no. 1, pp. 55–72.

Papademetriou, D.G. (1985) 'Illegal Caribbean Migration to the US and Caribbean Development', in Pastor ed. *Migration and Development in the Caribbean.*

Papademetriou, D.G. and Martin, Ph.L. (1991) eds. *The Unsettled Relationship: Labor Migration and Economic Development*, Contributions in Labour Studies, Nr. 33, Greenwood Press, Westport.

Parsons, T. (1951) *The Social System*. The Free Press, Glencoe, Ill.

Pastor, R.A. (1985) ed. *Migration and Development in the Caribbean: The Unexplored Connection*, Westview, Boulder.

Pastor, R.A. and Rogers, R. (1985) 'Using Migration to Enhance Economic Development in the Caribbean', in Pastor ed. *Migration and Development in the Caribbean.*

Pedraza, S. (1991) 'Women and Migration: The Social Consequences of Gender', in Scott, W.R. ed. *Annual Review of Sociology*, Annual Reviews Inc, Palo Alto, CA., vol. 17, pp. 303–25.

Pessar, P. (1986) 'The Role of Gender in Dominican Settlement on the United States', in Nash, J., Safa, N., South Hadley, M. eds. *Women and Change in Latin America*, Bergin Garvey, pp. 273–94.

—— (1988) 'The Constraints and Release of Female Labor Power: Dominican Migration to the United States', in Dwyer, D. and Bruce, J. eds. *A Home Divided. Women and Income in the Third World*, Stanford University Press, Stanford, pp. 195–215.

Peters, B. (1993) *Die Integration moderner Gesellschaften,* Suhrkamp, Frankfurt.

Petersen, W. (1958) 'A General Typology of Migration', *American Sociological Review,* vol. 23, pp. 256–66.

—— (1968) 'Migration: Social Aspects', in Sills, D.L. ed. *International Encyclopedia of the Social Sciences*, The Macmillan Company and

The Free Press, New York, vol. 10, pp. 286–92.

Phizacklea, A. (1983) ed. *One Way Ticket: Migration and Female Labour*, Routledge and Kegan Paul, London.

Piore, M.J. (1979) *Birds of Passage: Migrant Labor and Industrial Societies*, Cambridge University Press, New York.

Pischke, J.-S. and Velling, J. (1994) *Wage and Employment Effects of Immigration to Germany: An Analysis Based on Local Labour Markets*, CEPR Discussion Paper 935, London.

Plane, D.A. (1992) 'Demographic Influences on Migration', *Regional Studies*, vol. 27, pp. 375–83.

Pohjola, A. (1991) 'Social Networks – Help or Hindrance to the Migrant?', *International Migration*, vol. 29, no. 3, pp. 435–44.

Polanyi, K. (1957) with Arensberg, C.M. and Peason, H. *Trade and Markets in Early Empires*. The Free Press, Glencoe, Ill.

Pongsapich, A. (1988) *Social Effects of Migration in Countries of Origin: The Case of Asian Migrants to the Gulf Region*, Eighth ICM Seminar on Migration, Geneva.

Pope, D. and Withers, G. (1993) 'Do Migrants Rob Jobs? Lessons of Australian History 1861–1991', *Journal of Economic History*, vol. 53, pp. 719–42.

Popkin, S.L. (1979) *The Rational Peasant: The Political Economy of Rural Society in Vietnam*, University of California Press, Berkeley.

Popoola, D. (1988) 'International Migration of Skilled Personnel and the Development Process', in Fashoyin, T. ed. *Labour and Development in Nigeria*, Lagos, pp. 107–20.

Portes, A. (1995) ed. *The Economic Sociology of Immigration: Essays on Networks, Ethnicity, and Entrepreneurship*, Russell Sage Foundation, New York.

Portes, A. and Walton, J. (1981) *Labor, Class, and the International System*, Academic Books, New York.

Pred, A. (1981) 'Social Reproduction and the Time-Geography of Everyday Life', *Geografiska Annaler*, vol. 63b, 15–22.

Pries, L. (1996) 'Internationale Arbeitsmigration und das Entstehen transnationaler sozialer Räume: Das Beispiel Mexico–USA', in Faist, T., Hillmann F. and Zühlke-Robinet, K. eds. *Neue Formen der Arbeitsmigration*, ZeS-Arbeitspapier no. 2/1996, Zentrum für Sozialpolitik, Bremen.

Ramsey, F. (1928) 'A Mathematical Theory of Saving', *Economic Journal*, vol. 38, pp. 543–59.

Ranis, G. and Fei, J.C.H. (1961) 'A Theory of Economic Development', *American Economic Review*, vol. 51, pp. 533–65.

Ravenstein, E.G. (1889) 'The Laws of Migration', *Journal of the Royal Statistical Society*, vol. 52, no. 2, pp. 241–301.

—— (1885) 'The Laws of Migration', *Journal of the Royal Statistical Society*, vol. 48, no. 2, pp. 167–227.

Razin, A. and Sadka, E. (1995) *Resisting Migration: Wage Rigidity and Income Distribution*, CEPR Discussion Paper 1091, London.

Rees, W.E. and Wackernagel, M. (1992) *Appropriated Carrying Capacity: Measuring the Natural Capital Requirements of the Human Economy*, paper presented to The Second Meeting of the International Society for Ecological Economics, Stockholm.

Relph, E. (1976) *Place and Placelessness*, Pion, London.

Ritchey, P. (1976) 'Explanations of Migration', *Annual Review of Sociology*, vol. 2, pp. 363–404.

Roberts, B. (1995) *Making of Citizens; Cities of Peasants Revisited*, Arnold, London.

Robertson, A.F. (1991) *Beyond the Family. The Social Organization of Human Reproduction*. Polity, Cambridge.

Rocha-Trindade, M.B. (1993) 'Portugal and Spain: Culture of Migration', in Kubat, D. ed. *The Politics of Migration Policies: Settlement and Integration – the First World into the 1990s*, Centre for Migration Studies, New York, pp. 262–80.

Romer, P.M. (1994) 'The Origins of Endogenous Growth', *Journal of Economic Perspectives*, vol. 8, no. 1, pp. 3–22.

Rossi, P.H. (1980) *Why Families Move*, 2nd ed. Sage, Beverly Hills.

Rostow, W.W. (1960) *The Stages of Economic Growth. A Non-Communist Manifesto*, Cambridge University Press, Cambridge.

Rubin, G. (1975) 'The Traffic in Women: Notes on the "Political Economy" of Sex', in Reiter, R.R. ed. *Toward an Anthropology of Women*, Monthly Review Press, New York, pp. 157–210.

Runciman, W.G. (1966) *Relative Deprivation and Social Justice: A Study of Attitudes to Social Inequality in Twentieth-Century England*, Routledge, London.

Russel, S.S. (1992) 'Migrant Remittances and Development', *International Migration*, vol. XXX, No. 3–4.

Russel, S.S., Jacobsen, K. and Stanley, W.D. (1990) *International Migration and Development in Sub-Saharan Africa*, World Bank Discussion Papers 101, vol. I.

Russel, S.S. and Teitelbaum, M.S. (1992) *International Migration and International Trade*, World Bank Discussion Papers 160, World Bank, Washington D.C.

Rystad, G. (1990a) ed. *The Uprooted: Forced Migration as International Problem in the Post-War Era*, Lund University Press, Lund.

—— (1990b) 'Victims of Oppression or Ideological Weapons? Aspects of U.S. Refugee Policy in the Postwar Era', in Rystad, G. ed. *The Uprooted*, pp. 195–226.

Sahlins, M.D. (1965) 'On the Sociology of Primitive Exchange', in Banton, M. ed. *The Relevance of Models for Social Anthropology*, A.S.A. Monographs 1. Tavistock, London, pp. 139–227.

Salvatore, D. (1981) 'A Theoretical and Empirical Evaluation and Extension of the Todaro Migration Model', *Regional Science and Urban Economics*, vol. 11, pp. 499–508.

Sassen-Koob, S. (1984) 'Direct Foreign Investment: a Migration Push-Factor?', *Environment and Planning, Government and Planning*, vol. 2.

Schaeffer, P. (1985) 'Human Capital Accumulation and Job Mobility', *Journal of Regional Science*, vol. 25, pp. 103–14.

Schmink, M. (1984) 'Household Economic Strategies: A Review and Research Agenda', *Latin American Research Review*, vol. 19, pp. 87–101.

Scott, J.A. (1976) *The Moral Economy of the Peasant: Rebellion and Subsistence in Southeast Asia*, Yale University Press, New Haven.

Shah, N. (1994a) 'An Overview of Present and Future Emigration Dynamics in South Asia', *International Migration*, vol. 32, no. 2, pp. 217–68.

—— (1994b) 'Migration between Asian Countries', *Population Distribution and Migration,* UN 1994.

—— (1995) 'Emigration Dynamics from and within South Asia', *International Migration*, vol. 23, nos. 3/4, pp. 559–626.

Shils, E. (1957) 'Primordial, Personal, Sacred and Civil Ties', *British Journal of Sociology*, vol. 7.

Shrestha, N. (1988) 'A Structural Perspective on Labour Migration in Underdeveloped Countries', *Progress in Human Geography,* vol. 12, no. 2.

Siebert, H. (1993) 'Internationale Wanderungsbewegungen – Erklärungsansätze und Grundsatzfragen', *Schweizerische Zeitschrift für Volkswirtschaft und Statistik*, vol. 129, pp. 229–25.

—— (1994) *Migration: A Challenge for Europe*, Tübingen.

—— (1995) *Locational Competition in the World Economy,* Kiel Week Conference 1994, Tübingen.

Simkins (1970) 'Migration as a Response to Population Pressure; The Case of the Philippines', in Zelinsky, Kosinski and Prothero eds. *Geography and a Crowding World*, Oxford University Press, Oxford.

Simon, H.A. (1957) *Models of Man*, John Wiley, New York.

—— (1983) *Reason in Human Affairs*, Basil Blackwell, Oxford.

Simon, J.L. (1989) *The Economic Consequences of Immigration*, Blackwell and The Cato Institute, Oxford.

—— (1994) 'On the Economic Consequences of Immigration: Lessons for Immigration Policies', in Giersch, H. ed. *Economic Aspects of*

International Migration, pp. 227–48.

Sjaastad, L.A. (1962) 'The Costs and Returns of Human Migration', *Journal of Political Economy*, vol. 70, pp. 80–93.

Sjöholt, P. (1988) *Tropical Colonization: Problems and Achievements. The Case of Chanchamayo and Satipo in Peru*, Institute of Latin American Studies, Stockholm.

Skeldon, R. (1990) *Population Mobility in Developing Countries: A Reinterpretation,* Belhaven, London.

—— (1995) 'The challenge facing migration research: a case for greater awareness', *Progress in human geography,* vol. 19 no. 1, pp. 91–6.

Smith, A.D. (1983) *State and Nation in the Third World,* Wheatsheaf, London.

Smolny, W. (1991) 'Macroeconomic Consequences of International Labour Migration: Simulation Experience from an Econometric Disequilibrium Model', in Vosgerau, H.J. ed. *European Integration in the World Economy*, Springer, Berlin, pp. 376–412.

Solow, R.M. (1956) 'A Contribution to the Theory of Economic Growth', *Quarterly Journal of Economics*, vol. 70, pp. 65–94.

—— (1994) 'Perspectives on Growth Theory', *Journal of Economic Perspectives*, vol. 81, pp. 45–54.

Soto, I.M. (1987) 'West Indian Fostering: Its Role in Migrant Exchanges', in Sutton, C.R. and Chaney, E.M. eds. *Caribbean Life in New York City: Sociocultural Dimensions*, Center for Migration Studies, New York, pp. 131–49.

SOU (1991:1) *Refugee and Immigration Policy*, public investigation (in Swedish).

South Pacific Commission (1987) *Migration, Employment and Development in the South Pacific*, SPC, Noumea, 1987.

Sovani (1964) 'The Analysis of "Overurbanization"', *Economic Development and Cultural Change,* Syracuse.

Stahl, Ch. (1989) 'Overview: Economic Perspectives', in Appleyard, R. ed. *The Impact of International Migration on Developing Countries*, OECD, Paris.

Stahl, Ch. and Habib, A. (1992) 'Emigration and Development in South and Southeast Asia', in Papademetriou, D.G. and Martin, Ph.L. eds. *The Unsettled Relationship*, pp. 163–80.

Stark, O. (1984) 'Migration Decision Making: A Review Article', *Journal of Development Economics*, vol. 14, pp. 251–9.

—— (1986) ed. 'Migration, Human Capital and Development', in *Research in Human Capital and Development*, vol. 4, Jai Press Inc., London.

—— (1991) *The Migration of Labor*, Basil Blackwell, Cambridge, Mass.

—— (1994) 'Patterns of Labor Migration when Workers Differ in their

Skills and Information is Asymmetric', in *Economic Aspects of International Migration*, Berlin, pp. 57–74.

Stark, O. and Bloom, (1985) 'The New Economics of Labor Migration', *American Economic Review*, vol. 75, pp. 173–8.

Stark, O. and Levhari, D. (1982) 'On Migration and Risk in LDCs', *Economic Development and Cultural Change*, vol. 31, pp. 191–6.

Stark, O. and Taylor, J. (1991) 'Migration Incentives, Migration Types: The Role of Relative Deprivation', *The Economic Journal*, vol. 101, pp. 1163–78.

Stark, O. and Yitzhaki, S. (1988) 'Labour Migration as a Response to Relative Deprivation', *Journal of Population Economics*, vol. 1, pp. 57–70.

Statistisches Bundesamt (1955–95) *Statistisches Jahrbuch der Bundesrepublik Deutschland,* Steiner, Wiesbaden.

Stewart, F. (1991) 'The Many Faces of Adjustment', *World Development*, vol. 19, no. 12.

Stillwell, J. (1991) 'Spatial Interaction and the Propensity to Migrate over Distance', in Stillwell, J. and Congdon, P. eds. *Migration Models.*

Stillwell, J. and Congdon, P. (1991) eds. *Migration Models – Micro and Macro Approaches*, Belhaven, London.

Stouffer, S.A. (1940) 'Intervening Opportunities: A Theory Relating Mobility and Distance', *American Sociological Review,* vol. 5, pp. 845–67.

Straubhaar, Th. (1987) 'International Migration under Incomplete Information: A Comment, *Schweizerische Zeitschrift für Volkswirtschaft und Statistik*, vol. 123, pp. 219–26.

—— (1992) 'Allocational and Distributional Aspects of Future Immigration to Western Europe', *International Migration Review*, vol. 26, pp. 462–82.

—— (1993) 'Migration Pressure', *International Migration*, vol. 31, pp. 5–41.

—— (1994) *Neuere Entwicklungen in der Migrationstheorie*, Diskussionspapier des Instituts für Wirtschaftspolitik der Universität der Bundeswehr Nr. 41, Hamburg.

—— (1995) 'Migrationstheorie', in Berthold, N. ed. *Allgemeine Wirtschaftstheorie*, WiSt Taschenbücher, Ed. Franz Vahlen, Munich.

Suhrke, A. (1994) 'Towards a Comprehensive Refugee Policy: Conflict and Refugees in the Post-Cold War World', in Böhning, W.R. and Schloeter-Paredes, M.-L. eds. *Aid in Place of Migration?*, pp. 13–38.

Summerfield, H. (1993) 'Patterns of Adaptation: Somali and Bangladeshi Women in Britain', in Buijs, G. ed. *Migrant Women,* pp. 83–98.

Swedish Government (1990/1:195) *An Active Refugee and Immigration*

Policy (in Swedish).

Swedish Ministry of Labour (1990) *A Coordinated Refugee and Immigration Policy*, mimeo (in Swedish).

Tamas, K. (1996) *South to North Migration: Migration Potential and Economic Development*, Programme on Population and Development (PROP), PROP Reports No. 10, Department of Sociology, University of Lund.

Tapinos, G.P. (1992) 'Migratory Pressure: An Expression of Concern or an Analytical Concept?', in Tapinos, G.P. and Keely, C.B., *Migration and Population: Two Views on International Migration*, Working Paper of the World Employment Programme Research, ILO, May.

—— (1993) 'Can International Cooperation be an Alternative to the Emigration of Workers?', in OECD, *The Changing Course of International Migration*.

Taylor, A.M. and Williamson, J.G. (1994) *Convergence in the Age of Mass Migration*, NBER Working Paper, no. 474.

Taylor, J.E. (1986) 'Differential Migration, Networks, Information and Risk', in Stark, O. ed. pp. 147–71.

—— (1995) *Micro Economy-Wide Models for Migration and Policy Analysis: An Application to Rural Mexico*, Development Centre Studies, OECD Development Centre, Paris.

Taylor, P. (1989) 'The Error of Developmentalism in Human Geography', in Gregory, D. and Walford, R. eds. *Horizons in Human Geography,* Macmillan, London.

Thadani, V.N. and Todaro, M.P. (1984) 'Female Migration: A Conceptual Framework', in Fawcett, J.T., Siew-Ean, K. and Smith, P.C. eds. *Women in the Cities of Asia: Migration and Urban Adaptation*, Westview, Boulder, CO.

Thistlethwaite, F. (1991) 'Migration from Europe Overseas in the Nineteenth and Twentieth Centuries', reprinted in Vecoli, R.J. and Williamson, J.G. eds. *A Century of European Migrations, 1830–1930*, University of Illinois Press, Urbana (originally published in 1960).

Thomas, B. (1961) *International Migration and Economic Development*, UNESCO, Paris.

—— (1973) *Migration and Economic Growth*, Cambridge University Press, New York.

Thomas, W.I. and Znaniecki, F. (1918–20) *The Polish Peasant in Europe and America*, 5 Vols. University of Chicago Press, Chicago and Badger Press, Boston.

Tienda, M. and Booth, K. (1991) 'Gender, Migration and Social Change', *International Sociology,* vol. 6, pp. 51–72.

Tilly, C. (1978) 'Migration in Modern European History', in McNeil, W.H. and Adams, R.H. eds. *Human Migration: Patterns and Policies*,

Indiana University Press, Bloomington, pp. 48–72.

—— (1990) 'Transplanted Networks', in Yans-McLaughlin, V. ed. *Immigration Reconsidered. History, Sociology, and Politics*, Oxford University Press, New York, pp. 79–95.

—— (1996) *Big Transitions,* CSSC Working Paper, New School for Social Research, New York.

Tinker, I. (1990) ed. *Persistent Inequalities. Women and World Development*, Oxford University Press, Oxford etc.

Todaro, M.P. (1969) 'A Model of Labor Migration and Urban Unemployment in Less Developed Countries', *American Economic Review*, vol. 59, pp. 138–48.

—— (1976) *International Migration in Developing Countries: A Review of Theory*, ILO, Geneva.

—— (1989) *Economic Development in the Third World*, Longman, New York.

Todaro, M.P. and Maruszko, L. (1987) 'Illegal Immigration and US Immigration Reform: A Conceptual Framework', *Population and Development Review*, vol. 13, pp. 101–14.

Tuan, Yi-Fu (1991) 'Language and the Making of Place: A Narrative Descriptive Approach', *Annals of the Association of American Geographers*, vol. 81, no. 4, pp. 684–96.

Tucker, S.K. (1991) 'The Potential of Trade Expansion as a Generator of Added Employment in the Caribbean Basin', in Díaz-Briquets, S. and Weintraub, S. eds. *Migration Impacts of Trade and Foreign Investment*, pp. 91–112.

Tung, R. K.-C. (1981) *Exit-Voice Catastrophes: Dilemma between Migration and Participation*, University of Stockholm, Stockholm.

UN (1986) *International Co-operation to Avert New Flows of Refugees*, Ref No. A/41/324.

—— (1994) *Population Distribution and Migration*, mimeo to be published as ST/ESA/SER.R/133.

—— (1995) *Review of Population Trends, Policies and Programmes: Monitoring of World Population Trends and Policies*, Population Commission twenty-eighth session, 21 Feb.–2 March 1995, electronic version obtained through the Population Information Network (POPIN) Gopher of the United Nations Population Division, Department for Economic and Social Information and Policy Analysis.

—— (1996) *South to North Migration Flows,* Electronic version obtained through the Population Information Network (POPIN) Gopher of the United Nations Population Division, Department for Economic and Social Information and Policy Analysis.

UNDP (1992, 1993, 1994) *Human Development Report 1992, 1993,*

1994, Oxford University Press, Oxford.

UNESCO (1988) *International Migration Today*, vol. I, Paris.

—— (1984) *Population Distribution, Migration and Development*, Paris.

UNFPA (1993) *The State of World Population – 1993*, United Nations, New York.

United Nations, Department for Economic and Social Information and Policy Analysis, Population Division (1995) *International Migration Policies and the Status of Female Migrants*, Proceedings of the United Nations Expert Group Meeting on International Migration Policies and the Status of Female Migrants, San Miniato, Italy, 28–31 March 1990.

United Nations/ESCAP (1980–4) *National Migration Survey Manuals 1–10*, New York, United Nations. Bangkok, Economic and Social Commission for Asia and the Pacific.

United Nations International Covenant on Civil and Political Rights, (1966).

United Nations International Covenant on Economic, Social, and Cultural Rights, (1966).

United Nations Universal Declaration of Human Rights, (1948).

US Commission for the Study of International Migration and Cooperative Economic Development (1990) *Unauthorized Migration: An Economic Development Response*, Washington.

USA (1992) *The US Perspective on 'Migration and Development'*, Tenth IOM Seminar on Migration, Geneva, September 1992.

Waever, O., Buzan, B., Kelstrup, M. and Lemaitre, P. (1993) *Identity, Migration and the New Security Agenda in Europe*, Pinter, London.

Wall, K.D. (1993) 'A Model of Decision Making under Bounded Rationality', *Journal of Economic Behaviour and Organization*, vol. 21, pp. 331–52.

Wallerstein, I. (1974) *The Modern World-System: Capitalist Agriculture and the Origins of the European World Economy in the Sixteenth Century*, Academic Press, New York.

Warnes, T. (1992) 'Migration and the Life Course', in Champion, T. and Fielding, T. eds. *Migration Processes and Patterns*, Research Progress and Prospects, vol. I, Belhaven, London, pp. 175–87.

Watts, S. J. (1983) 'Marriage Migration: A Neglected Form of Long Term Mobility', *International Migration Review*, vol. 17, no. 4, pp. 682–98.

Weber, M. (1978) 'Basic Categories of Social Organisation', in Runciman, W.G. ed. *Weber, Selections in Translation*, Cambridge University Press, Cambridge.

Weber, R. (1993) *Einwanderung und staatliche Umverteilung*, Chur/

Zürich.

Weiner, M. (1993a) ed. *International Migration and Security*, Westview, Boulder.

—— (1993b) 'Security, Stability and International Migration', in Weiner, M. ed. *International Migration and Security*, pp. 1–35.

Weintraub, S. and Díaz-Briquets, S. (1994) 'The Use of Foreign Aid for Reducing Incentives to Emigrate from Central America', in Böhning, W.R. and Schloeter-Paredes, M.-L. eds. *Aid in Place of Migration?*, pp. 119–50.

White, P. and Woods, R. (1980) eds. *The Geographical Impact of Migration,* Longman, London.

White, S. (1980) 'A Philosophical Dichotomy in Migration Research', *Professional Geographer,* vol. 32, pp. 6–13.

Widgren, J. (1987) 'International Migration: New Challenges to Europe', Report prepared for the Third Conference of European Ministers Responsible for Migration, organized by the Council of Europe, Porto, Portugal, 13–15 May, Reprinted in *Migration News* (2), International Catholic Migration Commission, Geneva.

—— (1989) 'Europe and International Migration in the Future: The Necessity for Merging Migration, Refugee, and Development Policies', in Loescher, G. and Monahan, L. eds. *Refugees and International Relations,* pp. 49–63.

Wilkinson, R.C. (1977) *Poverty and Progress: An Ecological Model of Economic Development,* Methuen, London.

Willis, K.G. (1974) *Problems in Migration Analysis,* Saxon House/Lexington Books, Farnborough, Lexington.

Wilson, S. (1974) *Urban and Regional Models in Geography and Planning,* John Wiley, London.

Winkelmann, R. and Zimmermann, K.F. (1993) 'Ageing, Migration and Labour Mobility', in Johnson, P. and Zimmermann, K.F. eds. *Labour Markets in an Ageing Europe*, Cambridge University Press, Cambridge, pp. 255–83.

Winter-Ebmer, R. (1994) 'Motivation for Migration and Economic Success', *Journal of Economic Psychology*, vol. 15, pp. 269–84.

Wolburg, M. (1996) *Effects of Brain Drain on Macroeconomic Development*, Diskussionspapier des Instituts für Wirtschaftspolitik, Universität der Bundeswehr, Hamburg.

Wolpert, J. (1975) 'Behavioural Aspects of the Decision to Migrate', in Jones E. ed. *Readings in Social Geography,* Oxford University Press, Oxford, pp. 191–9.

Wood, W. (1994) 'Forced Migration: Local Conflicts and International Dilemmas', *Annals of the Association of American Geographers*, vol. 84, no. 4, pp. 607–34.

World Bank (1979, 1992, 1994, 1995) *World Development Report 1979, 1992, 1994, 1995*, Oxford.

Xu, C. (1992) *Risk Aversion, Rural–Urban Wage Differentiation and Migration*, CEPR Discussion Paper no. 108, London.

Yanagisako, S.J. (1979) 'The Family and Household: The Analysis of Domestic Groups', *Annual Review of Anthropology*, vol. 8, pp. 161–205.

Yanagisako, S.J. and Collier, J.F. (1987) 'Toward a Unified Analysis of Gender and Kinship', in Collier, J.F. and Yanagisako, S.J. eds. *Gender and Kinship: Essays Toward a Unified Analysis*, Stanford University Press, Stanford.

Yoon, B.-S.L. (1992) 'Reverse Brain Drain in South Korea: State-Led Model', *Studies in Comparative International Development*, Spring 1992, vol. 27, no. 1, pp. 4–26.

Zelinsky, W. (1971) 'The Hypothesis of the Mobility Transistion', *Geographical Review*, vol. 61, pp. 219–49.

Zimmermann, K.F. (1993) 'Industrial Restructuring, Unemployment and Migration', in Beckmans, L. and Tsoukalis, L. eds. *Europe and Global Economic Interdependence*, College of Europe and European Interuniversity Press, Bruges, pp. 25–52.

—— (1995) 'Tackling the European Migration Problem', *Journal of Economic Perspectives*, vol. 9, no. 2, pp. 45–62.

Zinn, D.L. (1994) 'The Senegalese Immigrants in Bari. What Happens When the Africans Peer Back', in Benmayor, R. and Skotnes, A. eds. *Migration and Identity*, pp. 53–68.

Zlotnik, H. (1995) 'The South-to-North Migration of Women', *International Migration Review*, vol. 24, no. 1, pp. 229–54.

Zolberg, A.R. (1992) 'Labour Regimes and International Regimes: Bretton Woods and After', in Kritz, M.M., Lim, L.L. and Zlotnik, H. eds. *International Migration Systems: A Global Approach*, Clarendon Press, Oxford, pp. 315–34.

Zolberg, A.R., Suhrke, A. and Aguayo, S. (1989) *Escape from Violence. Conflict and the Refugee Crisis in the Developing World*, Cambridge University Press, New York.

Index

adjustment, in situ, 216
Afghanistan, 165, 184
Africa, 6, 7, 95, 134–6, 160, 165, 205, 209, 259
    Sub-Saharan, 138, 148, 165–6
    North, 3, 7, 148, 187
age, 31–2, 64, 257
Aguayo, 173
Ahmadiyya, 183
Algeria, 170, 213, 215
alienation, 177
aliens control,
    see control
aliens legislation, 16
aliens rights, 259
allocation effect, 106–7
allocational aspects, 103–4, 114
Amazonas, 24
America, 95
    Central, 138, 143, 148
    Latin, 138, 148, 170, 205
    North, 11, 172, 188, 217, 230
anthropology, 13, 219–23, 251
Appleyard, 140
Argentina, 148
Armenians, 173
arms sales, 154
Asia, 165
    East, 157, 241
    South, 3, 6, 138, 241
    Southeast, 147, 157
    West, 3, 6, 7
assimilation, 273
asylum seekers, 11, 16, 167
Australia, 7, 11, 165, 172, 230, 241
Austro-Hungarian empire, 173
autism, 175, 184, 262

Bahai, 183
balance of payment, 128, 152
balance of trade, 136

Ballard, 244
Banfield, 214
Bangladesh, 12, 230–1, 237, 244,
barriers, 265
Bauböck, 161
behavioural dynamics, 14, 28
Belgium, 7
border control, 11, 34, 164
border disputes, 180
Bracero Program, 266
brain drain and brain gain, 12, 92, 99, 107, 123, 127–8, 170, 239
Brandt commission, 133, 152, 156
Brazil, 148
Brundtland, 155–6
Bulgaria, 166
Böcker, 229
Böhning, 137

Canada, 7, 165, 209
capital,
    cultural, 207, 248
    economic, 248
    financial, 207
    human, 60, 62–3, 76, 86, 92, 104, 120, 207, 248, 263
    mobility, 59
    political, 207
    social, 188, 199–203, 248, 251, 254, 256, 263
    transnational, 133
capitalism, 258
capitalist labour-market, 37
capitalist world system, 47
Caribbean, 138, 143, 195, 210, 215, 231, 241, 244, 246
carriers, 265
caste system, 227
Catholics, 165
centre-periphery, 93, 119, 169, 270
ceteris paribus, 13, 18, 220, 257

Index

Index

underclass, 177
unemployment, 3, 6, 58–9, 65, 110, 123, 150, 200, 238, 253
   see also employment
United Kingdom, 7, 17, 154, 170, 192, 213, 215, 231, 236–7, 244
United Nations, 163
United States, 7, 122, 143, 154, 165–7, 170–2, 178, 197–8, 205–6, 213, 216, 231, 241, 244
upbringing, 231
urbanisation, 38, 142
utility maximiser, 249

value-expectancy, 66, 189, 253
Venezuela, 148
Vietnam, 174
violence, 173, 174
visa system, 11
voice, 198, 216, 248, 251

   see also exit-voice-loyalty

Wackernagel, 155
wage differences, 50, 54–6, 59, 62, 88, 94, 105, 118, 253
   see also income differentials
Weber, 161
West India, 231
Williamson, 195
World Bank, 133
world population, 156–7
world system theory, 192, 258

xenophobia, 12

Yugoslavia, 184

Zelinsky, 36
Znaniecki, 197, 203, 214, 216
Zolberg, 173